DAZZLE

Vol. 1

Minari Endoh

TOKYOPOP®

HAMBURG // LONDON // LOS ANGELES // TOKYO

Contents

破天荒遊戯

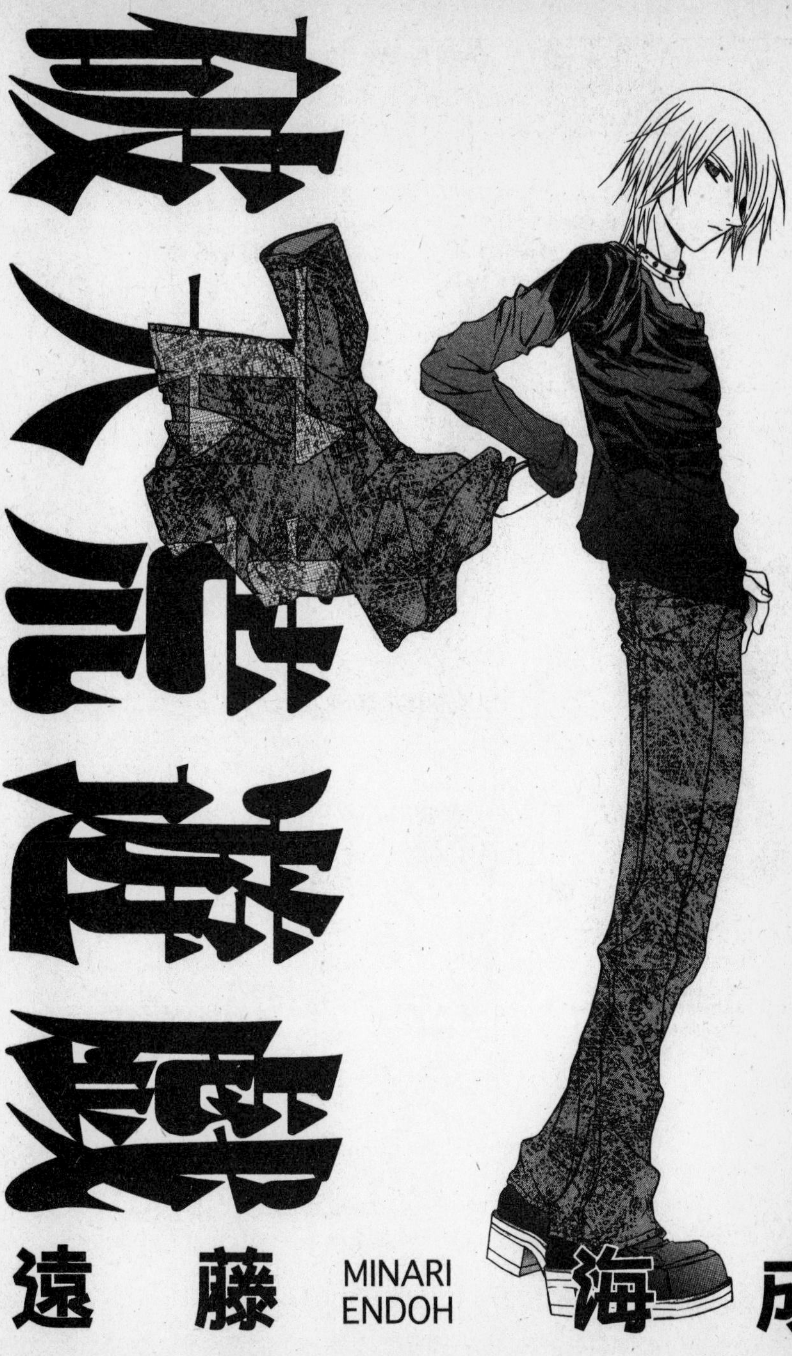

遠藤 海成
MINARI ENDOH

Dazzle Vol. 1
Created by Minari Endoh

Translation - Yoohae Yang
English Adaptation - Peter Ahlstrom
Retouch and Lettering - Creative Circle
Production Artist - Lucas Rivera and Alyson Stetz
Cover Design - Seth Cable

Editor - Troy Lewter
Digital Imaging Manager - Chris Buford
Production Managers - Jennifer Miller and Mutsumi Miyazaki
Managing Editor - Lindsey Johnston
VP of Production - Ron Klamert
Publisher and E.I.C. - Mike Kiley
President and C.O.O. - John Parker
C.E.O. - Stuart Levy

A  Manga

TOKYOPOP Inc.
5900 Wilshire Blvd. Suite 2000
Los Angeles, CA 90036

E-mail: info@TOKYOPOP.com
Come visit us online at www.TOKYOPOP.com

ISBN: 1-59816-092-3

First TOKYOPOP printing: January 2006
10 9 8 7 6 5 4 3 2 1
Printed in the USA

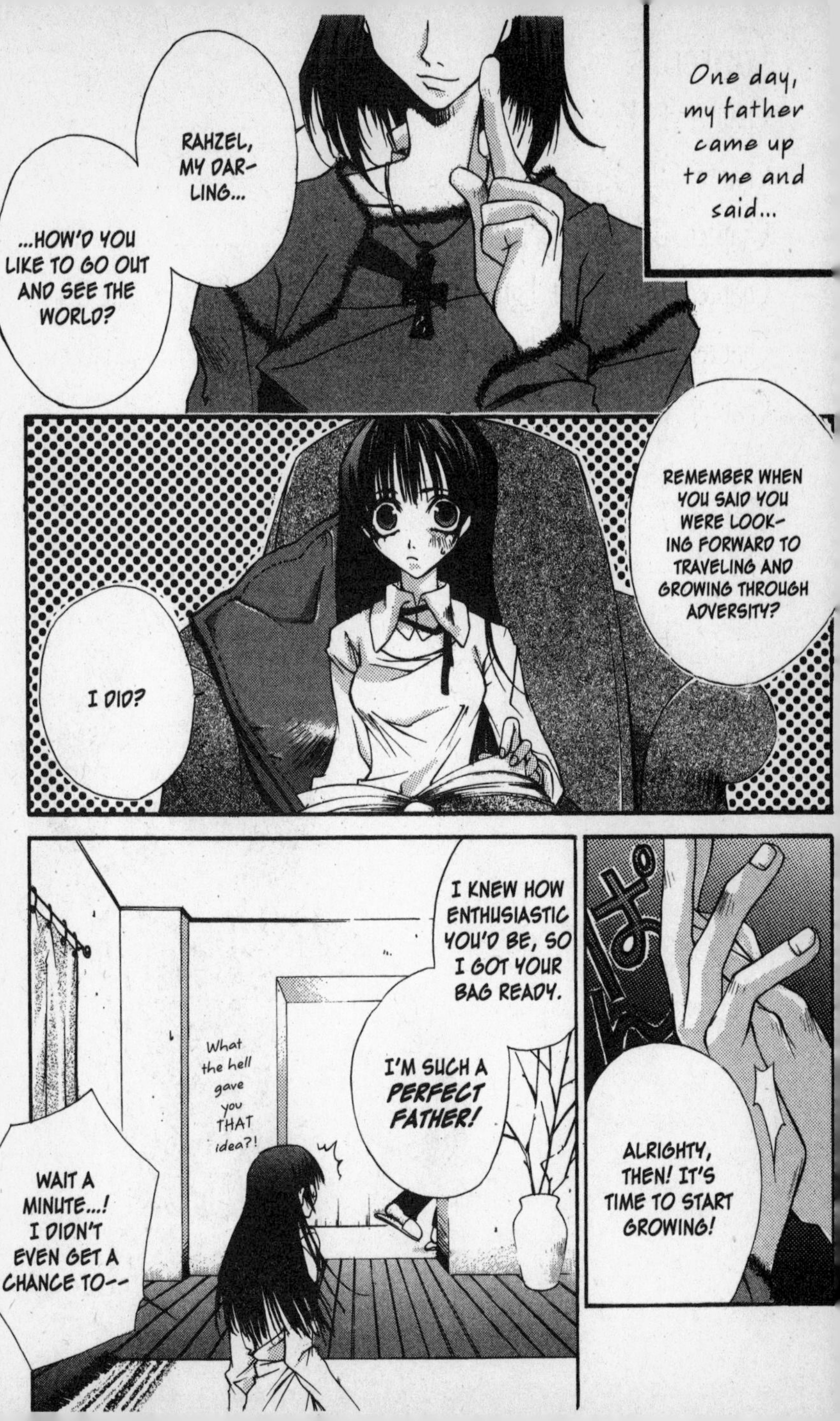
One day, my father came up to me and said...
RAHZEL, MY DARLING...
...HOW'D YOU LIKE TO GO OUT AND SEE THE WORLD?
REMEMBER WHEN YOU SAID YOU WERE LOOKING FORWARD TO TRAVELING AND GROWING THROUGH ADVERSITY?
I DID?
ALRIGHTY, THEN! IT'S TIME TO START GROWING!
I KNEW HOW ENTHUSIASTIC YOU'D BE, SO I GOT YOUR BAG READY.
I'M SUCH A PERFECT FATHER!
What the hell gave you THAT idea?!
WAIT A MINUTE...! I DIDN'T EVEN GET A CHANCE TO--

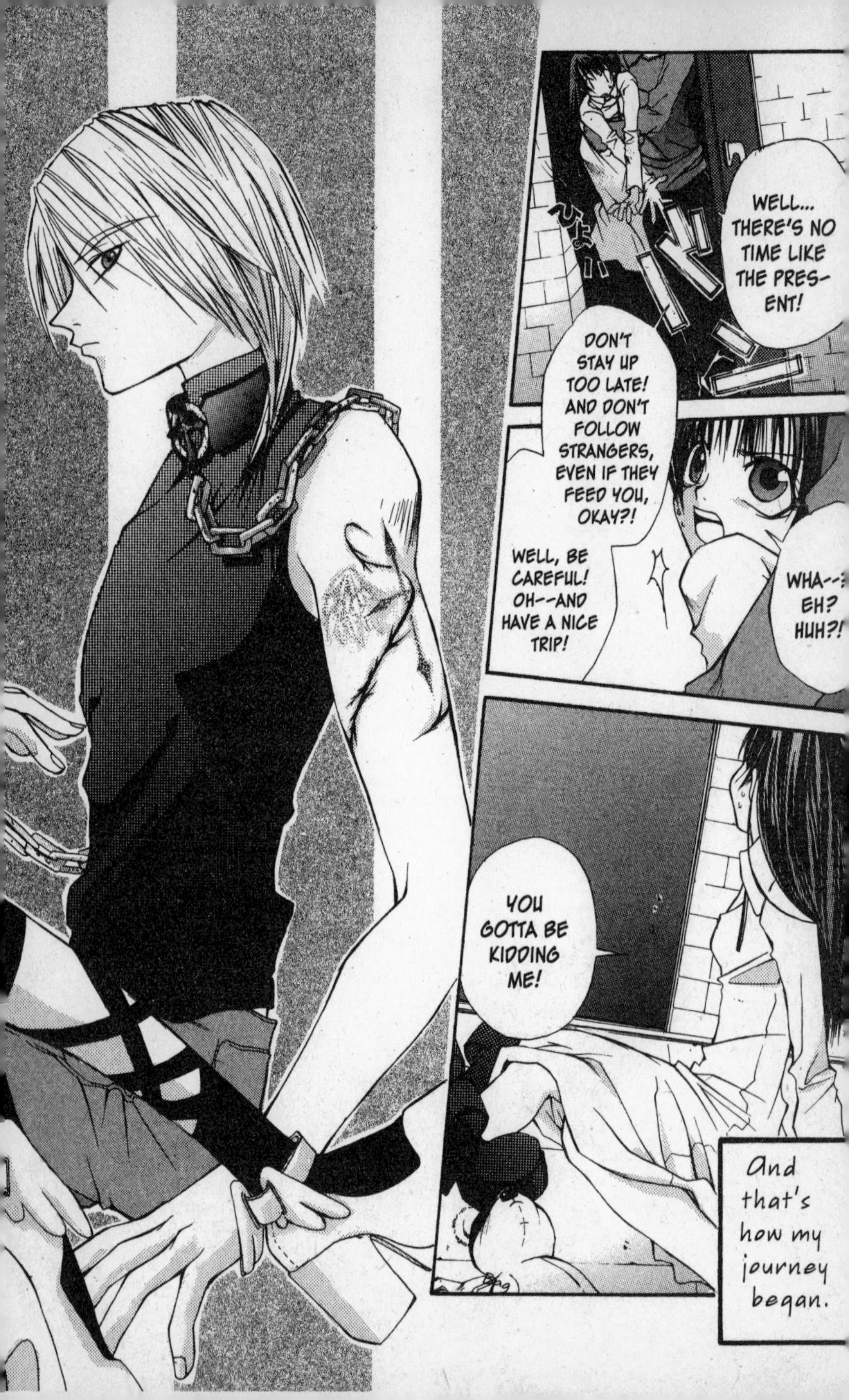
WELL... THERE'S NO TIME LIKE THE PRES-ENT!
DON'T STAY UP TOO LATE! AND DON'T FOLLOW STRANGERS, EVEN IF THEY FEED YOU, OKAY?!
WELL, BE CAREFUL! OH--AND HAVE A NICE TRIP!
WHA--? EH? HUH?!
YOU GOTTA BE KIDDING ME!
And that's how my journey began.

Chapter 1: Prelude

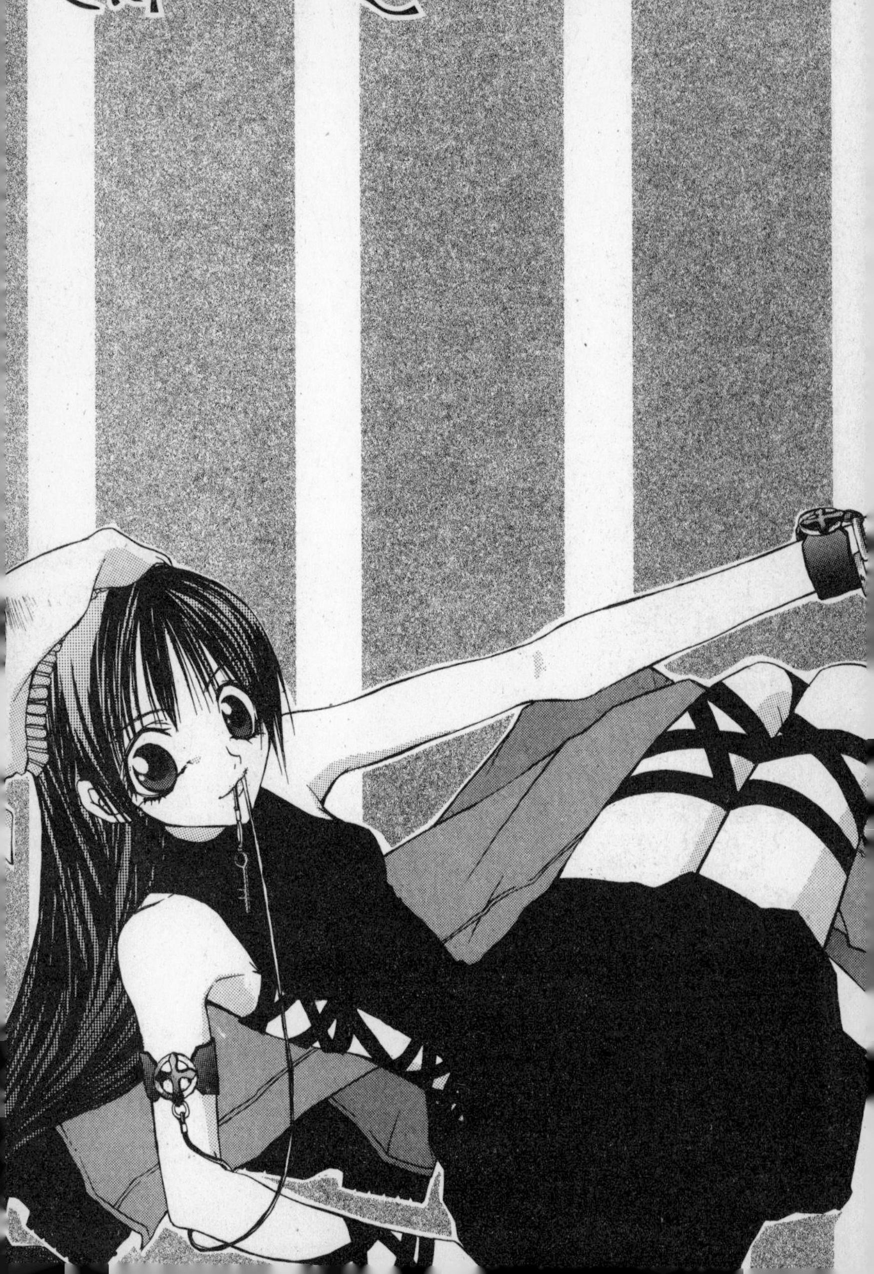

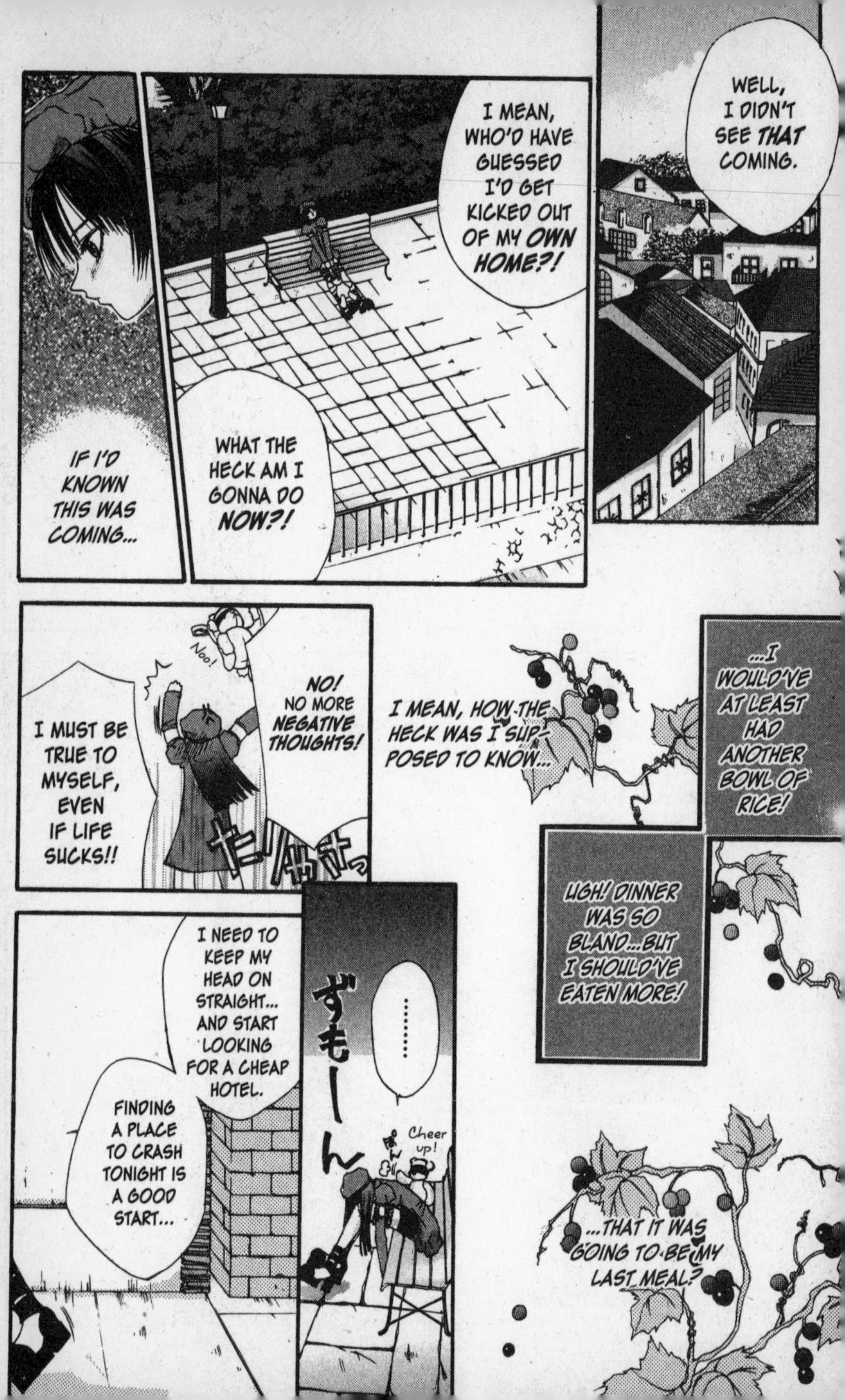
WELL, I DIDN'T SEE THAT COMING.
I MEAN, WHO'D HAVE GUESSED I'D GET KICKED OUT OF MY OWN HOME?!
WHAT THE HECK AM I GONNA DO NOW?!
IF I'D KNOWN THIS WAS COMING...
...I WOULD'VE AT LEAST HAD ANOTHER BOWL OF RICE!
I MEAN, HOW THE HECK WAS I SUP-POSED TO KNOW...
UGH! DINNER WAS SO BLAND...BUT I SHOULD'VE EATEN MORE!
...THAT IT WAS GOING TO BE MY LAST MEAL?
NO! NO MORE NEGATIVE THOUGHTS!
Noo!
I MUST BE TRUE TO MYSELF, EVEN IF LIFE SUCKS!!
ずもーん
....
Cheer up!
I NEED TO KEEP MY HEAD ON STRAIGHT... AND START LOOKING FOR A CHEAP HOTEL.
FINDING A PLACE TO CRASH TONIGHT IS A GOOD START...

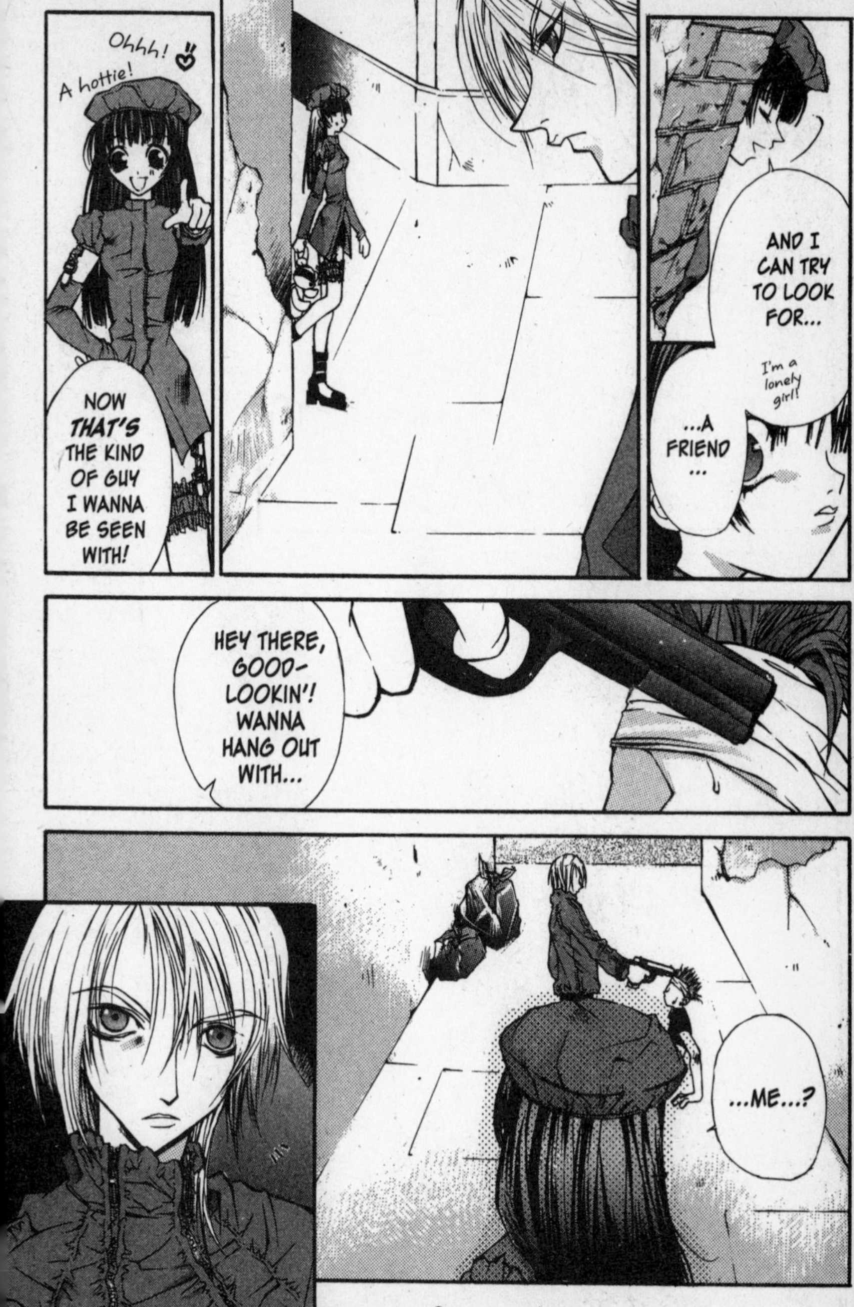
AND I CAN TRY TO LOOK FOR...
I'm a lonely girl!
...A FRIEND...
Ohhh!
A hottie!
NOW THAT'S THE KIND OF GUY I WANNA BE SEEN WITH!
HEY THERE, GOOD-LOOKIN'! WANNA HANG OUT WITH...
...ME...?

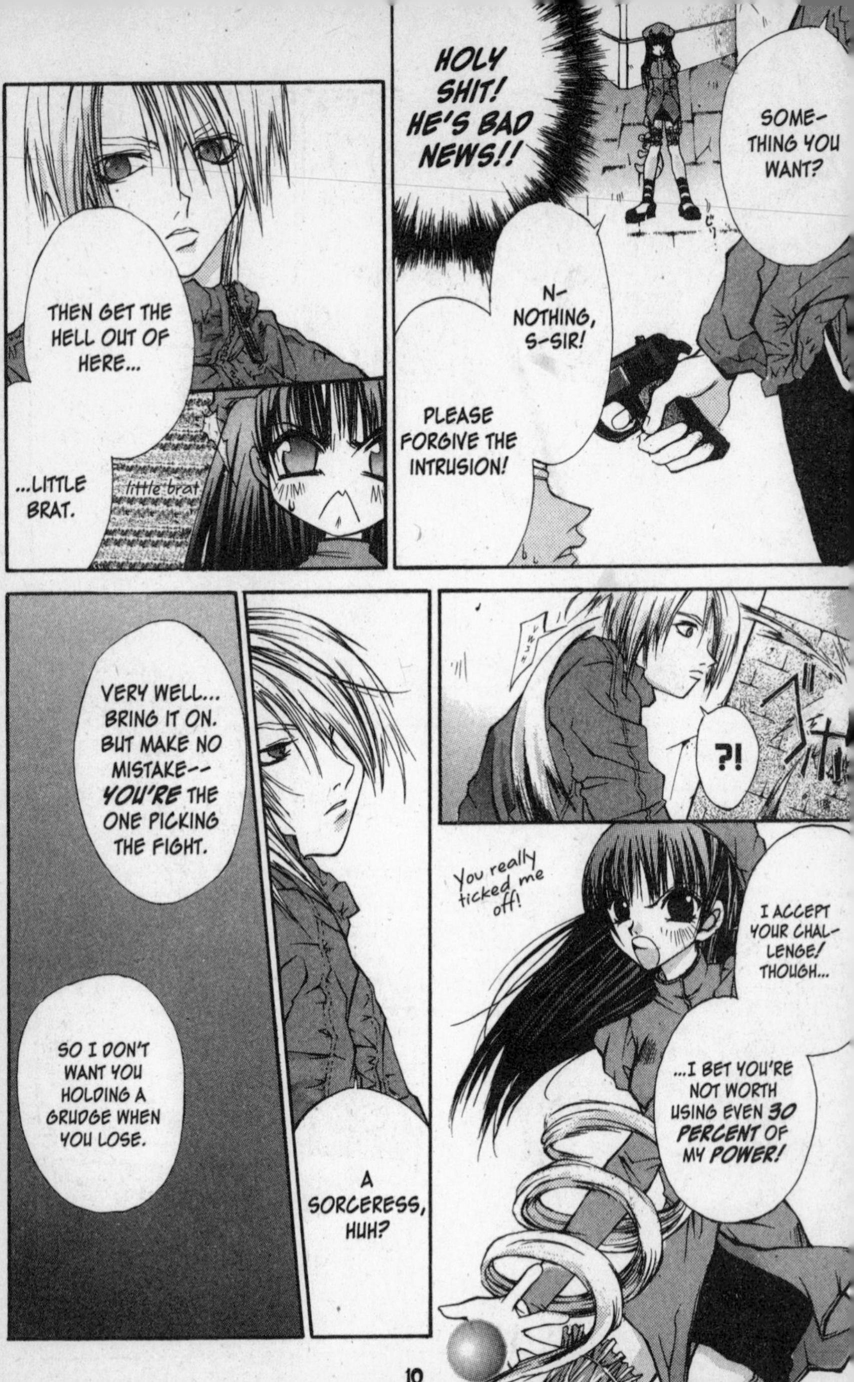
SOME-THING YOU WANT?
HOLY SHIT! HE'S BAD NEWS!!
N-NOTHING, S-SIR!
PLEASE FORGIVE THE INTRUSION!
THEN GET THE HELL OUT OF HERE...
...LITTLE BRAT.
little brat
?!
You really ticked me off!
I ACCEPT YOUR CHAL-LENGE! THOUGH...
...I BET YOU'RE NOT WORTH USING EVEN 30 PERCENT OF MY POWER!
A SORCERESS, HUH?
VERY WELL... BRING IT ON. BUT MAKE NO MISTAKE-- YOU'RE THE ONE PICKING THE FIGHT.
SO I DON'T WANT YOU HOLDING A GRUDGE WHEN YOU LOSE.

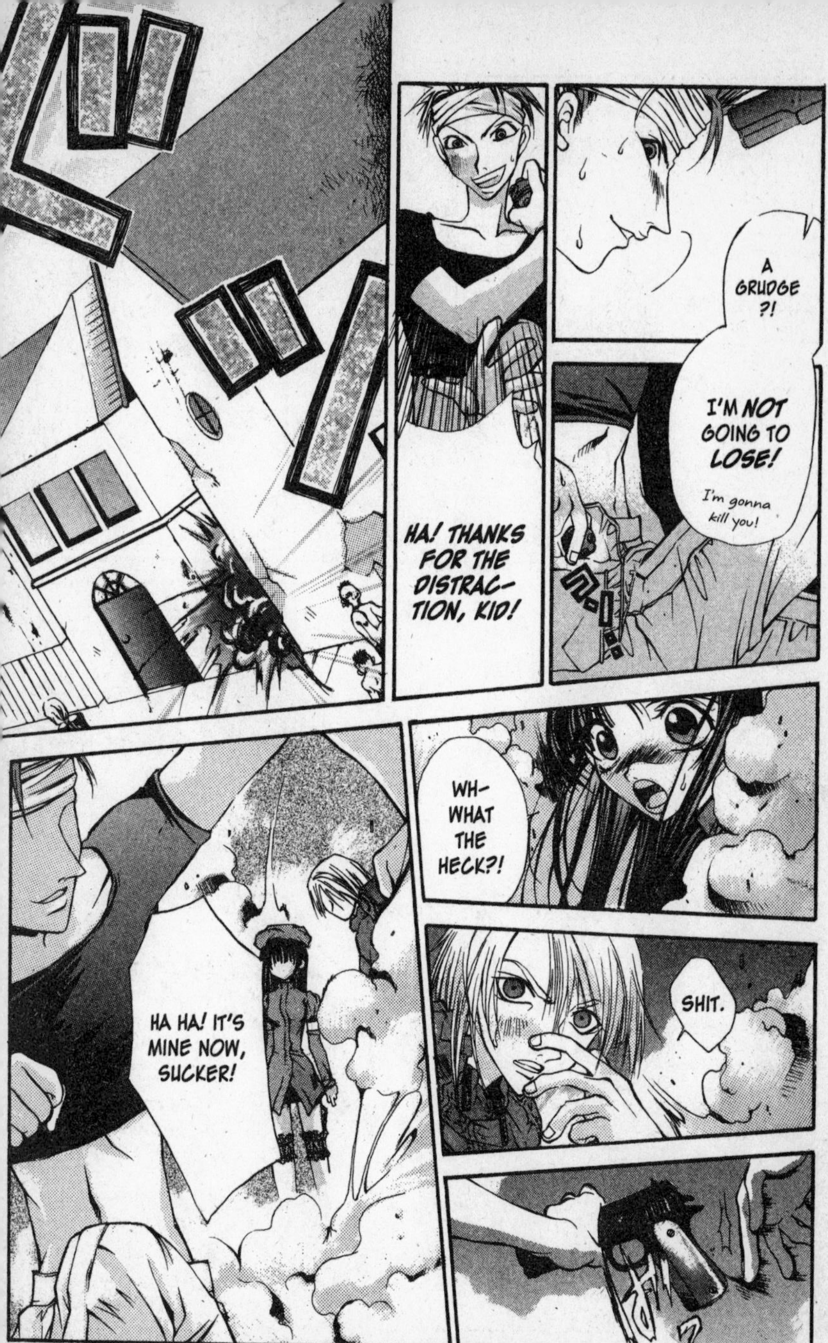

A GRUDGE ?!
I'M NOT GOING TO LOSE!
I'm gonna kill you!
HA! THANKS FOR THE DISTRAC- TION, KID!
WH- WHAT THE HECK?!
SHIT.
HA HA! IT'S MINE NOW, SUCKER!

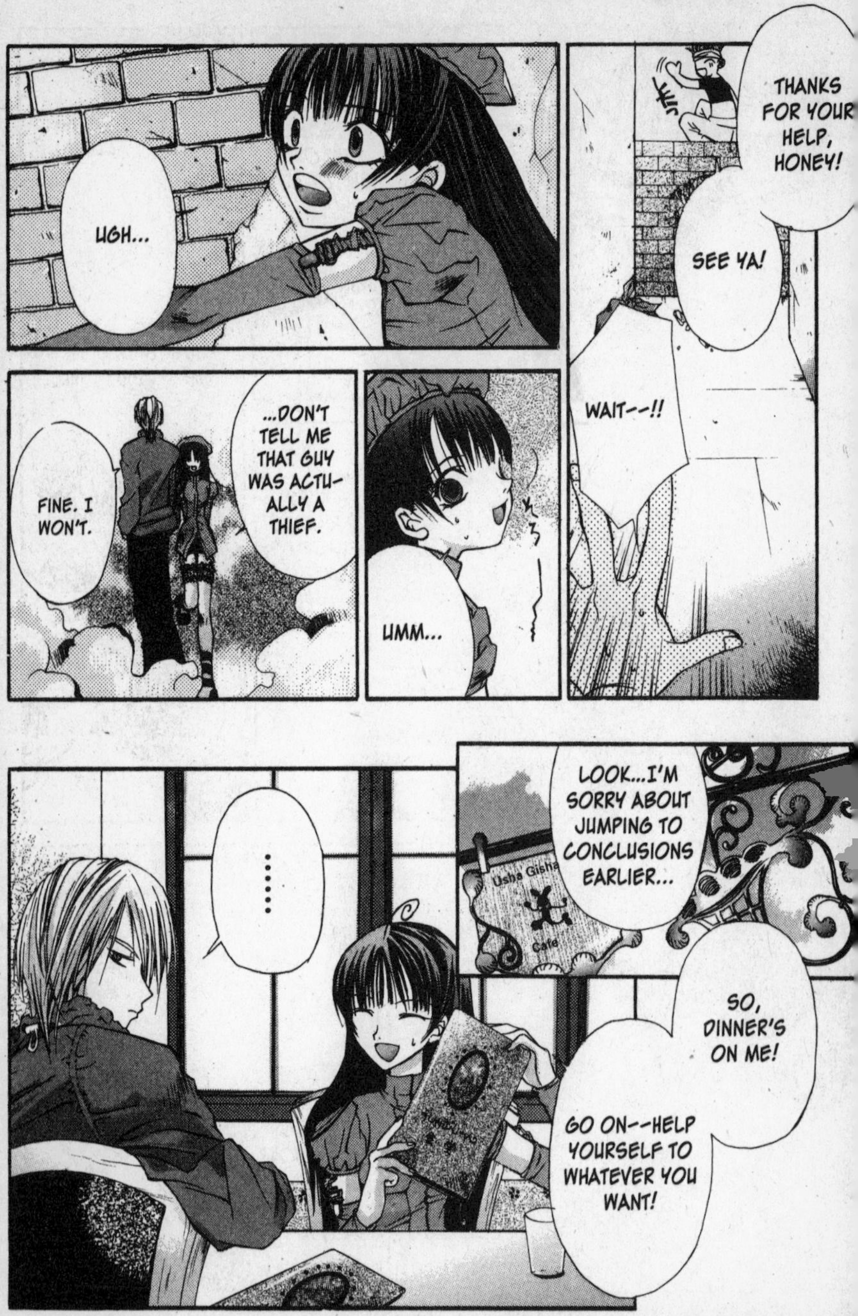
THANKS FOR YOUR HELP, HONEY!
SEE YA!
WAIT--!!
UGH...
UMM...
...DON'T TELL ME THAT GUY WAS ACTU-ALLY A THIEF.
FINE. I WON'T.
LOOK...I'M SORRY ABOUT JUMPING TO CONCLUSIONS EARLIER...
Usha Gisha
Cafe
SO, DINNER'S ON ME!
GO ON--HELP YOURSELF TO WHATEVER YOU WANT!
......

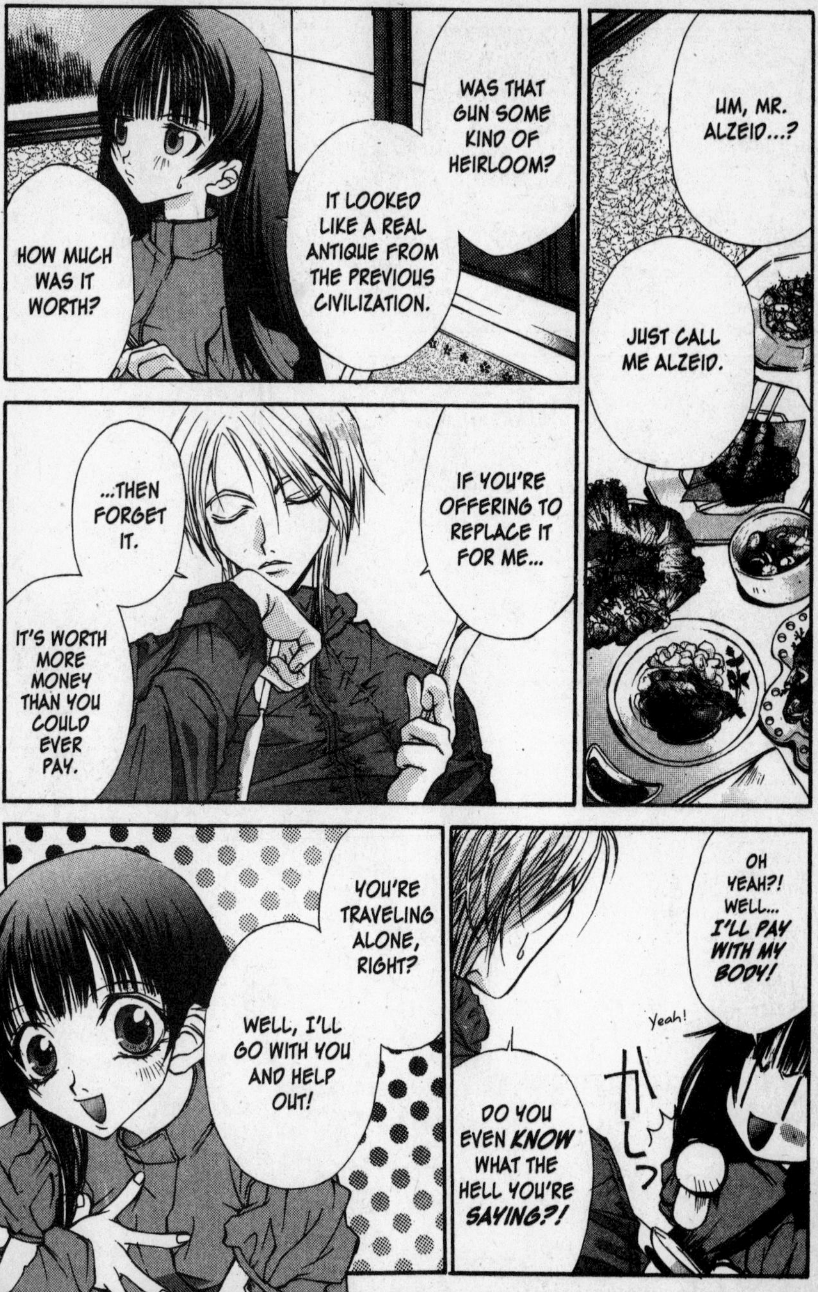
UM, MR. ALZEID...?
JUST CALL ME ALZEID.
WAS THAT GUN SOME KIND OF HEIRLOOM?
IT LOOKED LIKE A REAL ANTIQUE FROM THE PREVIOUS CIVILIZATION.
HOW MUCH WAS IT WORTH?
IF YOU'RE OFFERING TO REPLACE IT FOR ME...
...THEN FORGET IT.
IT'S WORTH MORE MONEY THAN YOU COULD EVER PAY.
OH YEAH?! WELL... *I'LL PAY WITH MY BODY!*
Yeah!
かしっ
DO YOU EVEN *KNOW* WHAT THE HELL YOU'RE *SAYING?!*
YOU'RE TRAVELING ALONE, RIGHT?
WELL, I'LL GO WITH YOU AND HELP OUT!

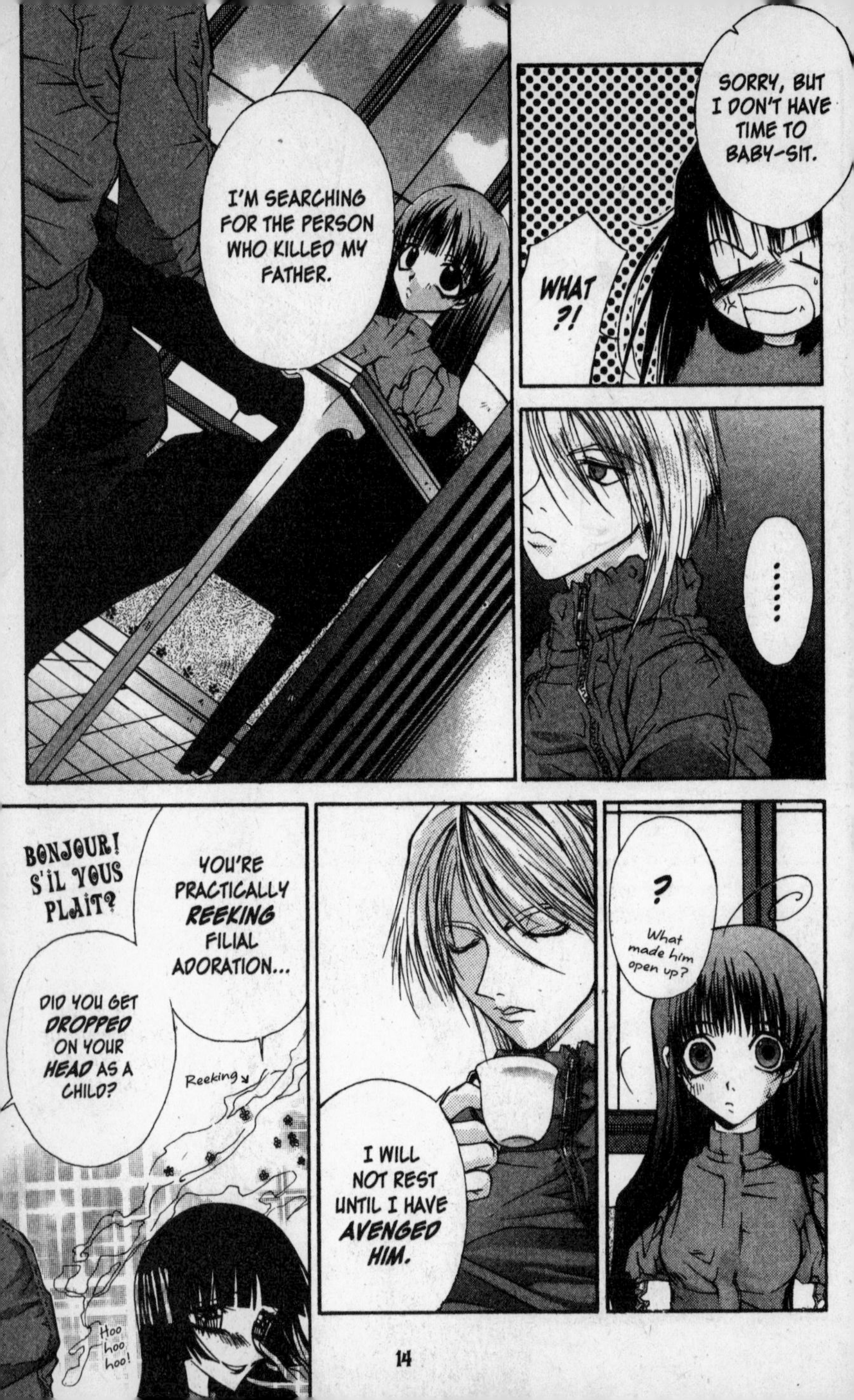
SORRY, BUT I DON'T HAVE TIME TO BABY-SIT.
WHAT ?!
......
I'M SEARCHING FOR THE PERSON WHO KILLED MY FATHER.
?
What made him open up?
I WILL NOT REST UNTIL I HAVE AVENGED HIM.
YOU'RE PRACTICALLY REEKING FILIAL ADORATION...
BONJOUR! S'IL VOUS PLAIT?
DID YOU GET DROPPED ON YOUR HEAD AS A CHILD?
Reeking
Hoo hoo hoo!

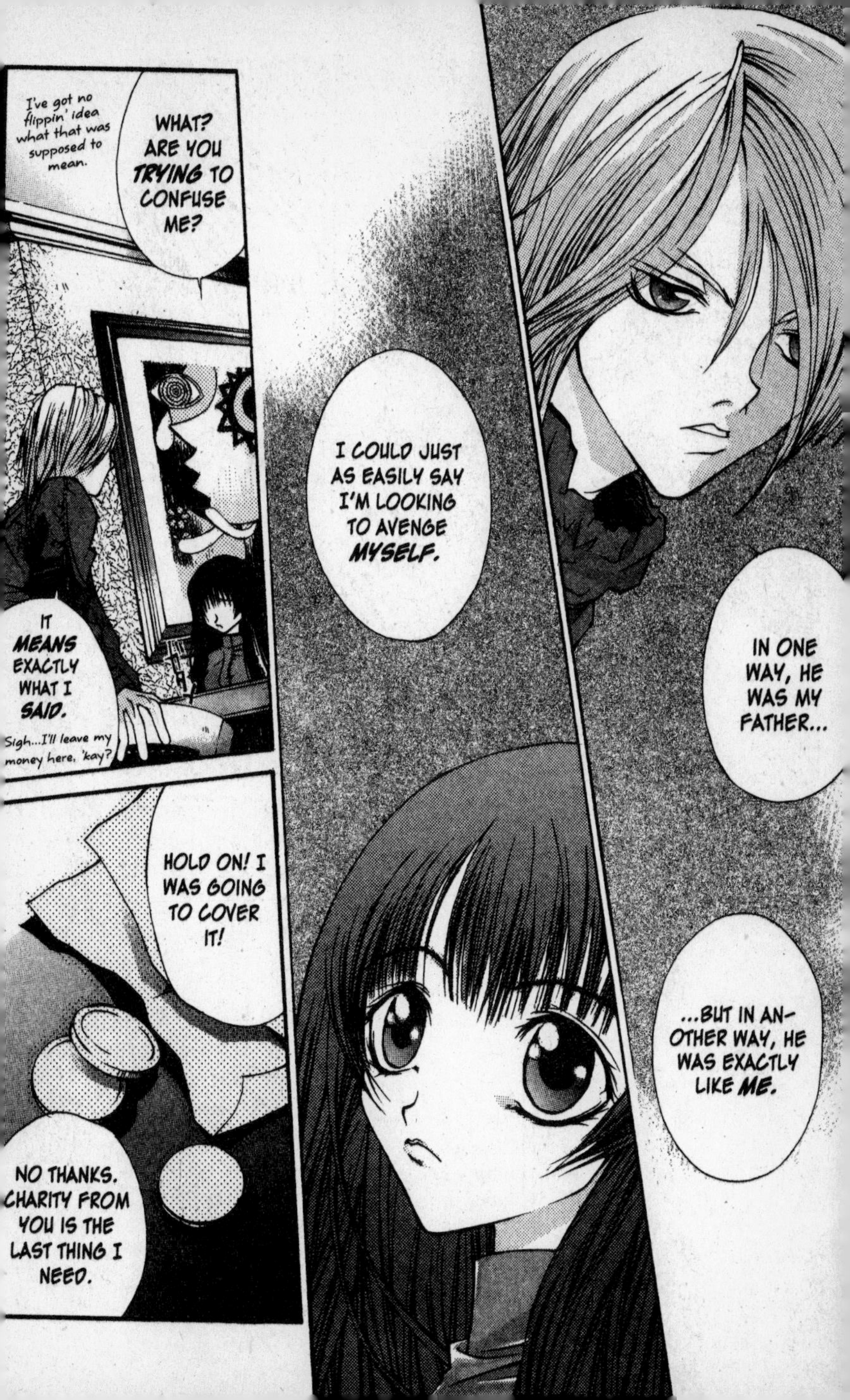

IN ONE WAY, HE WAS MY FATHER...
...BUT IN ANOTHER WAY, HE WAS EXACTLY LIKE ME.
I COULD JUST AS EASILY SAY I'M LOOKING TO AVENGE MYSELF.
WHAT? ARE YOU TRYING TO CONFUSE ME?
I've got no flippin' idea what that was supposed to mean.
IT MEANS EXACTLY WHAT I SAID.
Sigh...I'll leave my money here, 'kay?
HOLD ON! I WAS GOING TO COVER IT!
NO THANKS. CHARITY FROM YOU IS THE LAST THING I NEED.

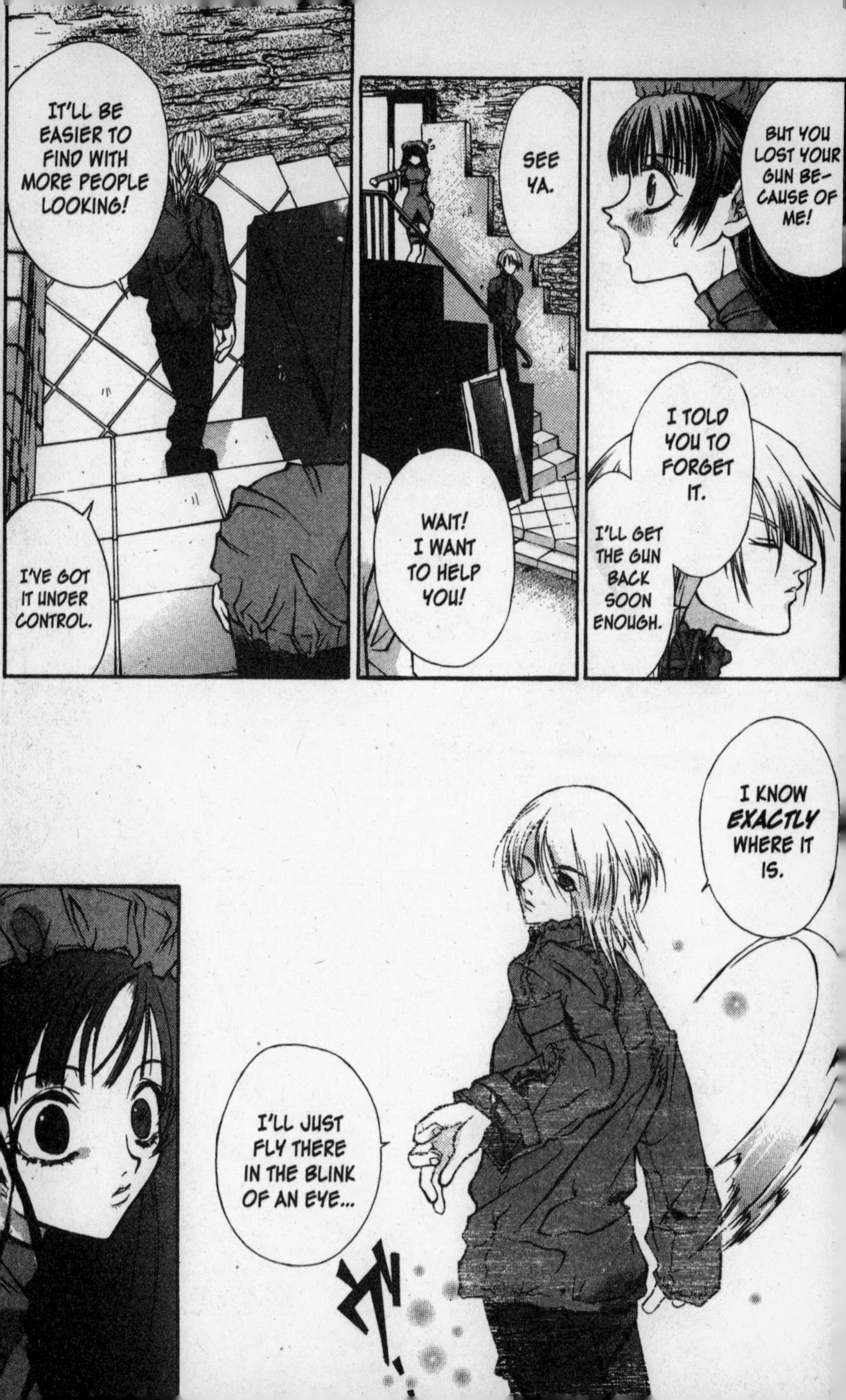
BUT YOU LOST YOUR GUN BE-CAUSE OF ME!
I TOLD YOU TO FORGET IT.
I'LL GET THE GUN BACK SOON ENOUGH.
SEE YA.
WAIT! I WANT TO HELP YOU!
IT'LL BE EASIER TO FIND WITH MORE PEOPLE LOOKING!
I'VE GOT IT UNDER CONTROL.
I KNOW *EXACTLY* WHERE IT IS.
I'LL JUST FLY THERE IN THE BLINK OF AN EYE...

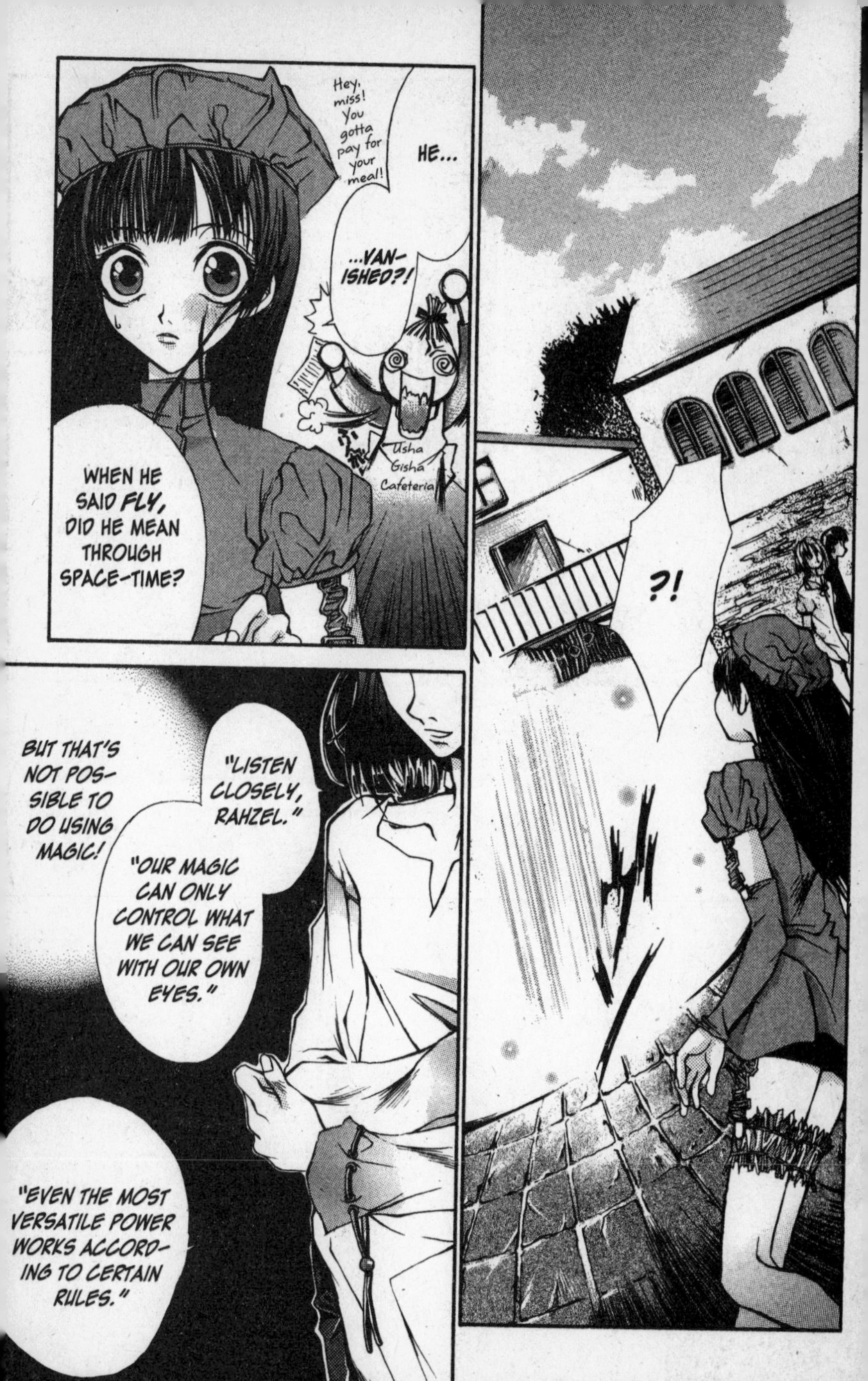
?!
Hey, miss! You gotta pay for your meal!
HE...
...VAN-ISHED?!
Usha Gisha Cafeteria
WHEN HE SAID FLY, DID HE MEAN THROUGH SPACE-TIME?
"LISTEN CLOSELY, RAHZEL."
BUT THAT'S NOT POS-SIBLE TO DO USING MAGIC!
"OUR MAGIC CAN ONLY CONTROL WHAT WE CAN SEE WITH OUR OWN EYES."
"EVEN THE MOST VERSATILE POWER WORKS ACCORD-ING TO CERTAIN RULES."

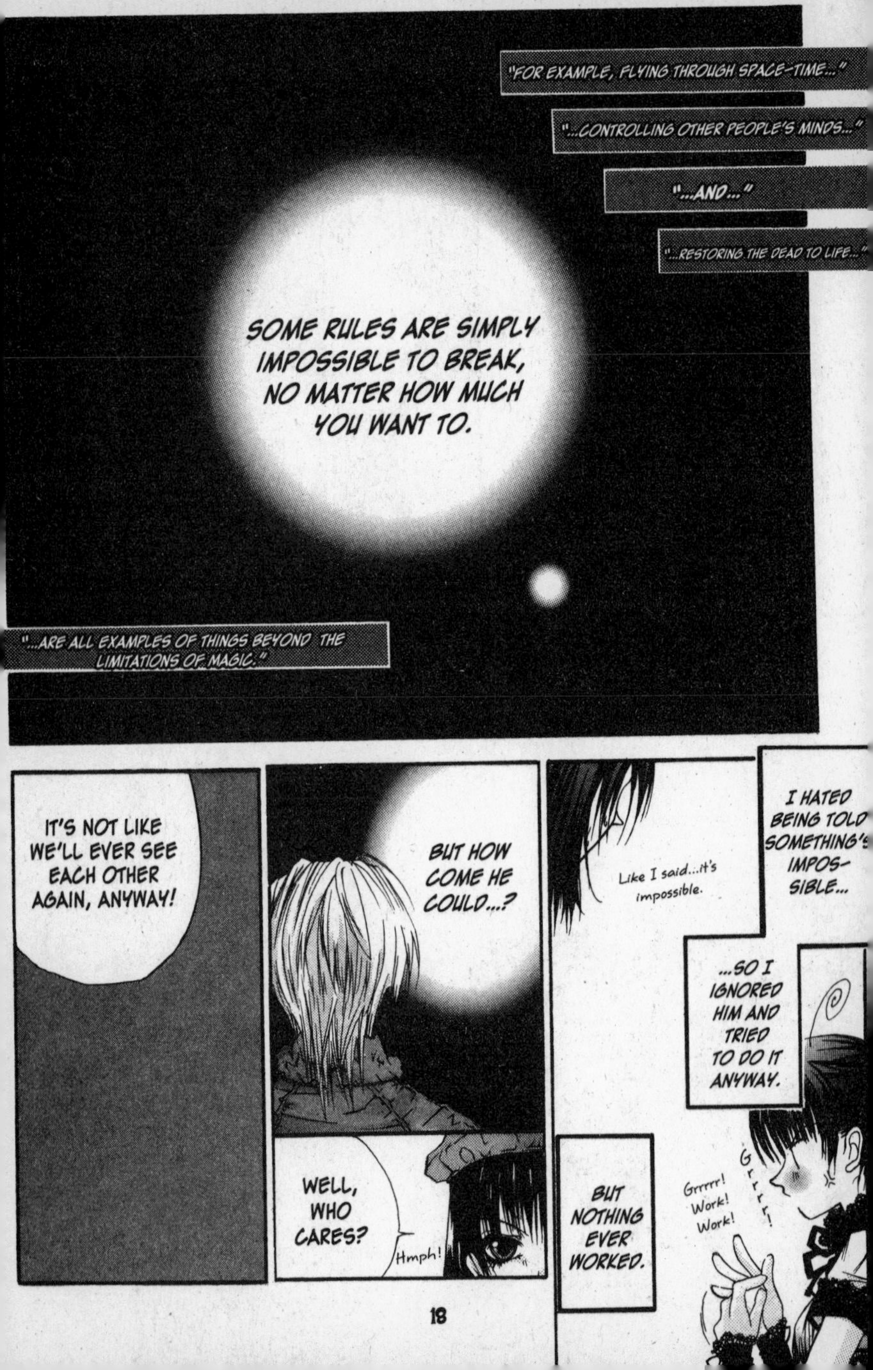
"FOR EXAMPLE, FLYING THROUGH SPACE-TIME..."
"...CONTROLLING OTHER PEOPLE'S MINDS..."
"...AND..."
"...RESTORING THE DEAD TO LIFE..."
SOME RULES ARE SIMPLY IMPOSSIBLE TO BREAK, NO MATTER HOW MUCH YOU WANT TO.
"...ARE ALL EXAMPLES OF THINGS BEYOND THE LIMITATIONS OF MAGIC."
I HATED BEING TOLD SOMETHING'S IMPOS-SIBLE...
Like I said...it's impossible.
...SO I IGNORED HIM AND TRIED TO DO IT ANYWAY.
Grrrrr! Work! Work!
Grrrr!
BUT NOTHING EVER WORKED.
BUT HOW COME HE COULD...?
WELL, WHO CARES?
Hmph!
IT'S NOT LIKE WE'LL EVER SEE EACH OTHER AGAIN, ANYWAY!

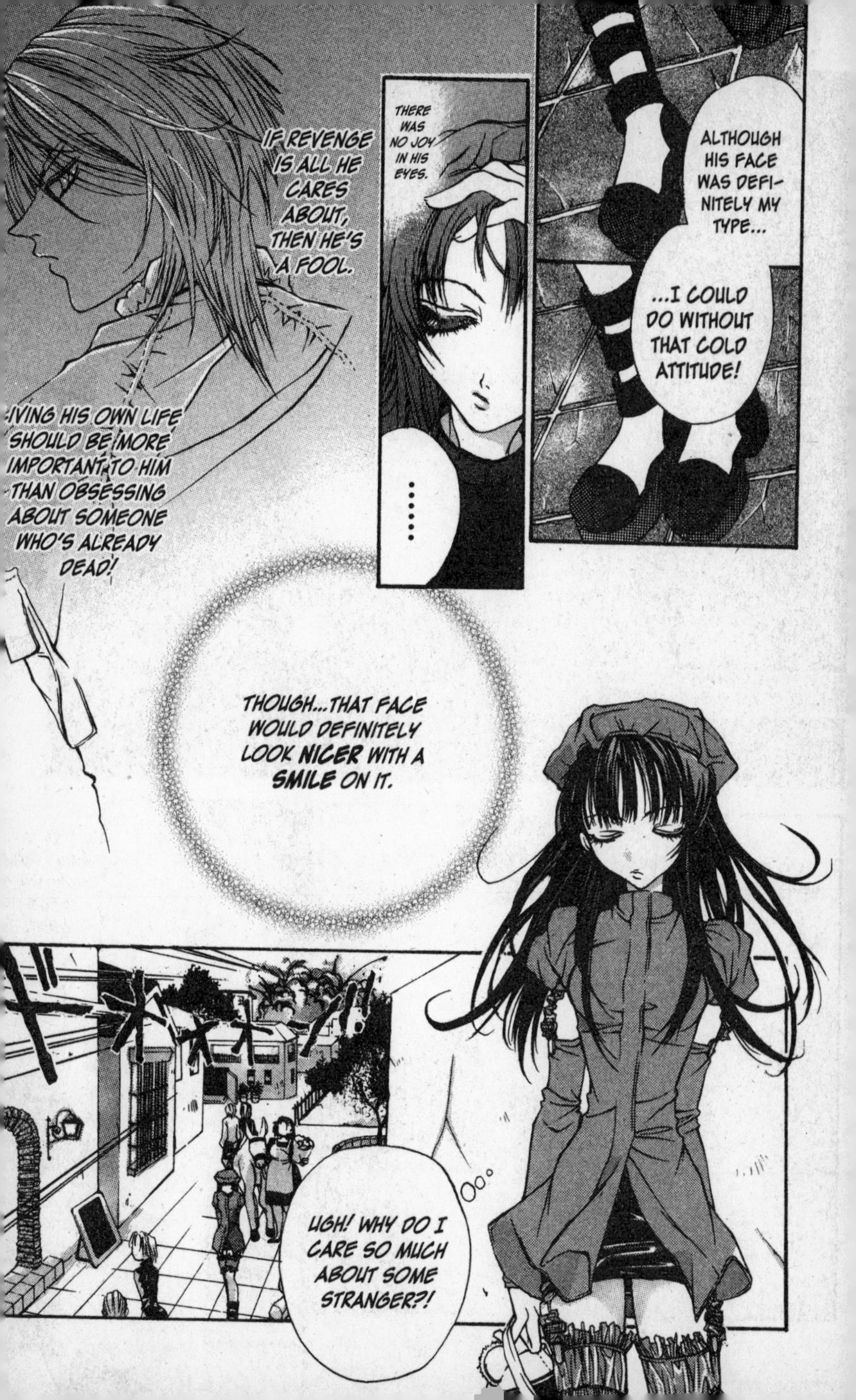
ALTHOUGH HIS FACE WAS DEFINITELY MY TYPE...
...I COULD DO WITHOUT THAT COLD ATTITUDE!
THERE WAS NO JOY IN HIS EYES.
......
IF REVENGE IS ALL HE CARES ABOUT, THEN HE'S A FOOL.
LIVING HIS OWN LIFE SHOULD BE MORE IMPORTANT TO HIM THAN OBSESSING ABOUT SOMEONE WHO'S ALREADY DEAD!
THOUGH...THAT FACE WOULD DEFINITELY LOOK NICER WITH A SMILE ON IT.
UGH! WHY DO I CARE SO MUCH ABOUT SOME STRANGER?!

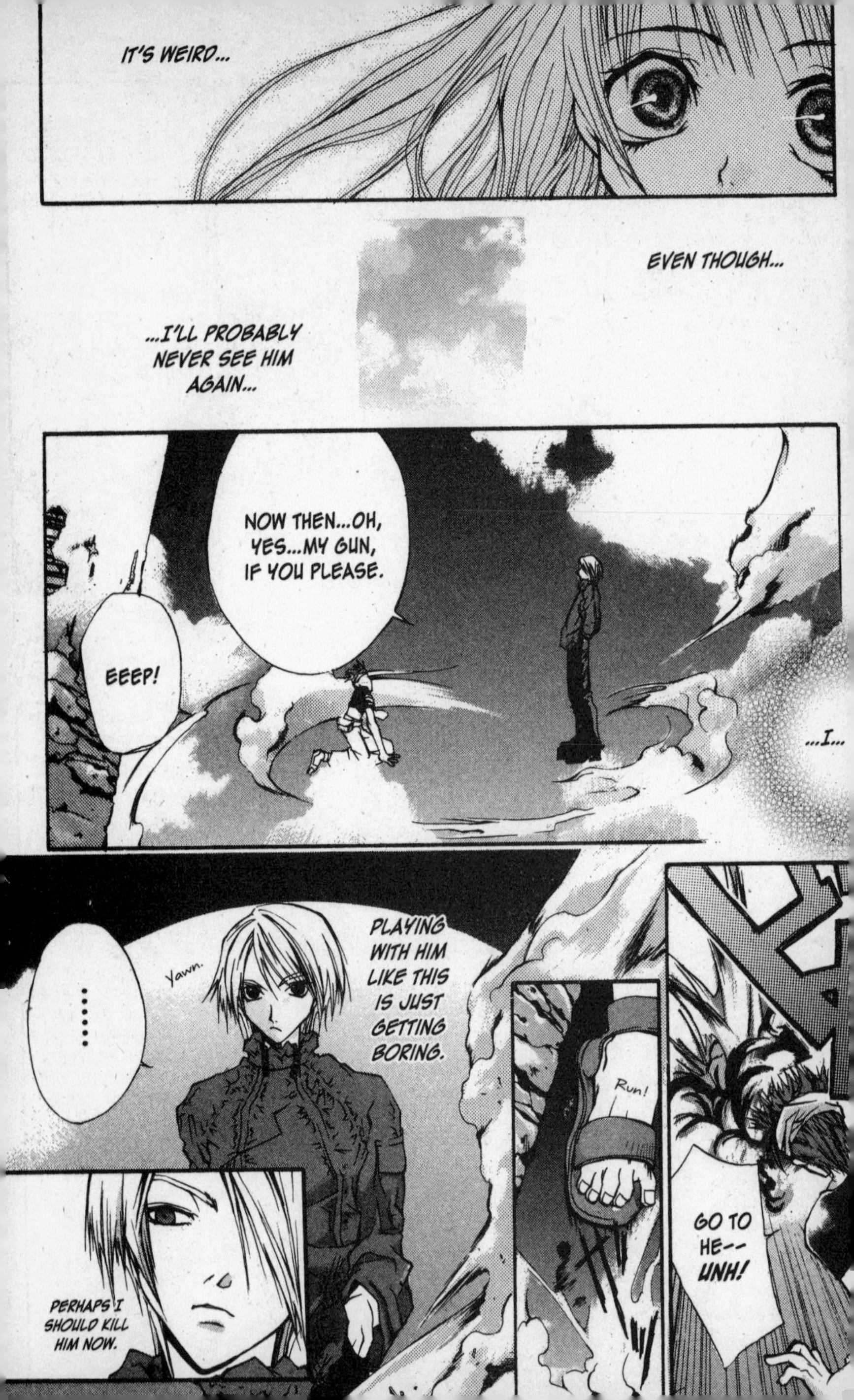
IT'S WEIRD...
EVEN THOUGH...
...I'LL PROBABLY NEVER SEE HIM AGAIN...
...I...
NOW THEN...OH, YES...MY GUN, IF YOU PLEASE.
EEEP!
GO TO HE-- UNH!
Run!
PLAYING WITH HIM LIKE THIS IS JUST GETTING BORING.
Yawn.
......
PERHAPS I SHOULD KILL HIM NOW.

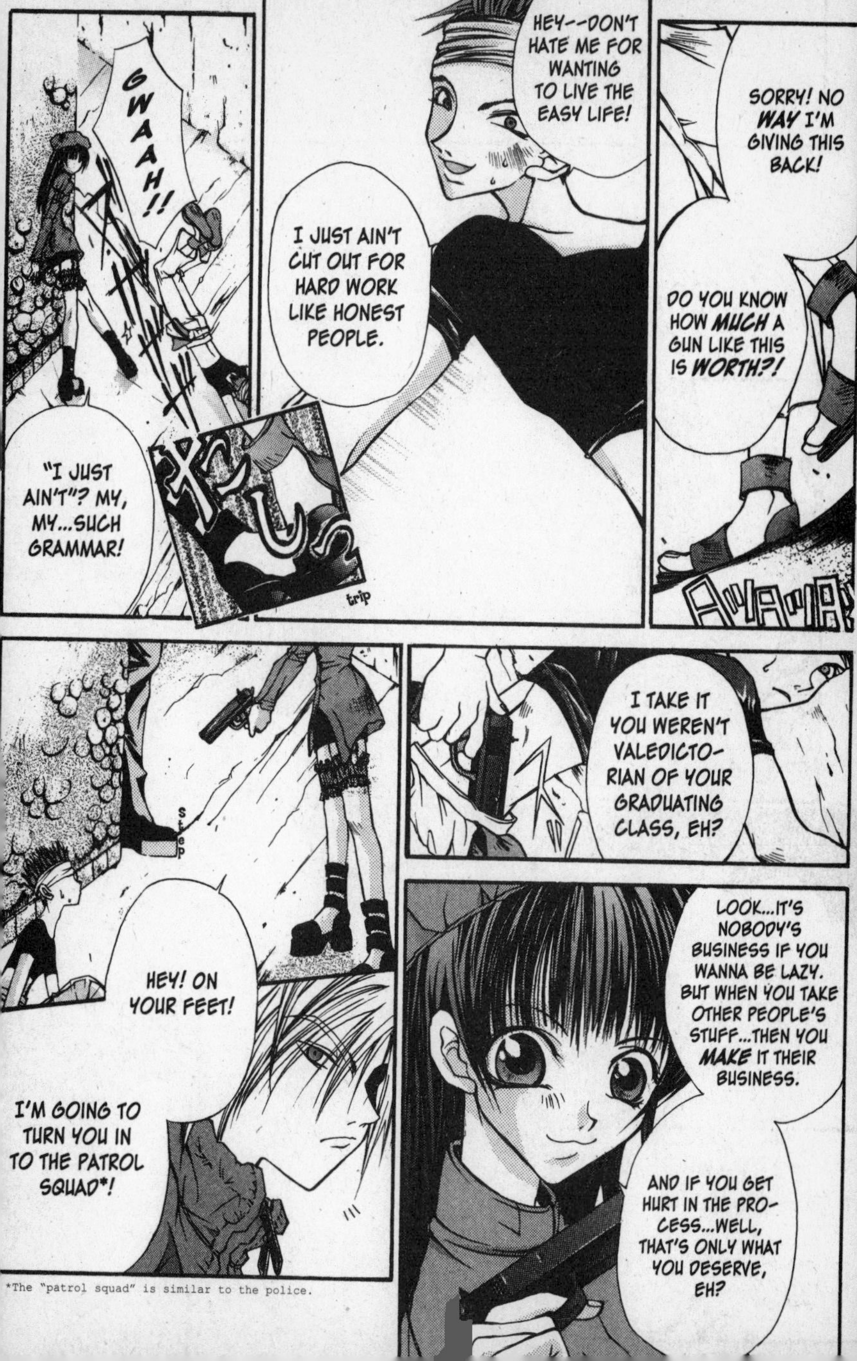
SORRY! NO WAY I'M GIVING THIS BACK!
DO YOU KNOW HOW MUCH A GUN LIKE THIS IS WORTH?!
HEY--DON'T HATE ME FOR WANTING TO LIVE THE EASY LIFE!
I JUST AIN'T CUT OUT FOR HARD WORK LIKE HONEST PEOPLE.
GWAAH!!
"I JUST AIN'T"? MY, MY...SUCH GRAMMAR!
trip
I TAKE IT YOU WEREN'T VALEDICTO-RIAN OF YOUR GRADUATING CLASS, EH?
LOOK...IT'S NOBODY'S BUSINESS IF YOU WANNA BE LAZY. BUT WHEN YOU TAKE OTHER PEOPLE'S STUFF...THEN YOU MAKE IT THEIR BUSINESS.
AND IF YOU GET HURT IN THE PRO-CESS...WELL, THAT'S ONLY WHAT YOU DESERVE, EH?
step
HEY! ON YOUR FEET!
I'M GOING TO TURN YOU IN TO THE PATROL SQUAD*!

*The "patrol squad" is similar to the police.

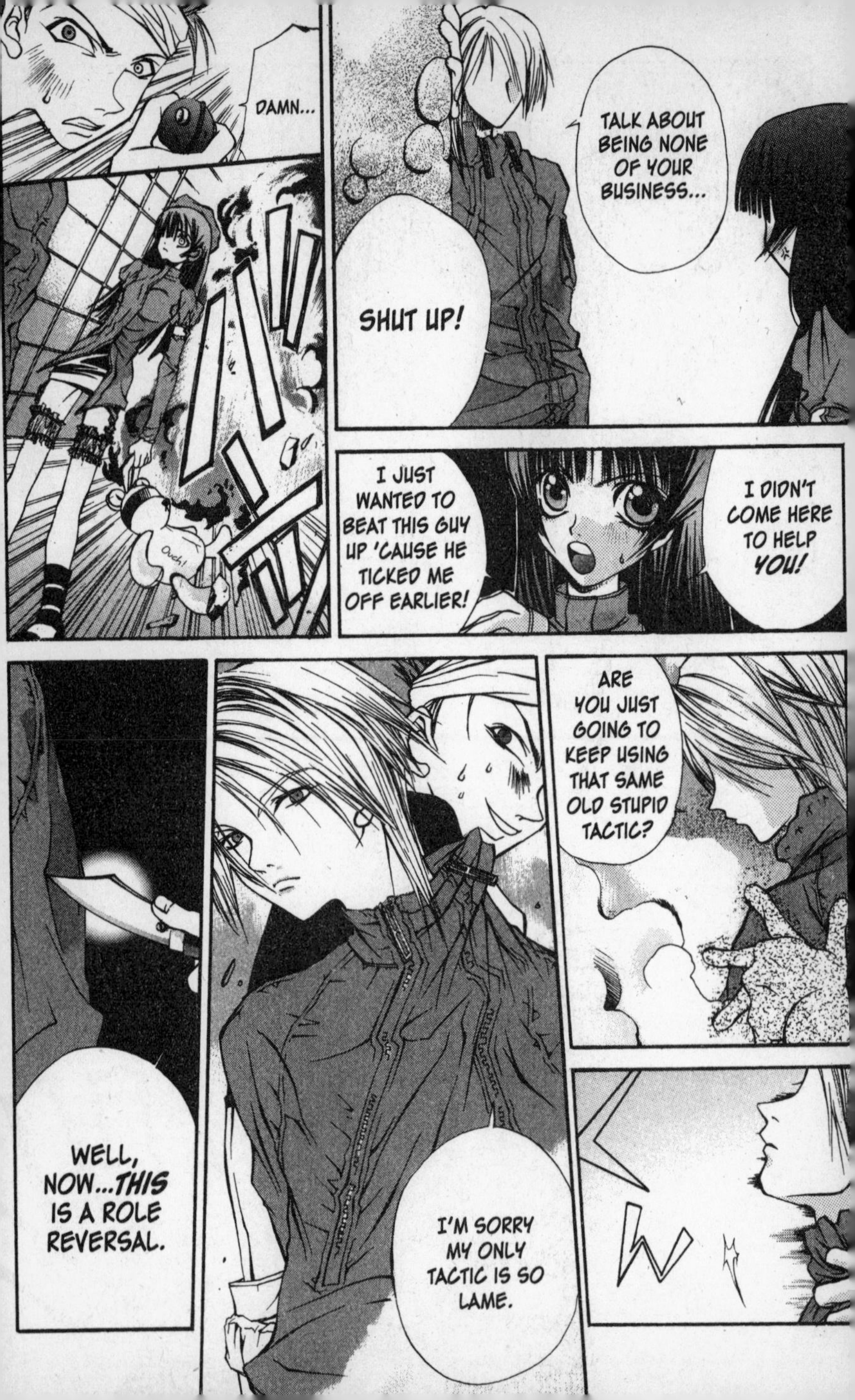
TALK ABOUT BEING NONE OF YOUR BUSINESS...
SHUT UP!
DAMN...
Ouch!
I DIDN'T COME HERE TO HELP *YOU!*
I JUST WANTED TO BEAT THIS GUY UP 'CAUSE HE TICKED ME OFF EARLIER!
ARE YOU JUST GOING TO KEEP USING THAT SAME OLD STUPID TACTIC?
I'M SORRY MY ONLY TACTIC IS SO LAME.
WELL, NOW...*THIS* IS A ROLE REVERSAL.

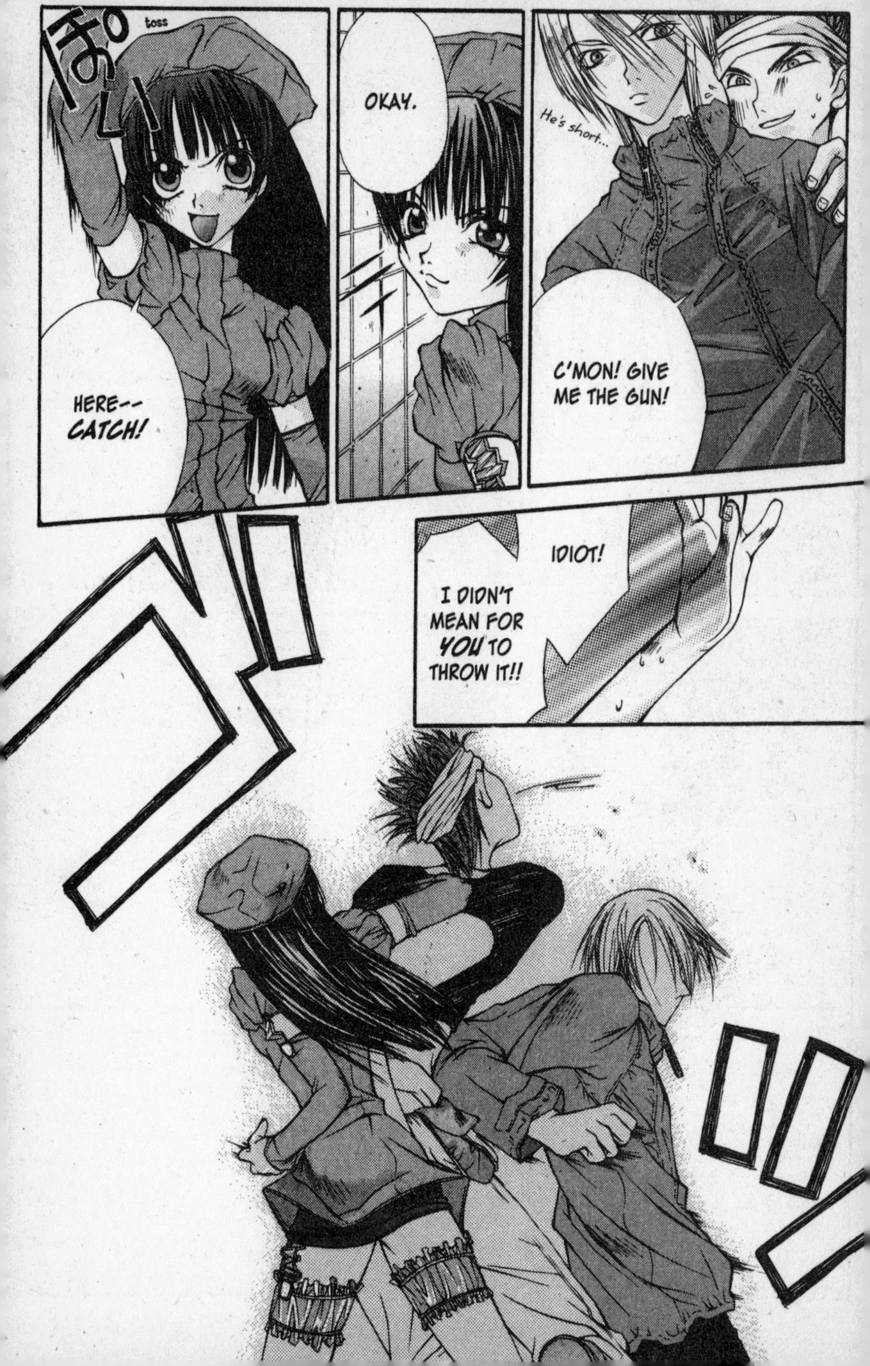
He's short...
C'MON! GIVE ME THE GUN!
OKAY.
ぽい
toss
HERE-- CATCH!
IDIOT!
I DIDN'T MEAN FOR YOU TO THROW IT!!

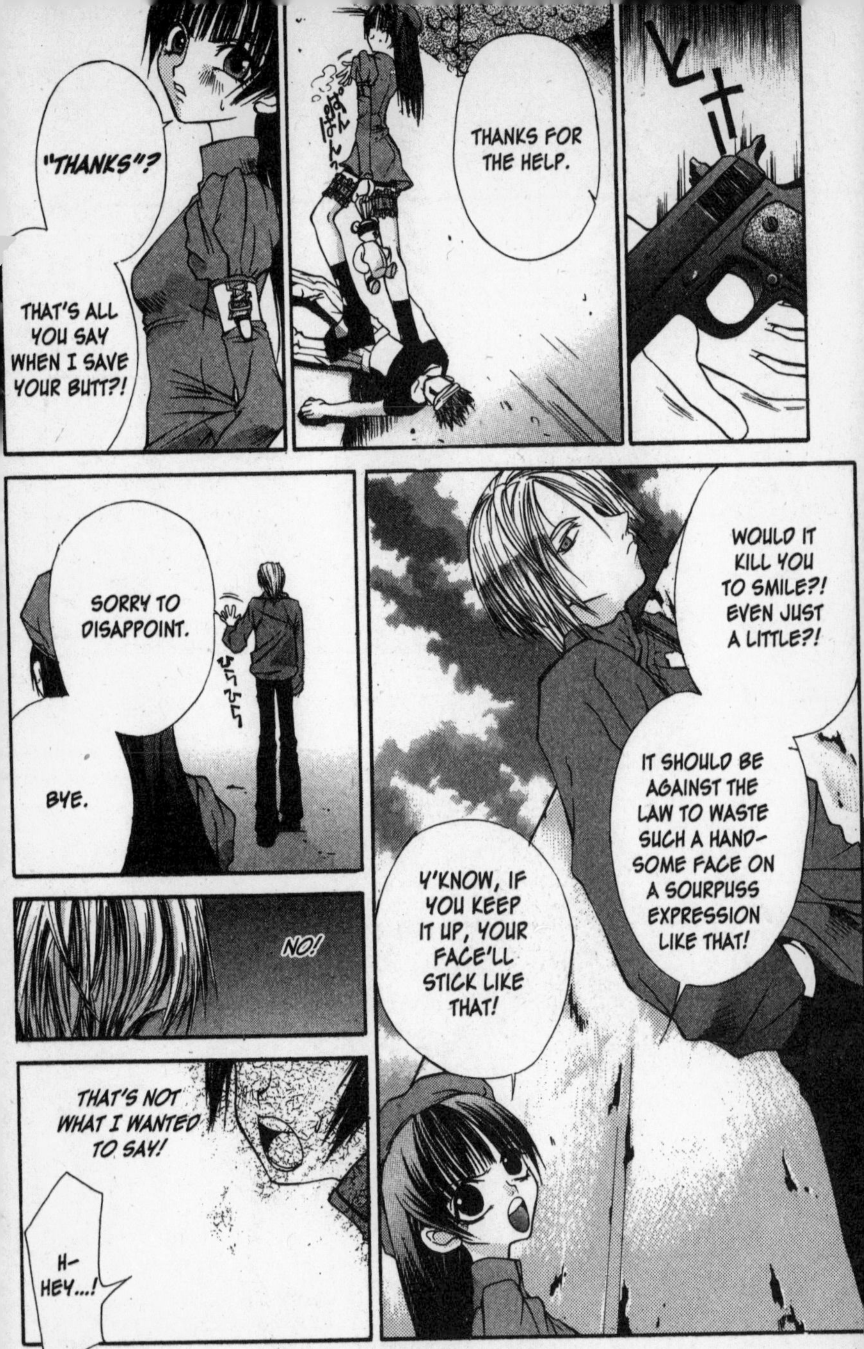
THANKS FOR THE HELP.
"THANKS"?
THAT'S ALL YOU SAY WHEN I SAVE YOUR BUTT?!
WOULD IT KILL YOU TO SMILE?! EVEN JUST A LITTLE?!
IT SHOULD BE AGAINST THE LAW TO WASTE SUCH A HAND-SOME FACE ON A SOURPUSS EXPRESSION LIKE THAT!
Y'KNOW, IF YOU KEEP IT UP, YOUR FACE'LL STICK LIKE THAT!
SORRY TO DISAPPOINT.
BYE.
NO!
THAT'S NOT WHAT I WANTED TO SAY!
H-HEY...!

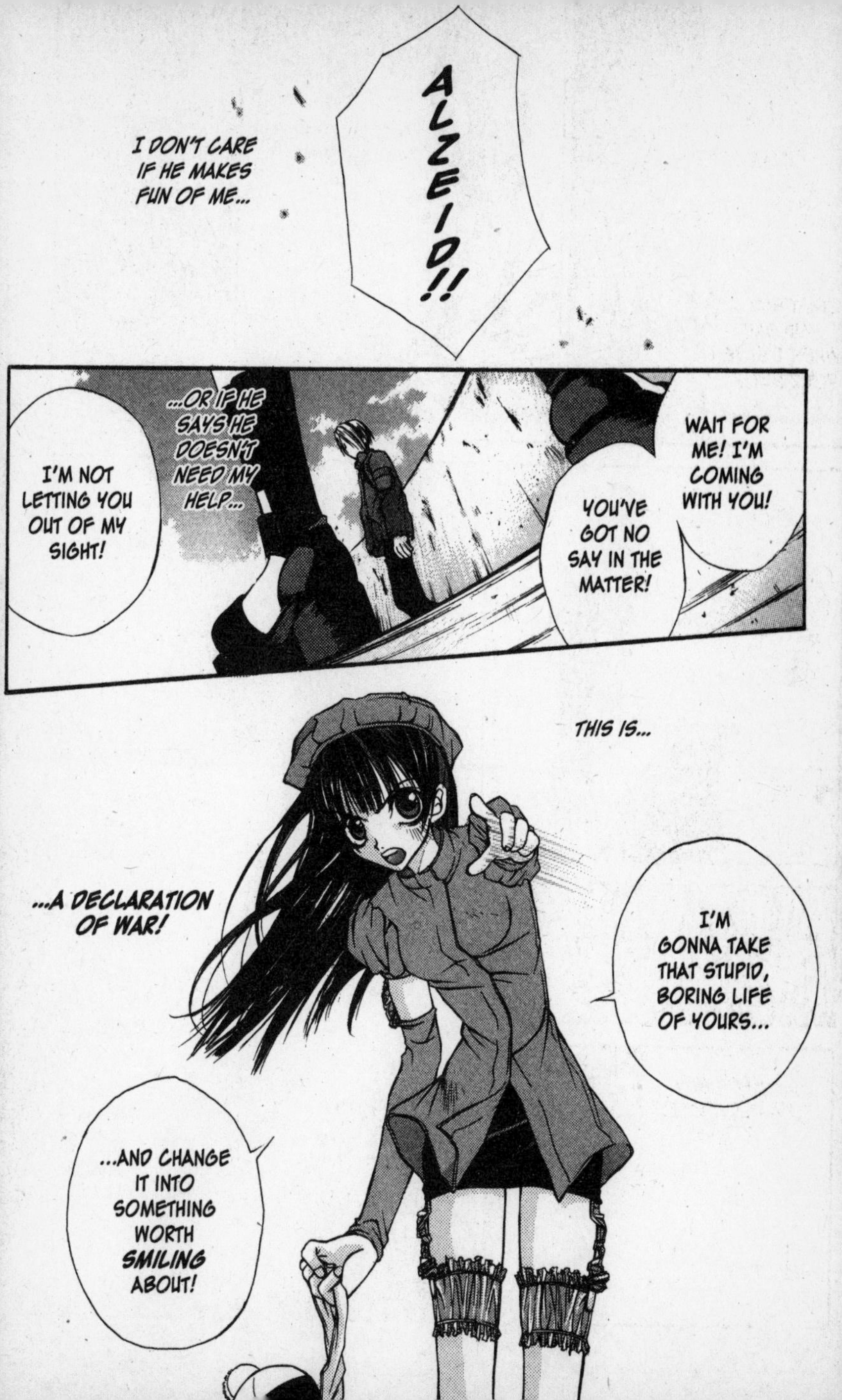
ALZEID!!
I DON'T CARE IF HE MAKES FUN OF ME...
WAIT FOR ME! I'M COMING WITH YOU!
YOU'VE GOT NO SAY IN THE MATTER!
...OR IF HE SAYS HE DOESN'T NEED MY HELP...
I'M NOT LETTING YOU OUT OF MY SIGHT!
THIS IS...
I'M GONNA TAKE THAT STUPID, BORING LIFE OF YOURS...
...A DECLARATION OF WAR!
...AND CHANGE IT INTO SOMETHING WORTH SMILING ABOUT!

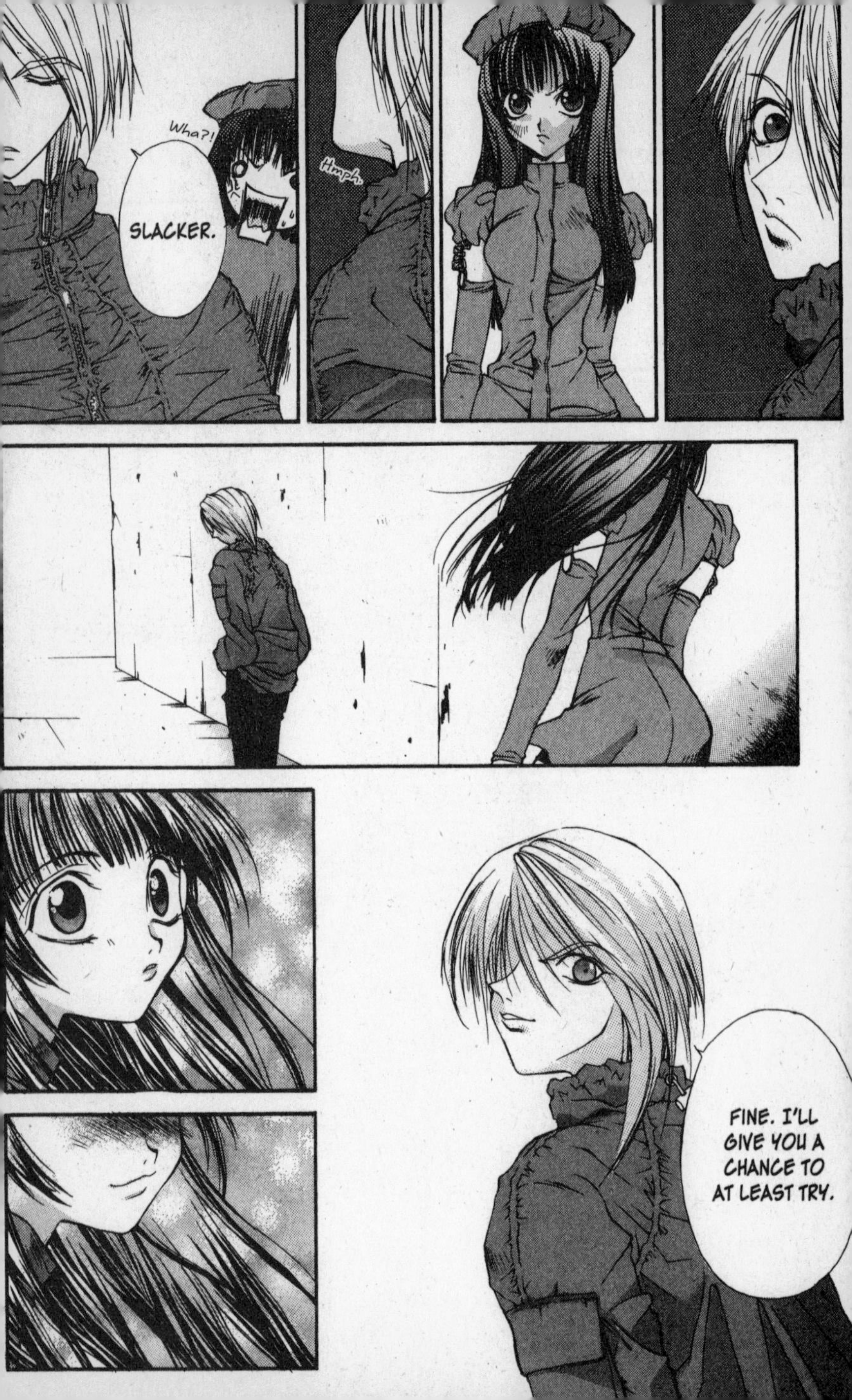
Hmph.
Wha?!
SLACKER.
FINE. I'LL GIVE YOU A CHANCE TO AT LEAST TRY.

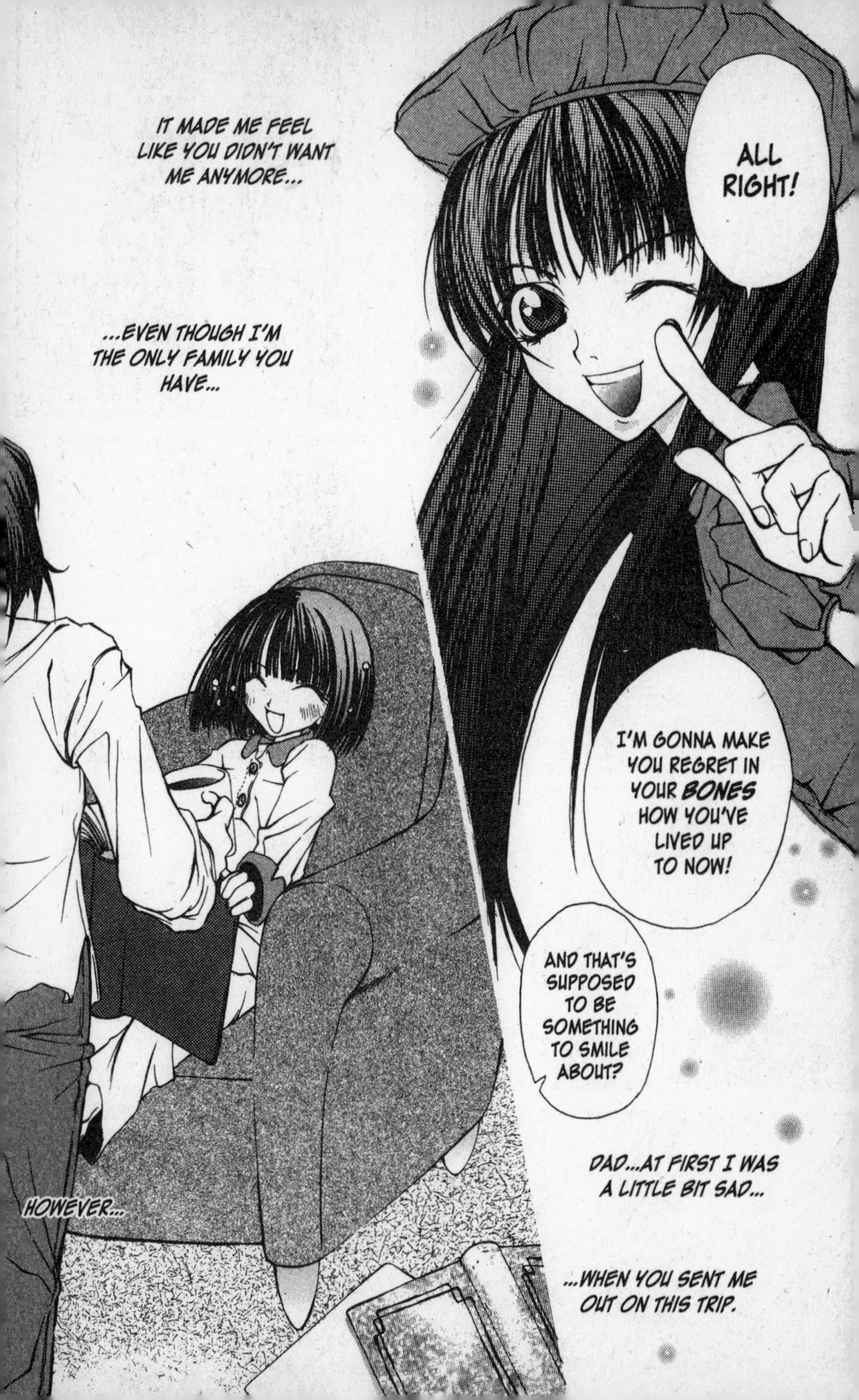
ALL RIGHT!
I'M GONNA MAKE YOU REGRET IN YOUR **BONES** HOW YOU'VE LIVED UP TO NOW!
AND THAT'S SUPPOSED TO BE SOMETHING TO SMILE ABOUT?
DAD...AT FIRST I WAS A LITTLE BIT SAD...
...WHEN YOU SENT ME OUT ON THIS TRIP.
IT MADE ME FEEL LIKE YOU DIDN'T WANT ME ANYMORE...
...EVEN THOUGH I'M THE ONLY FAMILY YOU HAVE...
HOWEVER...

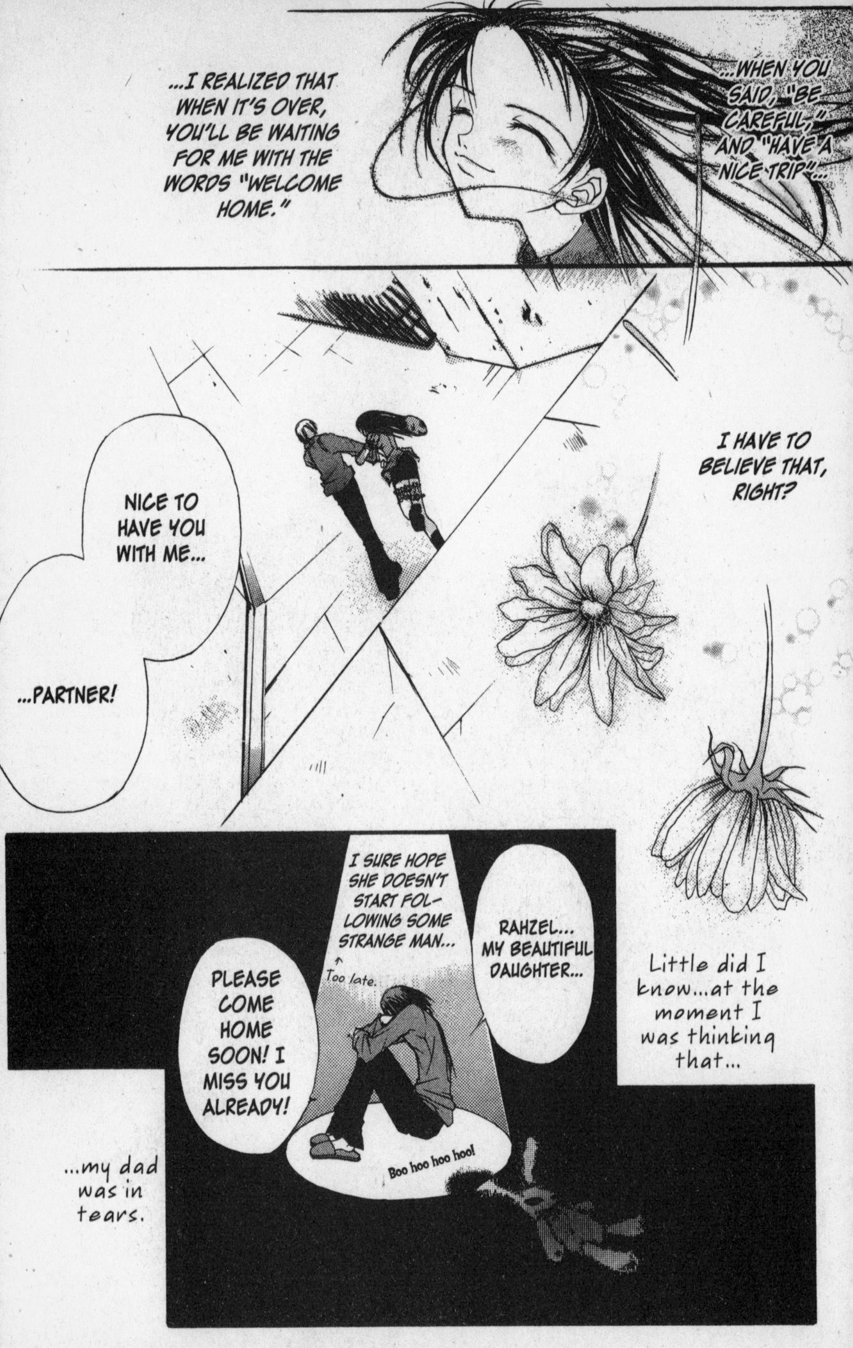
...WHEN YOU SAID, "BE CAREFUL," AND "HAVE A NICE TRIP"...
...I REALIZED THAT WHEN IT'S OVER, YOU'LL BE WAITING FOR ME WITH THE WORDS "WELCOME HOME."
I HAVE TO BELIEVE THAT, RIGHT?
NICE TO HAVE YOU WITH ME...
...PARTNER!
Little did I know...at the moment I was thinking that...
RAHZEL... MY BEAUTIFUL DAUGHTER...
I SURE HOPE SHE DOESN'T START FOL-LOWING SOME STRANGE MAN...
Too late.
PLEASE COME HOME SOON! I MISS YOU ALREADY!
Boo hoo hoo hoo!
...my dad was in tears.

Chapter 2: Separation

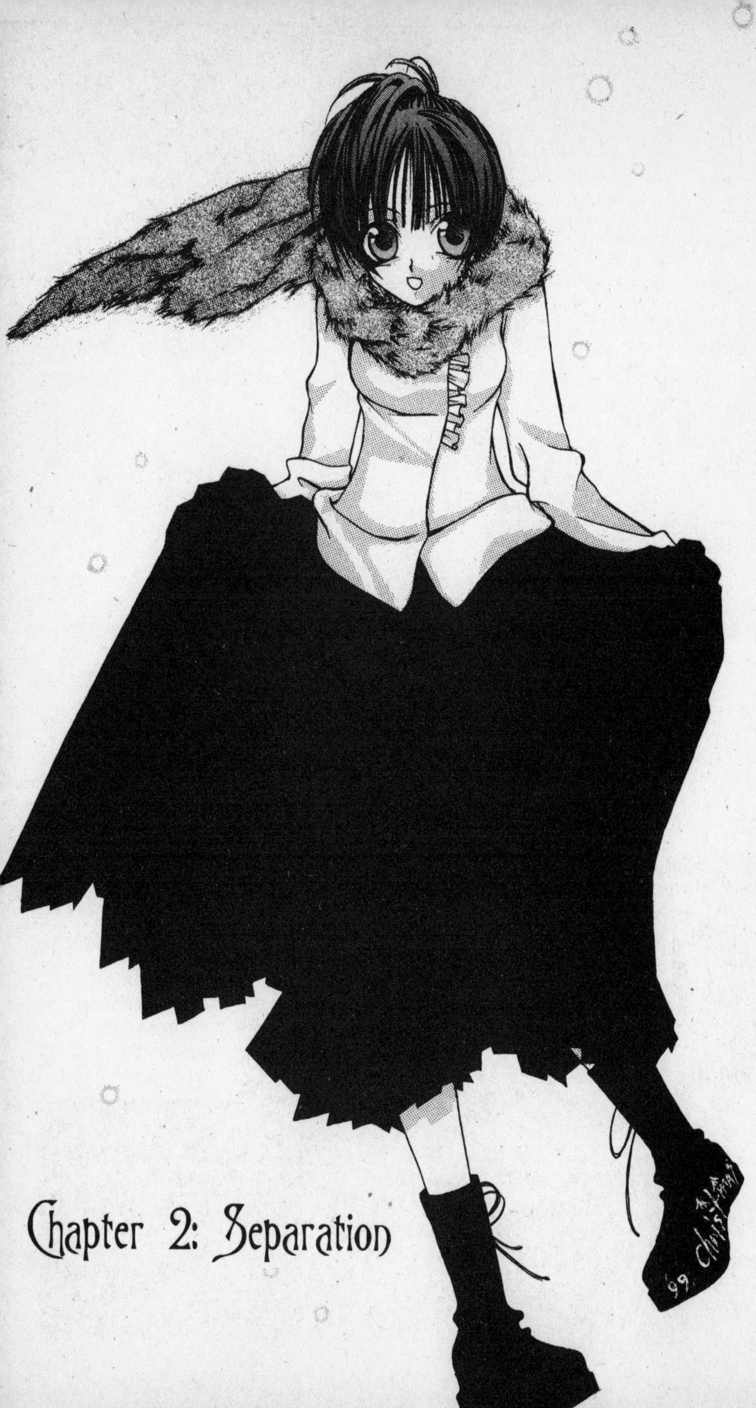

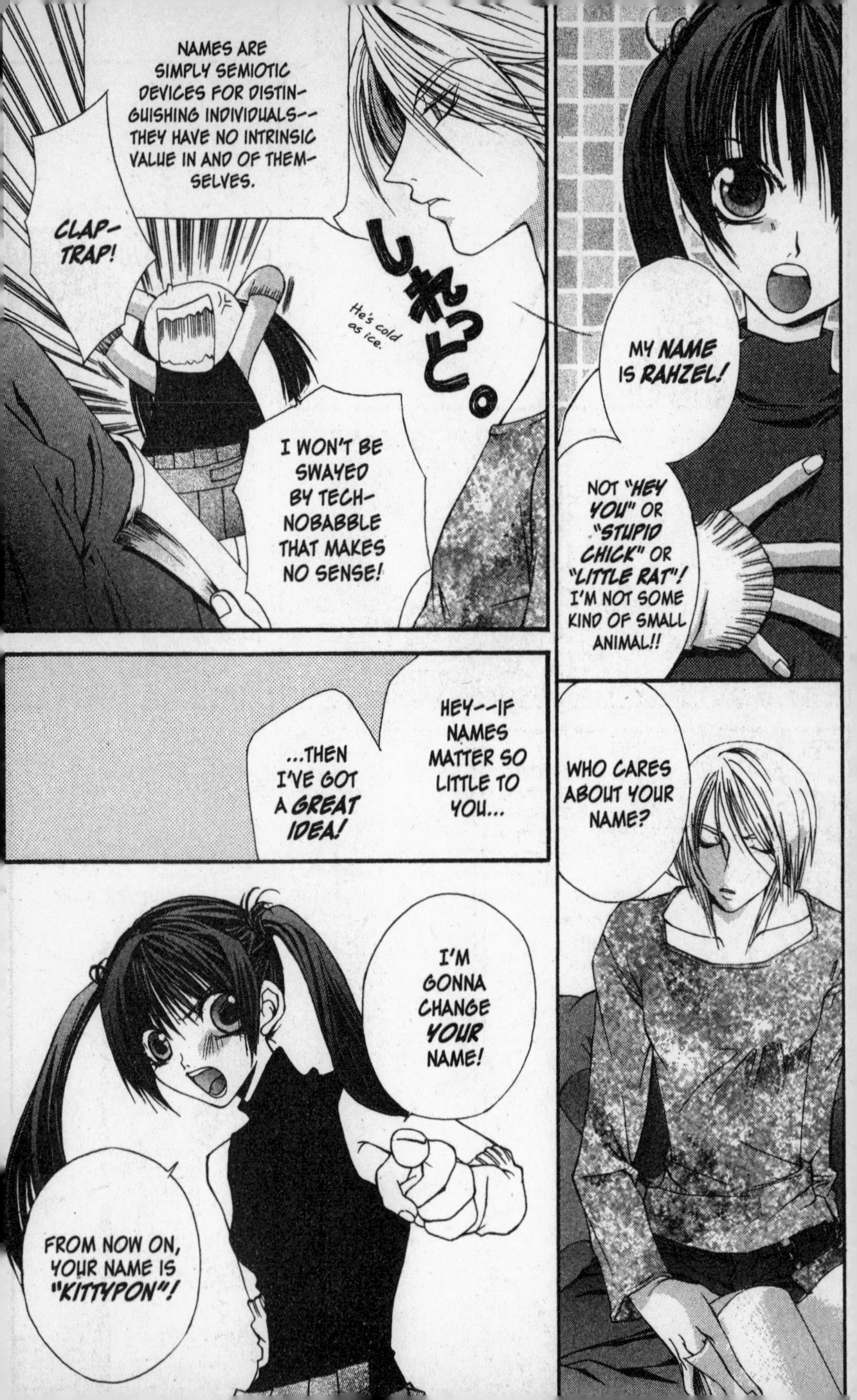
MY NAME IS RAHZEL!
NOT "HEY YOU" OR "STUPID CHICK" OR "LITTLE RAT"! I'M NOT SOME KIND OF SMALL ANIMAL!!
NAMES ARE SIMPLY SEMIOTIC DEVICES FOR DISTIN-GUISHING INDIVIDUALS--THEY HAVE NO INTRINSIC VALUE IN AND OF THEM-SELVES.
しれっと。
He's cold as ice.
CLAP-TRAP!
I WON'T BE SWAYED BY TECH-NOBABBLE THAT MAKES NO SENSE!
WHO CARES ABOUT YOUR NAME?
HEY--IF NAMES MATTER SO LITTLE TO YOU...
...THEN I'VE GOT A GREAT IDEA!
I'M GONNA CHANGE YOUR NAME!
FROM NOW ON, YOUR NAME IS "KITTYPON"!

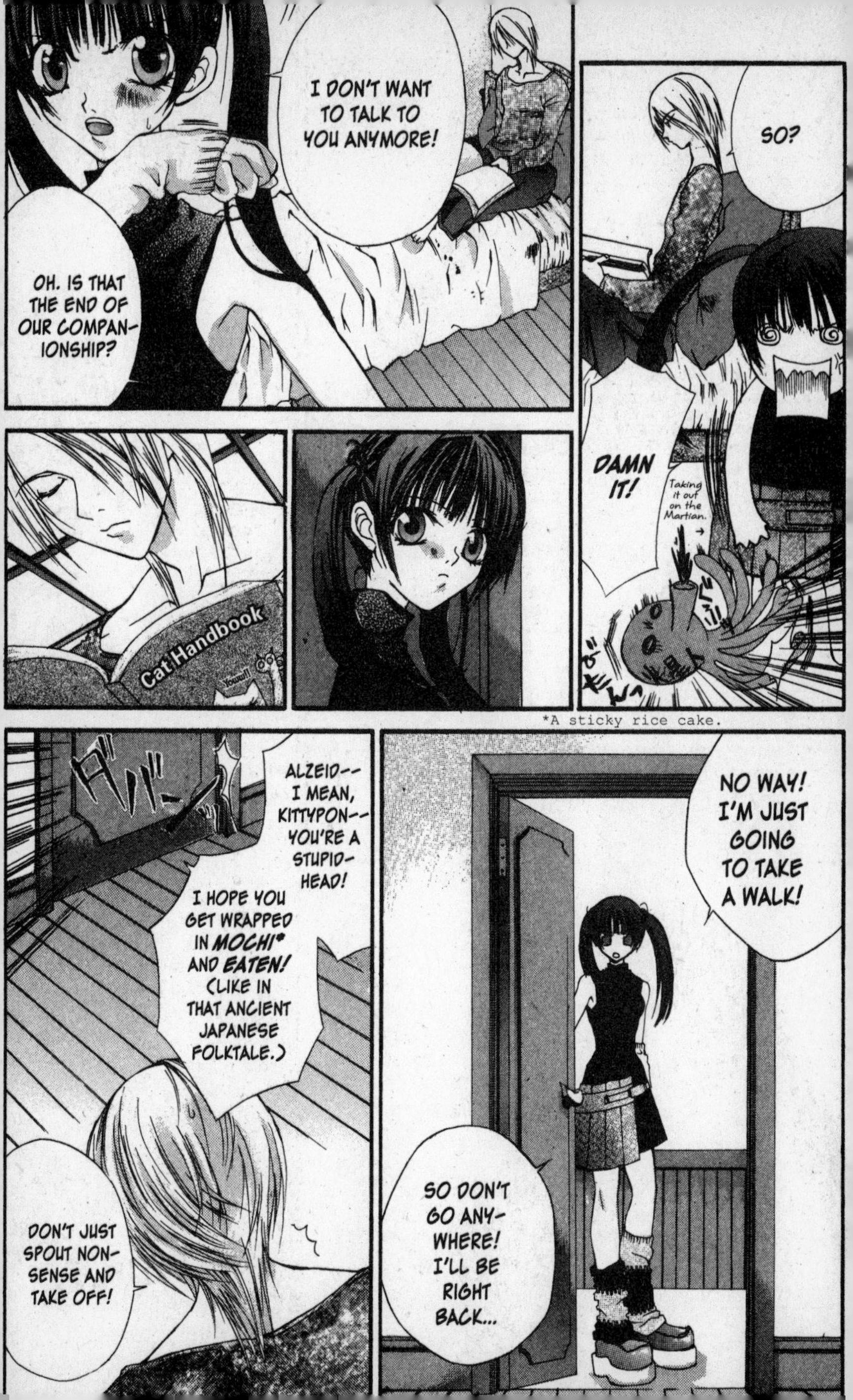
SO?
DAMN IT!
Taking it out on the Martian.
I DON'T WANT TO TALK TO YOU ANYMORE!
OH. IS THAT THE END OF OUR COMPANIONSHIP?
Cat Handbook
*A sticky rice cake.
NO WAY! I'M JUST GOING TO TAKE A WALK!
SO DON'T GO ANYWHERE! I'LL BE RIGHT BACK...
ALZEID-- I MEAN, KITTYPON-- YOU'RE A STUPID-HEAD!
I HOPE YOU GET WRAPPED IN MOCHI* AND EATEN! (LIKE IN THAT ANCIENT JAPANESE FOLKTALE.)
DON'T JUST SPOUT NONSENSE AND TAKE OFF!

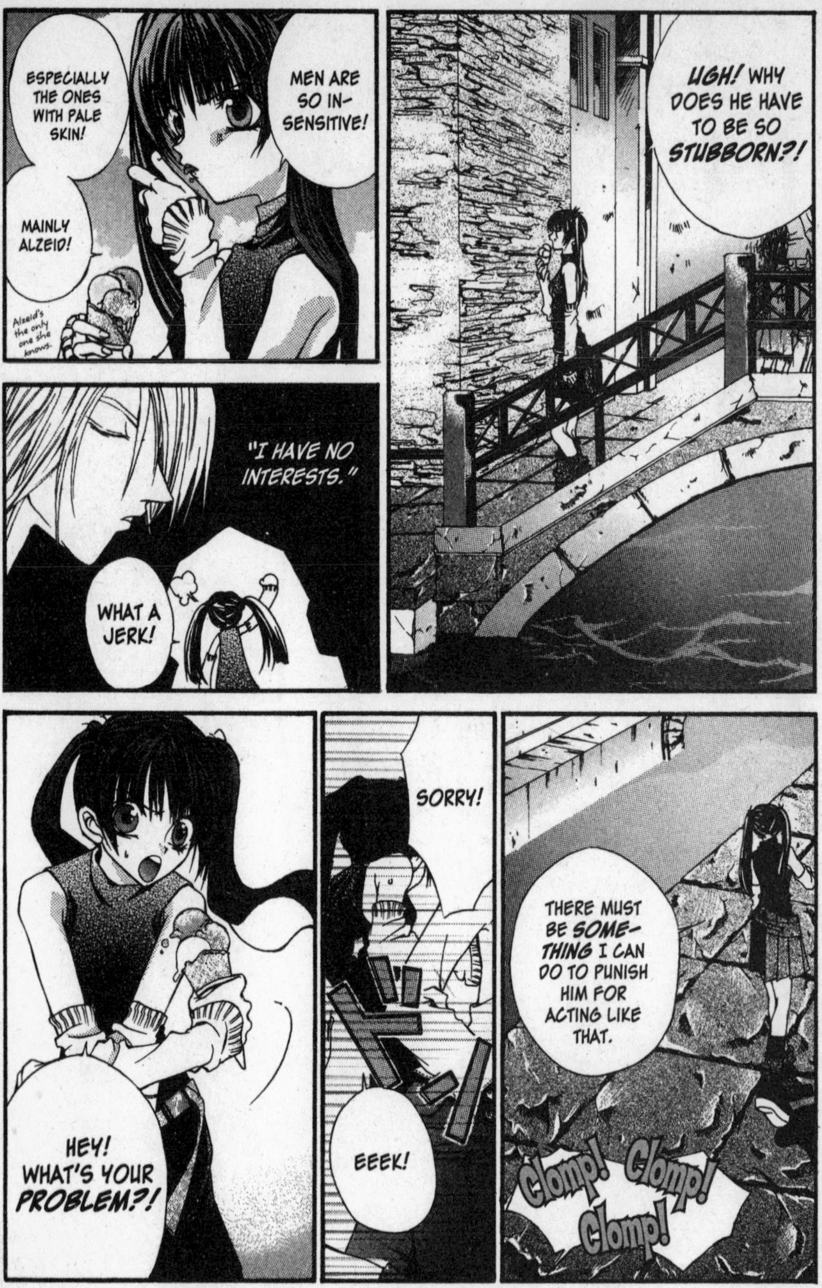
UGH! WHY DOES HE HAVE TO BE SO STUBBORN?!
MEN ARE SO IN-SENSITIVE!
ESPECIALLY THE ONES WITH PALE SKIN!
MAINLY ALZEID!
Alzeid's the only one she knows.
"I HAVE NO INTERESTS."
WHAT A JERK!
THERE MUST BE SOME-THING I CAN DO TO PUNISH HIM FOR ACTING LIKE THAT.
Clomp! Clomp! Clomp!
SORRY!
EEEK!
HEY! WHAT'S YOUR PROBLEM?!

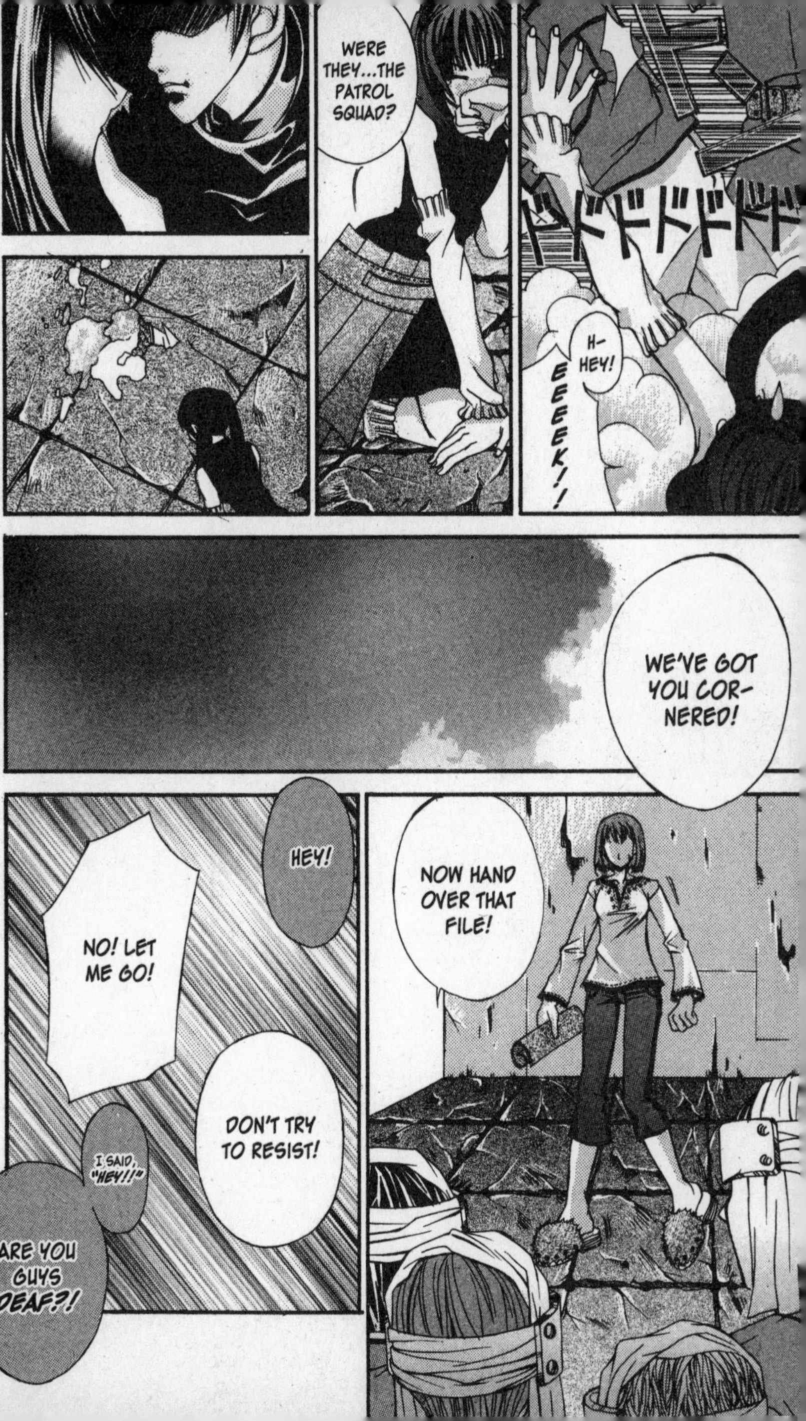
ドドドドドドド
H-HEY!
EEEEEK!!
WERE THEY...THE PATROL SQUAD?
WE'VE GOT YOU COR-NERED!
NOW HAND OVER THAT FILE!
HEY!
NO! LET ME GO!
DON'T TRY TO RESIST!
I SAID, "HEY!!"
ARE YOU GUYS DEAF?!

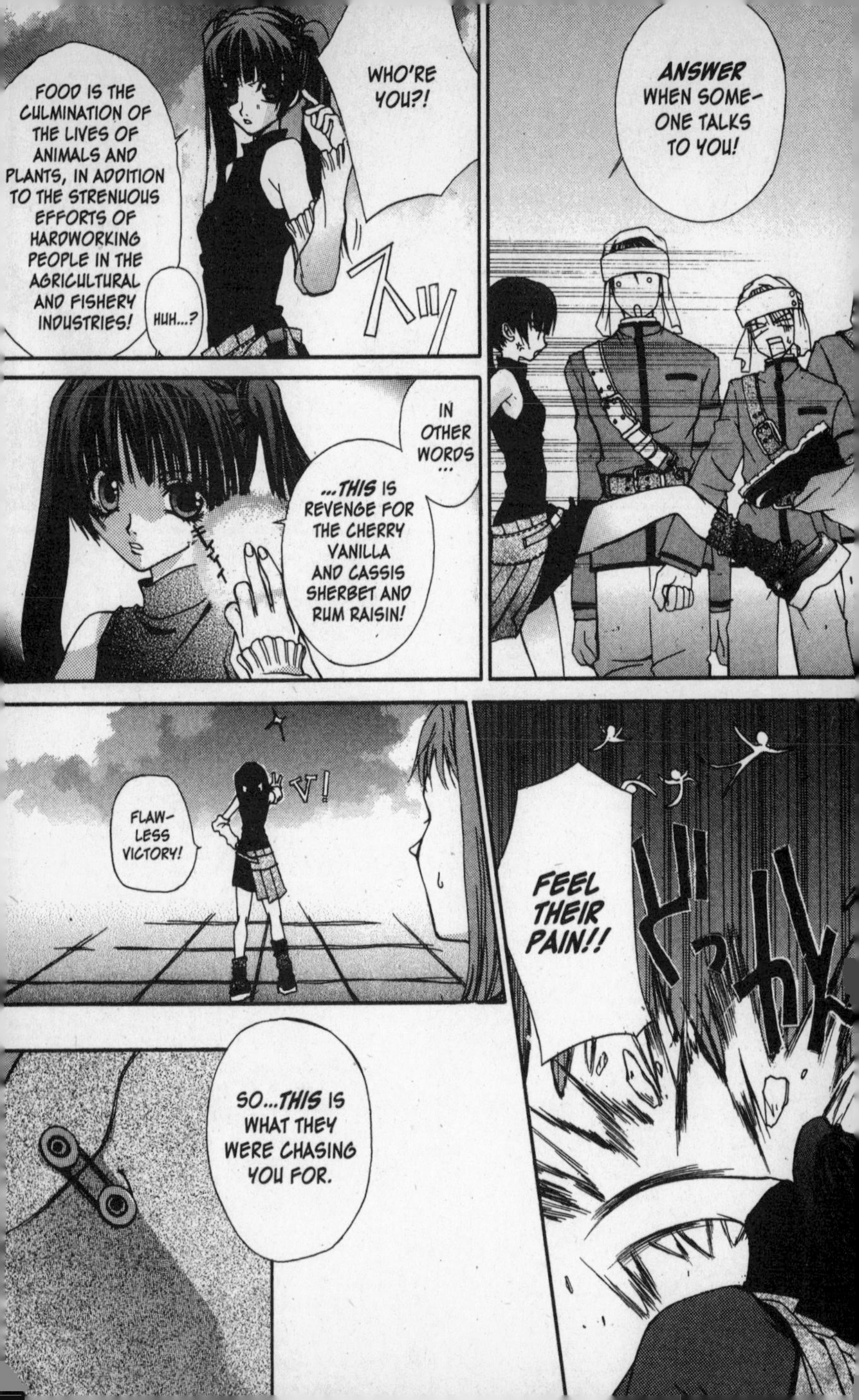
ANSWER WHEN SOME-ONE TALKS TO YOU!
WHO'RE YOU?!
FOOD IS THE CULMINATION OF THE LIVES OF ANIMALS AND PLANTS, IN ADDITION TO THE STRENUOUS EFFORTS OF HARDWORKING PEOPLE IN THE AGRICULTURAL AND FISHERY INDUSTRIES!
HUH...?
IN OTHER WORDS...
...THIS IS REVENGE FOR THE CHERRY VANILLA AND CASSIS SHERBET AND RUM RAISIN!
FEEL THEIR PAIN!!
FLAW-LESS VICTORY!
SO...THIS IS WHAT THEY WERE CHASING YOU FOR.

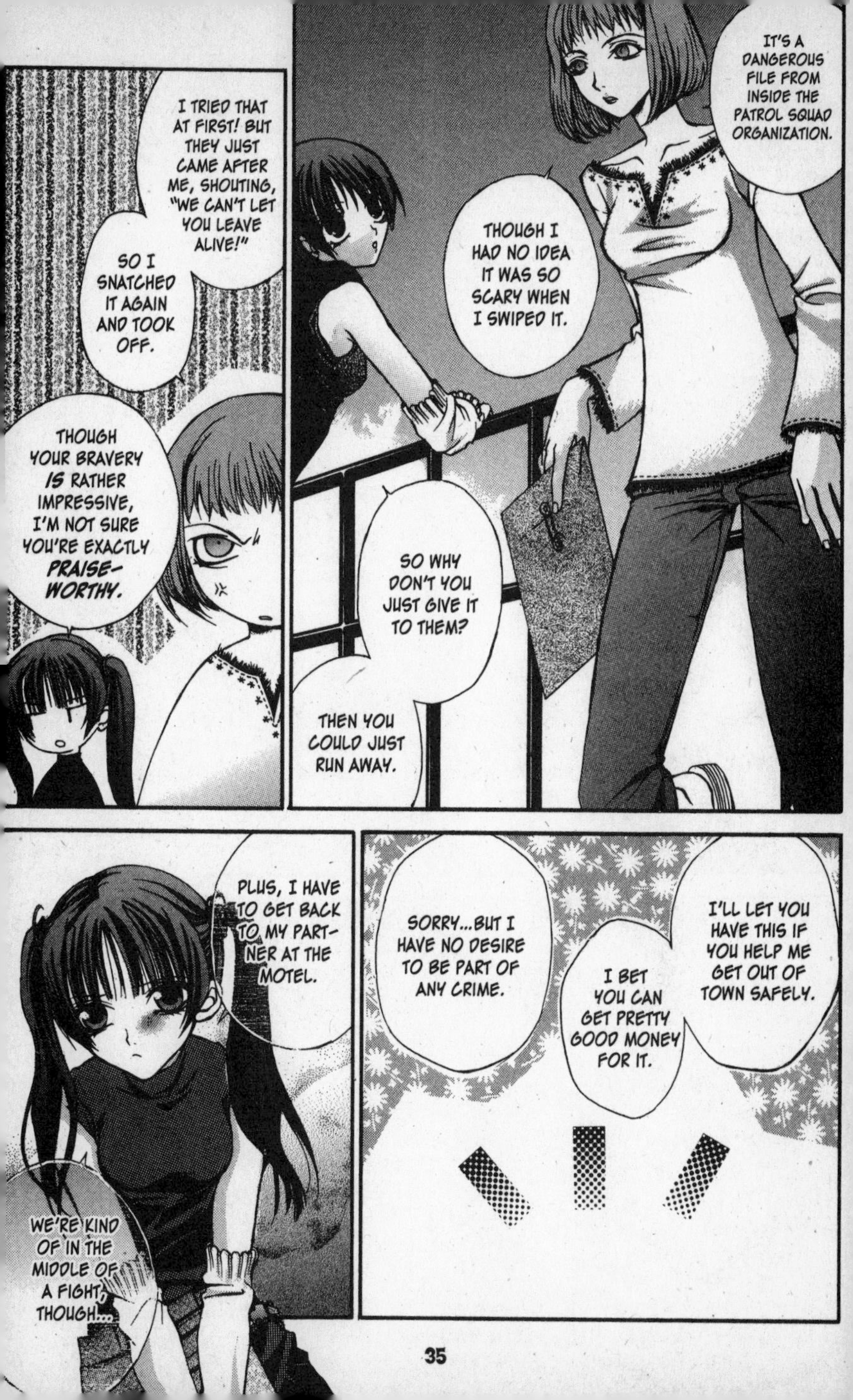

IT'S A DANGEROUS FILE FROM INSIDE THE PATROL SQUAD ORGANIZATION.
THOUGH I HAD NO IDEA IT WAS SO SCARY WHEN I SWIPED IT.
SO WHY DON'T YOU JUST GIVE IT TO THEM?
THEN YOU COULD JUST RUN AWAY.
I TRIED THAT AT FIRST! BUT THEY JUST CAME AFTER ME, SHOUTING, "WE CAN'T LET YOU LEAVE ALIVE!"
SO I SNATCHED IT AGAIN AND TOOK OFF.
THOUGH YOUR BRAVERY *IS* RATHER IMPRESSIVE, I'M NOT SURE YOU'RE EXACTLY *PRAISE-WORTHY.*
I'LL LET YOU HAVE THIS IF YOU HELP ME GET OUT OF TOWN SAFELY.
I BET YOU CAN GET PRETTY GOOD MONEY FOR IT.
SORRY...BUT I HAVE NO DESIRE TO BE PART OF ANY CRIME.
PLUS, I HAVE TO GET BACK TO MY PART-NER AT THE MOTEL.
WE'RE KIND OF IN THE MIDDLE OF A FIGHT, THOUGH...

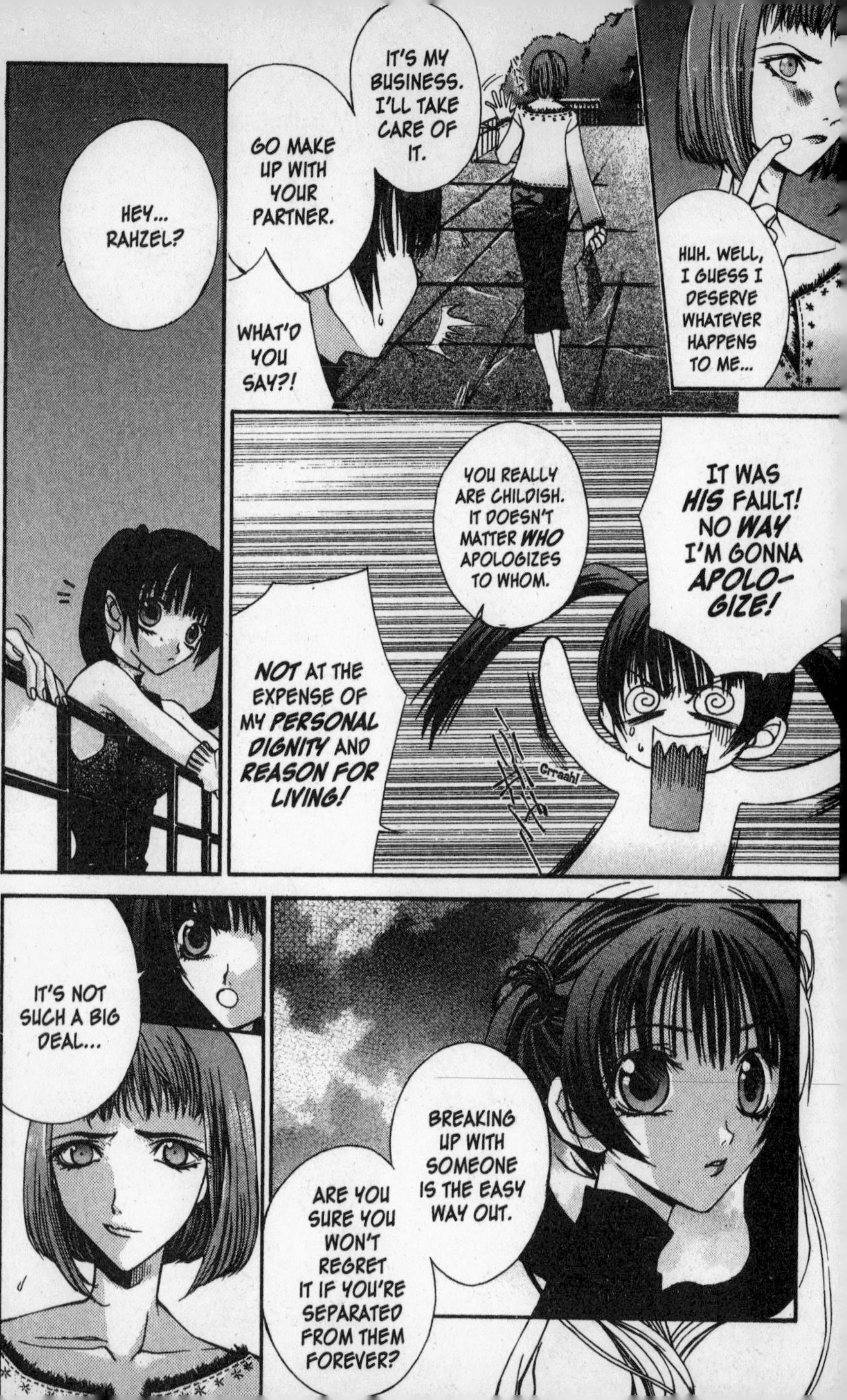
HUH. WELL, I GUESS I DESERVE WHATEVER HAPPENS TO ME...
IT'S MY BUSINESS. I'LL TAKE CARE OF IT.
GO MAKE UP WITH YOUR PARTNER.
WHAT'D YOU SAY?!
IT WAS HIS FAULT! NO WAY I'M GONNA APOLOGIZE!
YOU REALLY ARE CHILDISH. IT DOESN'T MATTER WHO APOLOGIZES TO WHOM.
NOT AT THE EXPENSE OF MY PERSONAL DIGNITY AND REASON FOR LIVING!
Grraah!
HEY... RAHZEL?
BREAKING UP WITH SOMEONE IS THE EASY WAY OUT.
ARE YOU SURE YOU WON'T REGRET IT IF YOU'RE SEPARATED FROM THEM FOREVER?
IT'S NOT SUCH A BIG DEAL...

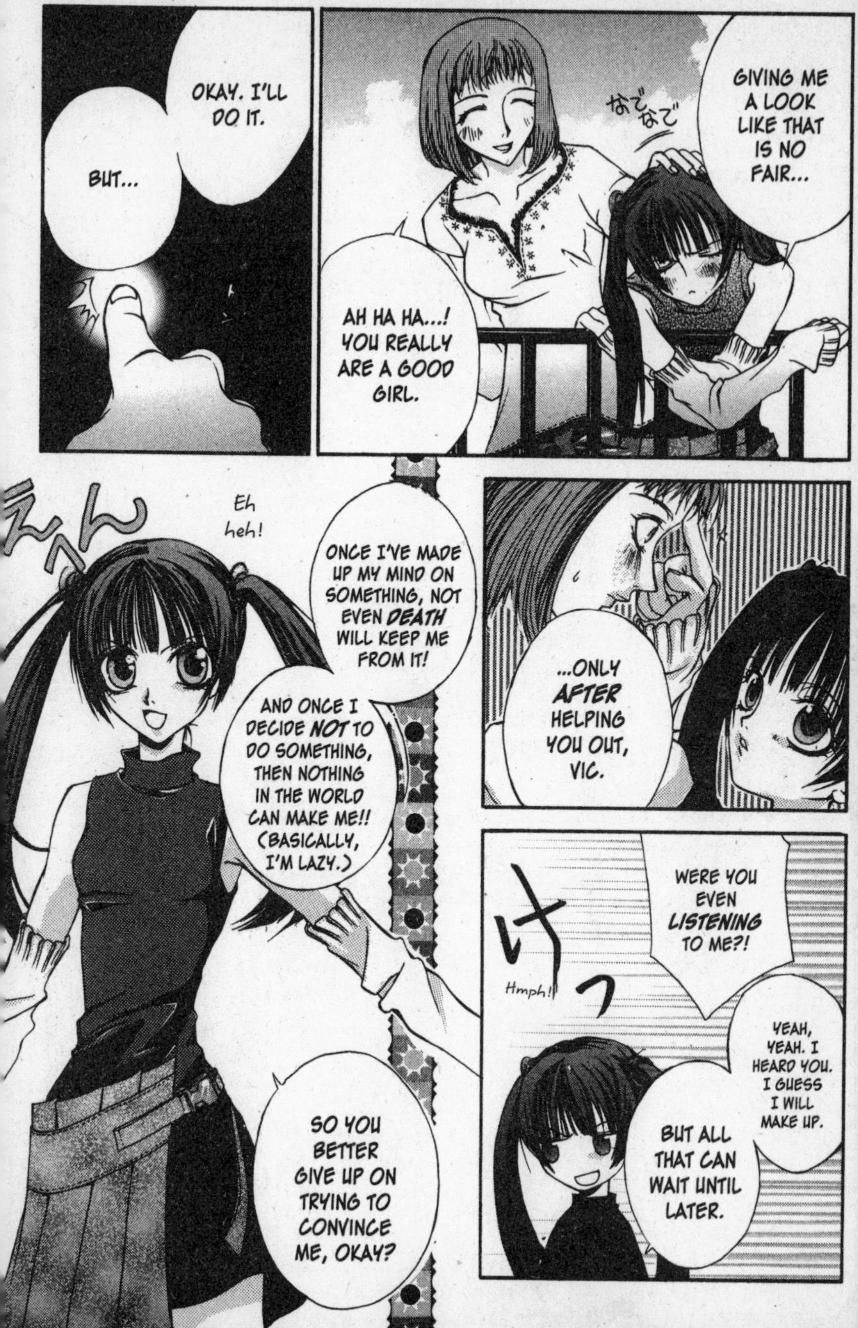
GIVING ME A LOOK LIKE THAT IS NO FAIR...
なでなで
AH HA HA...! YOU REALLY ARE A GOOD GIRL.
OKAY. I'LL DO IT.
BUT...
...ONLY AFTER HELPING YOU OUT, VIC.
WERE YOU EVEN LISTENING TO ME?!
けっ
Hmph!!
YEAH, YEAH. I HEARD YOU. I GUESS I WILL MAKE UP.
BUT ALL THAT CAN WAIT UNTIL LATER.
えへん
Eh heh!
ONCE I'VE MADE UP MY MIND ON SOMETHING, NOT EVEN DEATH WILL KEEP ME FROM IT!
AND ONCE I DECIDE NOT TO DO SOMETHING, THEN NOTHING IN THE WORLD CAN MAKE ME!! (BASICALLY, I'M LAZY.)
SO YOU BETTER GIVE UP ON TRYING TO CONVINCE ME, OKAY?

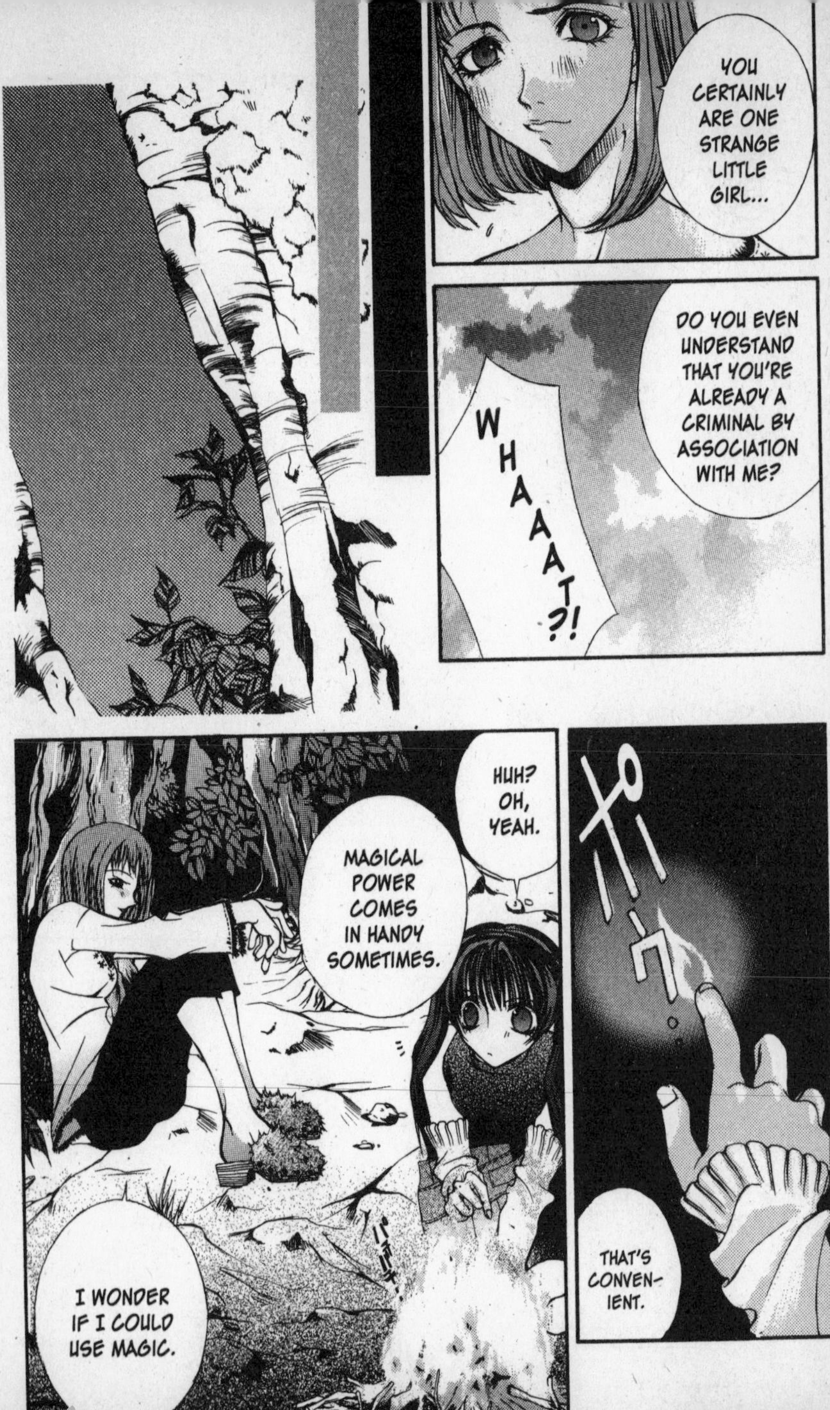
YOU CERTAINLY ARE ONE STRANGE LITTLE GIRL...
DO YOU EVEN UNDERSTAND THAT YOU'RE ALREADY A CRIMINAL BY ASSOCIATION WITH ME?
WHAAAAT?!
THAT'S CONVEN-IENT.
HUH? OH, YEAH.
MAGICAL POWER COMES IN HANDY SOMETIMES.
I WONDER IF I COULD USE MAGIC.

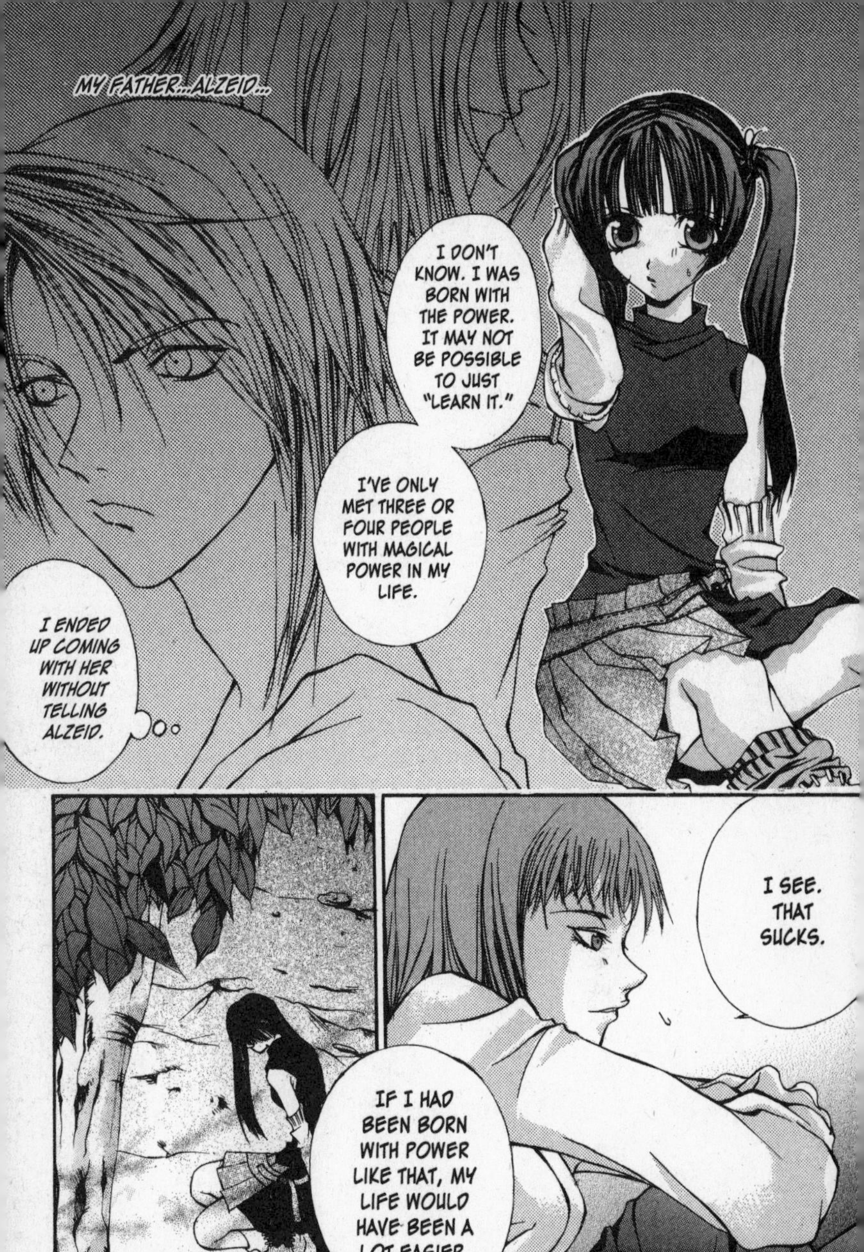
I DON'T KNOW. I WAS BORN WITH THE POWER. IT MAY NOT BE POSSIBLE TO JUST "LEARN IT."
I'VE ONLY MET THREE OR FOUR PEOPLE WITH MAGICAL POWER IN MY LIFE.
MY FATHER...ALZEID...
I ENDED UP COMING WITH HER WITHOUT TELLING ALZEID.
I SEE. THAT SUCKS.
IF I HAD BEEN BORN WITH POWER LIKE THAT, MY LIFE WOULD HAVE BEEN A LOT EASIER.

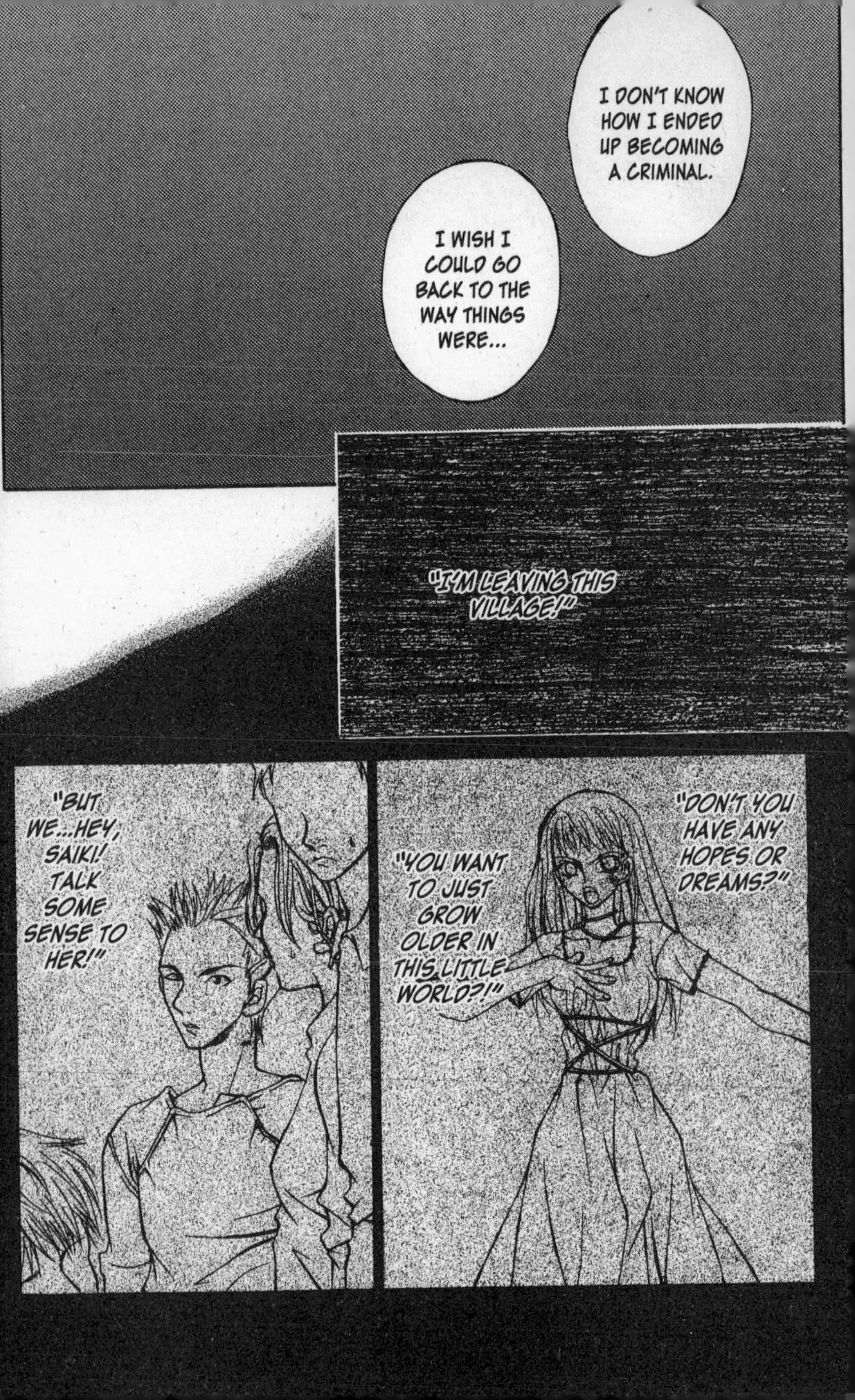
I DON'T KNOW HOW I ENDED UP BECOMING A CRIMINAL.
I WISH I COULD GO BACK TO THE WAY THINGS WERE...
"I'M LEAVING THIS VILLAGE!"
"DON'T YOU HAVE ANY HOPES OR DREAMS?"
"YOU WANT TO JUST GROW OLDER IN THIS LITTLE WORLD?!"
"BUT WE...HEY, SAIKI! TALK SOME SENSE TO HER!"

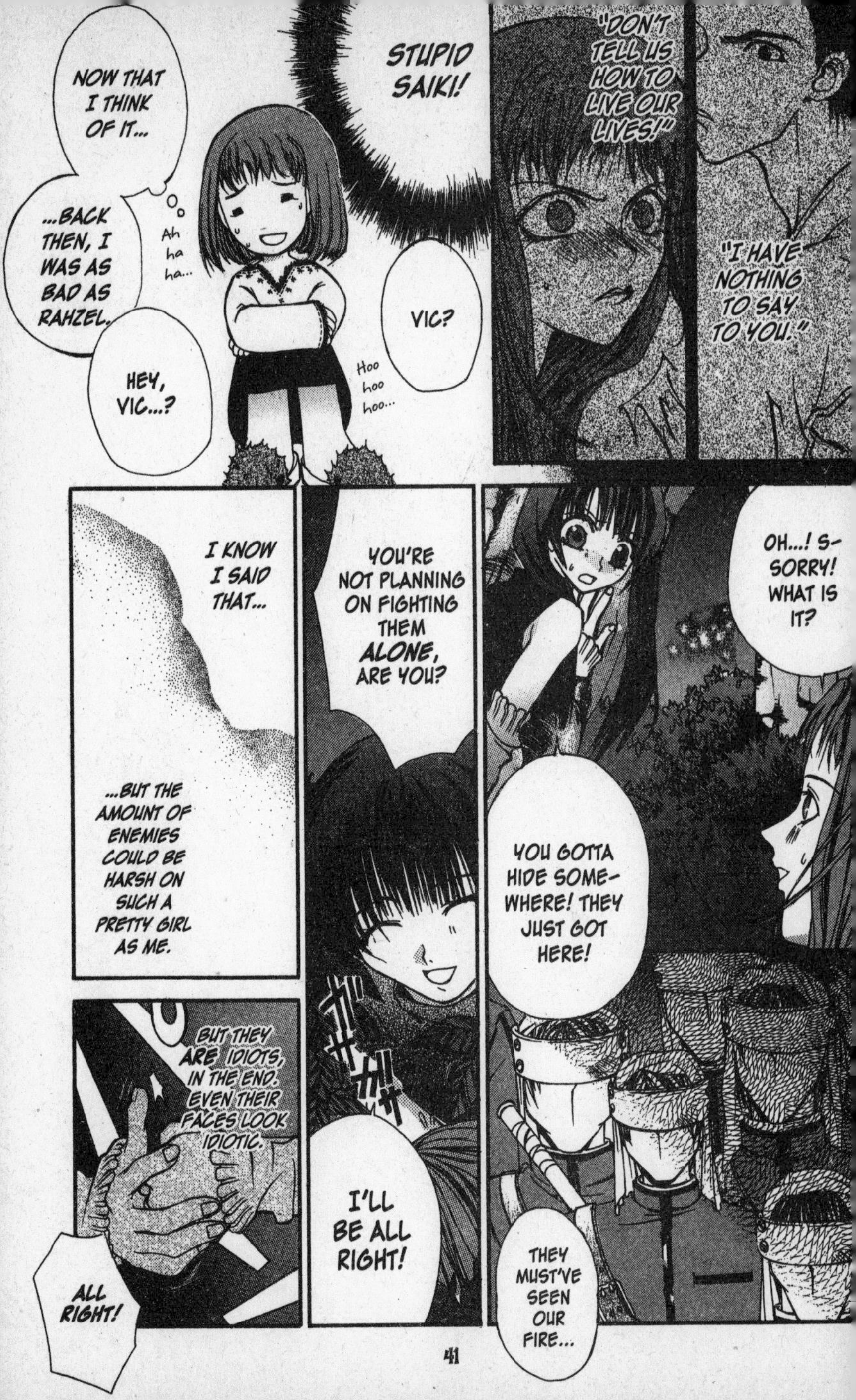
"DON'T TELL US HOW TO LIVE OUR LIVES!"
"I HAVE NOTHING TO SAY TO YOU."
STUPID SAIKI!
NOW THAT I THINK OF IT...
...BACK THEN, I WAS AS BAD AS RAHZEL.
Oo Ah ha ha...
VIC?
Hoo hoo hoo...
HEY, VIC...?
OH...! S-SORRY! WHAT IS IT?
YOU GOTTA HIDE SOME-WHERE! THEY JUST GOT HERE!
THEY MUST'VE SEEN OUR FIRE...
YOU'RE NOT PLANNING ON FIGHTING THEM ALONE, ARE YOU?
I'LL BE ALL RIGHT!
I KNOW I SAID THAT...
...BUT THE AMOUNT OF ENEMIES COULD BE HARSH ON SUCH A PRETTY GIRL AS ME.
BUT THEY ARE IDIOTS, IN THE END. EVEN THEIR FACES LOOK IDIOTIC.
ALL RIGHT!

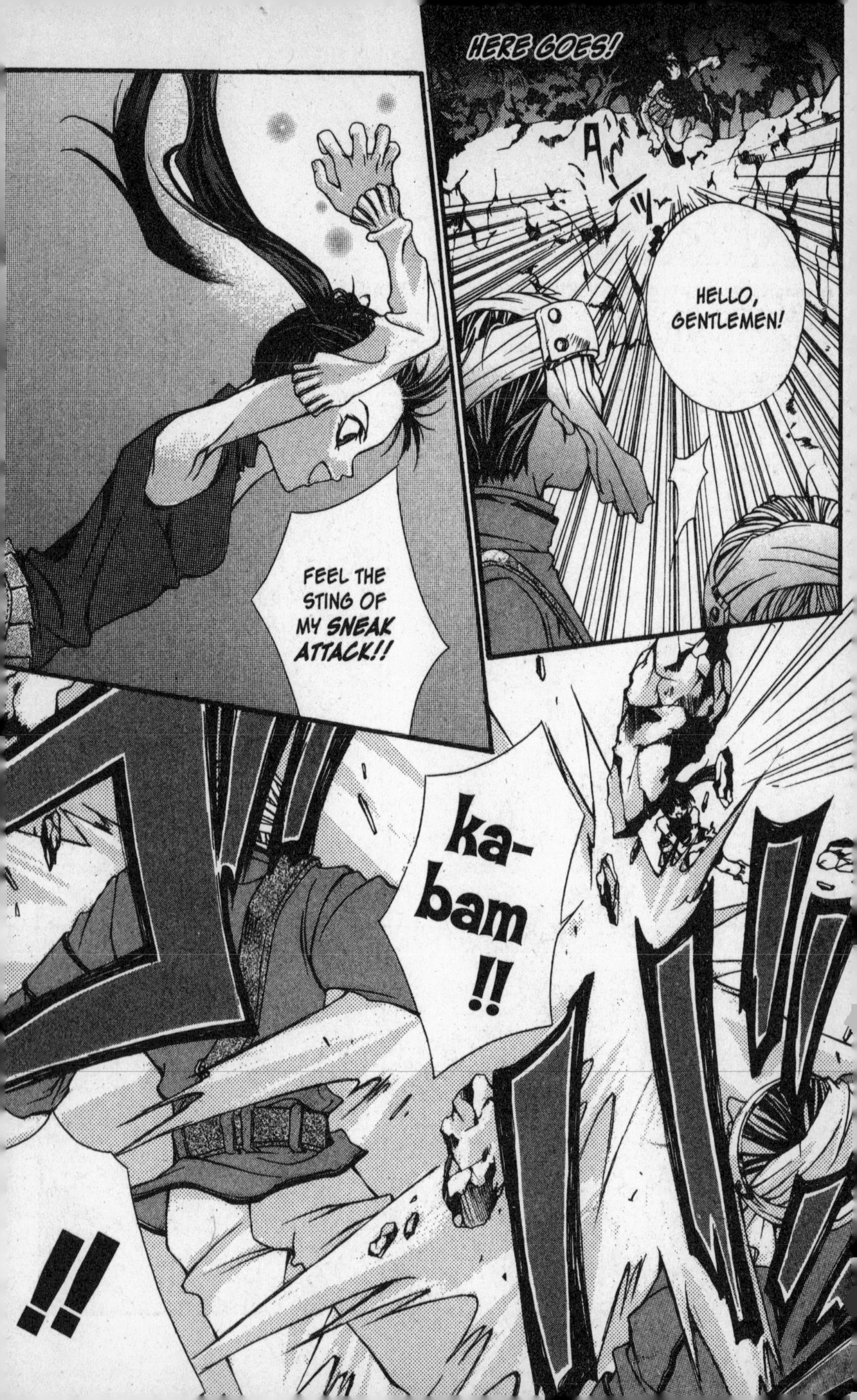
HERE GOES!
HELLO, GENTLEMEN!
FEEL THE STING OF MY SNEAK ATTACK!!
ka-bam !!
!!

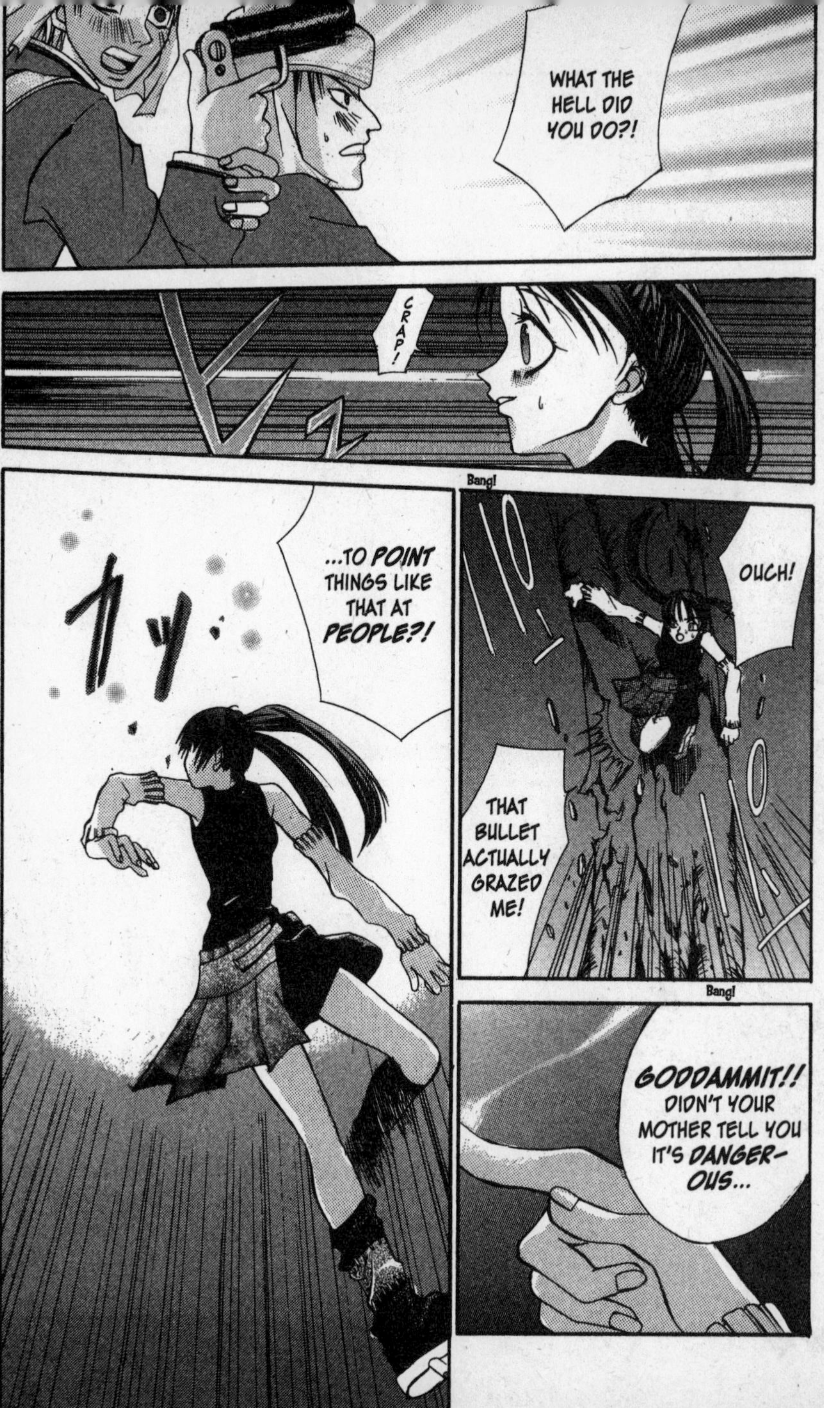
WHAT THE HELL DID YOU DO?!
CRAP!
Bang!
OUCH!
THAT BULLET ACTUALLY GRAZED ME!
Bang!
GODDAMMIT!! DIDN'T YOUR MOTHER TELL YOU IT'S DANGER-OUS...
...TO POINT THINGS LIKE THAT AT PEOPLE?!
カッ

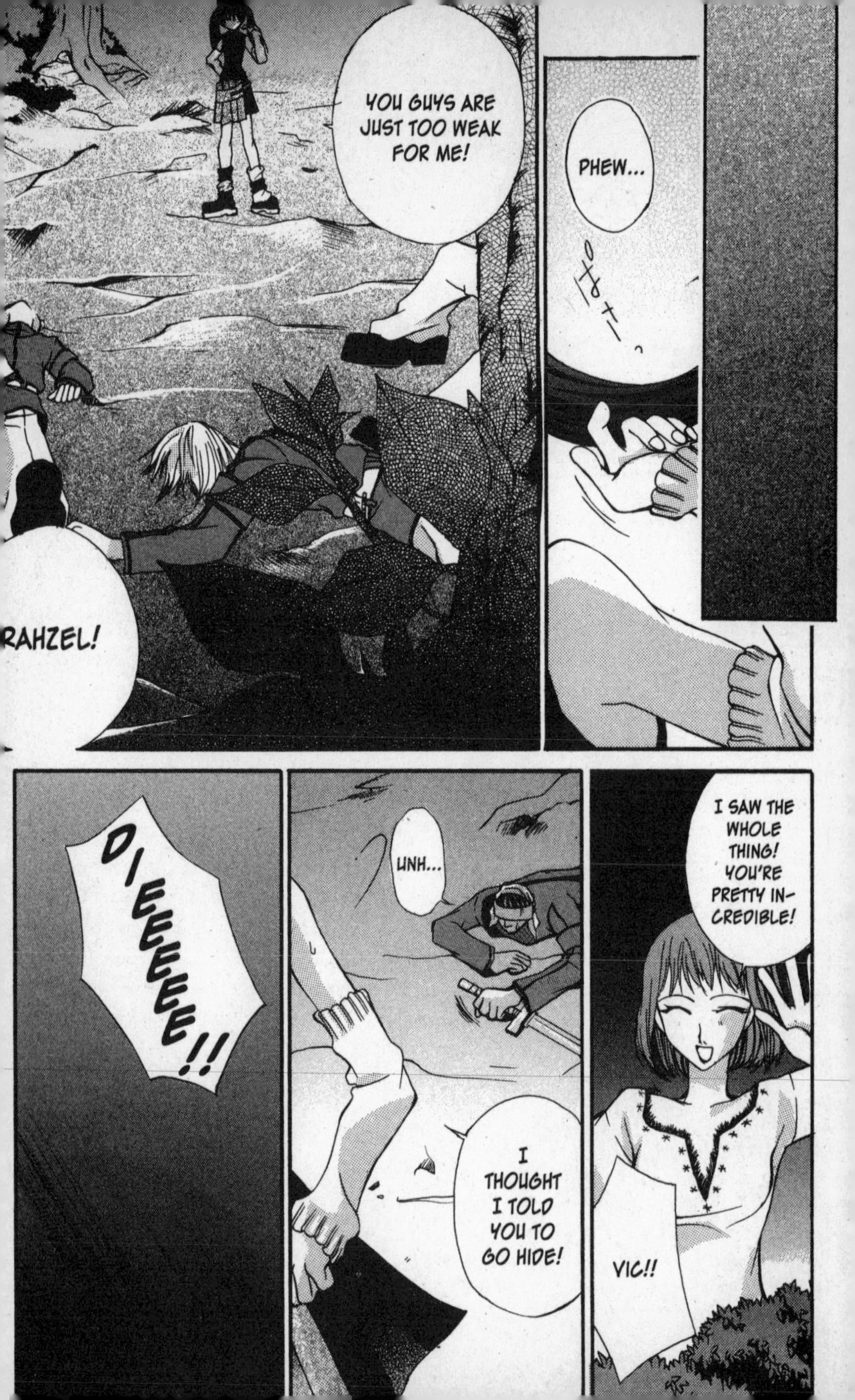
PHEW...
YOU GUYS ARE JUST TOO WEAK FOR ME!
RAHZEL!
I SAW THE WHOLE THING! YOU'RE PRETTY IN-CREDIBLE!
VIC!!
UNH...
I THOUGHT I TOLD YOU TO GO HIDE!
DIEEEEE!!

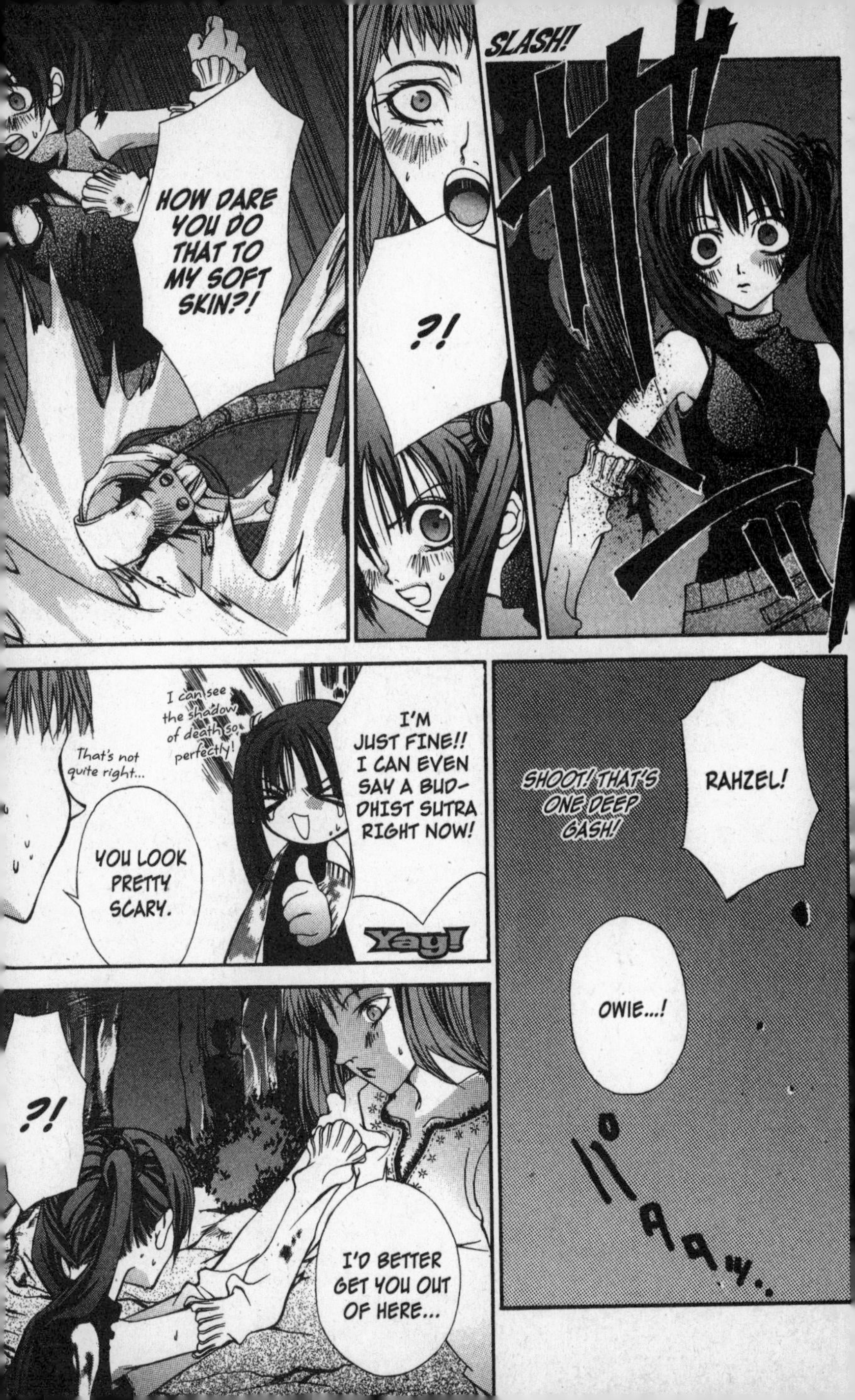
SLASH!
?!
HOW DARE YOU DO THAT TO MY SOFT SKIN?!
RAHZEL!
SHOOT! THAT'S ONE DEEP GASH!
OWIE...!
I'M JUST FINE!! I CAN EVEN SAY A BUD-DHIST SUTRA RIGHT NOW!
Yay!
I can see the shadow of death so perfectly!
That's not quite right...
YOU LOOK PRETTY SCARY.
I'D BETTER GET YOU OUT OF HERE...
?!

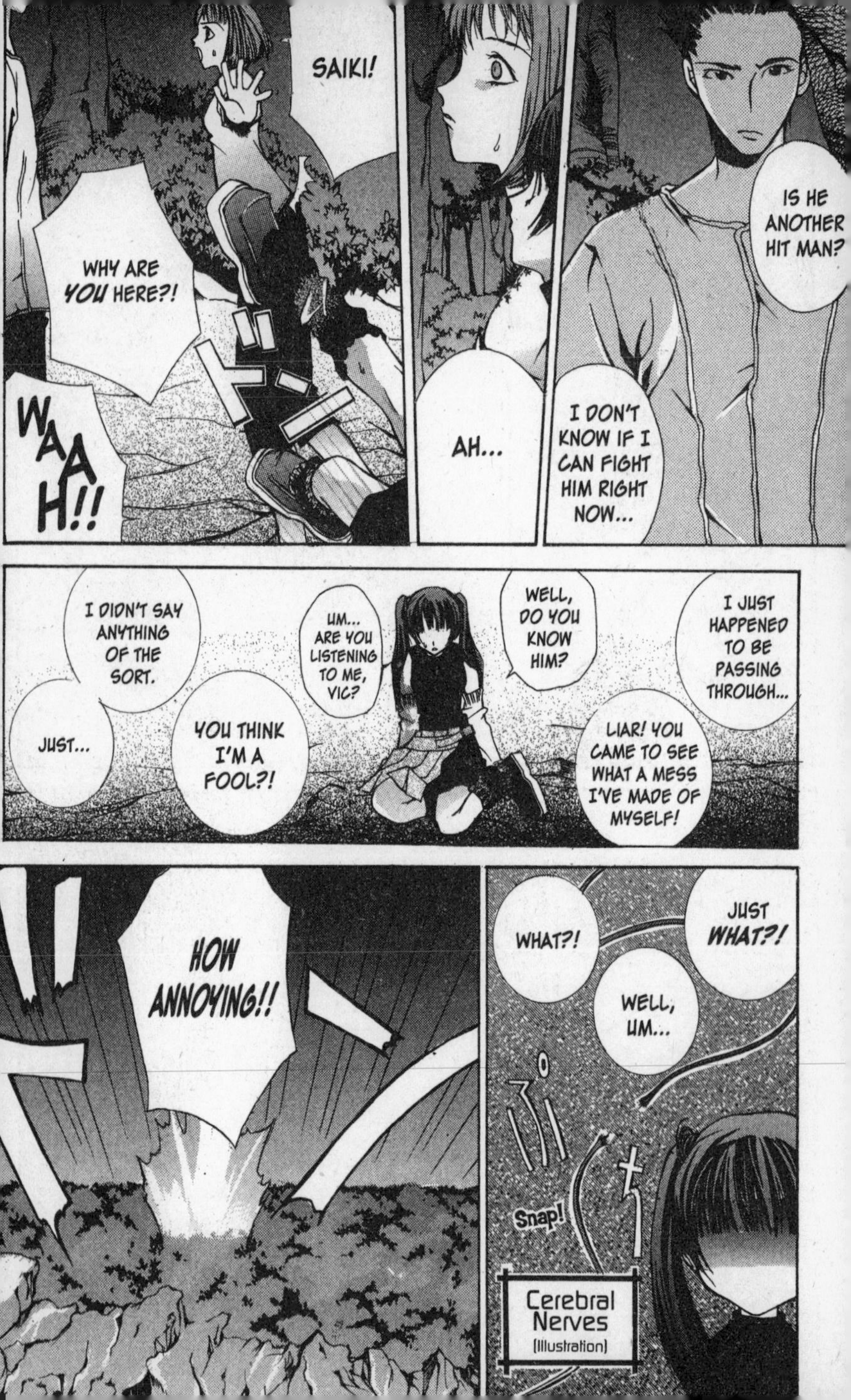
IS HE ANOTHER HIT MAN?
I DON'T KNOW IF I CAN FIGHT HIM RIGHT NOW...
AH...
SAIKI!
WHY ARE YOU HERE?!
WAAAH!!
I JUST HAPPENED TO BE PASSING THROUGH...
WELL, DO YOU KNOW HIM?
LIAR! YOU CAME TO SEE WHAT A MESS I'VE MADE OF MYSELF!
UM... ARE YOU LISTENING TO ME, VIC?
I DIDN'T SAY ANYTHING OF THE SORT.
YOU THINK I'M A FOOL?!
JUST...
JUST WHAT?!
WHAT?!
WELL, UM...
Snap!
Cerebral Nerves
(Illustration)
HOW ANNOYING!!

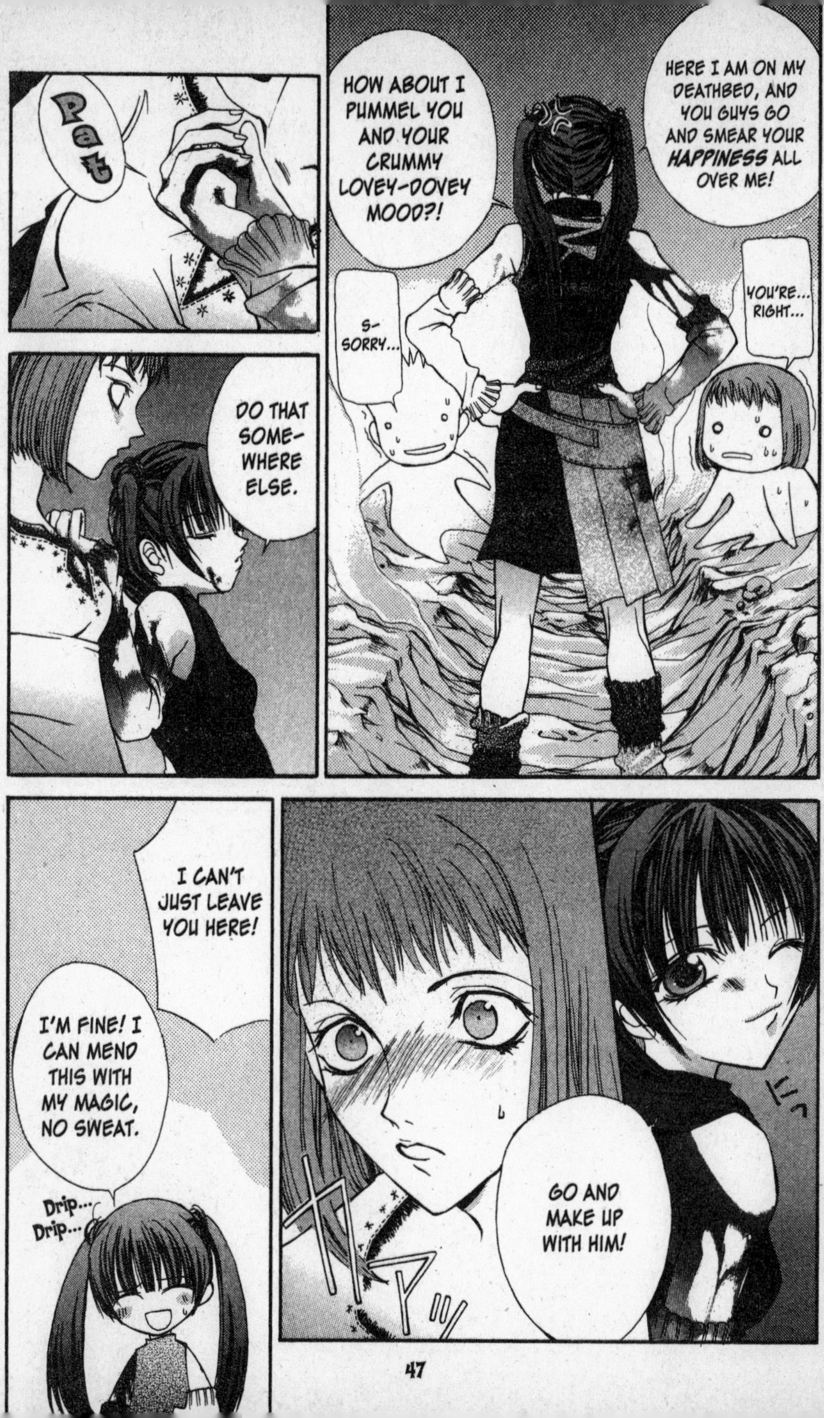
HERE I AM ON MY DEATHBED, AND YOU GUYS GO AND SMEAR YOUR *HAPPINESS* ALL OVER ME!
HOW ABOUT I PUMMEL YOU AND YOUR CRUMMY LOVEY-DOVEY MOOD?!
YOU'RE... RIGHT...
S-SORRY...
Pat
DO THAT SOME-WHERE ELSE.
GO AND MAKE UP WITH HIM!
I CAN'T JUST LEAVE YOU HERE!
I'M FINE! I CAN MEND THIS WITH MY MAGIC, NO SWEAT.
Drip... Drip...

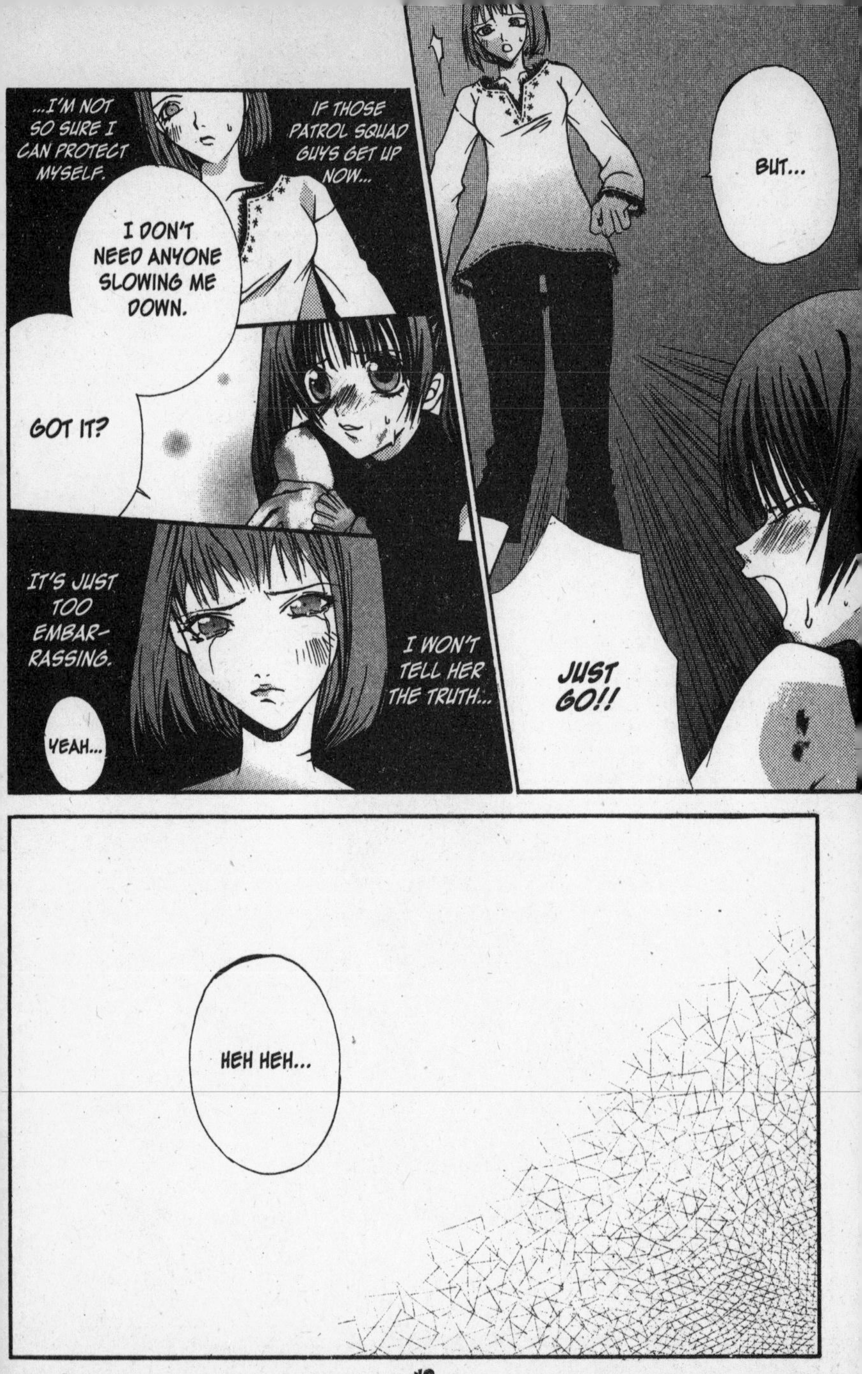

BUT...
JUST GO!!
IF THOSE PATROL SQUAD GUYS GET UP NOW...
...I'M NOT SO SURE I CAN PROTECT MYSELF.
I DON'T NEED ANYONE SLOWING ME DOWN.
GOT IT?
I WON'T TELL HER THE TRUTH...
IT'S JUST TOO EMBAR-RASSING.
YEAH...
HEH HEH...

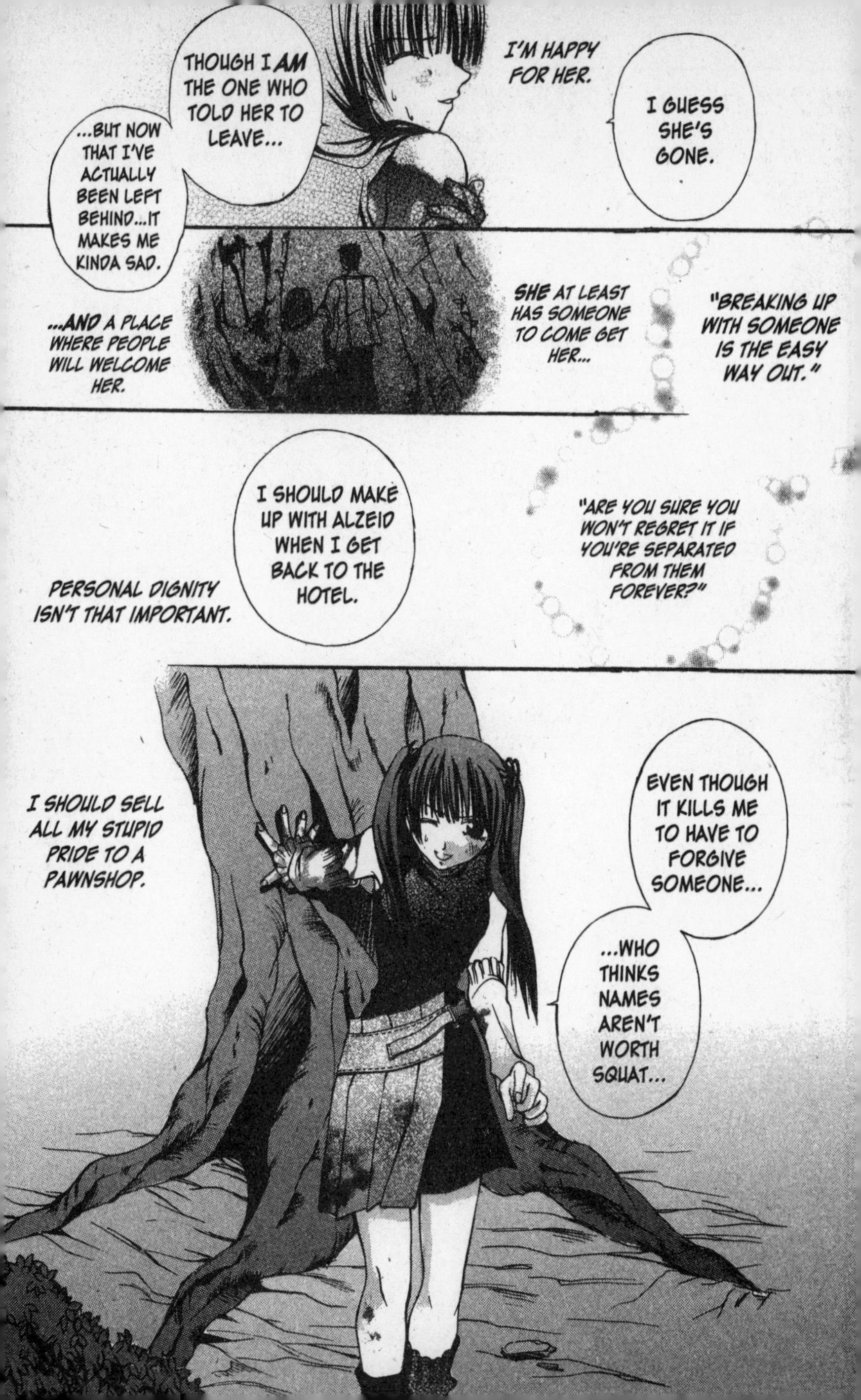
I GUESS SHE'S GONE.
I'M HAPPY FOR HER.
THOUGH I AM THE ONE WHO TOLD HER TO LEAVE...
...BUT NOW THAT I'VE ACTUALLY BEEN LEFT BEHIND...IT MAKES ME KINDA SAD.
"BREAKING UP WITH SOMEONE IS THE EASY WAY OUT."
SHE AT LEAST HAS SOMEONE TO COME GET HER...
...AND A PLACE WHERE PEOPLE WILL WELCOME HER.
"ARE YOU SURE YOU WON'T REGRET IT IF YOU'RE SEPARATED FROM THEM FOREVER?"
I SHOULD MAKE UP WITH ALZEID WHEN I GET BACK TO THE HOTEL.
PERSONAL DIGNITY ISN'T THAT IMPORTANT.
EVEN THOUGH IT KILLS ME TO HAVE TO FORGIVE SOMEONE...
...WHO THINKS NAMES AREN'T WORTH SQUAT...
I SHOULD SELL ALL MY STUPID PRIDE TO A PAWNSHOP.

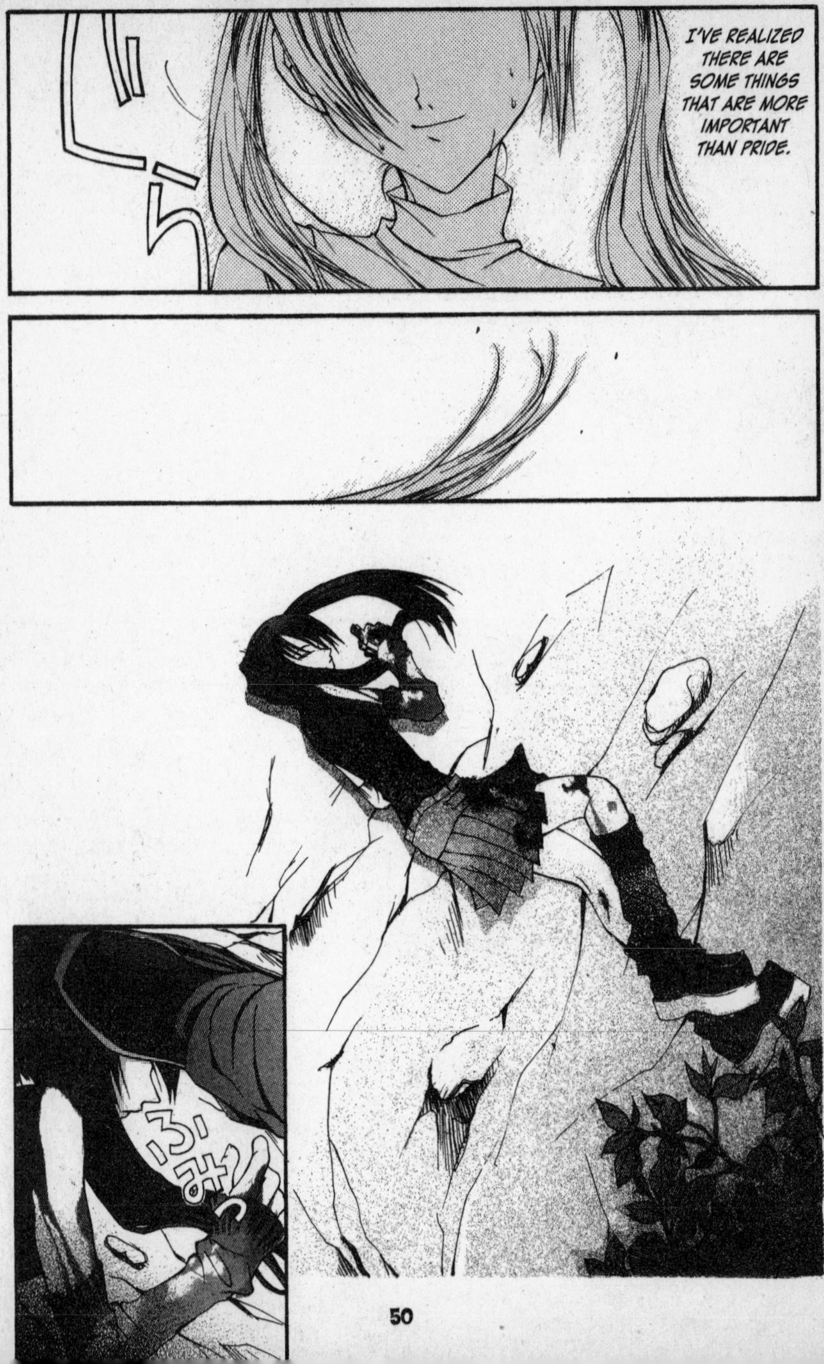
I'VE REALIZED THERE ARE SOME THINGS THAT ARE MORE IMPORTANT THAN PRIDE.
ふみっ

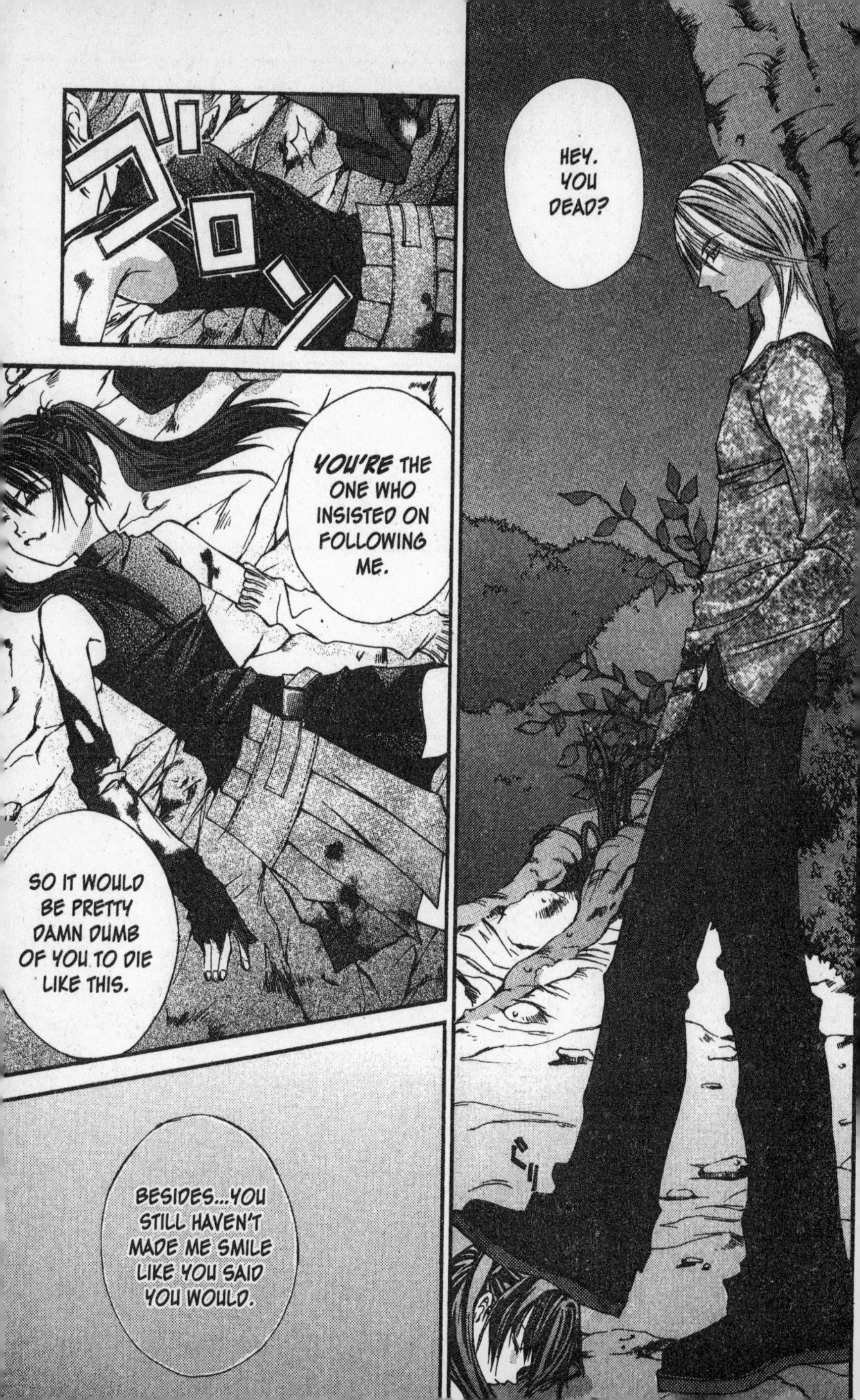
HEY. YOU DEAD?
YOU'RE THE ONE WHO INSISTED ON FOLLOWING ME.
SO IT WOULD BE PRETTY DAMN DUMB OF YOU TO DIE LIKE THIS.
BESIDES...YOU STILL HAVEN'T MADE ME SMILE LIKE YOU SAID YOU WOULD.

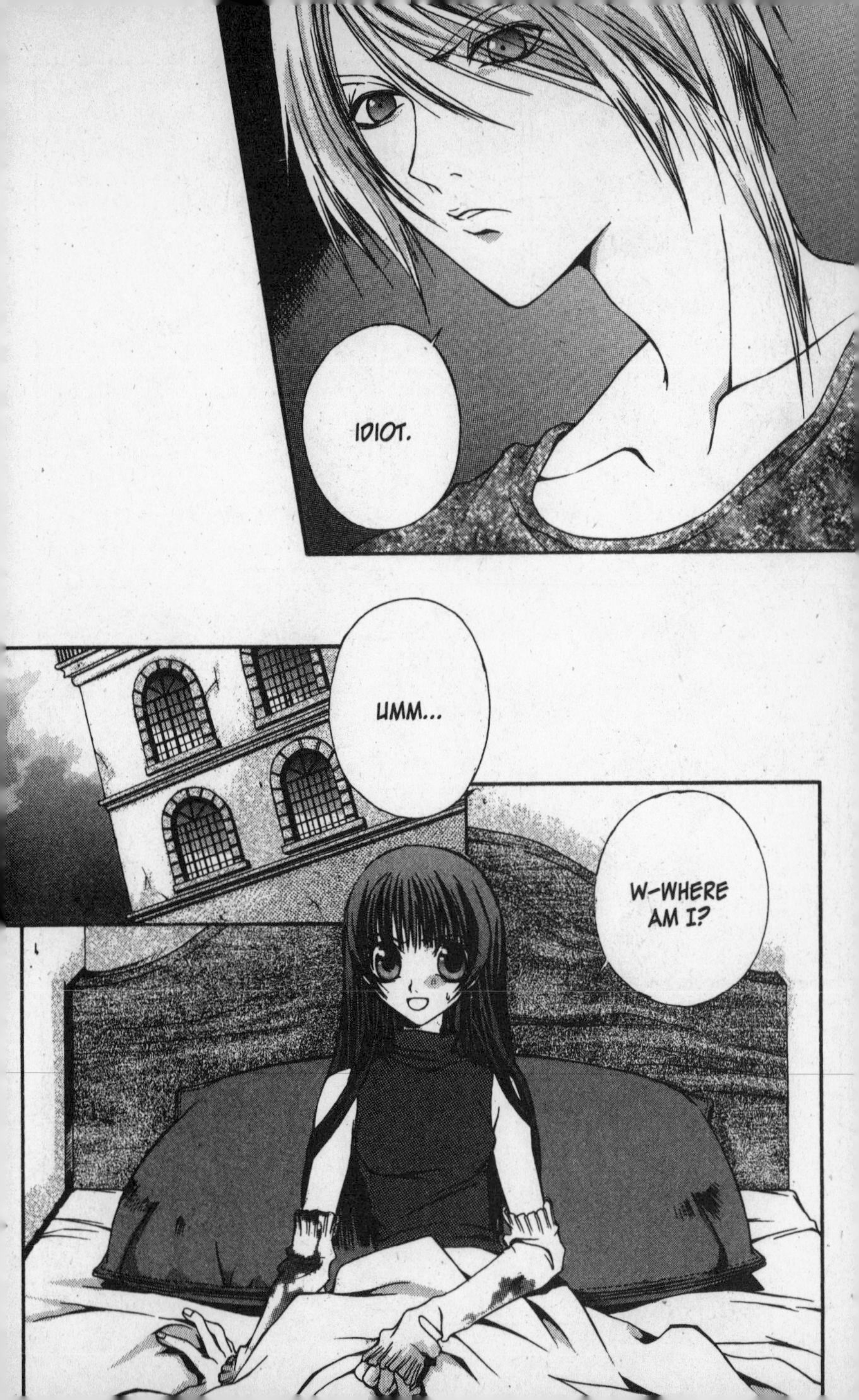
IDIOT.
UMM...
W-WHERE AM I?

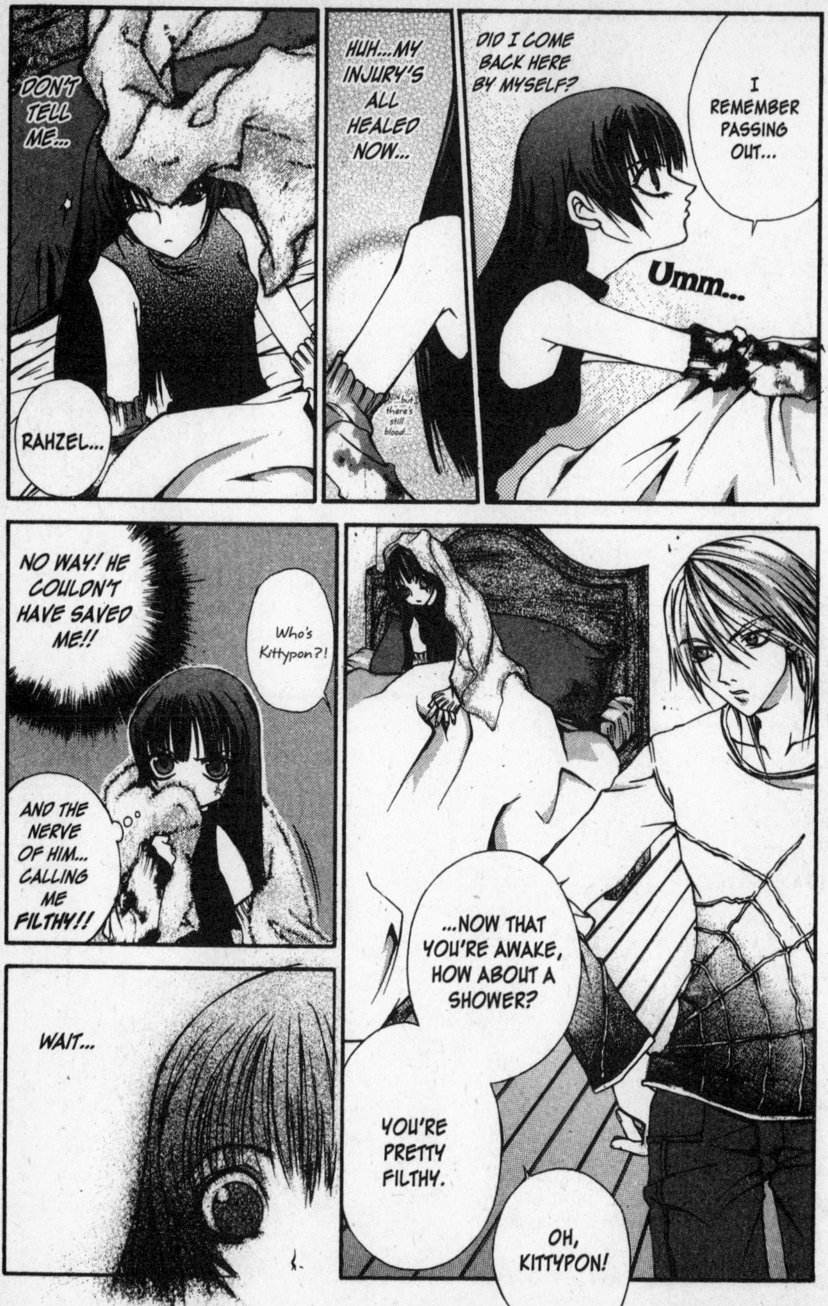
I REMEMBER PASSING OUT...
DID I COME BACK HERE BY MYSELF?
Umm...
HUH...MY INJURY'S ALL HEALED NOW...
...but there's still blood...
DON'T TELL ME...
RAHZEL...
...NOW THAT YOU'RE AWAKE, HOW ABOUT A SHOWER?
YOU'RE PRETTY FILTHY.
OH, KITTYPON!
NO WAY! HE COULDN'T HAVE SAVED ME!!
Who's Kittypon?!
AND THE NERVE OF HIM... CALLING ME FILTHY!!
WAIT...

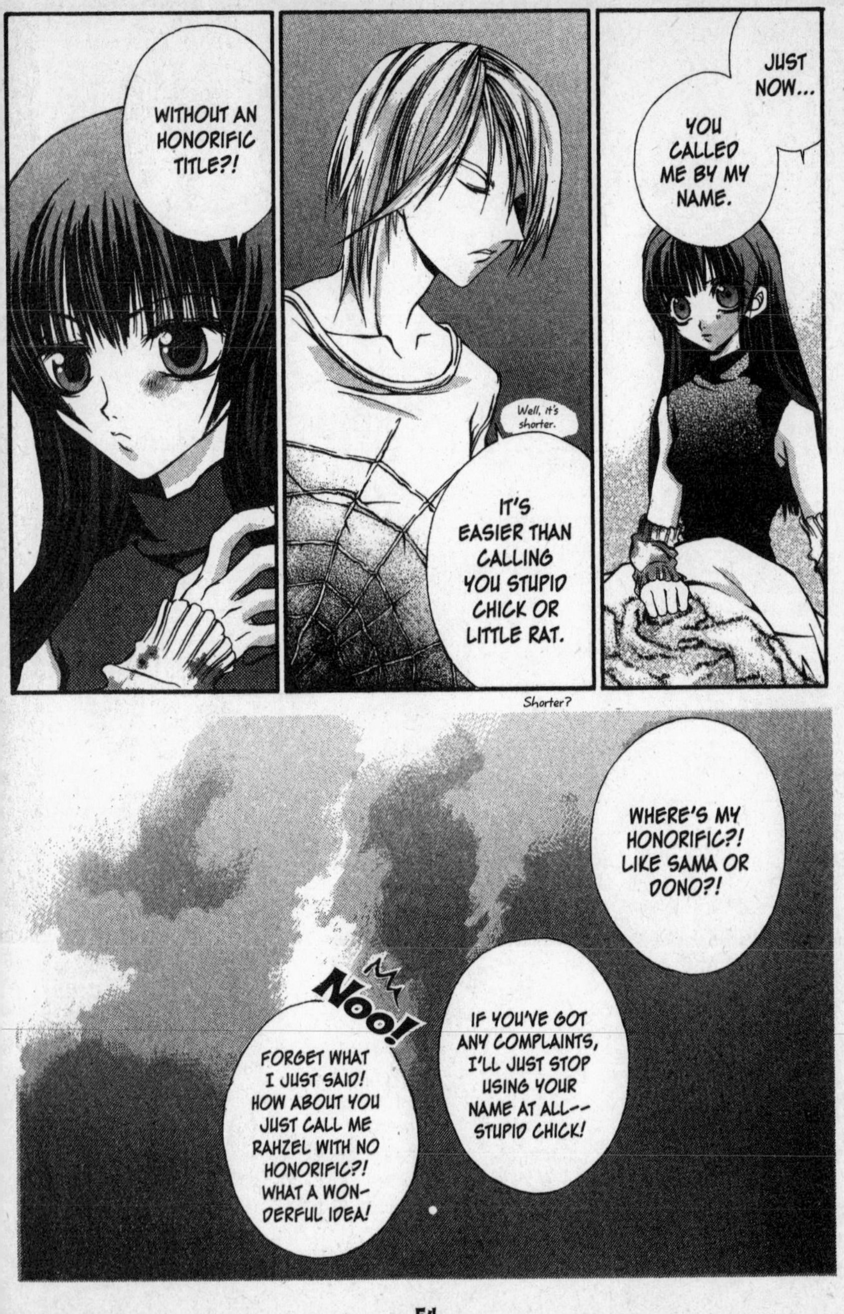
JUST NOW...
YOU CALLED ME BY MY NAME.
Well, it's shorter.
IT'S EASIER THAN CALLING YOU STUPID CHICK OR LITTLE RAT.
WITHOUT AN HONORIFIC TITLE?!
Shorter?
WHERE'S MY HONORIFIC?! LIKE SAMA OR DONO?!
IF YOU'VE GOT ANY COMPLAINTS, I'LL JUST STOP USING YOUR NAME AT ALL-- STUPID CHICK!
NOO!
FORGET WHAT I JUST SAID! HOW ABOUT YOU JUST CALL ME RAHZEL WITH NO HONORIFIC?! WHAT A WON-DERFUL IDEA!

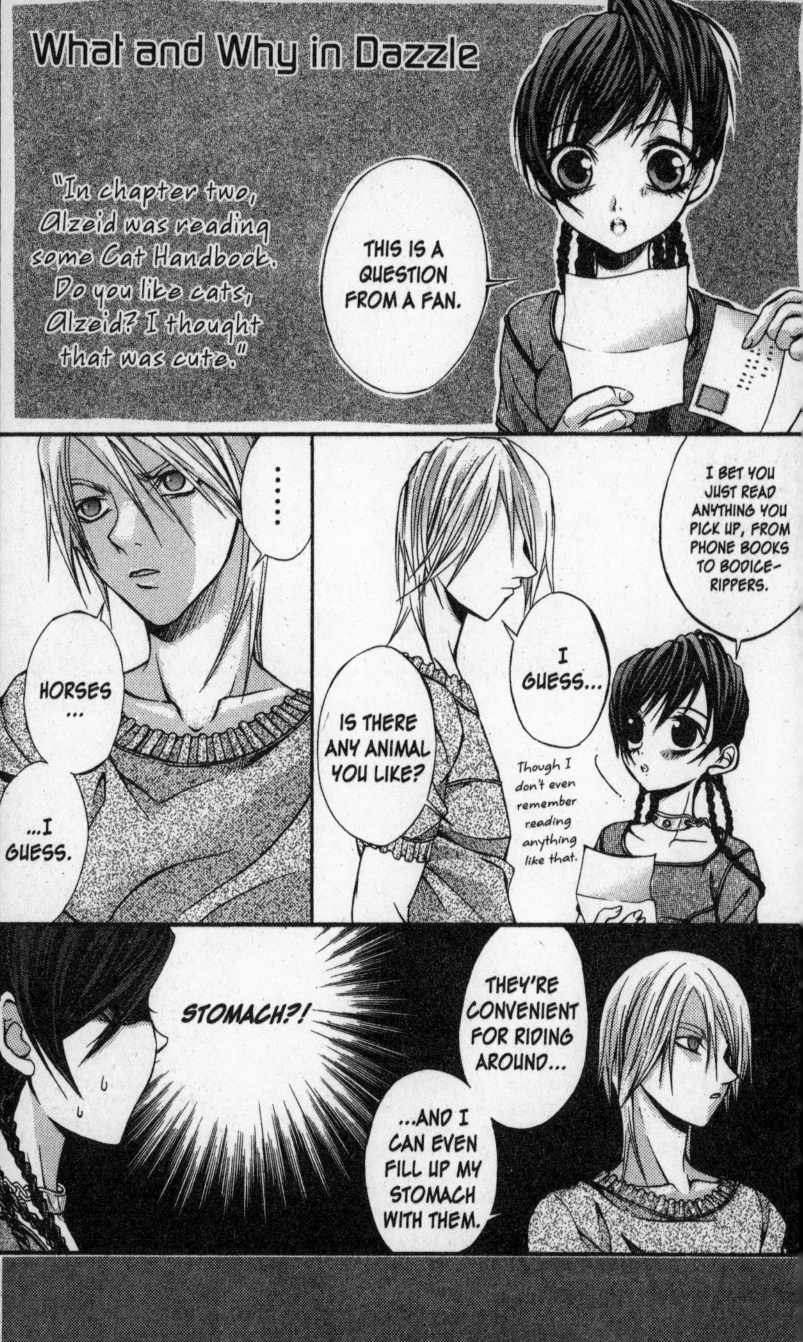
What and Why in Dazzle
THIS IS A QUESTION FROM A FAN.
"In chapter two, Alzeid was reading some Cat Handbook. Do you like cats, Alzeid? I thought that was cute."
I BET YOU JUST READ ANYTHING YOU PICK UP, FROM PHONE BOOKS TO BODICE-RIPPERS.
I GUESS...
Though I don't even remember reading anything like that.
IS THERE ANY ANIMAL YOU LIKE?
......
HORSES...
...I GUESS.
THEY'RE CONVENIENT FOR RIDING AROUND...
...AND I CAN EVEN FILL UP MY STOMACH WITH THEM.
STOMACH?!

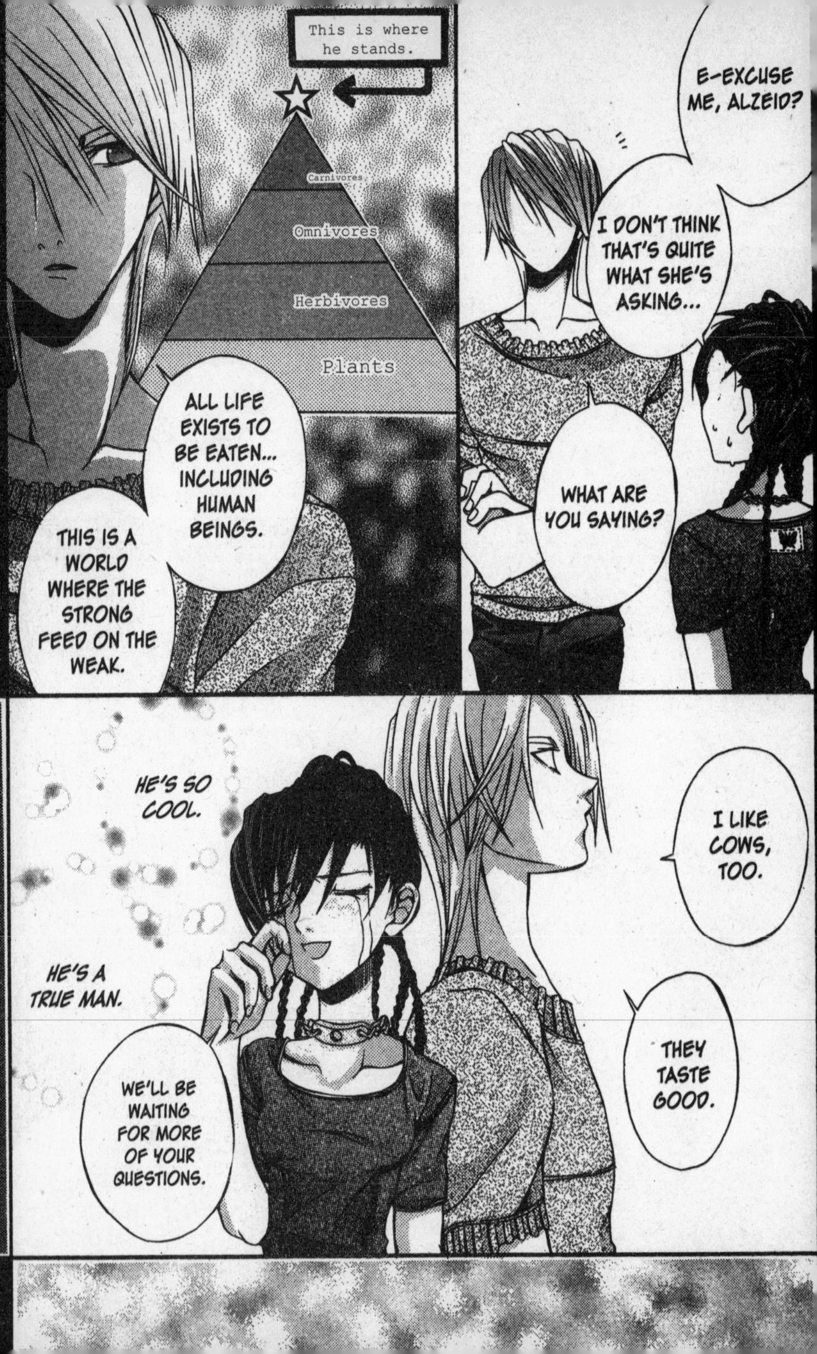
E-EXCUSE ME, ALZEID?
I DON'T THINK THAT'S QUITE WHAT SHE'S ASKING...
WHAT ARE YOU SAYING?
This is where he stands.
Carnivores
Omnivores
Herbivores
Plants
ALL LIFE EXISTS TO BE EATEN... INCLUDING HUMAN BEINGS.
THIS IS A WORLD WHERE THE STRONG FEED ON THE WEAK.
I LIKE COWS, TOO.
THEY TASTE GOOD.
HE'S SO COOL.
HE'S A TRUE MAN.
WE'LL BE WAITING FOR MORE OF YOUR QUESTIONS.

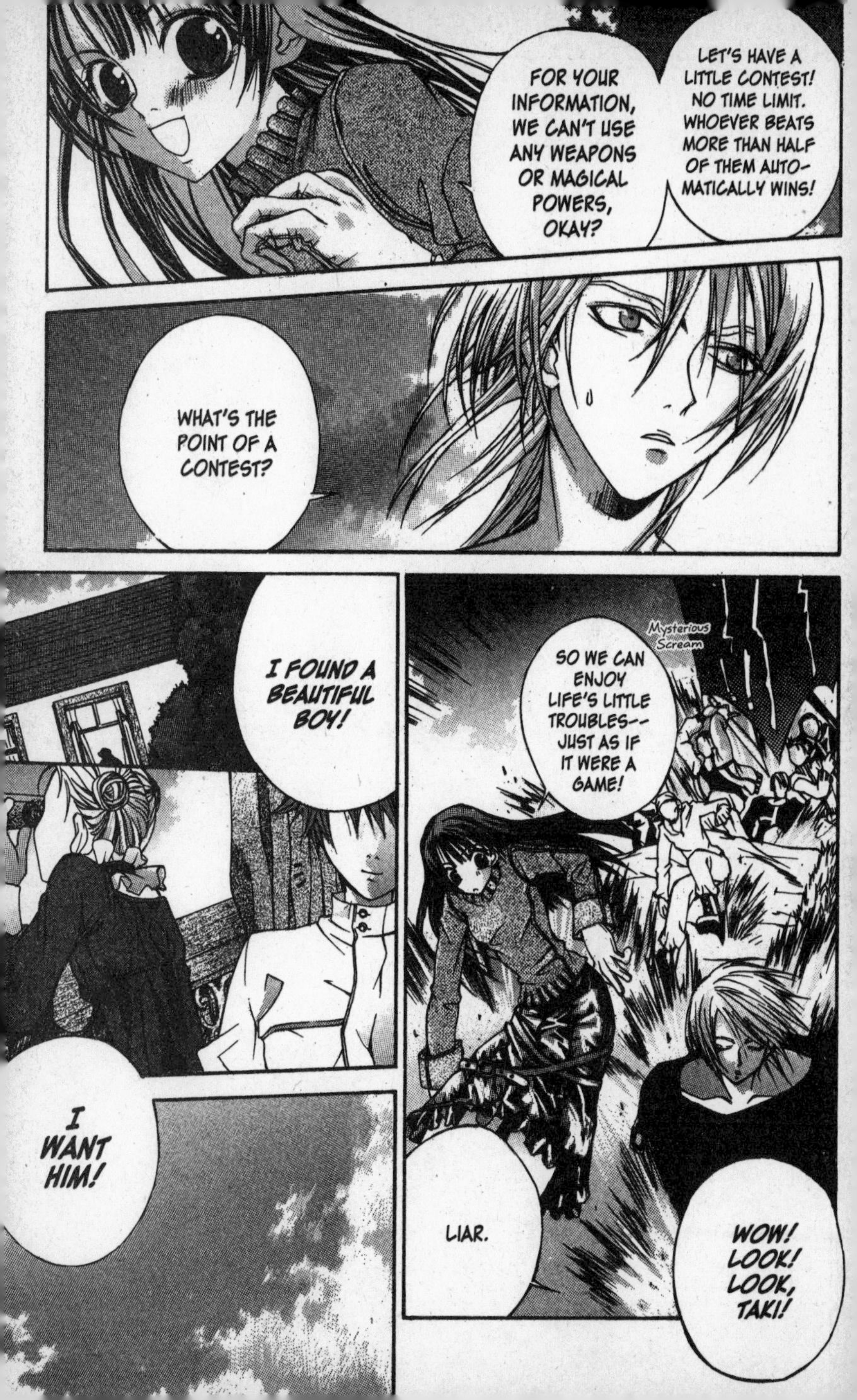
LET'S HAVE A LITTLE CONTEST! NO TIME LIMIT. WHOEVER BEATS MORE THAN HALF OF THEM AUTOMATICALLY WINS!
FOR YOUR INFORMATION, WE CAN'T USE ANY WEAPONS OR MAGICAL POWERS, OKAY?
WHAT'S THE POINT OF A CONTEST?
Mysterious Scream
SO WE CAN ENJOY LIFE'S LITTLE TROUBLES--JUST AS IF IT WERE A GAME!
WOW! LOOK! LOOK, TAKI!
LIAR.
I FOUND A BEAUTIFUL BOY!
I WANT HIM!

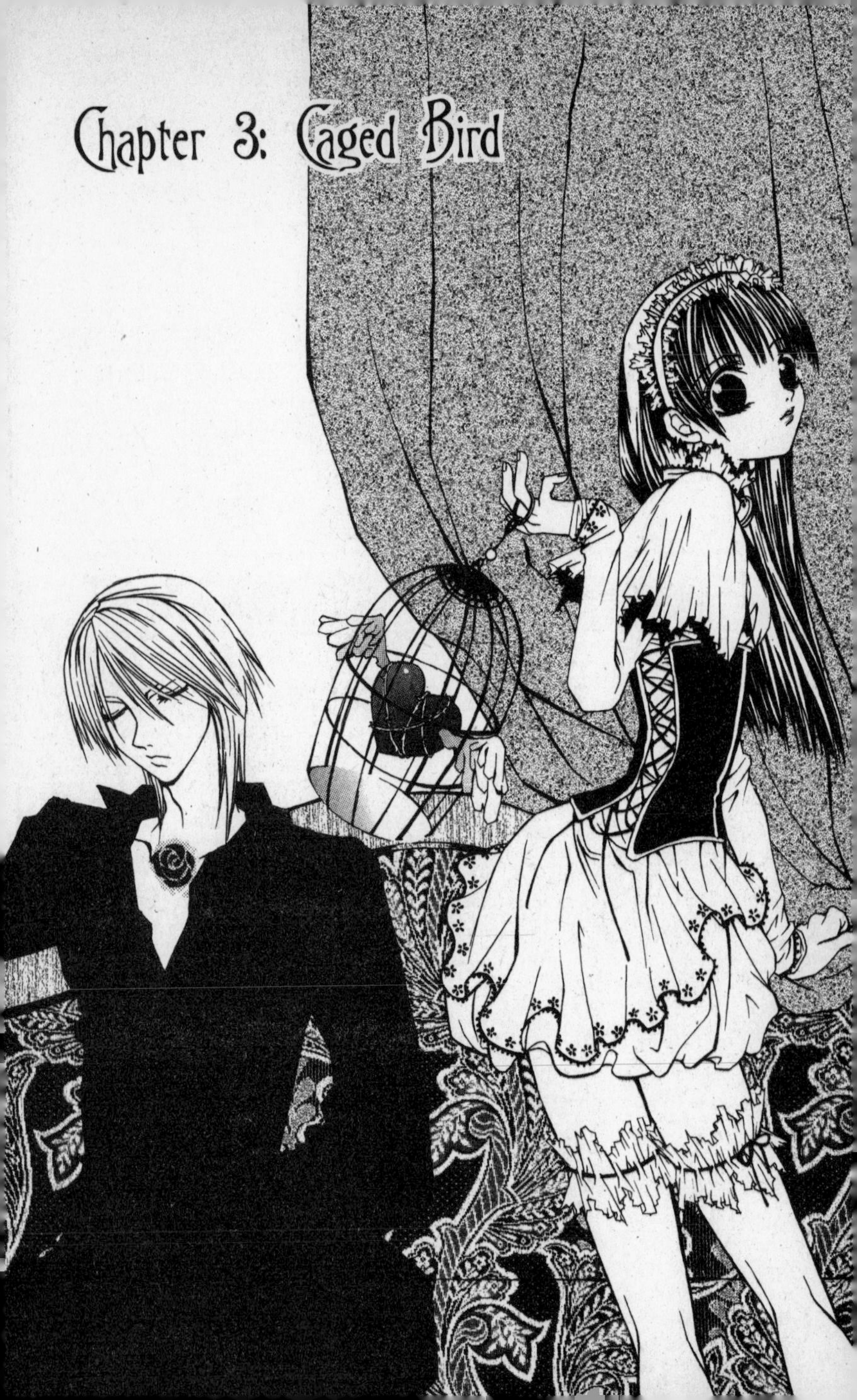
Chapter 3: Caged Bird

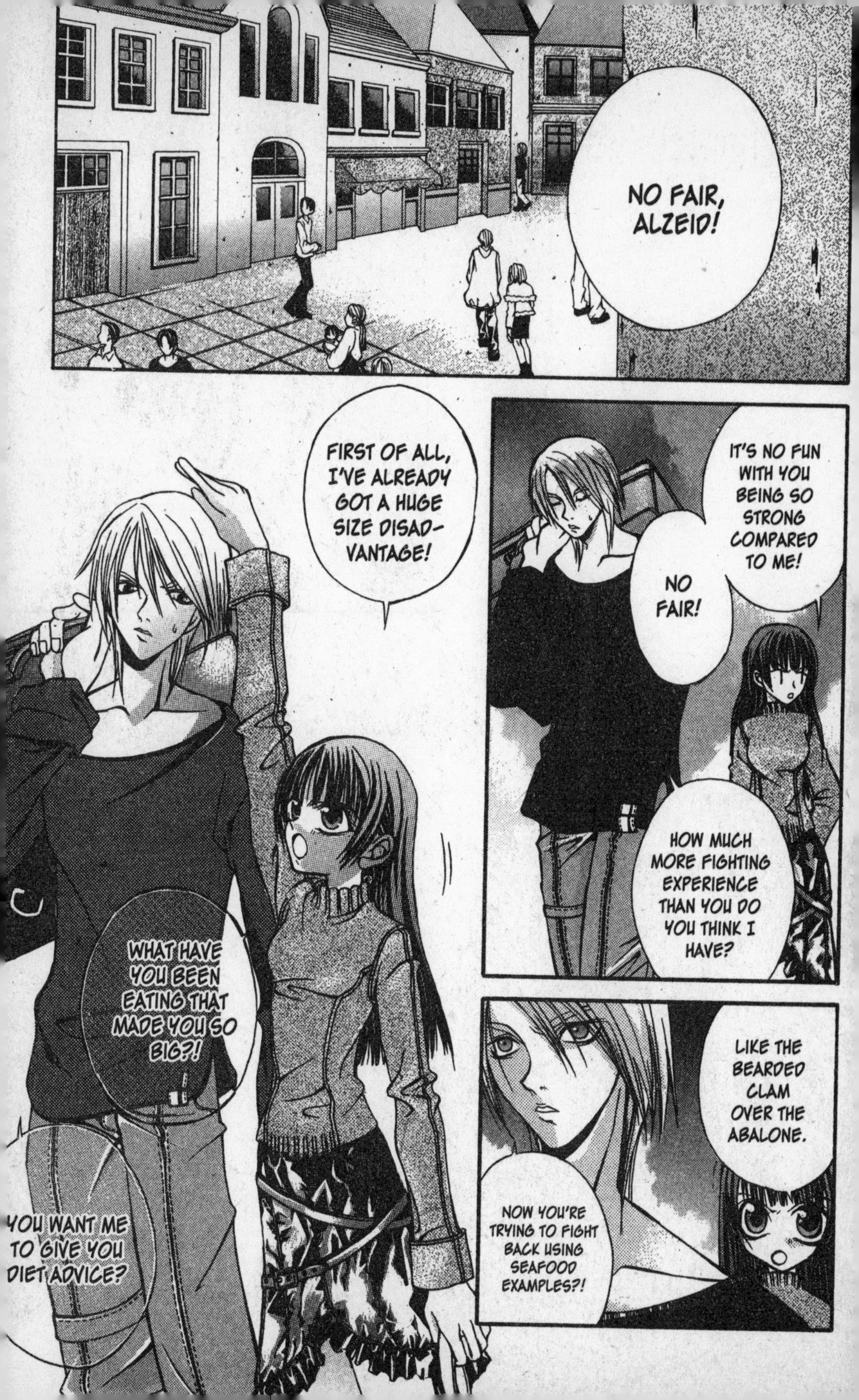
NO FAIR, ALZEID!
IT'S NO FUN WITH YOU BEING SO STRONG COMPARED TO ME!
NO FAIR!
HOW MUCH MORE FIGHTING EXPERIENCE THAN YOU DO YOU THINK I HAVE?
LIKE THE BEARDED CLAM OVER THE ABALONE.
NOW YOU'RE TRYING TO FIGHT BACK USING SEAFOOD EXAMPLES?!
FIRST OF ALL, I'VE ALREADY GOT A HUGE SIZE DISAD-VANTAGE!
WHAT HAVE YOU BEEN EATING THAT MADE YOU SO BIG?!
YOU WANT ME TO GIVE YOU DIET ADVICE?

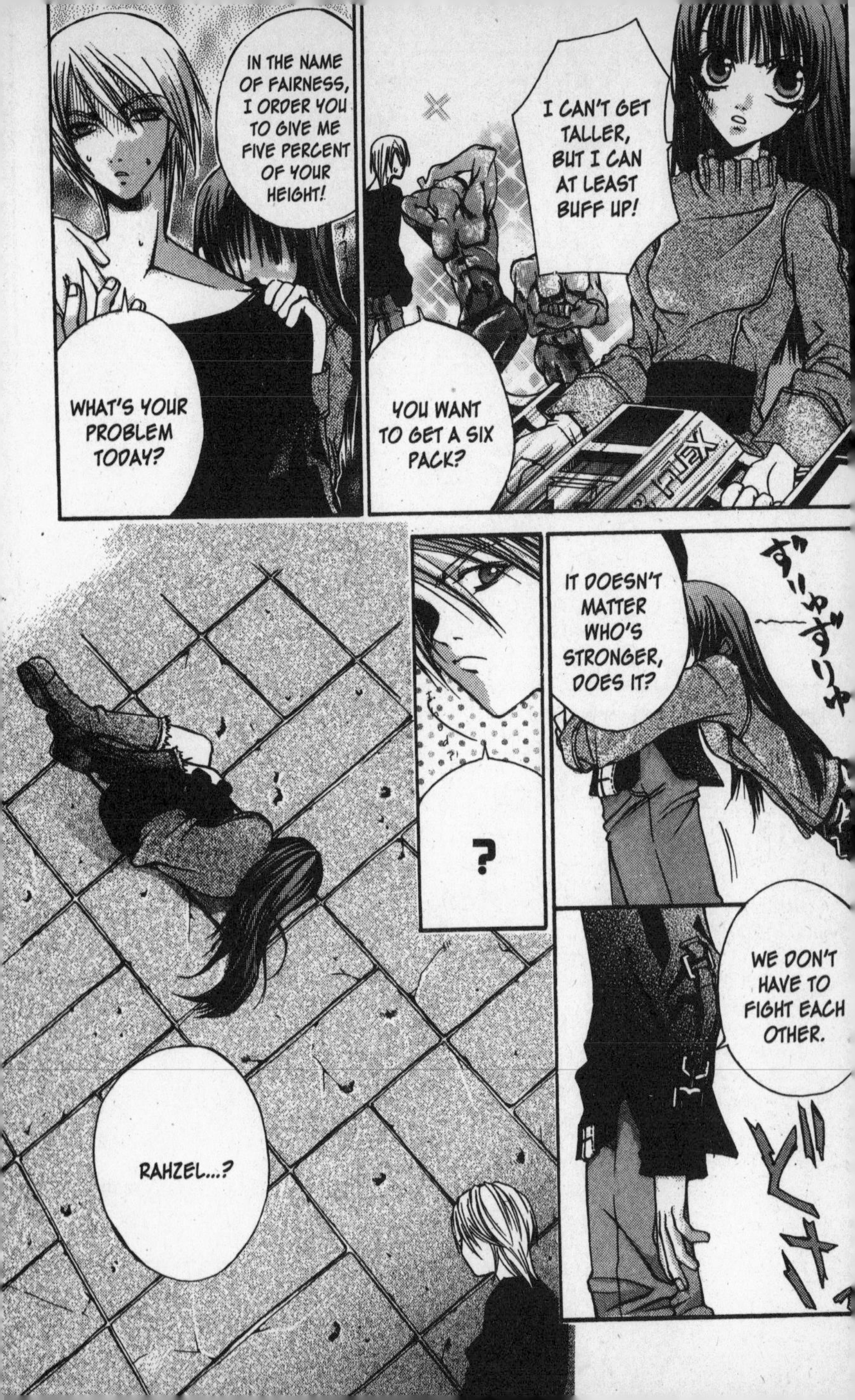
I CAN'T GET TALLER, BUT I CAN AT LEAST BUFF UP!
YOU WANT TO GET A SIX PACK?
IN THE NAME OF FAIRNESS, I ORDER YOU TO GIVE ME FIVE PERCENT OF YOUR HEIGHT!
WHAT'S YOUR PROBLEM TODAY?
IT DOESN'T MATTER WHO'S STRONGER, DOES IT?
?
WE DON'T HAVE TO FIGHT EACH OTHER.
RAHZEL...?

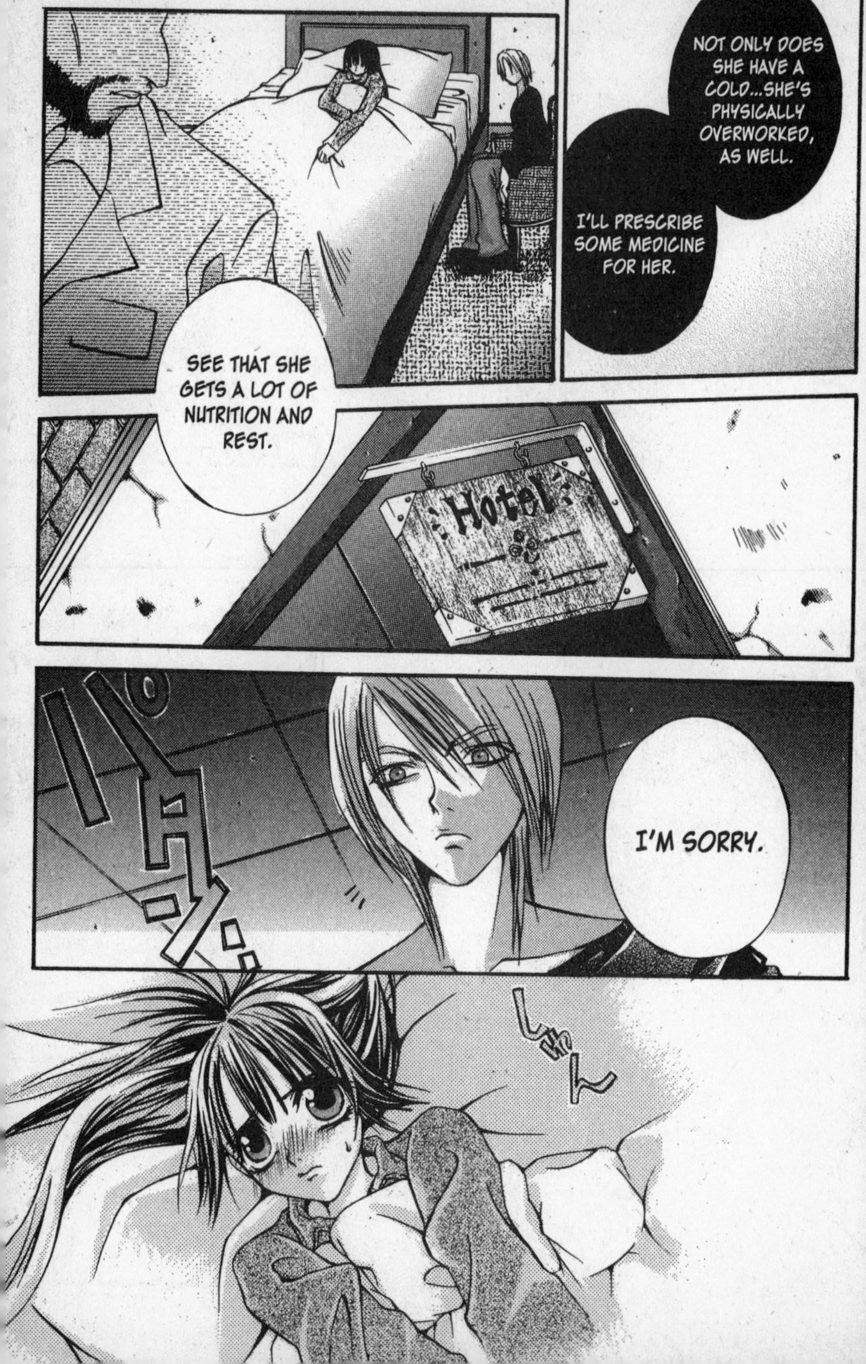
NOT ONLY DOES SHE HAVE A COLD...SHE'S PHYSICALLY OVERWORKED, AS WELL.
I'LL PRESCRIBE SOME MEDICINE FOR HER.
SEE THAT SHE GETS A LOT OF NUTRITION AND REST.
Hotel
I'M SORRY.

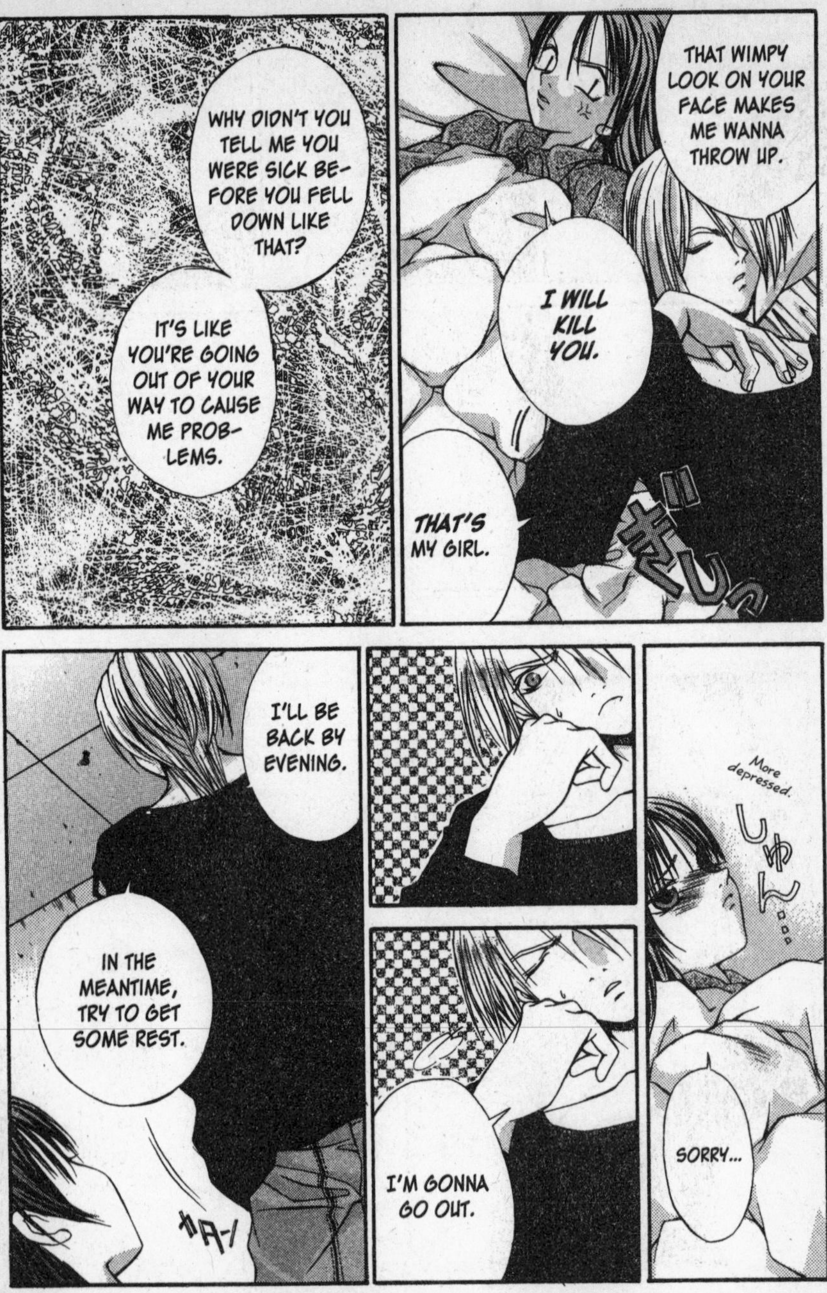
THAT WIMPY LOOK ON YOUR FACE MAKES ME WANNA THROW UP.
I WILL KILL YOU.
THAT'S MY GIRL.
WHY DIDN'T YOU TELL ME YOU WERE SICK BEFORE YOU FELL DOWN LIKE THAT?
IT'S LIKE YOU'RE GOING OUT OF YOUR WAY TO CAUSE ME PROBLEMS.
More depressed.
しゅん…
SORRY...
I'M GONNA GO OUT.
I'LL BE BACK BY EVENING.
IN THE MEANTIME, TRY TO GET SOME REST.

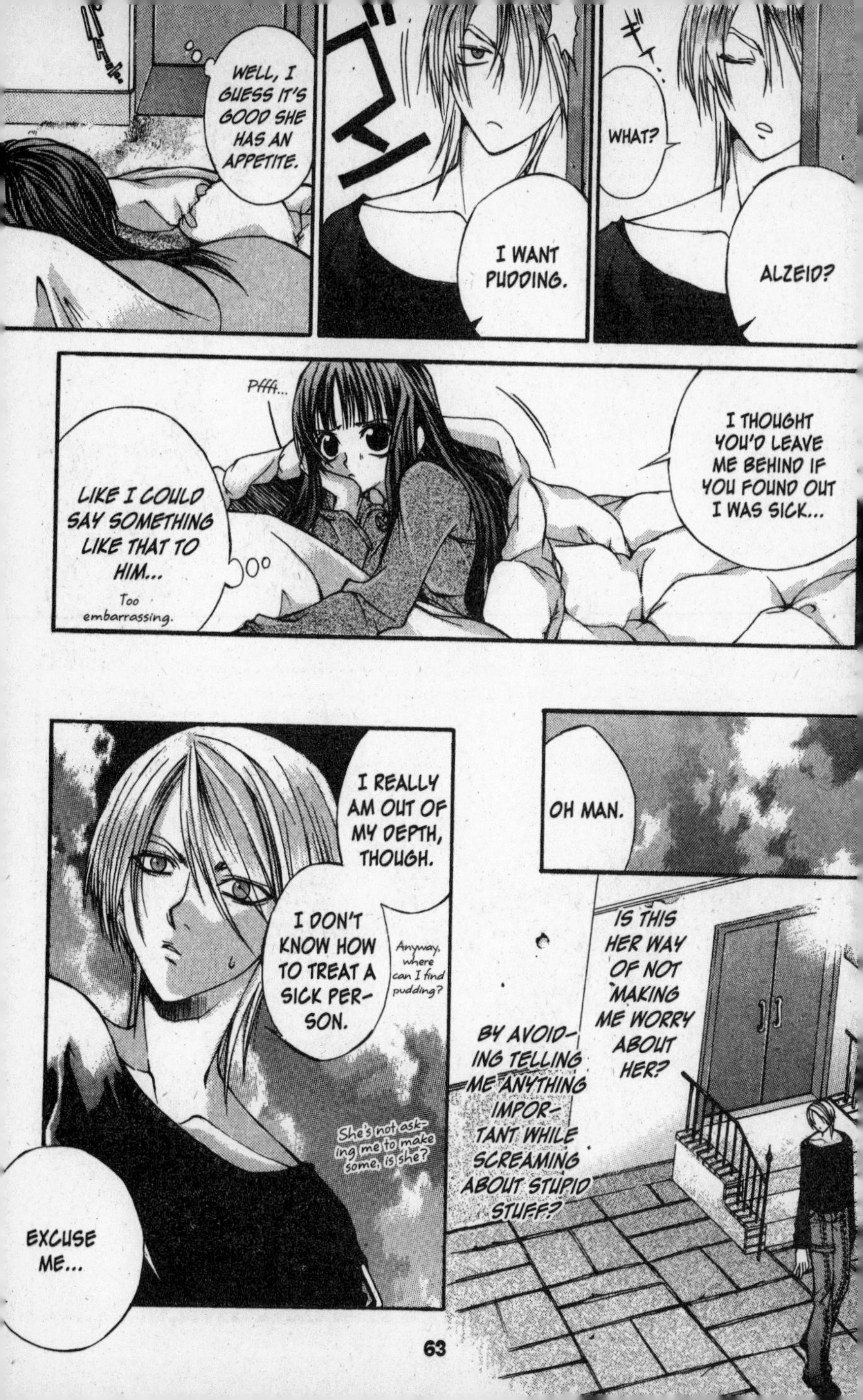
ALZEID?
WHAT?
I WANT PUDDING.
WELL, I GUESS IT'S GOOD SHE HAS AN APPETITE.
I THOUGHT YOU'D LEAVE ME BEHIND IF YOU FOUND OUT I WAS SICK...
Pfff...
LIKE I COULD SAY SOMETHING LIKE THAT TO HIM...
Too embarrassing.
OH MAN.
IS THIS HER WAY OF NOT MAKING ME WORRY ABOUT HER?
BY AVOID-ING TELLING ME ANYTHING IMPOR-TANT WHILE SCREAMING ABOUT STUPID STUFF?
I REALLY AM OUT OF MY DEPTH, THOUGH.
I DON'T KNOW HOW TO TREAT A SICK PER-SON.
Anyway, where can I find pudding?
She's not ask-ing me to make some, is she?
EXCUSE ME...

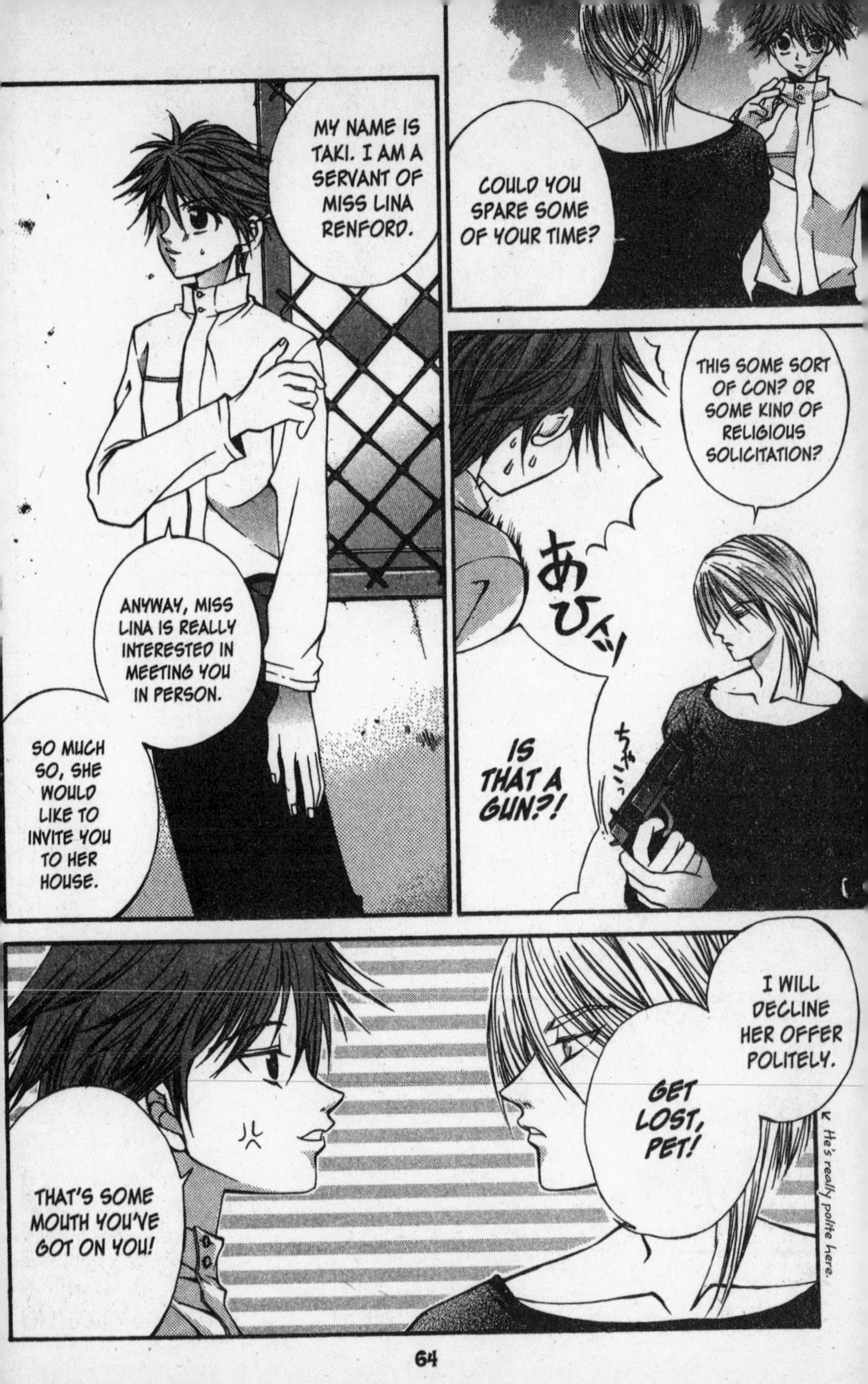
COULD YOU SPARE SOME OF YOUR TIME?
THIS SOME SORT OF CON? OR SOME KIND OF RELIGIOUS SOLICITATION?
あひっ
ちゃきっ
IS THAT A GUN?!
MY NAME IS TAKI. I AM A SERVANT OF MISS LINA RENFORD.
ANYWAY, MISS LINA IS REALLY INTERESTED IN MEETING YOU IN PERSON.
SO MUCH SO, SHE WOULD LIKE TO INVITE YOU TO HER HOUSE.
I WILL DECLINE HER OFFER POLITELY.
GET LOST, PET!
He's really polite here.
THAT'S SOME MOUTH YOU'VE GOT ON YOU!

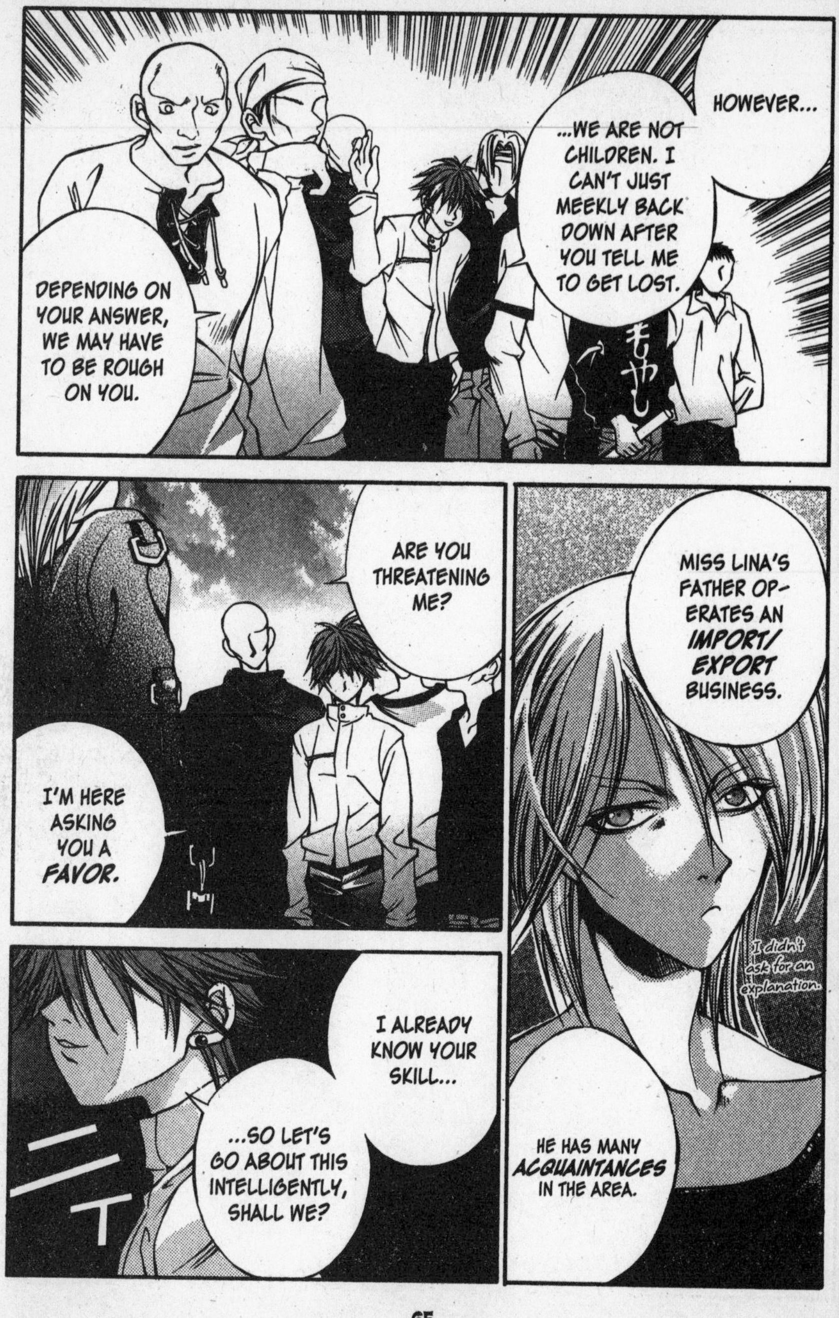
HOWEVER...
...WE ARE NOT CHILDREN. I CAN'T JUST MEEKLY BACK DOWN AFTER YOU TELL ME TO GET LOST.
もやし
DEPENDING ON YOUR ANSWER, WE MAY HAVE TO BE ROUGH ON YOU.
MISS LINA'S FATHER OP-ERATES AN *IMPORT/ EXPORT* BUSINESS.
I didn't ask for an explanation.
HE HAS MANY *ACQUAINTANCES* IN THE AREA.
ARE YOU THREATENING ME?
I'M HERE ASKING YOU A *FAVOR.*
I ALREADY KNOW YOUR SKILL...
...SO LET'S GO ABOUT THIS INTELLIGENTLY, SHALL WE?

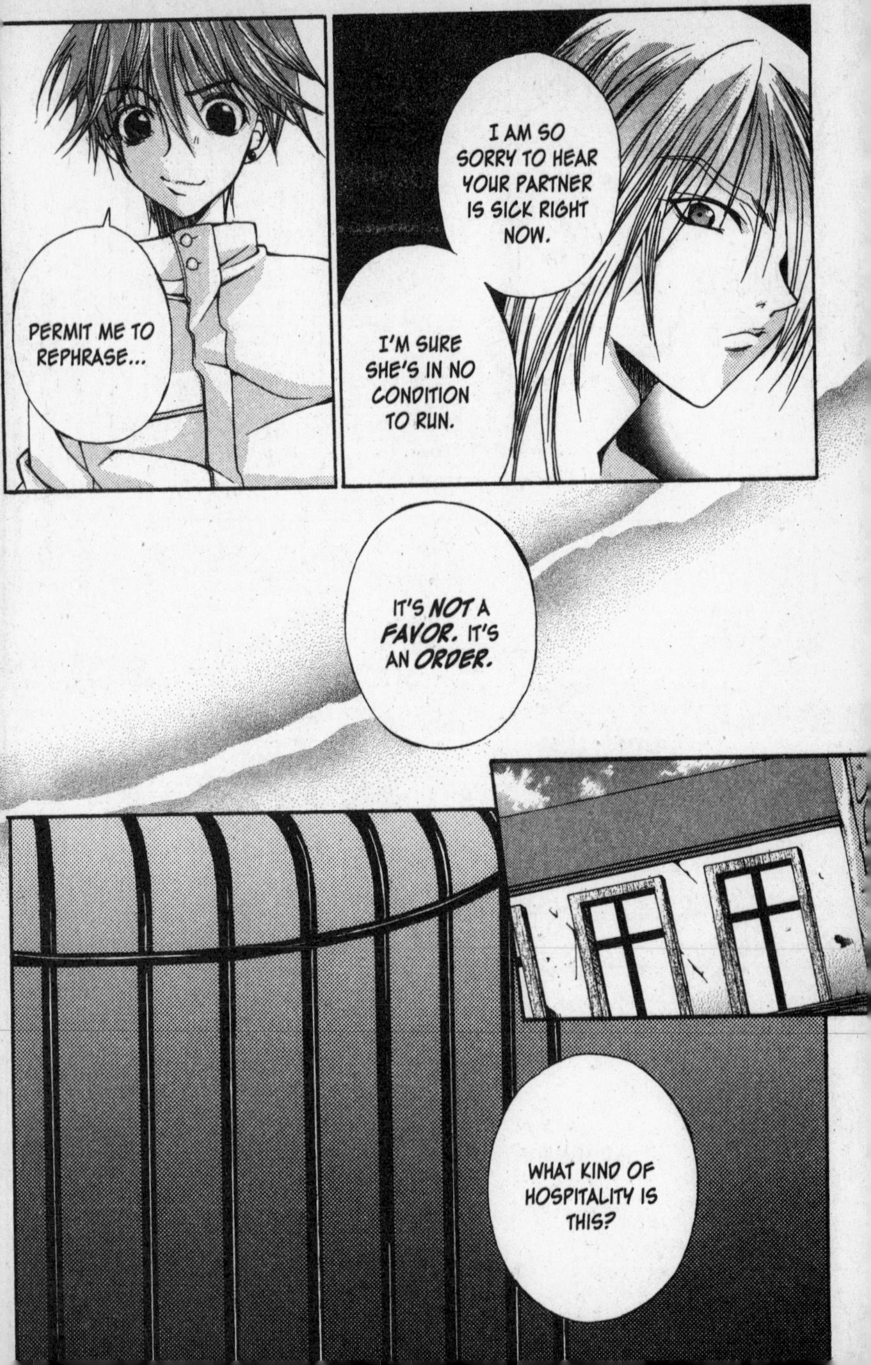
I AM SO SORRY TO HEAR YOUR PARTNER IS SICK RIGHT NOW.
I'M SURE SHE'S IN NO CONDITION TO RUN.
PERMIT ME TO REPHRASE...
IT'S *NOT* A *FAVOR.* IT'S AN *ORDER.*
WHAT KIND OF HOSPITALITY IS THIS?

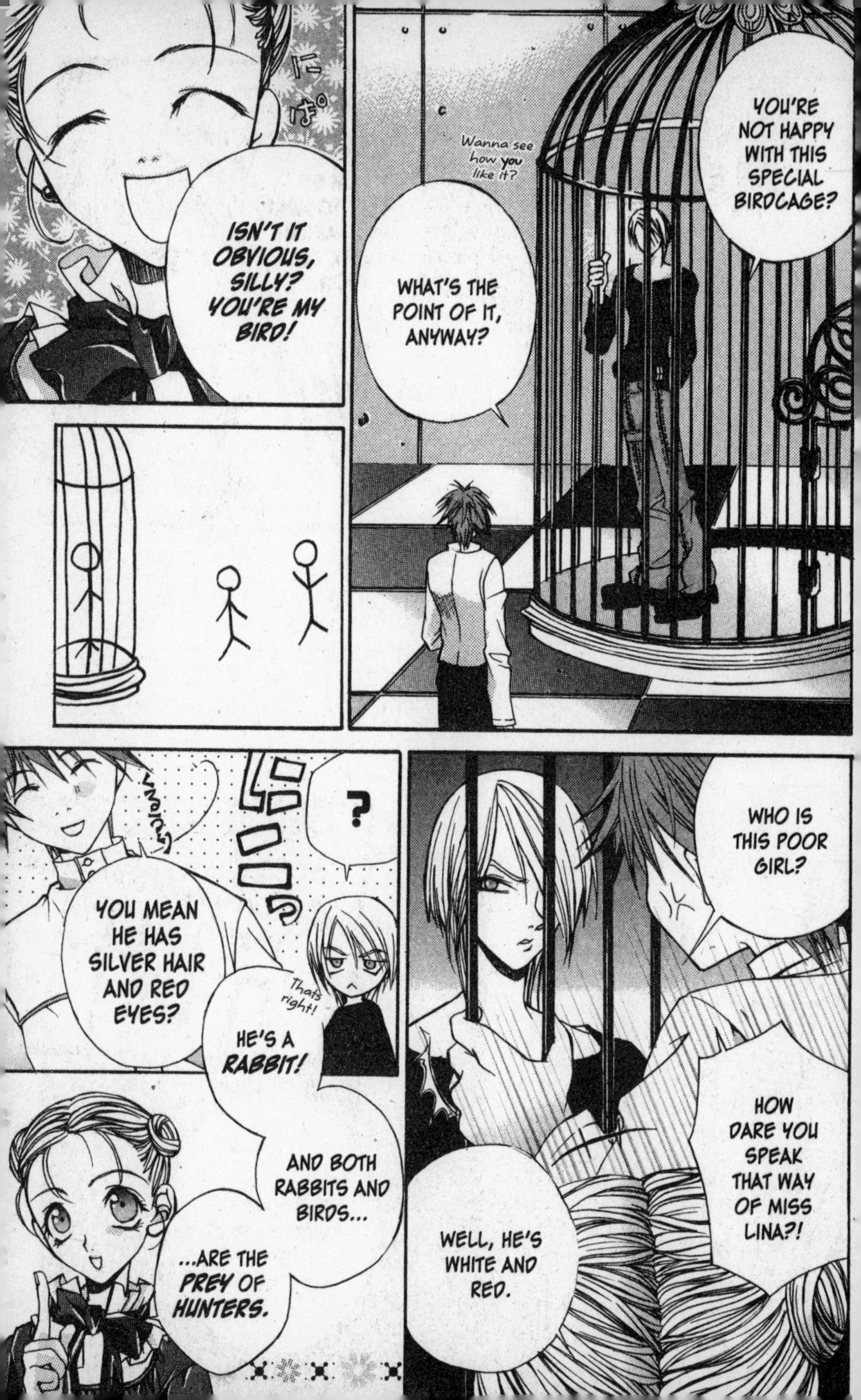
YOU'RE NOT HAPPY WITH THIS SPECIAL BIRDCAGE?
WHAT'S THE POINT OF IT, ANYWAY?
Wanna see how you like it?
にぱ
ISN'T IT OBVIOUS, SILLY? YOU'RE MY BIRD!
WHO IS THIS POOR GIRL?
HOW DARE YOU SPEAK THAT WAY OF MISS LINA?!
WELL, HE'S WHITE AND RED.
?
YOU MEAN HE HAS SILVER HAIR AND RED EYES?
Thats right!
HE'S A RABBIT!
AND BOTH RABBITS AND BIRDS...
...ARE THE PREY OF HUNTERS.

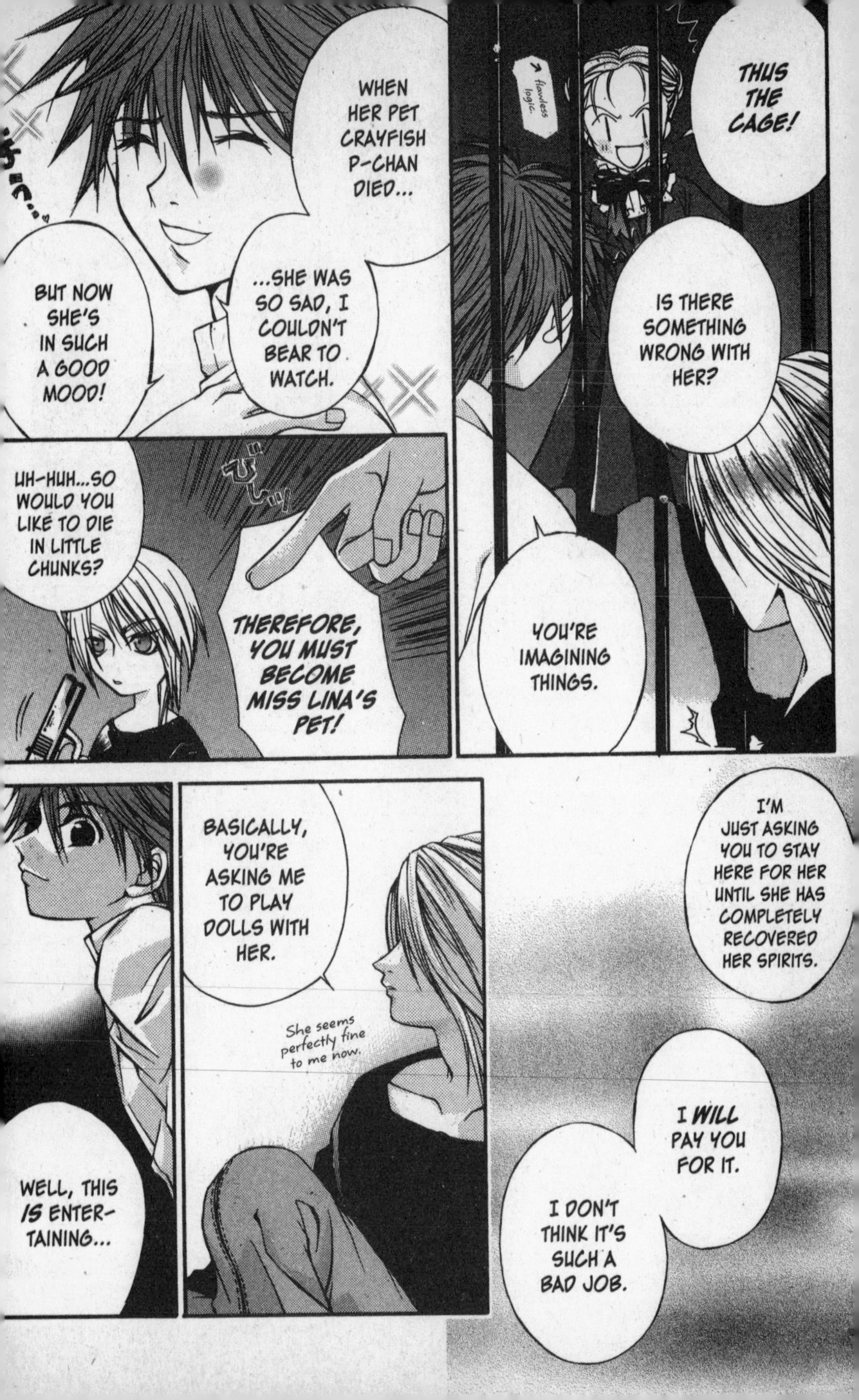
THUS THE CAGE!
→ flawless logic.
IS THERE SOMETHING WRONG WITH HER?
YOU'RE IMAGINING THINGS.
WHEN HER PET CRAYFISH P-CHAN DIED...
...SHE WAS SO SAD, I COULDN'T BEAR TO WATCH.
BUT NOW SHE'S IN SUCH A GOOD MOOD!
THEREFORE, YOU MUST BECOME MISS LINA'S PET!
UH-HUH...SO WOULD YOU LIKE TO DIE IN LITTLE CHUNKS?
I'M JUST ASKING YOU TO STAY HERE FOR HER UNTIL SHE HAS COMPLETELY RECOVERED HER SPIRITS.
I *WILL* PAY YOU FOR IT.
I DON'T THINK IT'S SUCH A BAD JOB.
BASICALLY, YOU'RE ASKING ME TO PLAY DOLLS WITH HER.
She seems perfectly fine to me now.
WELL, THIS *IS* ENTERTAINING...

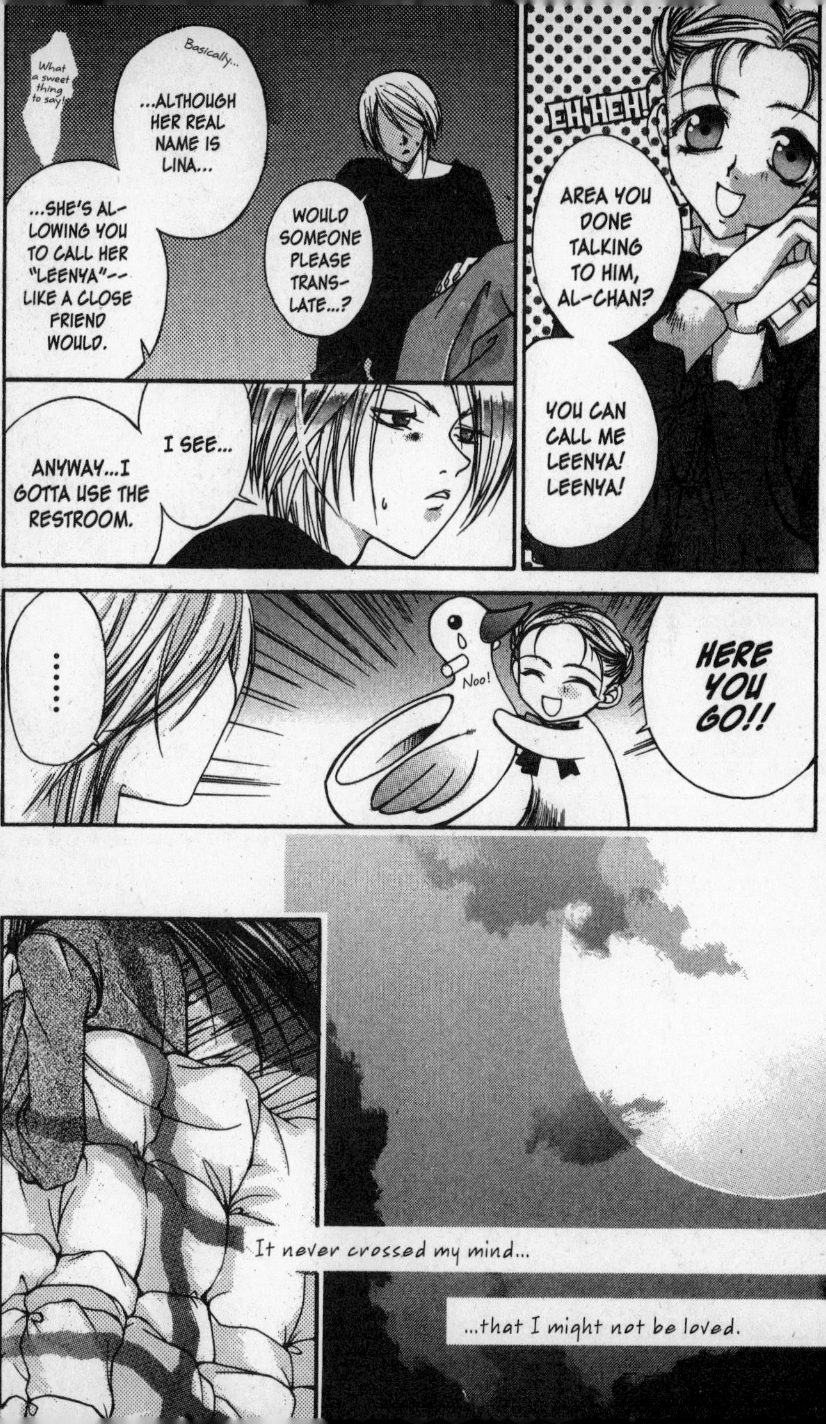
EH HEH!
AREA YOU DONE TALKING TO HIM, AL-CHAN?
YOU CAN CALL ME LEENYA! LEENYA!
WOULD SOMEONE PLEASE TRANS-LATE...?
Basically...
...ALTHOUGH HER REAL NAME IS LINA...
...SHE'S AL-LOWING YOU TO CALL HER "LEENYA"--LIKE A CLOSE FRIEND WOULD.
What a sweet thing to say!
I SEE...
ANYWAY...I GOTTA USE THE RESTROOM.
HERE YOU GO!!
Noo!
......
It never crossed my mind...
...that I might not be loved.

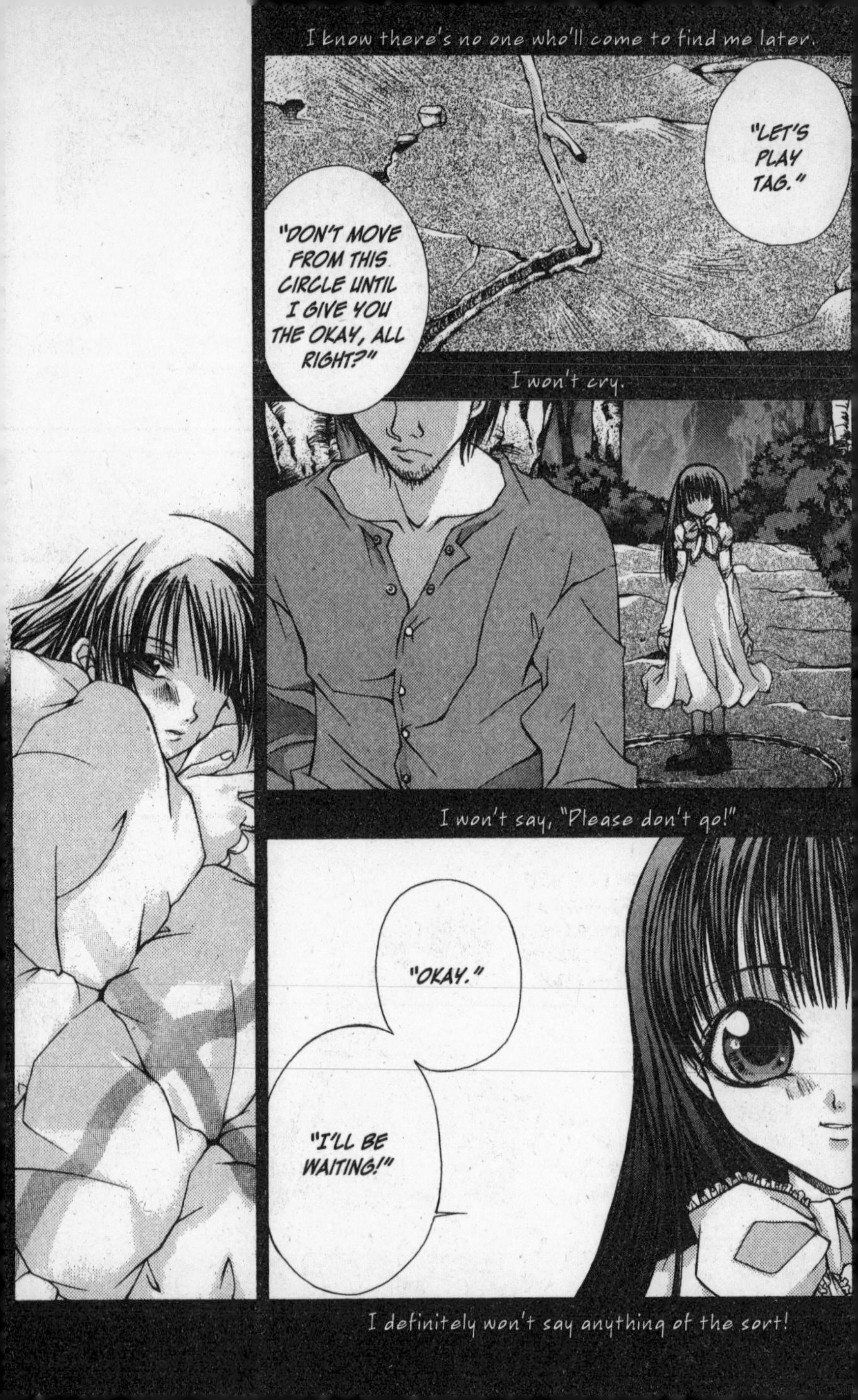
I know there's no one who'll come to find me later.
"LET'S PLAY TAG."
"DON'T MOVE FROM THIS CIRCLE UNTIL I GIVE YOU THE OKAY, ALL RIGHT?"
I won't cry.
I won't say, "Please don't go!"
"OKAY."
"I'LL BE WAITING!"
I definitely won't say anything of the sort!

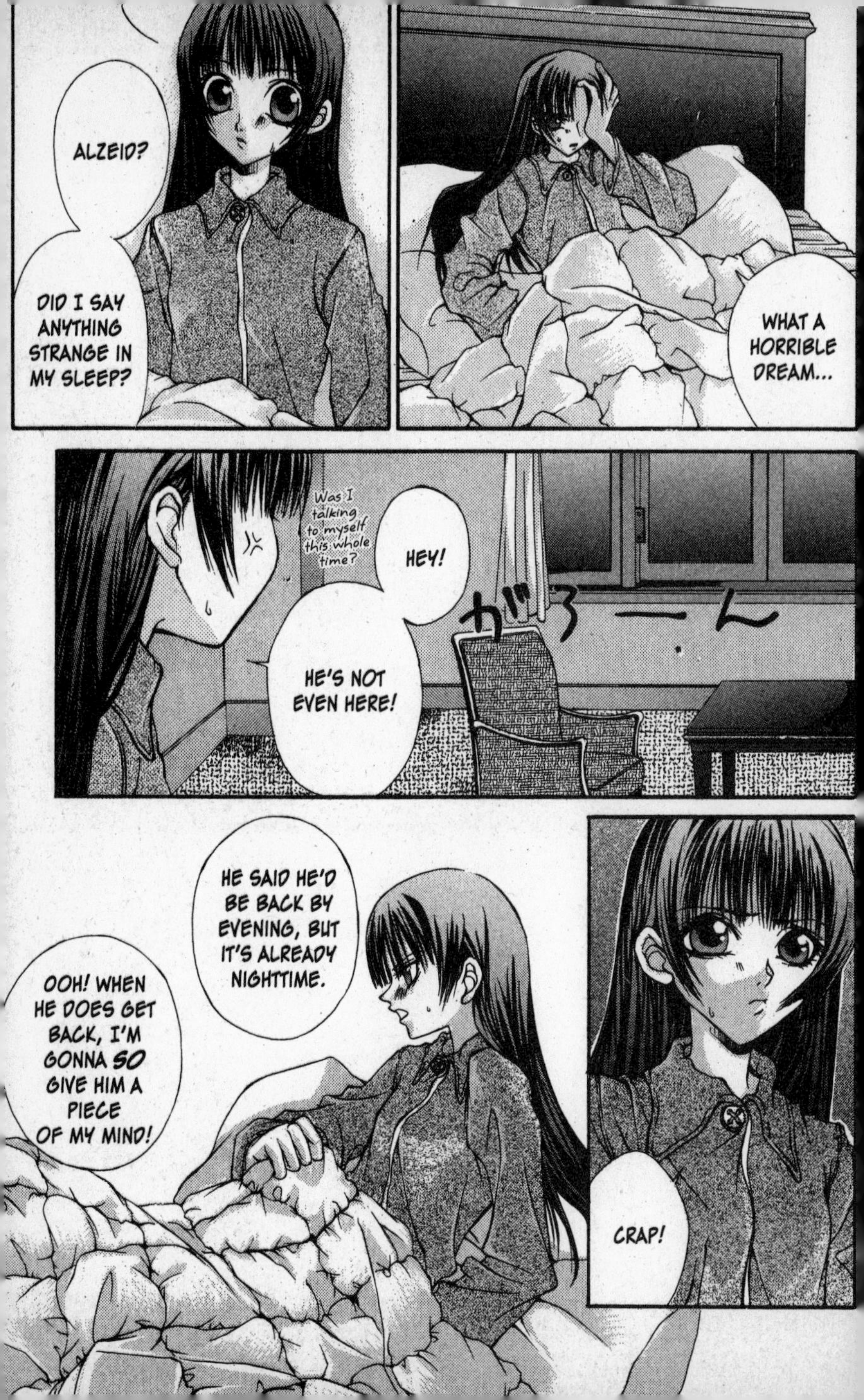
WHAT A HORRIBLE DREAM...
ALZEID?
DID I SAY ANYTHING STRANGE IN MY SLEEP?
がらーん
HEY!
Was I talking to myself this whole time?
HE'S NOT EVEN HERE!
CRAP!
HE SAID HE'D BE BACK BY EVENING, BUT IT'S ALREADY NIGHTTIME.
OOH! WHEN HE DOES GET BACK, I'M GONNA *SO* GIVE HIM A PIECE OF MY MIND!

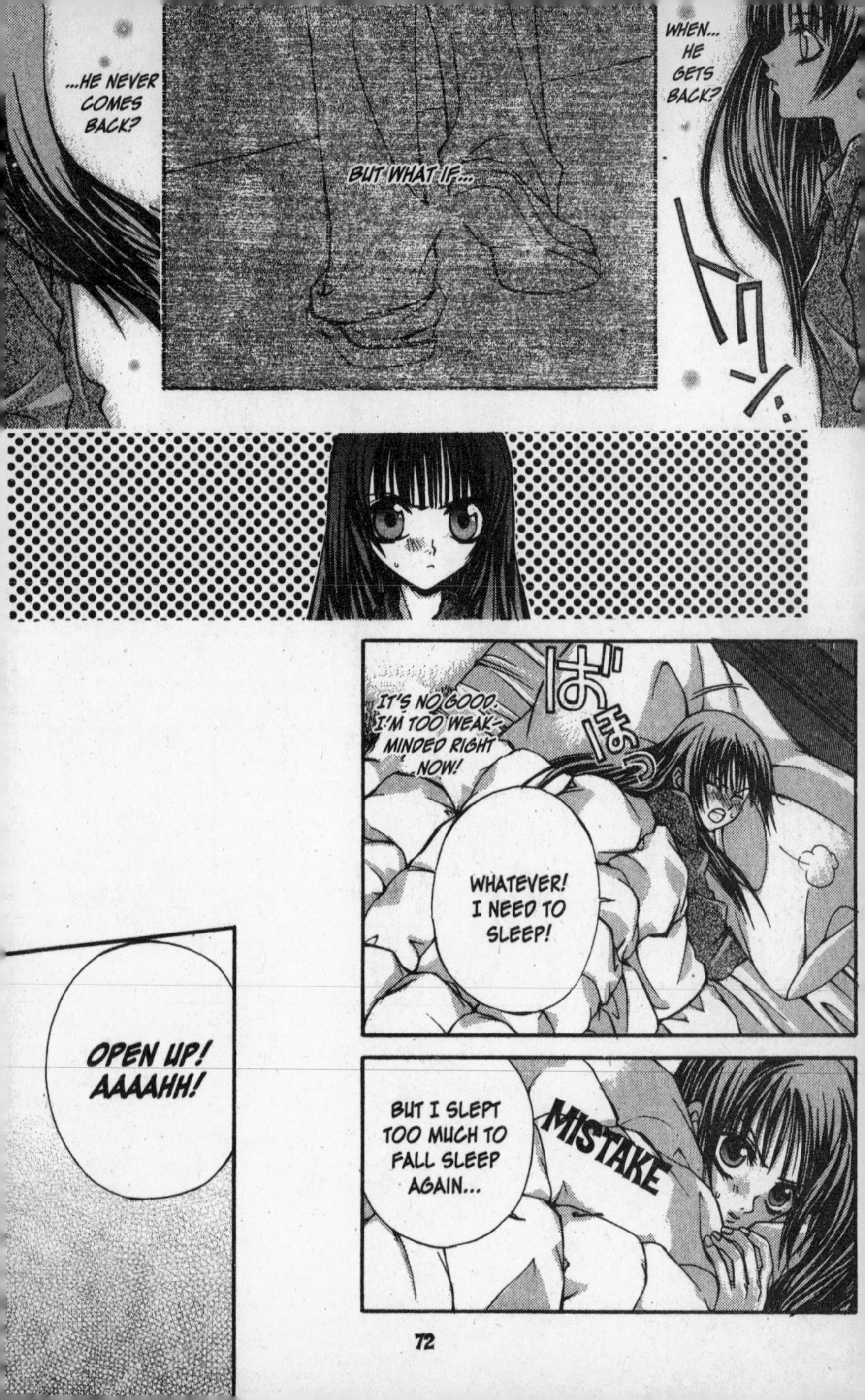
WHEN... HE GETS BACK?
BUT WHAT IF...
...HE NEVER COMES BACK?
IT'S NO GOOD. I'M TOO WEAK-MINDED RIGHT NOW!
WHATEVER! I NEED TO SLEEP!
BUT I SLEPT TOO MUCH TO FALL SLEEP AGAIN...
MISTAKE
OPEN UP! AAAAHH!

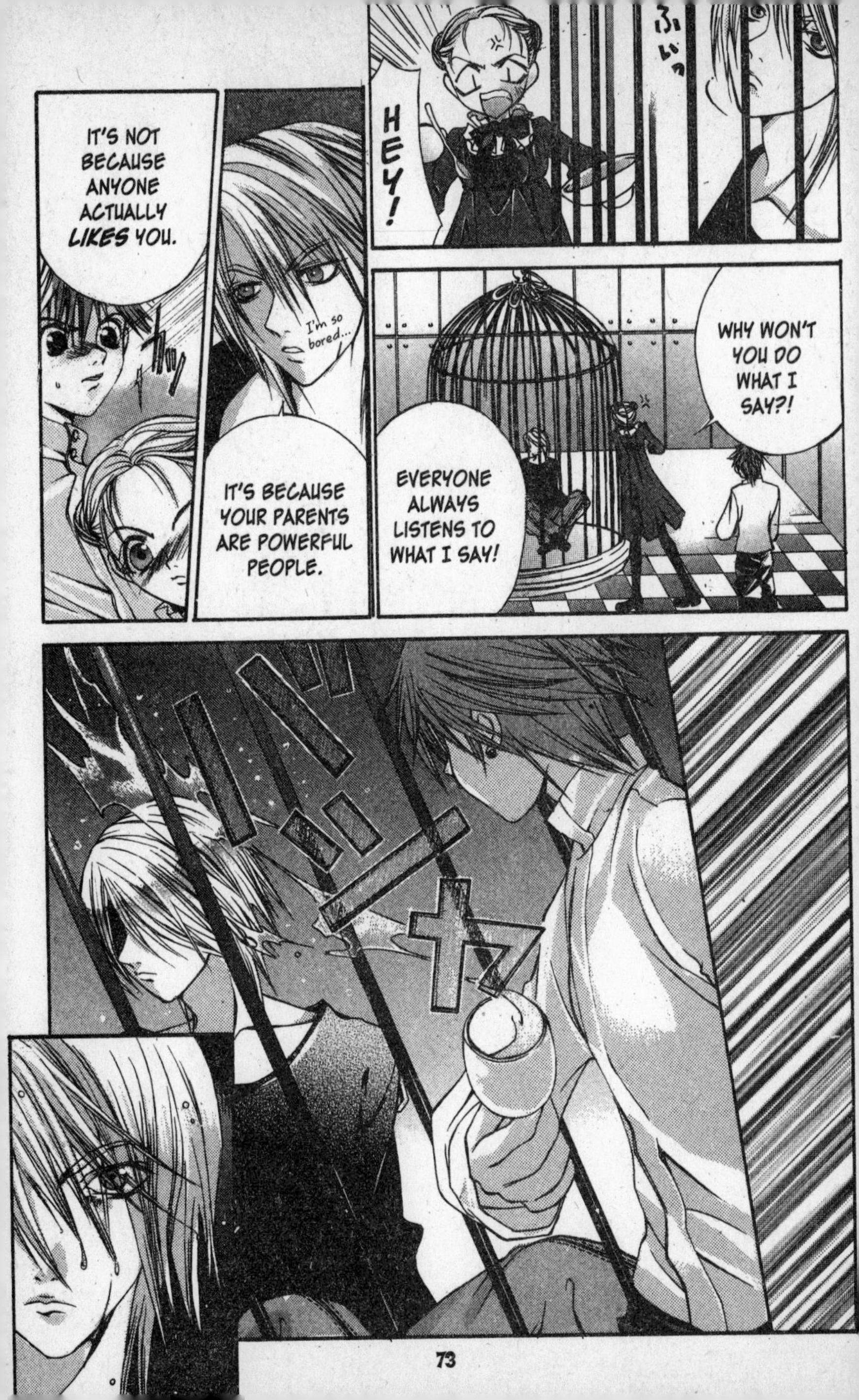
ふいっ
HEY!
WHY WON'T YOU DO WHAT I SAY?!
EVERYONE ALWAYS LISTENS TO WHAT I SAY!
I'm so bored...
IT'S BECAUSE YOUR PARENTS ARE POWERFUL PEOPLE.
IT'S NOT BECAUSE ANYONE ACTUALLY LIKES YOU.

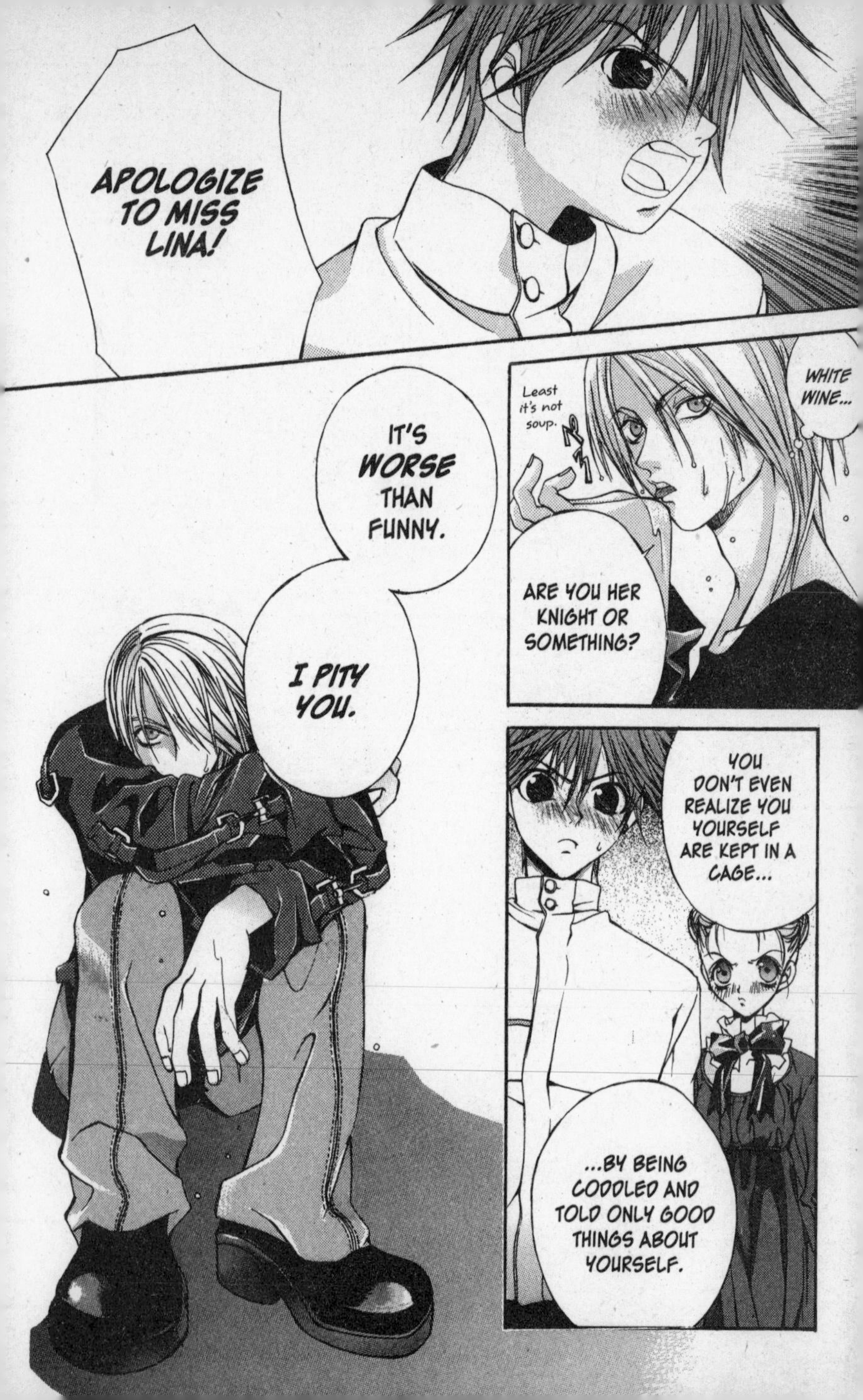
APOLOGIZE TO MISS LINA!
WHITE WINE...
Least it's not soup.
ARE YOU HER KNIGHT OR SOMETHING?
YOU DON'T EVEN REALIZE YOU YOURSELF ARE KEPT IN A CAGE...
...BY BEING CODDLED AND TOLD ONLY GOOD THINGS ABOUT YOURSELF.
IT'S WORSE THAN FUNNY.
I PITY YOU.

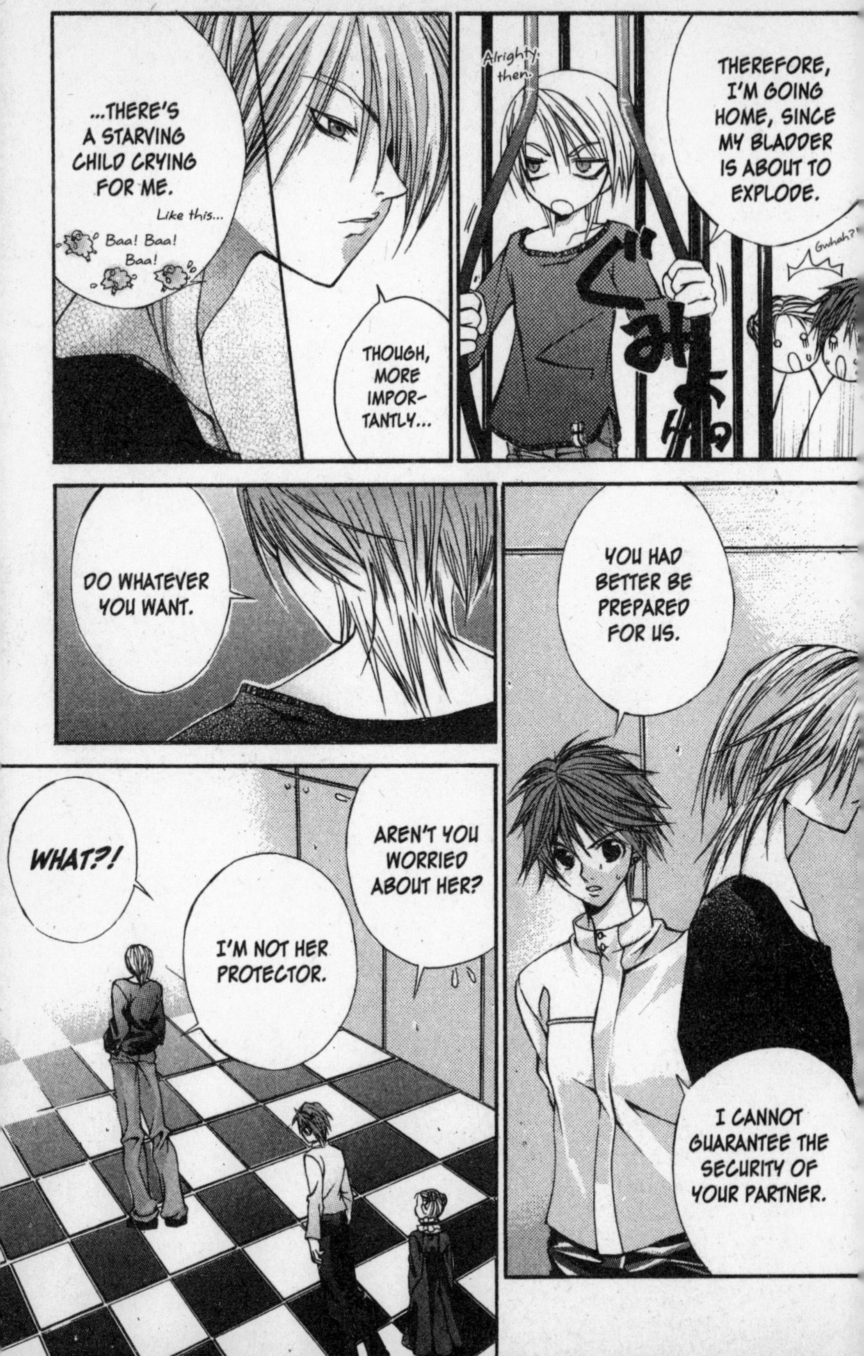
Alrighty, then.
THEREFORE, I'M GOING HOME, SINCE MY BLADDER IS ABOUT TO EXPLODE.
Gwhah?!
THOUGH, MORE IMPORTANTLY...
...THERE'S A STARVING CHILD CRYING FOR ME.
Like this...
Baa! Baa! Baa!
YOU HAD BETTER BE PREPARED FOR US.
I CANNOT GUARANTEE THE SECURITY OF YOUR PARTNER.
DO WHATEVER YOU WANT.
AREN'T YOU WORRIED ABOUT HER?
I'M NOT HER PROTECTOR.
WHAT?!

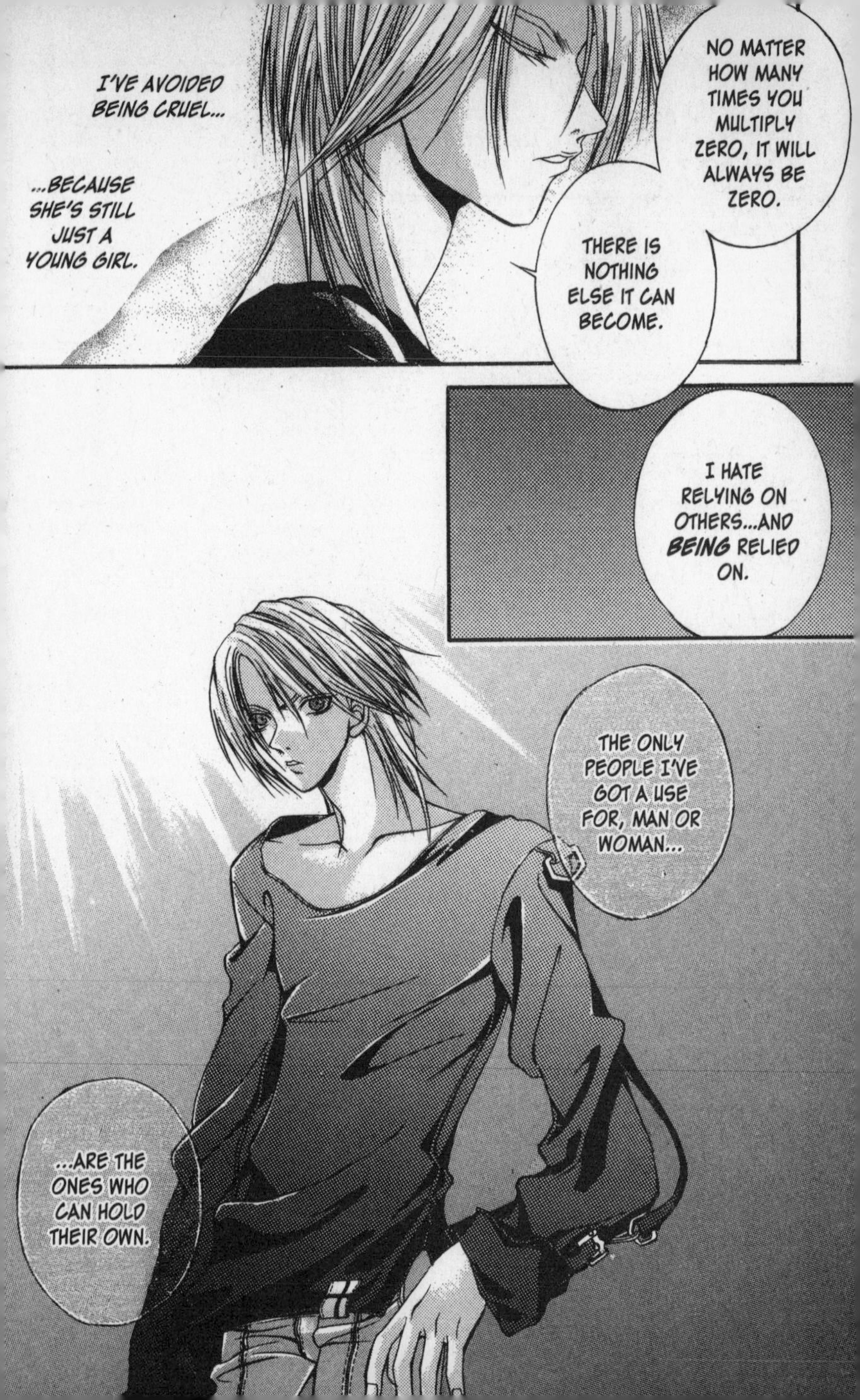
NO MATTER HOW MANY TIMES YOU MULTIPLY ZERO, IT WILL ALWAYS BE ZERO.
THERE IS NOTHING ELSE IT CAN BECOME.
I'VE AVOIDED BEING CRUEL...
...BECAUSE SHE'S STILL JUST A YOUNG GIRL.
I HATE RELYING ON OTHERS...AND *BEING* RELIED ON.
THE ONLY PEOPLE I'VE GOT A USE FOR, MAN OR WOMAN...
...ARE THE ONES WHO CAN HOLD THEIR OWN.

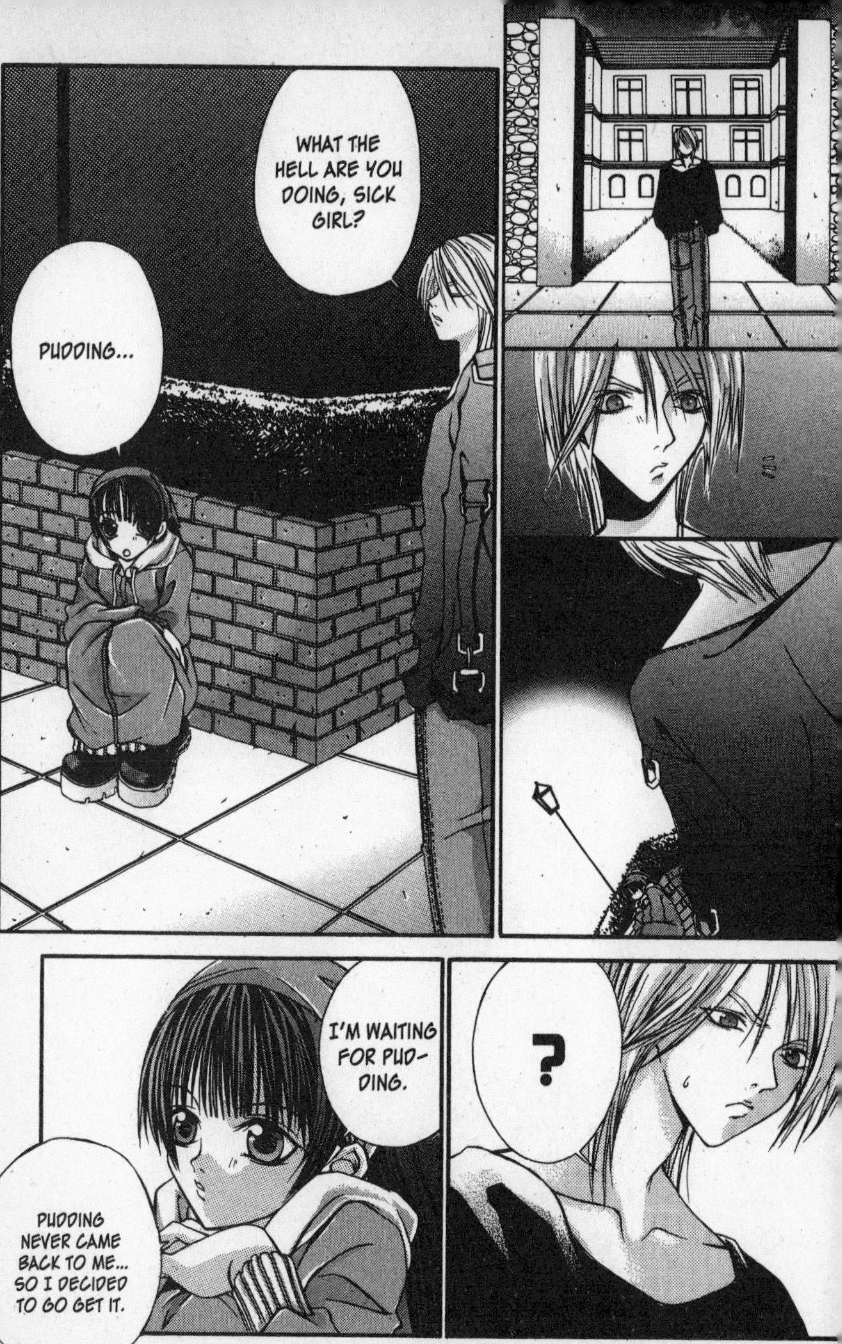
WHAT THE HELL ARE YOU DOING, SICK GIRL?
PUDDING...
?
I'M WAITING FOR PUD-DING.
PUDDING NEVER CAME BACK TO ME... SO I DECIDED TO GO GET IT.

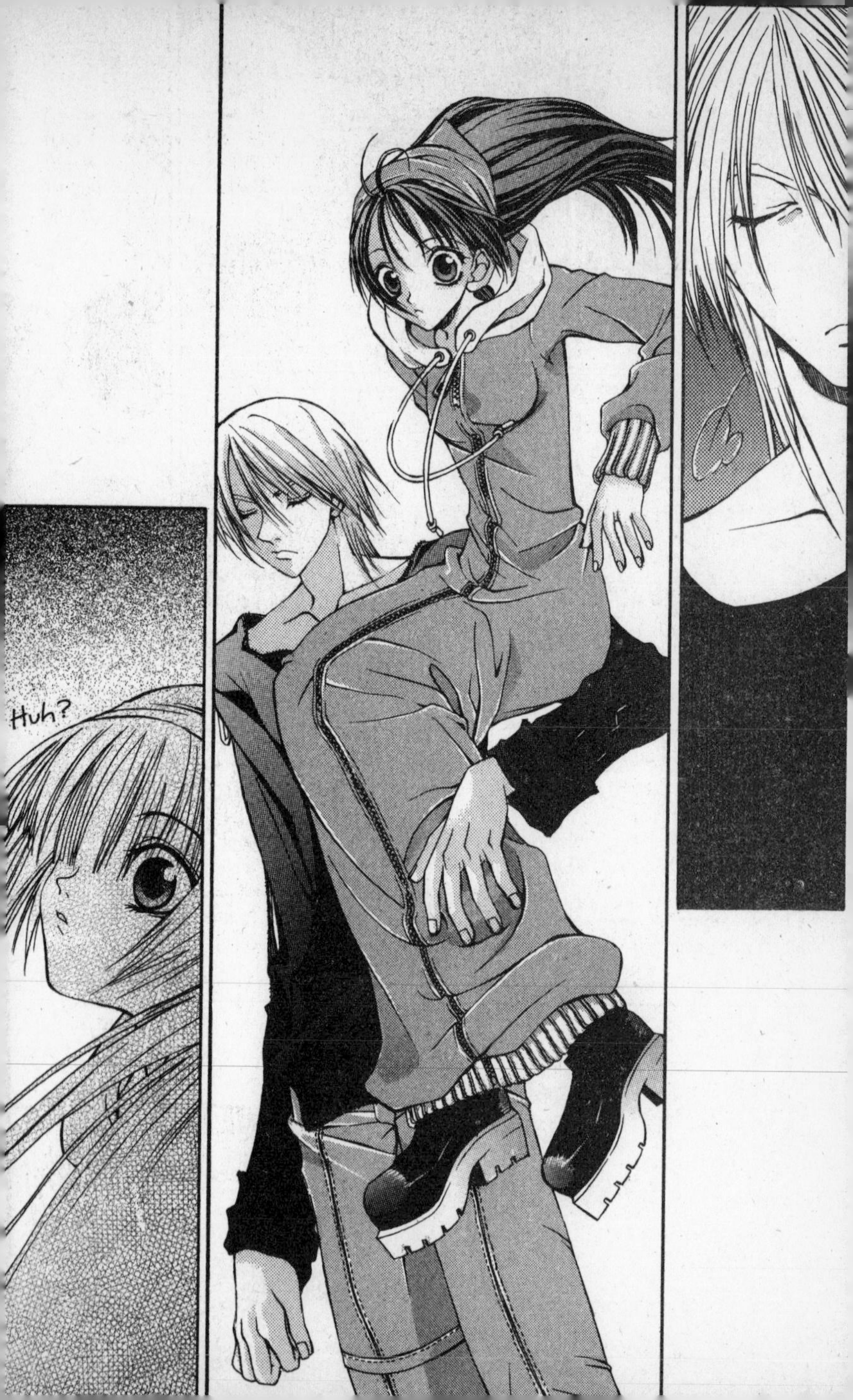
Huh?

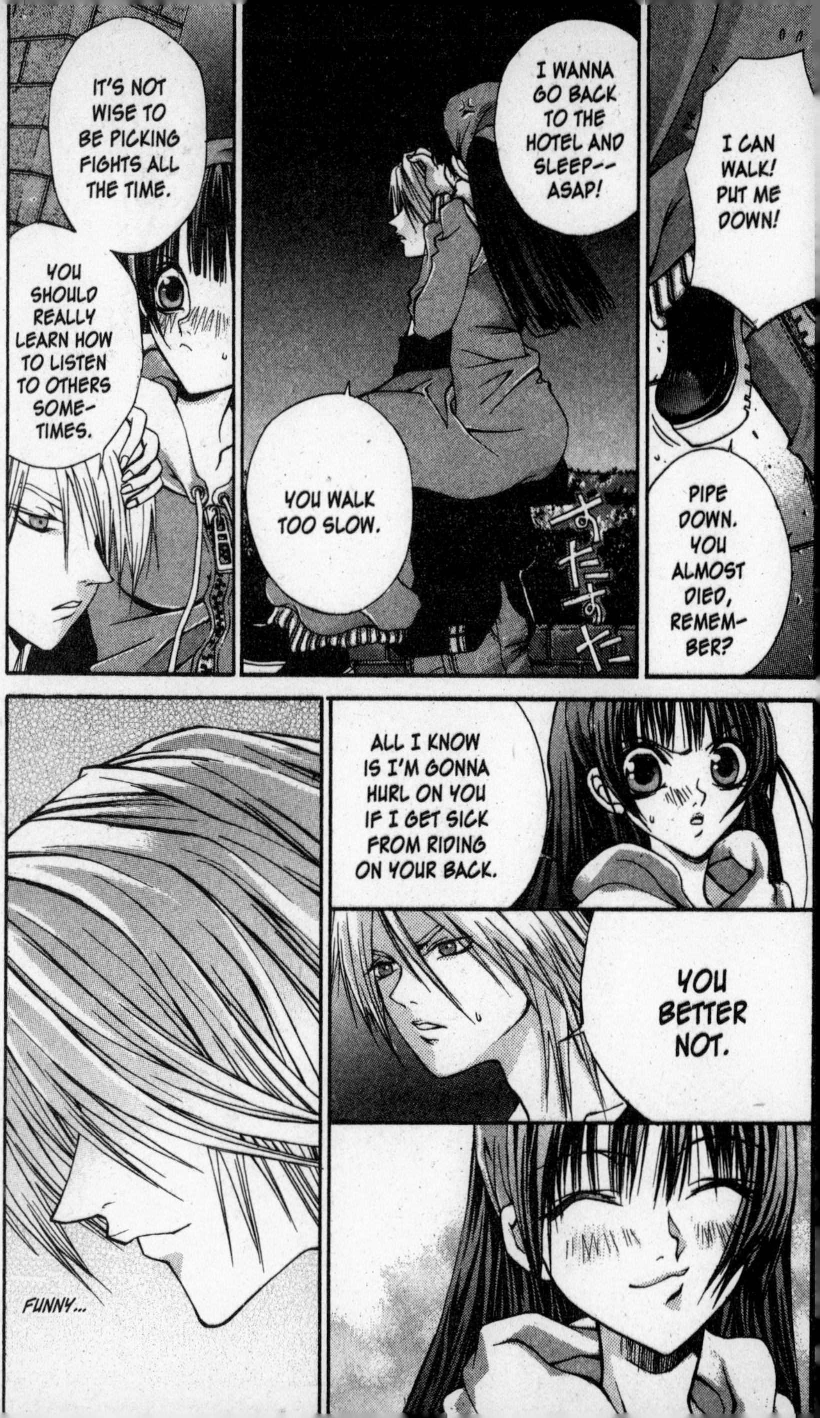
I CAN WALK! PUT ME DOWN!
PIPE DOWN. YOU ALMOST DIED, REMEMBER?
I WANNA GO BACK TO THE HOTEL AND SLEEP--ASAP!
YOU WALK TOO SLOW.
IT'S NOT WISE TO BE PICKING FIGHTS ALL THE TIME.
YOU SHOULD REALLY LEARN HOW TO LISTEN TO OTHERS SOMETIMES.
ALL I KNOW IS I'M GONNA HURL ON YOU IF I GET SICK FROM RIDING ON YOUR BACK.
YOU BETTER NOT.
FUNNY...

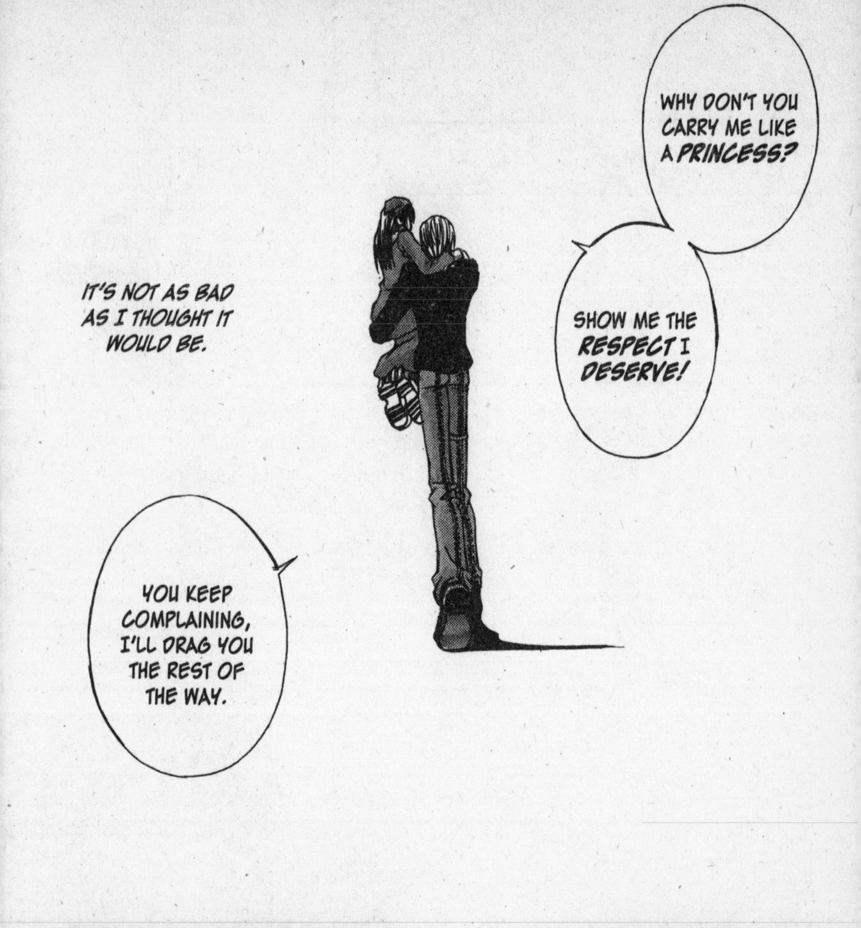
WHY DON'T YOU CARRY ME LIKE A PRINCESS?
SHOW ME THE RESPECT I DESERVE!
IT'S NOT AS BAD AS I THOUGHT IT WOULD BE.
YOU KEEP COMPLAINING, I'LL DRAG YOU THE REST OF THE WAY.

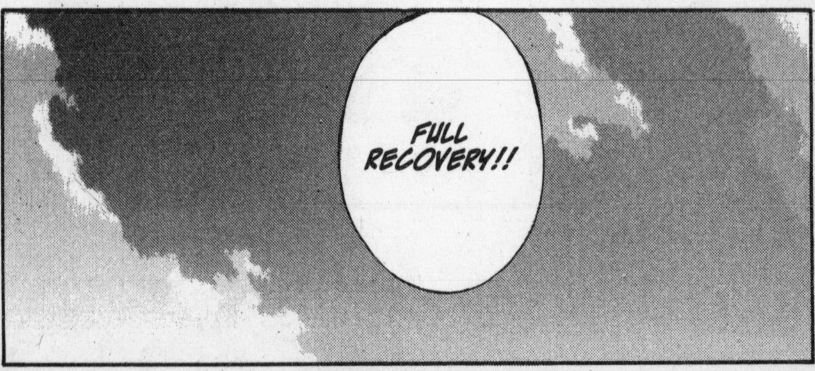
FULL RECOVERY!!

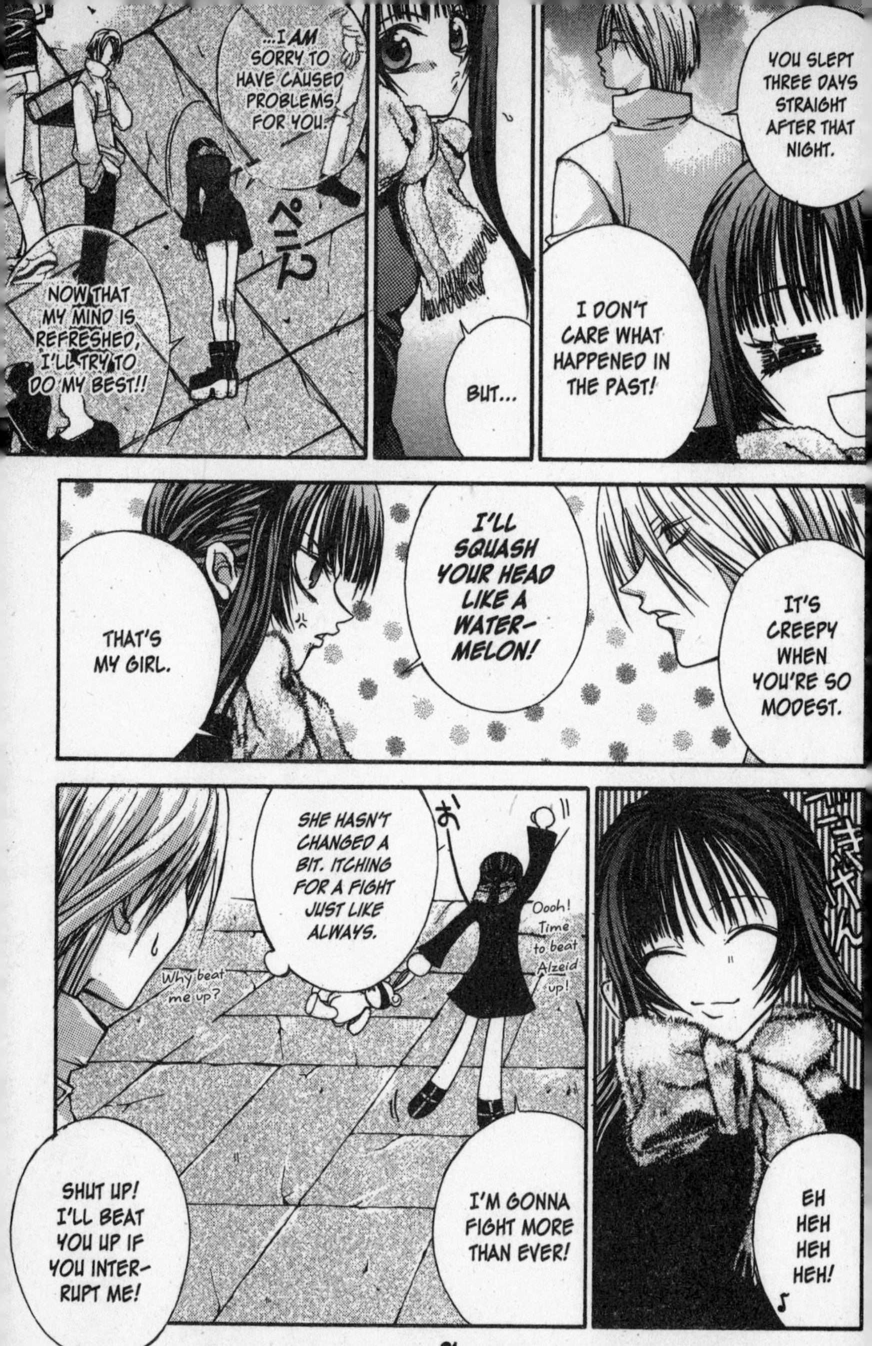
YOU SLEPT THREE DAYS STRAIGHT AFTER THAT NIGHT.
I DON'T CARE WHAT HAPPENED IN THE PAST!
BUT...
...I AM SORRY TO HAVE CAUSED PROBLEMS FOR YOU.
NOW THAT MY MIND IS REFRESHED, I'LL TRY TO DO MY BEST!!
IT'S CREEPY WHEN YOU'RE SO MODEST.
I'LL SQUASH YOUR HEAD LIKE A WATER-MELON!
THAT'S MY GIRL.
EH HEH HEH HEH!
I'M GONNA FIGHT MORE THAN EVER!
Oooh! Time to beat Alzeid up!
SHE HASN'T CHANGED A BIT. ITCHING FOR A FIGHT JUST LIKE ALWAYS.
Why beat me up?
SHUT UP! I'LL BEAT YOU UP IF YOU INTER-RUPT ME!

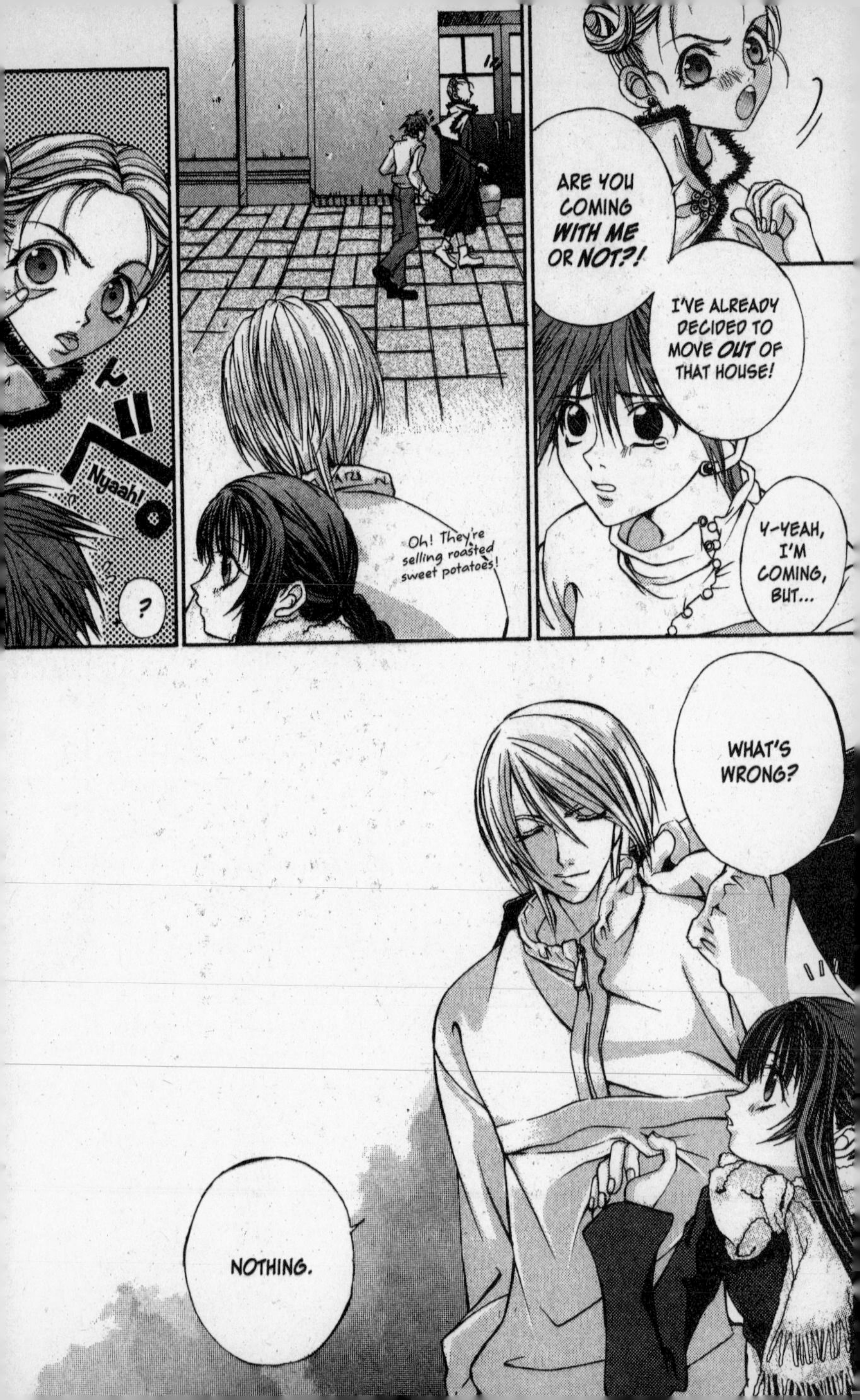
ARE YOU COMING WITH ME OR NOT?!
I'VE ALREADY DECIDED TO MOVE OUT OF THAT HOUSE!
Y-YEAH, I'M COMING, BUT...
Oh! They're selling roasted sweet potatoes!
Nyaah!
?
WHAT'S WRONG?
NOTHING.

Chapter 4: Eternal Light—Part 1: Waiting for Spring

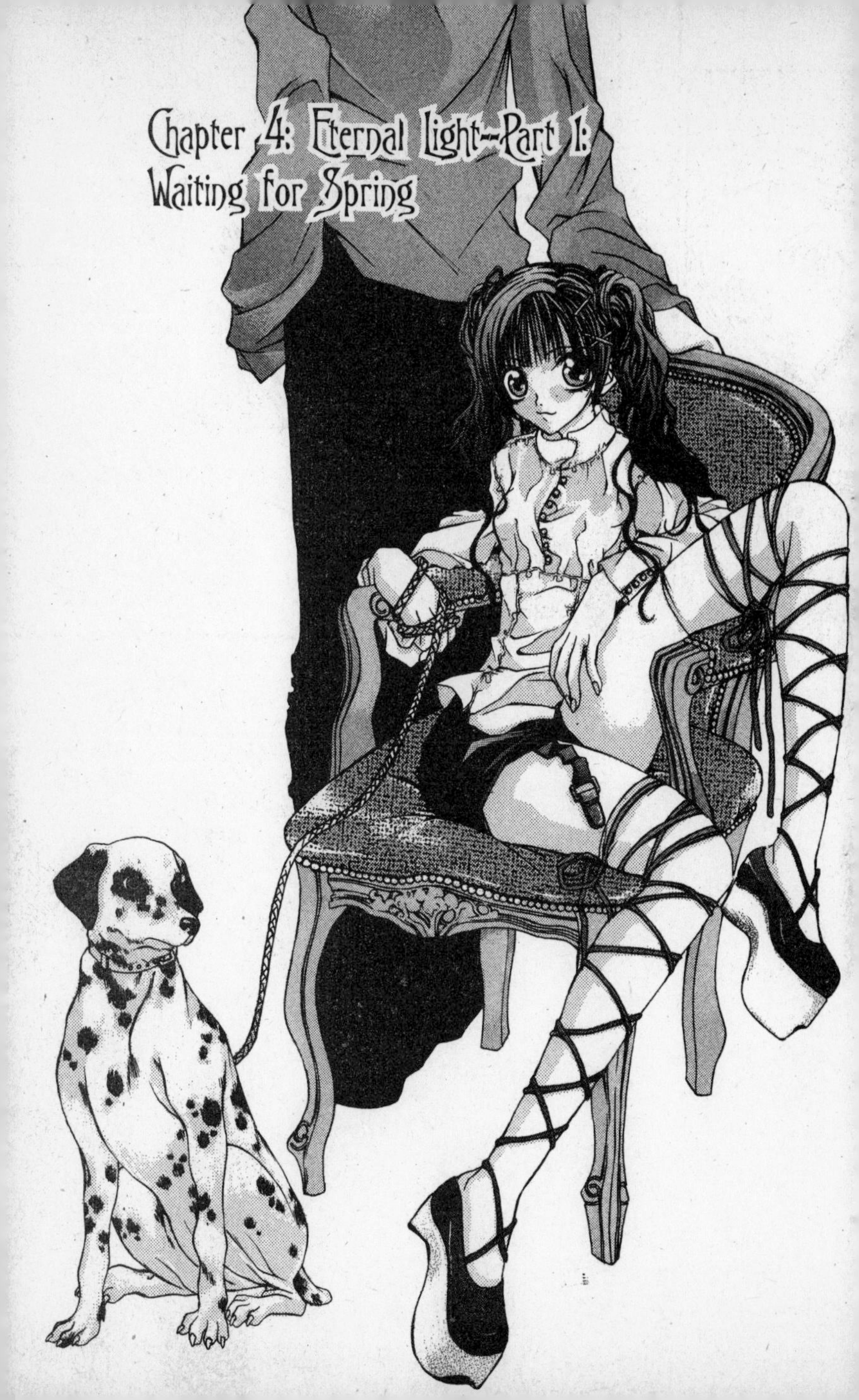

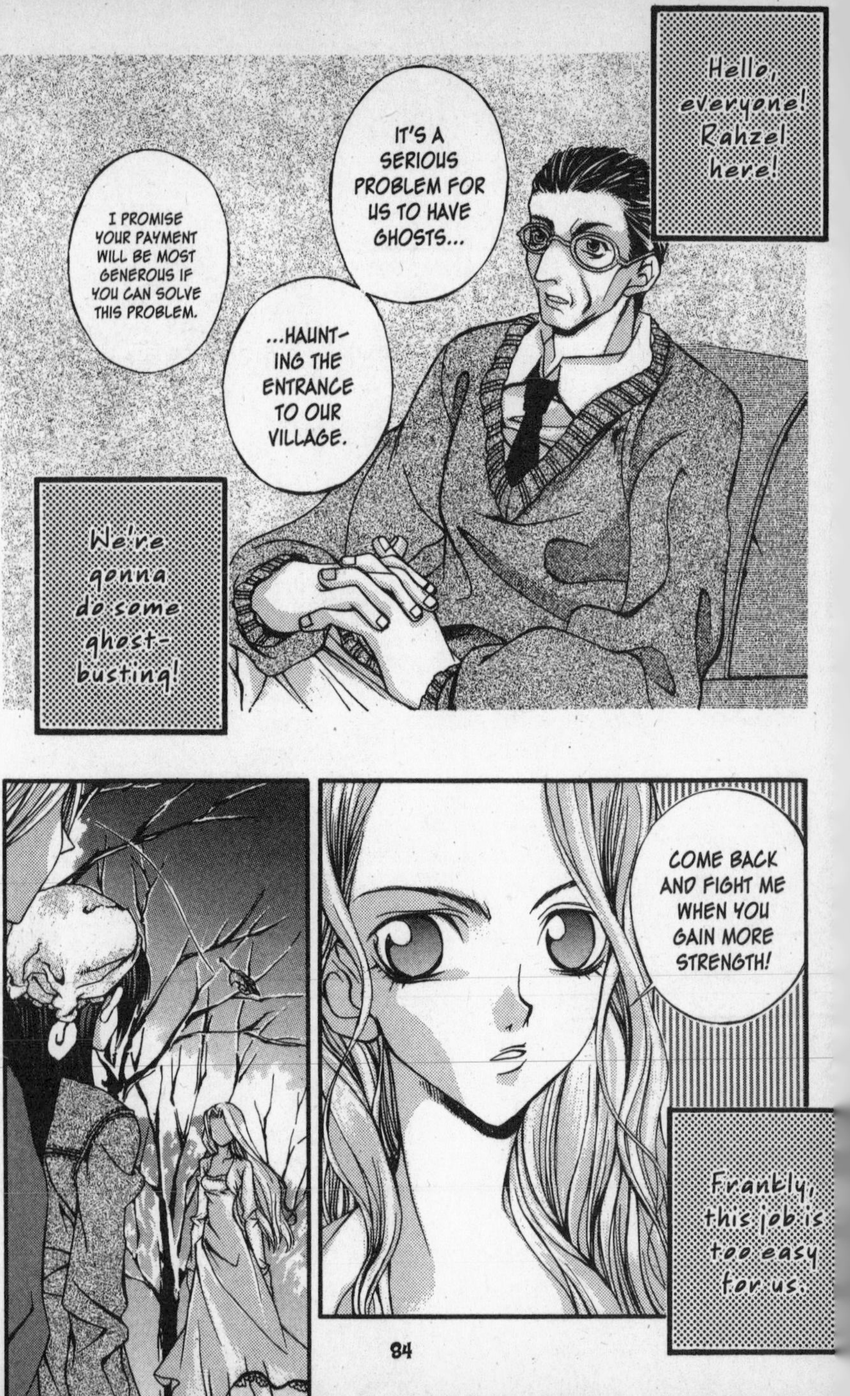
Hello, everyone! Rahzel here!
IT'S A SERIOUS PROBLEM FOR US TO HAVE GHOSTS...
...HAUNTING THE ENTRANCE TO OUR VILLAGE.
I PROMISE YOUR PAYMENT WILL BE MOST GENEROUS IF YOU CAN SOLVE THIS PROBLEM.
We're gonna do some ghost-busting!
COME BACK AND FIGHT ME WHEN YOU GAIN MORE STRENGTH!
Frankly, this job is too easy for us.

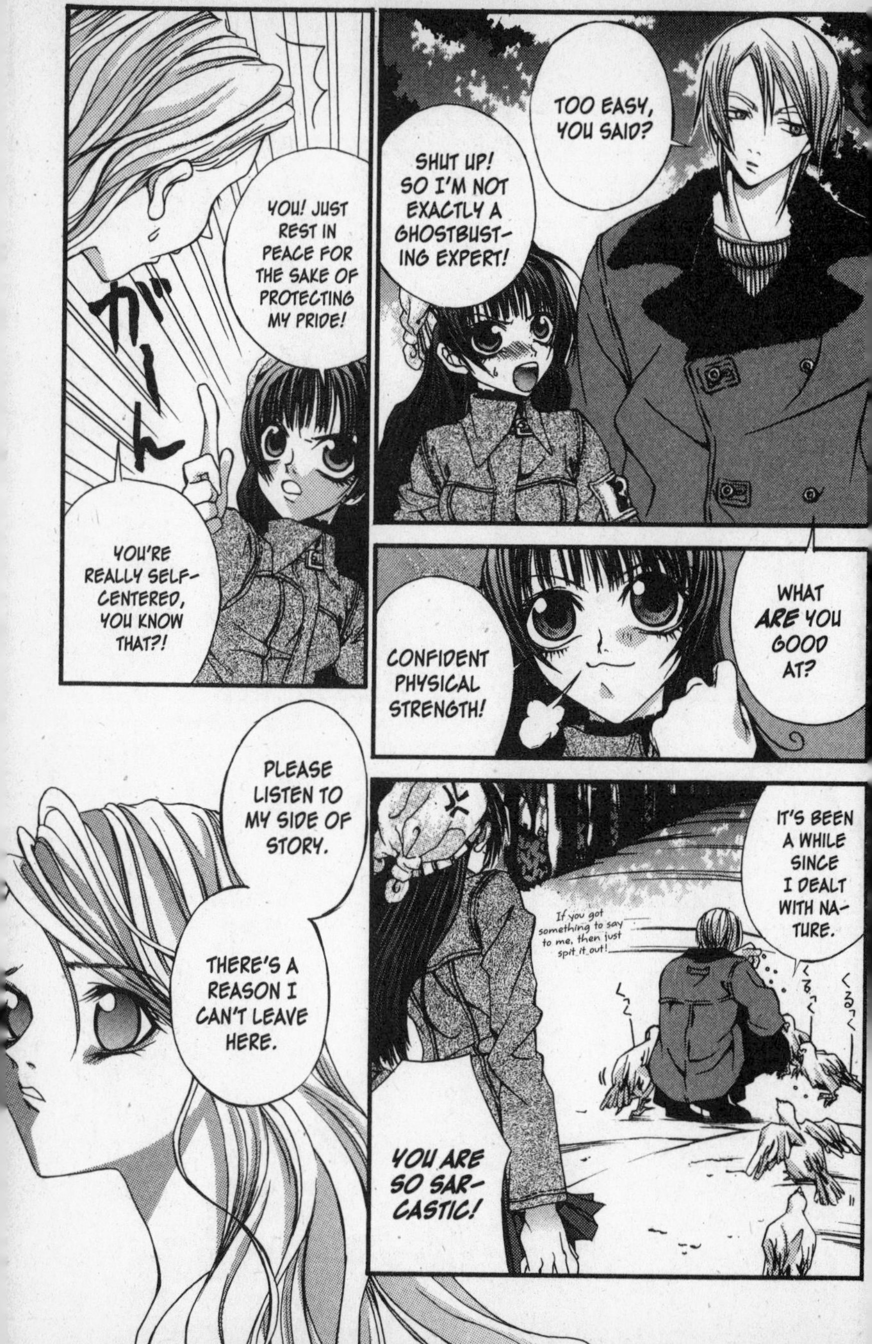

TOO EASY, YOU SAID?
SHUT UP! SO I'M NOT EXACTLY A GHOSTBUSTING EXPERT!
WHAT ARE YOU GOOD AT?
CONFIDENT PHYSICAL STRENGTH!
YOU! JUST REST IN PEACE FOR THE SAKE OF PROTECTING MY PRIDE!
がーん
YOU'RE REALLY SELF-CENTERED, YOU KNOW THAT?!
IT'S BEEN A WHILE SINCE I DEALT WITH NATURE.
If you got something to say to me, then just spit it out!
YOU ARE SO SARCASTIC!
PLEASE LISTEN TO MY SIDE OF STORY.
THERE'S A REASON I CAN'T LEAVE HERE.

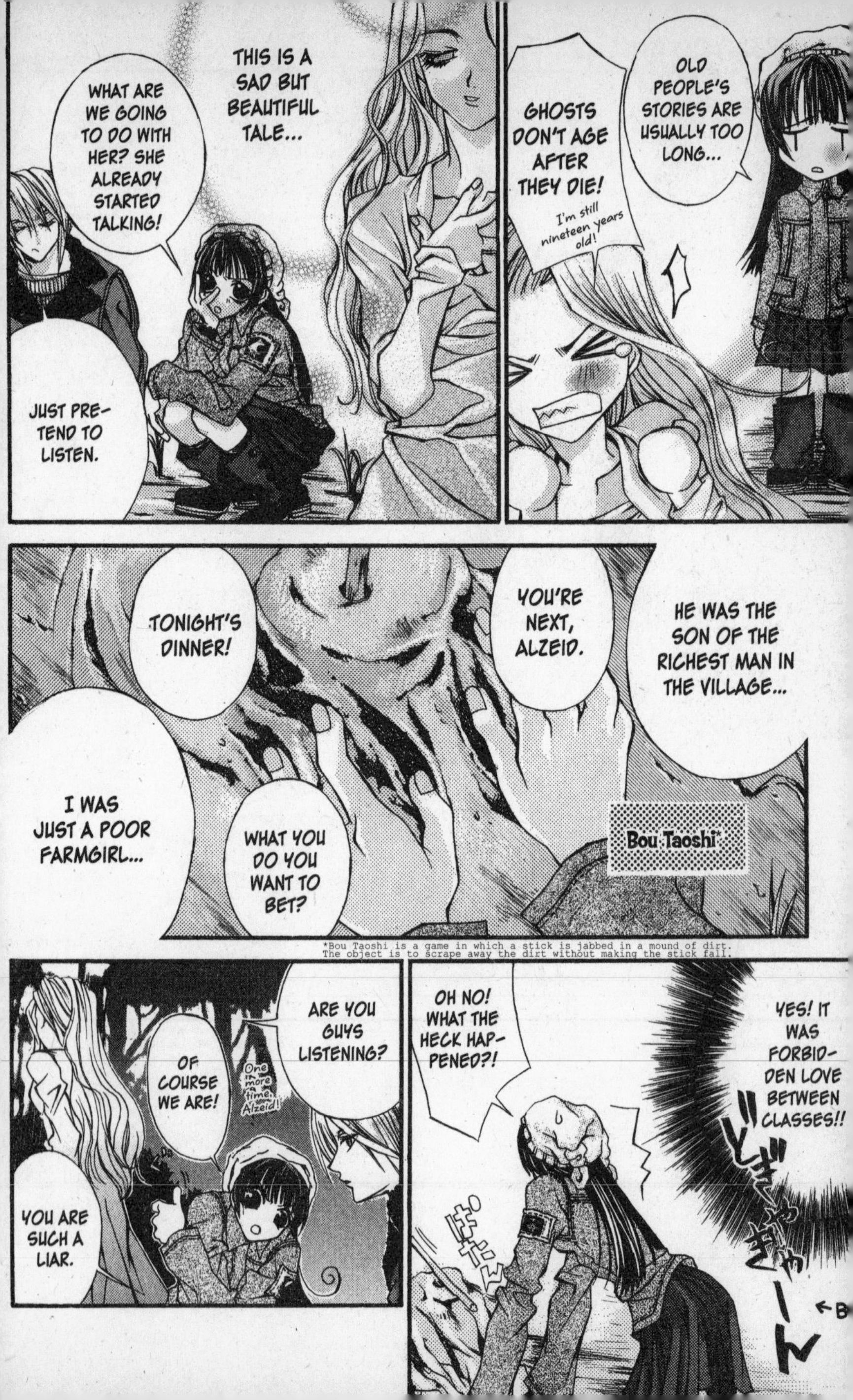
OLD PEOPLE'S STORIES ARE USUALLY TOO LONG...
GHOSTS DON'T AGE AFTER THEY DIE!
I'm still nineteen years old!
THIS IS A SAD BUT BEAUTIFUL TALE...
WHAT ARE WE GOING TO DO WITH HER? SHE ALREADY STARTED TALKING!
JUST PRE-TEND TO LISTEN.
HE WAS THE SON OF THE RICHEST MAN IN THE VILLAGE...
YOU'RE NEXT, ALZEID.
TONIGHT'S DINNER!
Bou Taoshi*
I WAS JUST A POOR FARMGIRL...
WHAT YOU DO YOU WANT TO BET?
YES! IT WAS FORBID-DEN LOVE BETWEEN CLASSES!!
OH NO! WHAT THE HECK HAP-PENED?!
ARE YOU GUYS LISTENING?
OF COURSE WE ARE!
One more time, Alzeid!
YOU ARE SUCH A LIAR.

*Bou Taoshi is a game in which a stick is jabbed in a mound of dirt. The object is to scrape away the dirt without making the stick fall.

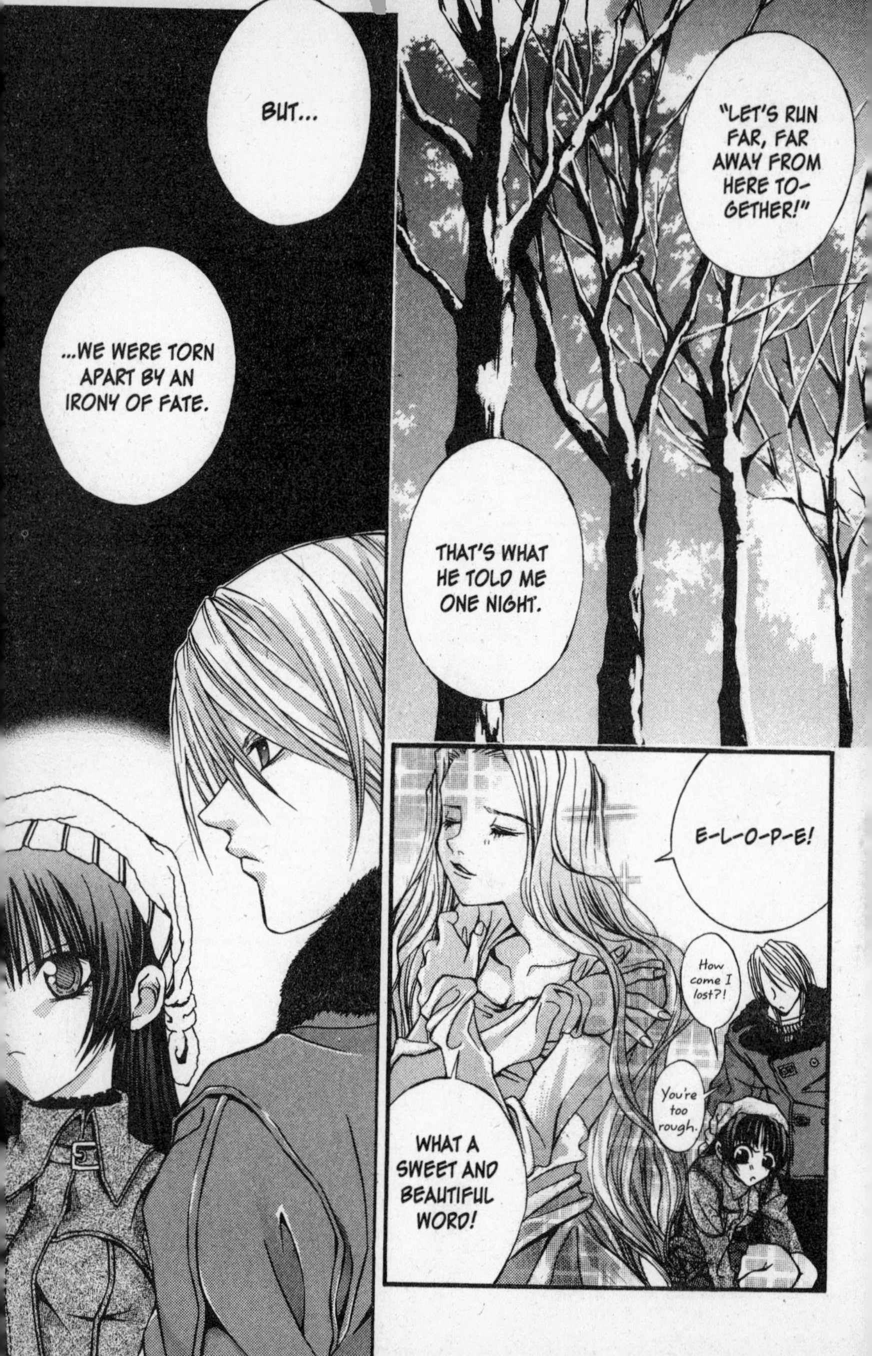
"LET'S RUN FAR, FAR AWAY FROM HERE TO-GETHER!"
THAT'S WHAT HE TOLD ME ONE NIGHT.
E-L-O-P-E!
How come I lost?!
You're too rough.
WHAT A SWEET AND BEAUTIFUL WORD!
BUT...
...WE WERE TORN APART BY AN IRONY OF FATE.

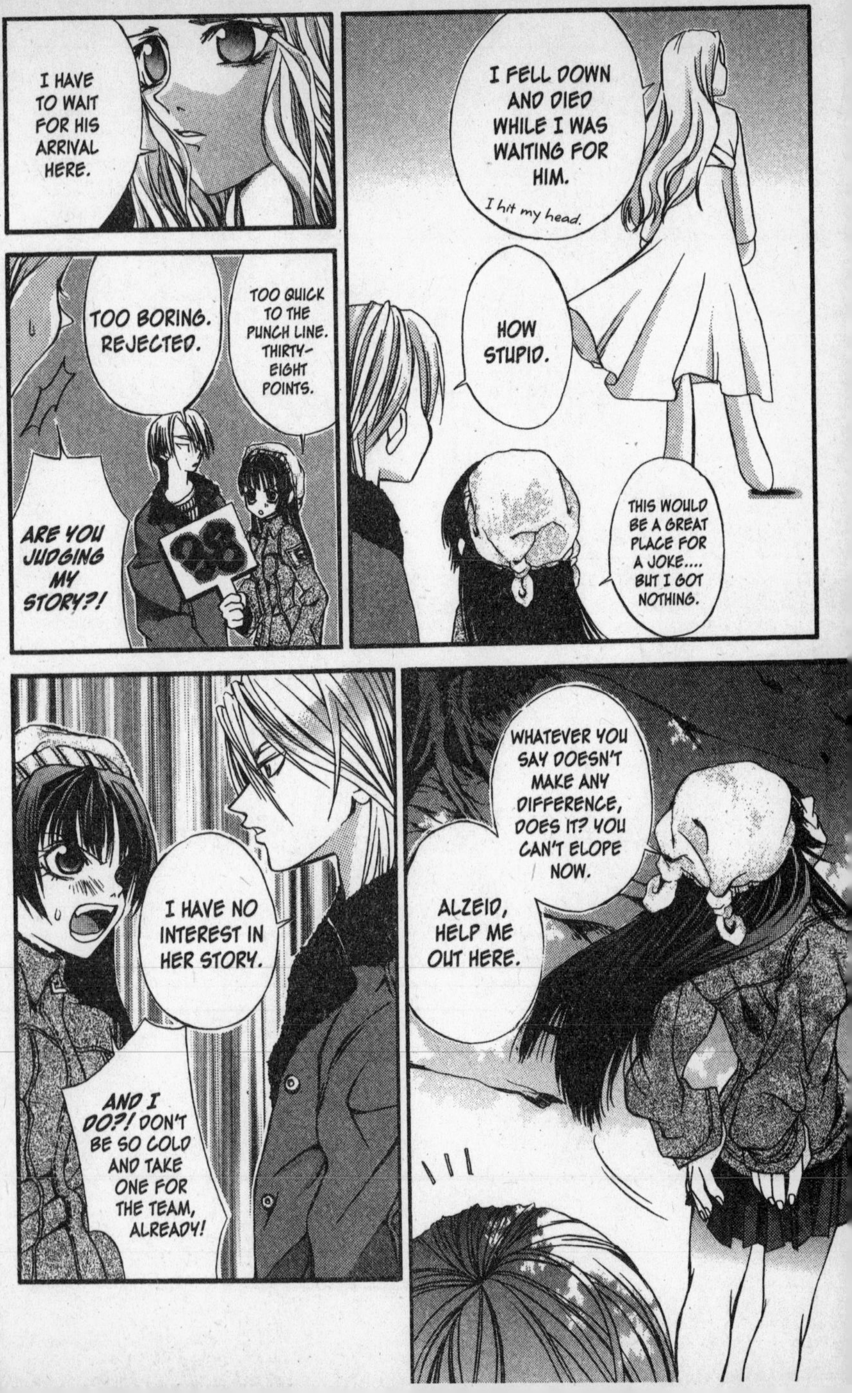
I FELL DOWN AND DIED WHILE I WAS WAITING FOR HIM.
I hit my head.
HOW STUPID.
THIS WOULD BE A GREAT PLACE FOR A JOKE.... BUT I GOT NOTHING.
I HAVE TO WAIT FOR HIS ARRIVAL HERE.
TOO QUICK TO THE PUNCH LINE. THIRTY-EIGHT POINTS.
TOO BORING. REJECTED.
38
ARE YOU JUDGING MY STORY?!
WHATEVER YOU SAY DOESN'T MAKE ANY DIFFERENCE, DOES IT? YOU CAN'T ELOPE NOW.
ALZEID, HELP ME OUT HERE.
I HAVE NO INTEREST IN HER STORY.
AND I DO?! DON'T BE SO COLD AND TAKE ONE FOR THE TEAM, ALREADY!

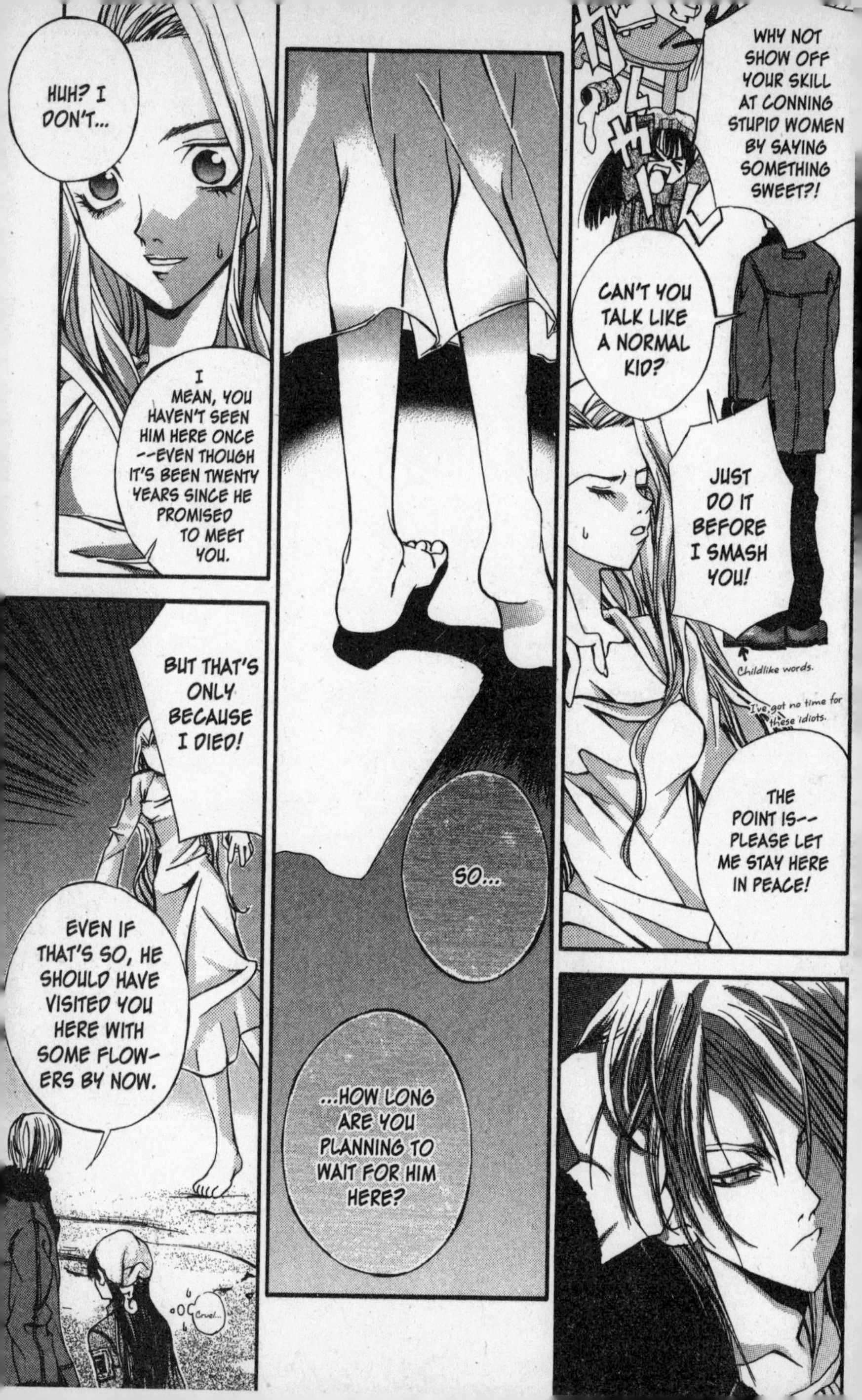
WHY NOT SHOW OFF YOUR SKILL AT CONNING STUPID WOMEN BY SAYING SOMETHING SWEET?!
CAN'T YOU TALK LIKE A NORMAL KID?
JUST DO IT BEFORE I SMASH YOU!
Childlike words.
I've got no time for these idiots.
THE POINT IS-- PLEASE LET ME STAY HERE IN PEACE!
SO...
...HOW LONG ARE YOU PLANNING TO WAIT FOR HIM HERE?
HUH? I DON'T...
I MEAN, YOU HAVEN'T SEEN HIM HERE ONCE--EVEN THOUGH IT'S BEEN TWENTY YEARS SINCE HE PROMISED TO MEET YOU.
BUT THAT'S ONLY BECAUSE I DIED!
EVEN IF THAT'S SO, HE SHOULD HAVE VISITED YOU HERE WITH SOME FLOWERS BY NOW.
Cruel...

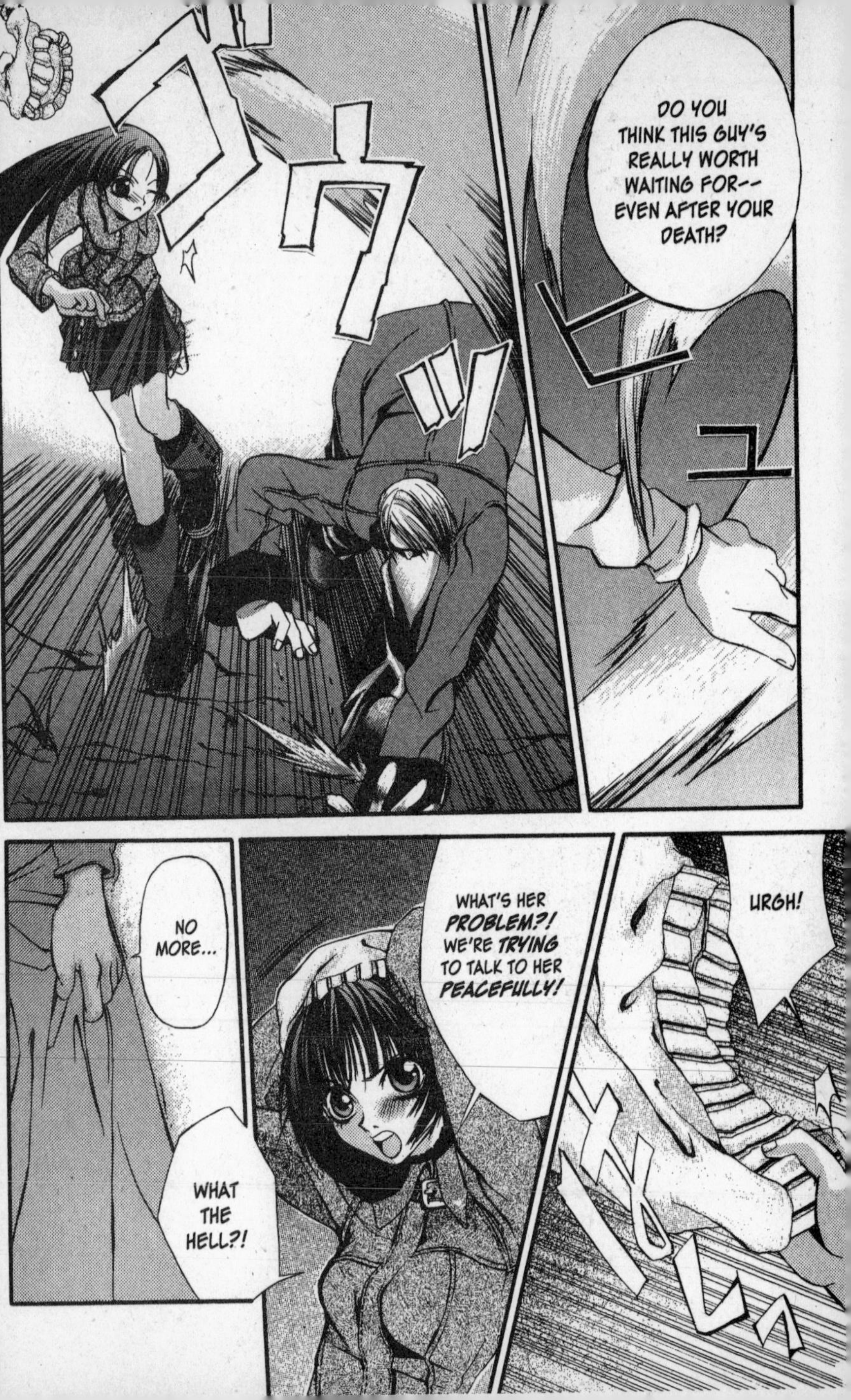
DO YOU THINK THIS GUY'S REALLY WORTH WAITING FOR-- EVEN AFTER YOUR DEATH?
URGH!
WHAT'S HER *PROBLEM?!* WE'RE *TRYING* TO TALK TO HER *PEACEFULLY!*
WHAT THE HELL?!
NO MORE...

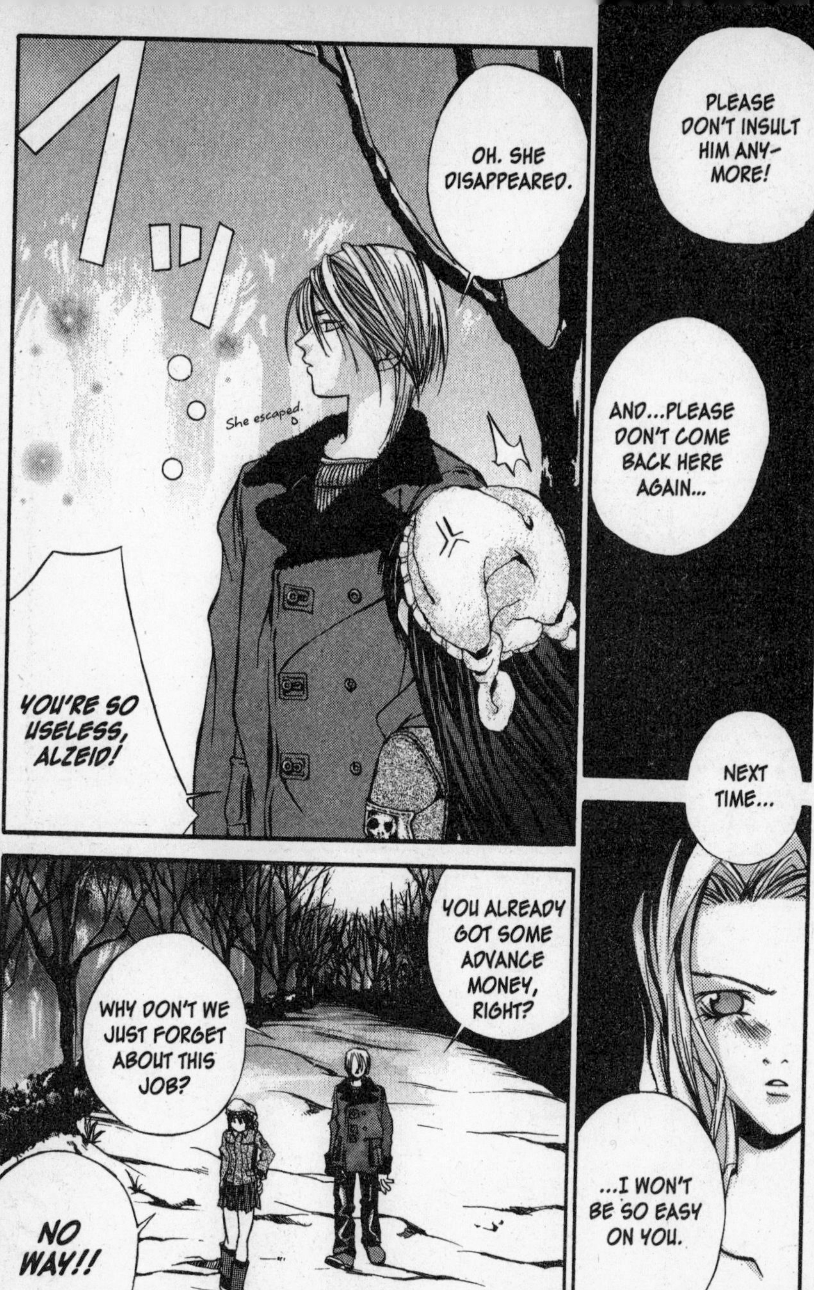
PLEASE DON'T INSULT HIM ANY-MORE!
AND...PLEASE DON'T COME BACK HERE AGAIN...
OH. SHE DISAPPEARED.
She escaped.
YOU'RE SO USELESS, ALZEID!
NEXT TIME...
...I WON'T BE SO EASY ON YOU.
YOU ALREADY GOT SOME ADVANCE MONEY, RIGHT?
WHY DON'T WE JUST FORGET ABOUT THIS JOB?
NO WAY!!
The advance money wasn't enough!

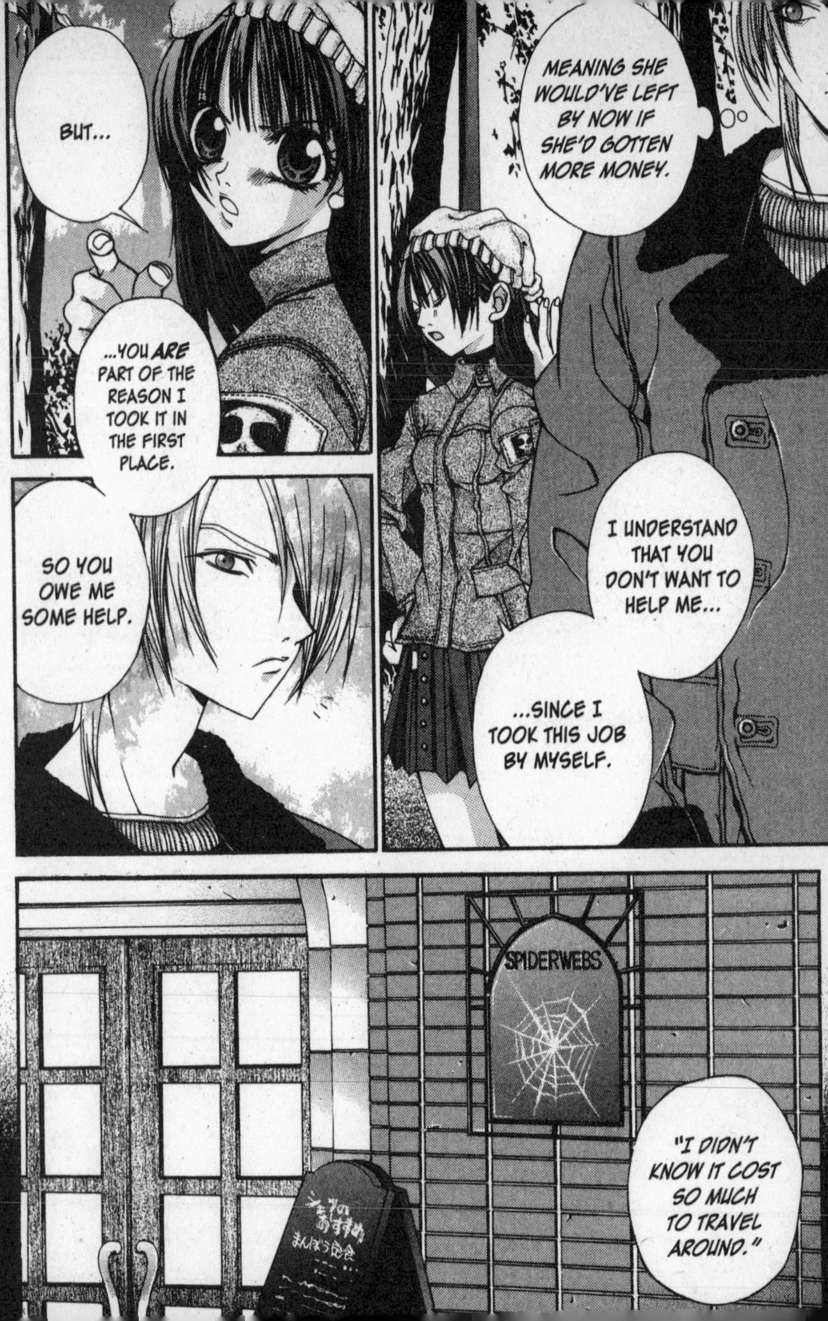

MEANING SHE WOULD'VE LEFT BY NOW IF SHE'D GOTTEN MORE MONEY.
I UNDERSTAND THAT YOU DON'T WANT TO HELP ME...
...SINCE I TOOK THIS JOB BY MYSELF.
BUT...
...YOU ARE PART OF THE REASON I TOOK IT IN THE FIRST PLACE.
SO YOU OWE ME SOME HELP.
SPIDERWEBS
"I DIDN'T KNOW IT COST SO MUCH TO TRAVEL AROUND."

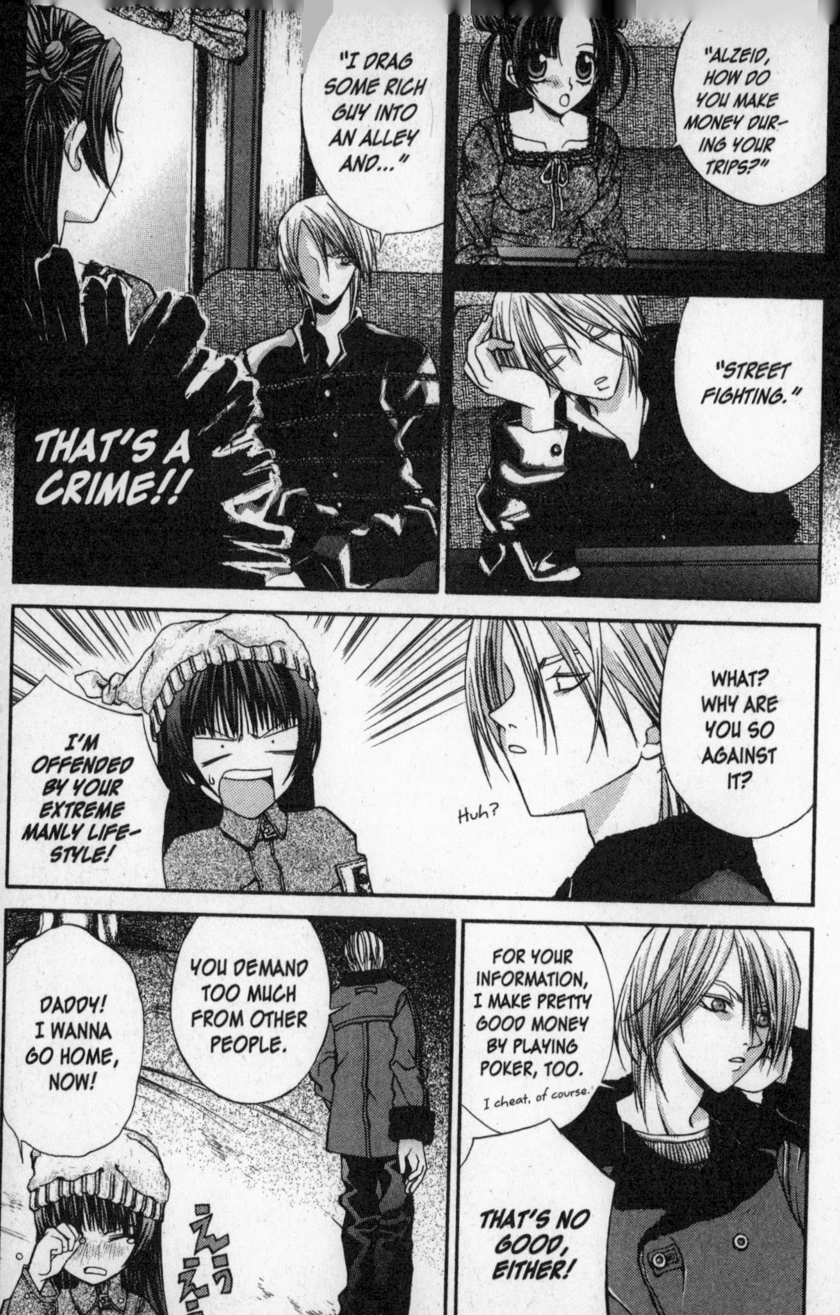
"ALZEID, HOW DO YOU MAKE MONEY DURING YOUR TRIPS?"
"STREET FIGHTING."
"I DRAG SOME RICH GUY INTO AN ALLEY AND..."
THAT'S A CRIME!!
WHAT? WHY ARE YOU SO AGAINST IT?
Huh?
I'M OFFENDED BY YOUR EXTREME MANLY LIFE-STYLE!
FOR YOUR INFORMATION, I MAKE PRETTY GOOD MONEY BY PLAYING POKER, TOO.
I cheat, of course.
THAT'S NO GOOD, EITHER!
YOU DEMAND TOO MUCH FROM OTHER PEOPLE.
DADDY! I WANNA GO HOME, NOW!
えぅえぅっ

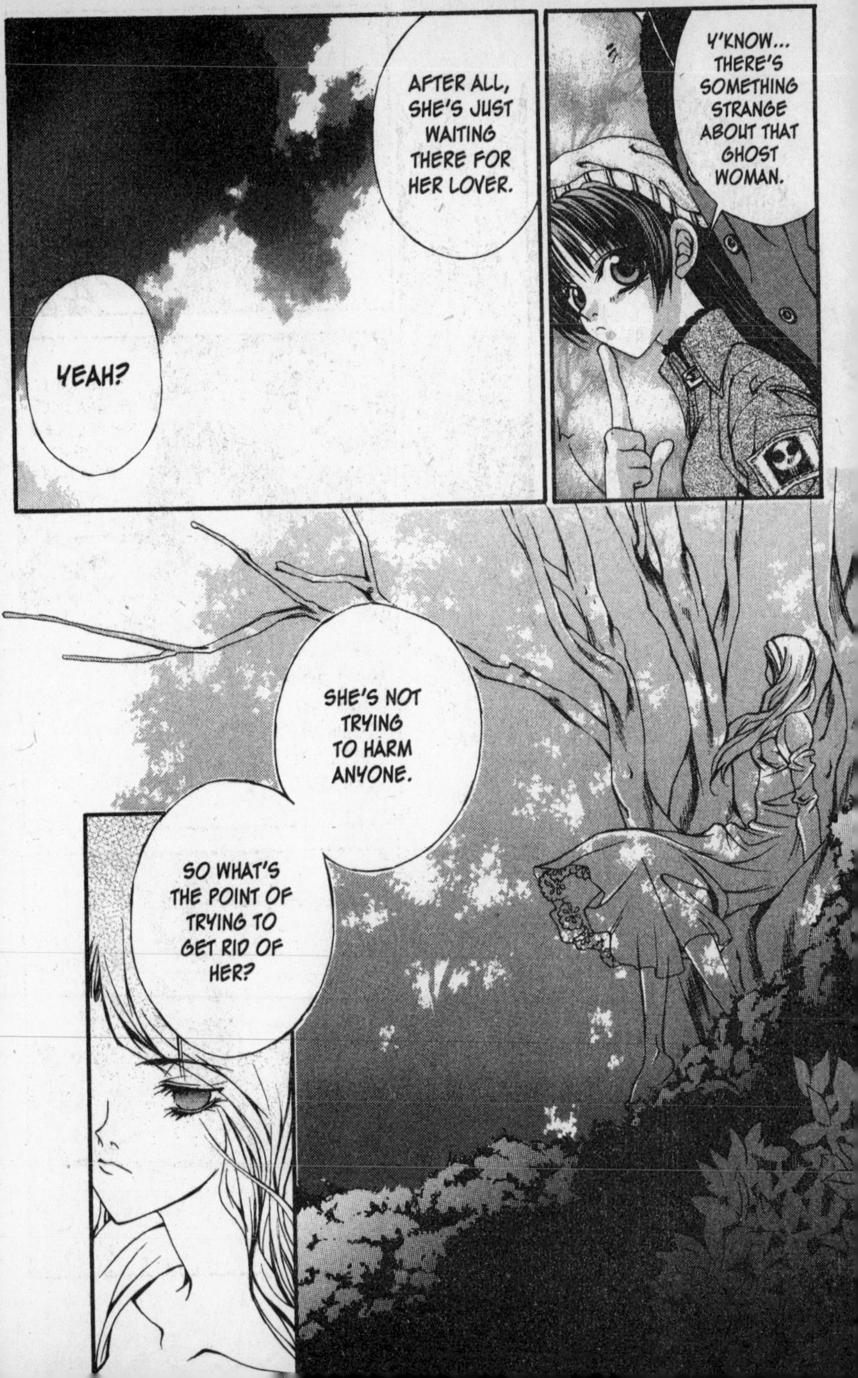
Y'KNOW... THERE'S SOMETHING STRANGE ABOUT THAT GHOST WOMAN.
AFTER ALL, SHE'S JUST WAITING THERE FOR HER LOVER.
YEAH?
SHE'S NOT TRYING TO HARM ANYONE.
SO WHAT'S THE POINT OF TRYING TO GET RID OF HER?

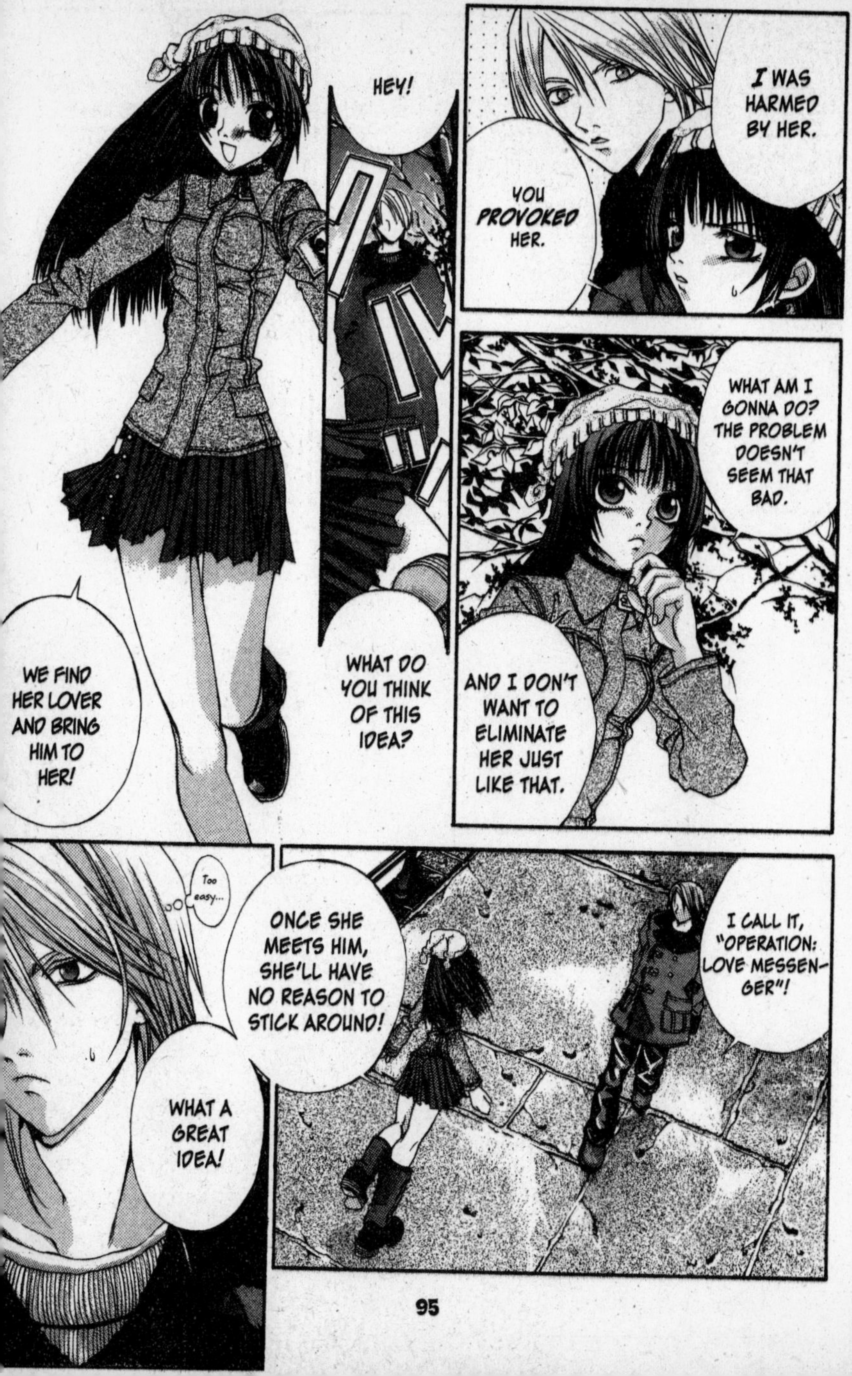
I WAS HARMED BY HER.
YOU *PROVOKED* HER.
WHAT AM I GONNA DO? THE PROBLEM DOESN'T SEEM THAT BAD.
AND I DON'T WANT TO ELIMINATE HER JUST LIKE THAT.
HEY!
WHAT DO YOU THINK OF THIS IDEA?
WE FIND HER LOVER AND BRING HIM TO HER!
I CALL IT, "OPERATION: LOVE MESSENGER"!
ONCE SHE MEETS HIM, SHE'LL HAVE NO REASON TO STICK AROUND!
Too easy...
WHAT A GREAT IDEA!

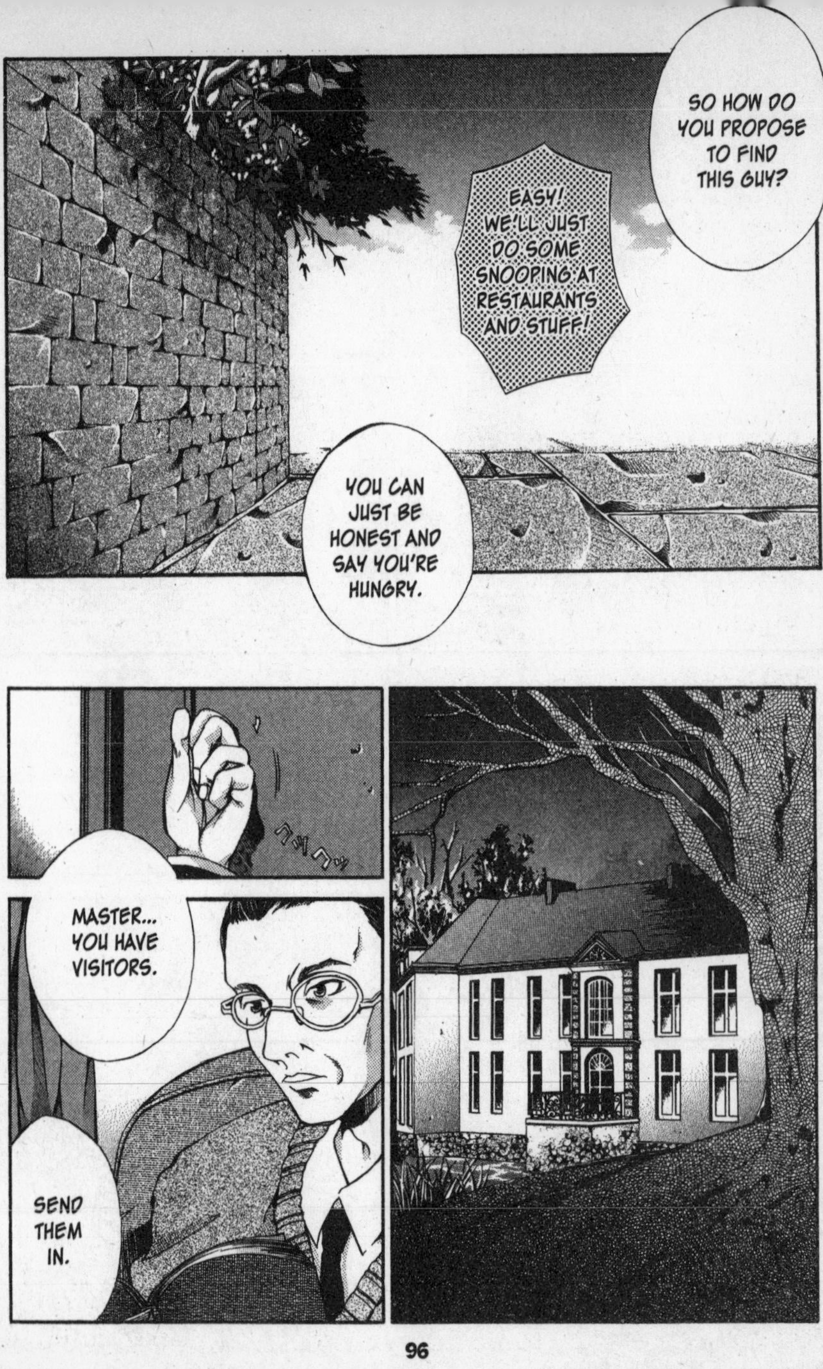
SO HOW DO YOU PROPOSE TO FIND THIS GUY?
EASY! WE'LL JUST DO SOME SNOOPING AT RESTAURANTS AND STUFF!
YOU CAN JUST BE HONEST AND SAY YOU'RE HUNGRY.
MASTER... YOU HAVE VISITORS.
SEND THEM IN.

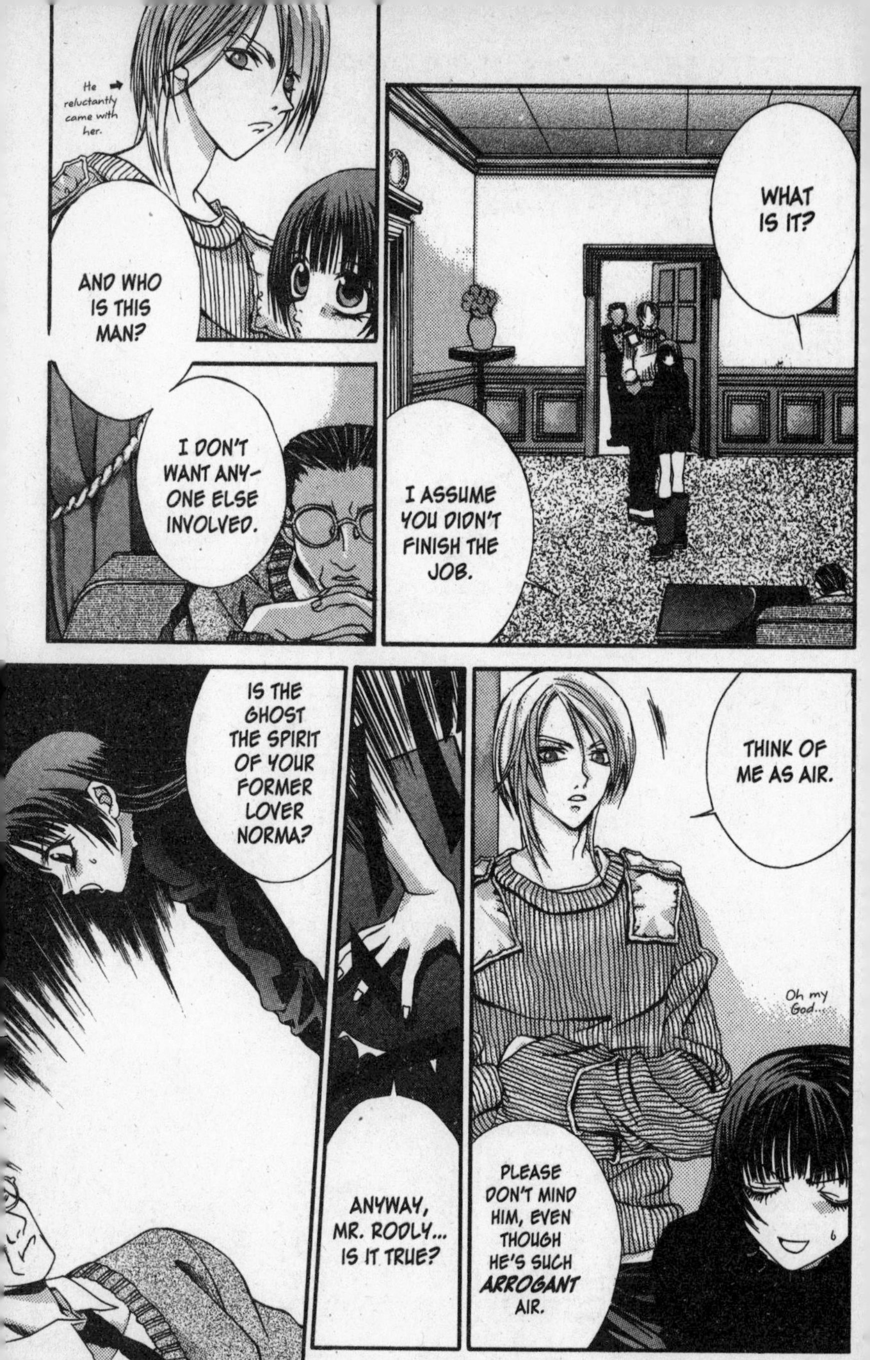
WHAT IS IT?
I ASSUME YOU DIDN'T FINISH THE JOB.
He reluctantly came with her.
AND WHO IS THIS MAN?
I DON'T WANT ANY-ONE ELSE INVOLVED.
THINK OF ME AS AIR.
Oh my God...
PLEASE DON'T MIND HIM, EVEN THOUGH HE'S SUCH ARROGANT AIR.
ANYWAY, MR. RODLY... IS IT TRUE?
IS THE GHOST THE SPIRIT OF YOUR FORMER LOVER NORMA?

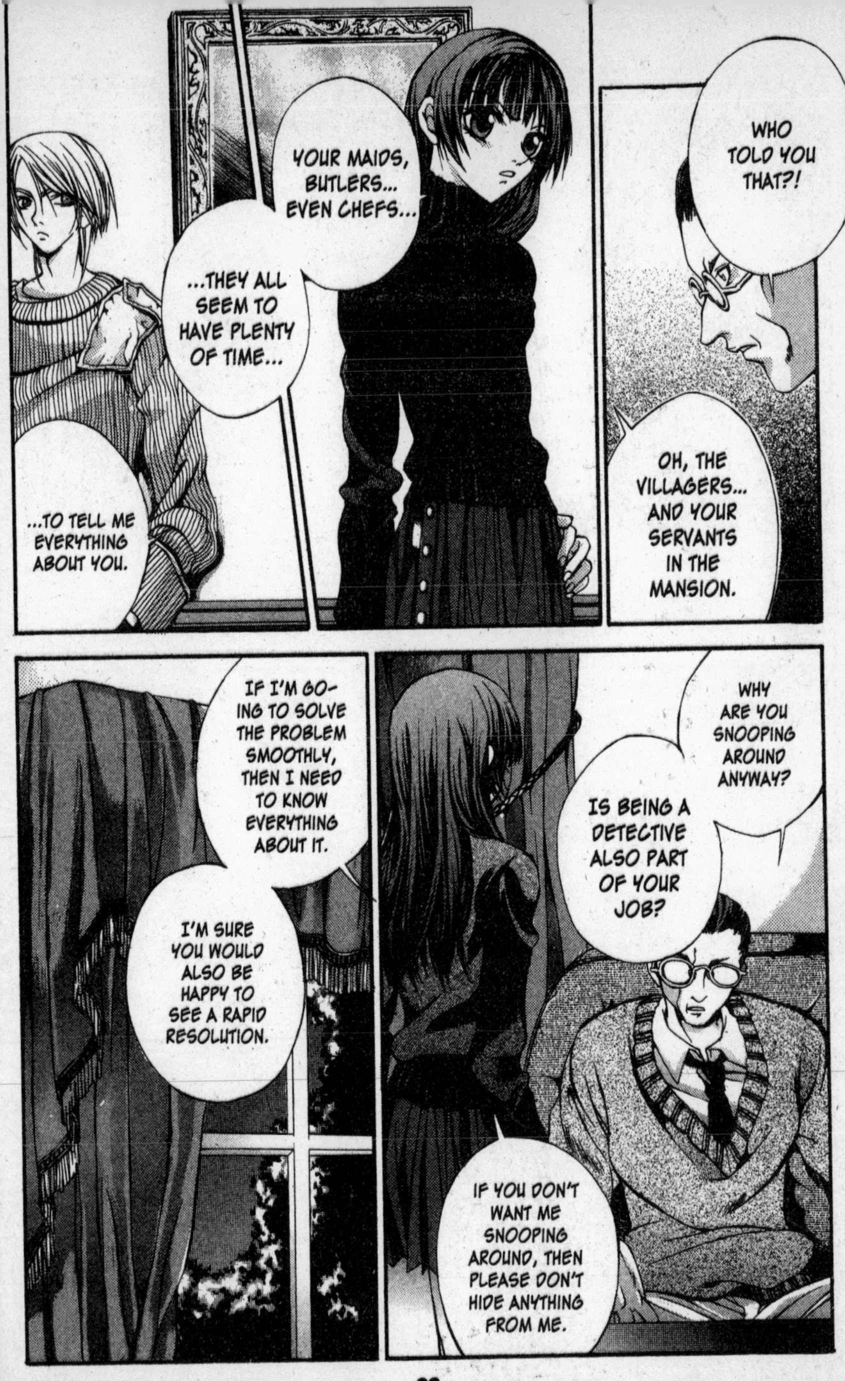
WHO TOLD YOU THAT?!
OH, THE VILLAGERS... AND YOUR SERVANTS IN THE MANSION.
YOUR MAIDS, BUTLERS... EVEN CHEFS...
...THEY ALL SEEM TO HAVE PLENTY OF TIME...
...TO TELL ME EVERYTHING ABOUT YOU.
WHY ARE YOU SNOOPING AROUND ANYWAY?
IS BEING A DETECTIVE ALSO PART OF YOUR JOB?
IF YOU DON'T WANT ME SNOOPING AROUND, THEN PLEASE DON'T HIDE ANYTHING FROM ME.
IF I'M GO-ING TO SOLVE THE PROBLEM SMOOTHLY, THEN I NEED TO KNOW EVERYTHING ABOUT IT.
I'M SURE YOU WOULD ALSO BE HAPPY TO SEE A RAPID RESOLUTION.

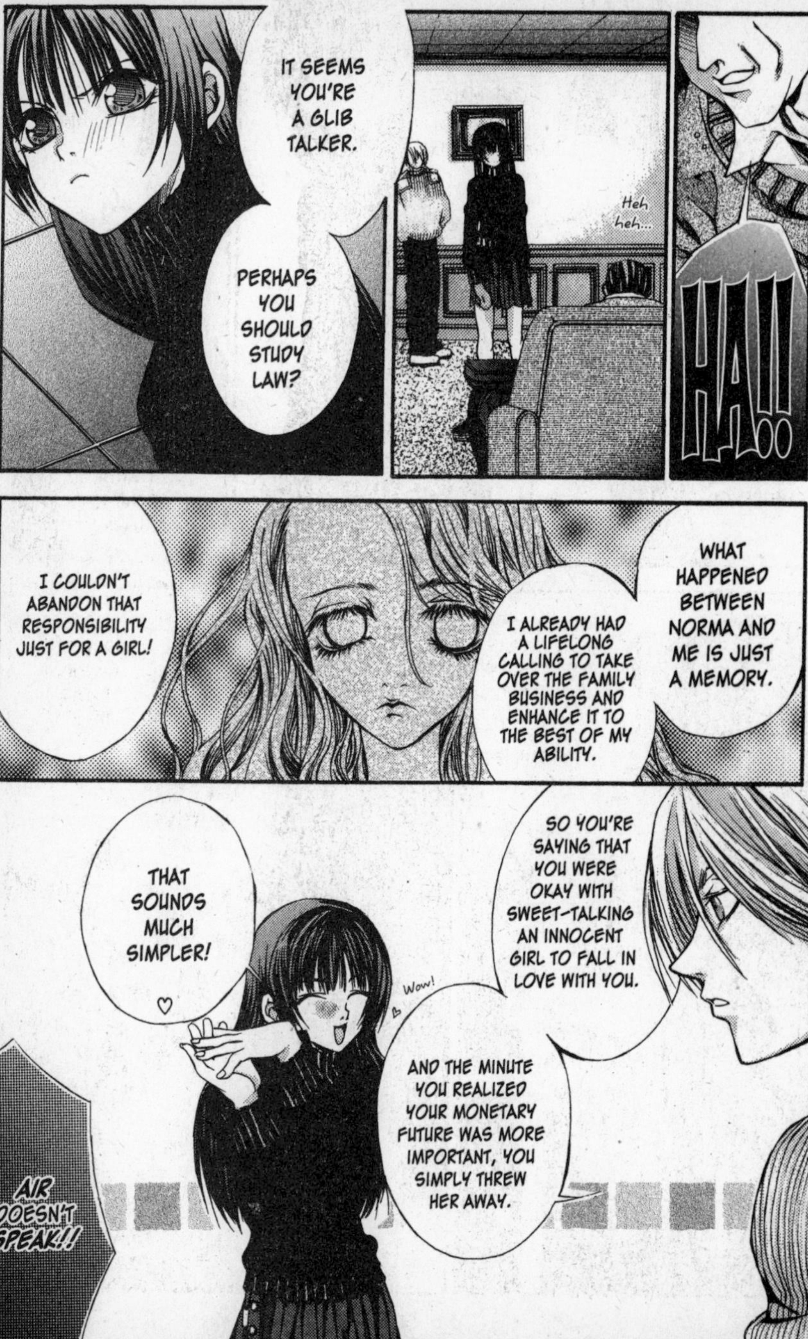
HA!!
Heh heh...
IT SEEMS YOU'RE A GLIB TALKER.
PERHAPS YOU SHOULD STUDY LAW?
WHAT HAPPENED BETWEEN NORMA AND ME IS JUST A MEMORY.
I ALREADY HAD A LIFELONG CALLING TO TAKE OVER THE FAMILY BUSINESS AND ENHANCE IT TO THE BEST OF MY ABILITY.
I COULDN'T ABANDON THAT RESPONSIBILITY JUST FOR A GIRL!
SO YOU'RE SAYING THAT YOU WERE OKAY WITH SWEET-TALKING AN INNOCENT GIRL TO FALL IN LOVE WITH YOU.
AND THE MINUTE YOU REALIZED YOUR MONETARY FUTURE WAS MORE IMPORTANT, YOU SIMPLY THREW HER AWAY.
Wow!
THAT SOUNDS MUCH SIMPLER! ♡
AIR DOESN'T SPEAK!!

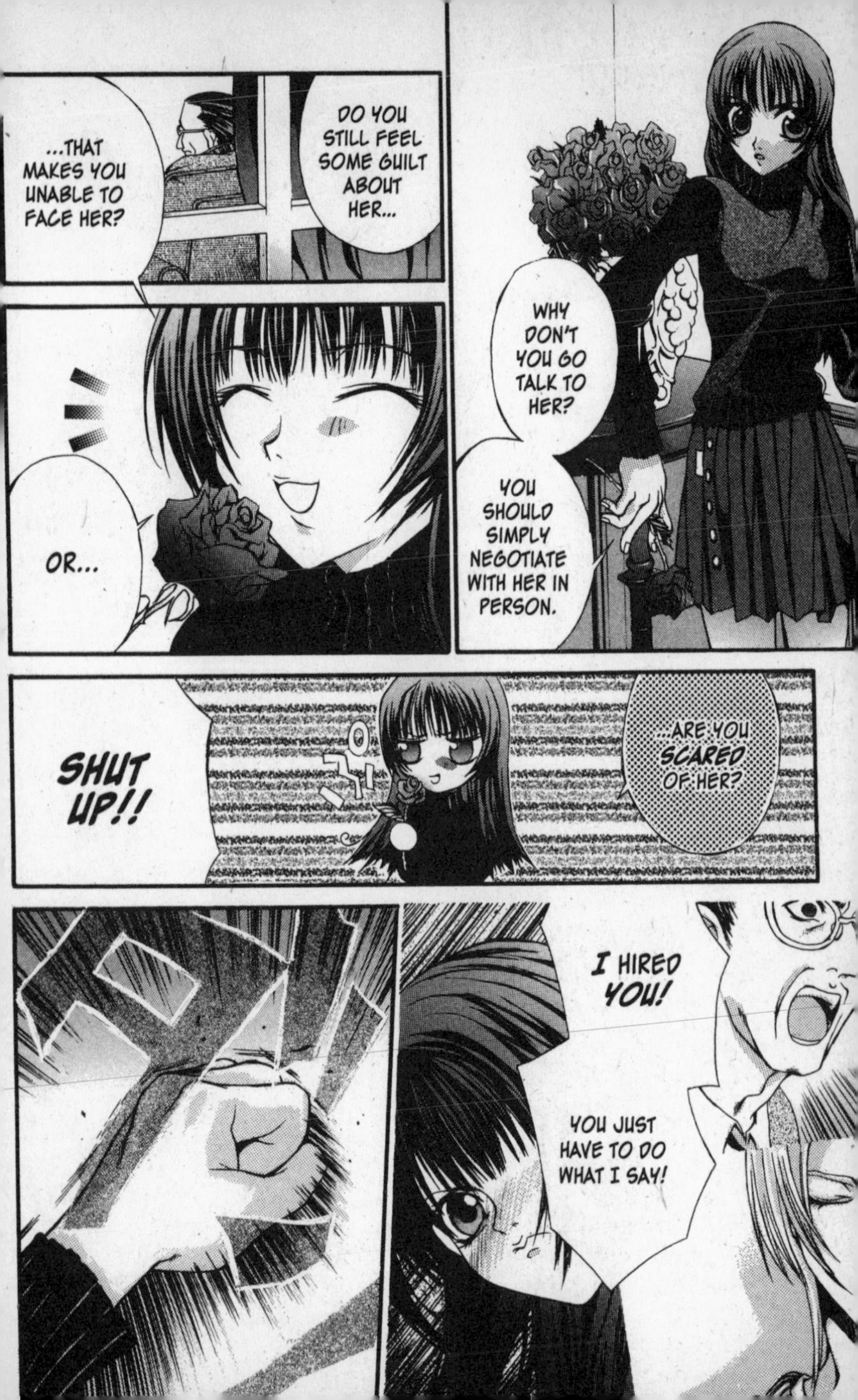
WHY DON'T YOU GO TALK TO HER?
YOU SHOULD SIMPLY NEGOTIATE WITH HER IN PERSON.
DO YOU STILL FEEL SOME GUILT ABOUT HER...
...THAT MAKES YOU UNABLE TO FACE HER?
OR...
...ARE YOU SCARED OF HER?
SHUT UP!!
I HIRED YOU!
YOU JUST HAVE TO DO WHAT I SAY!

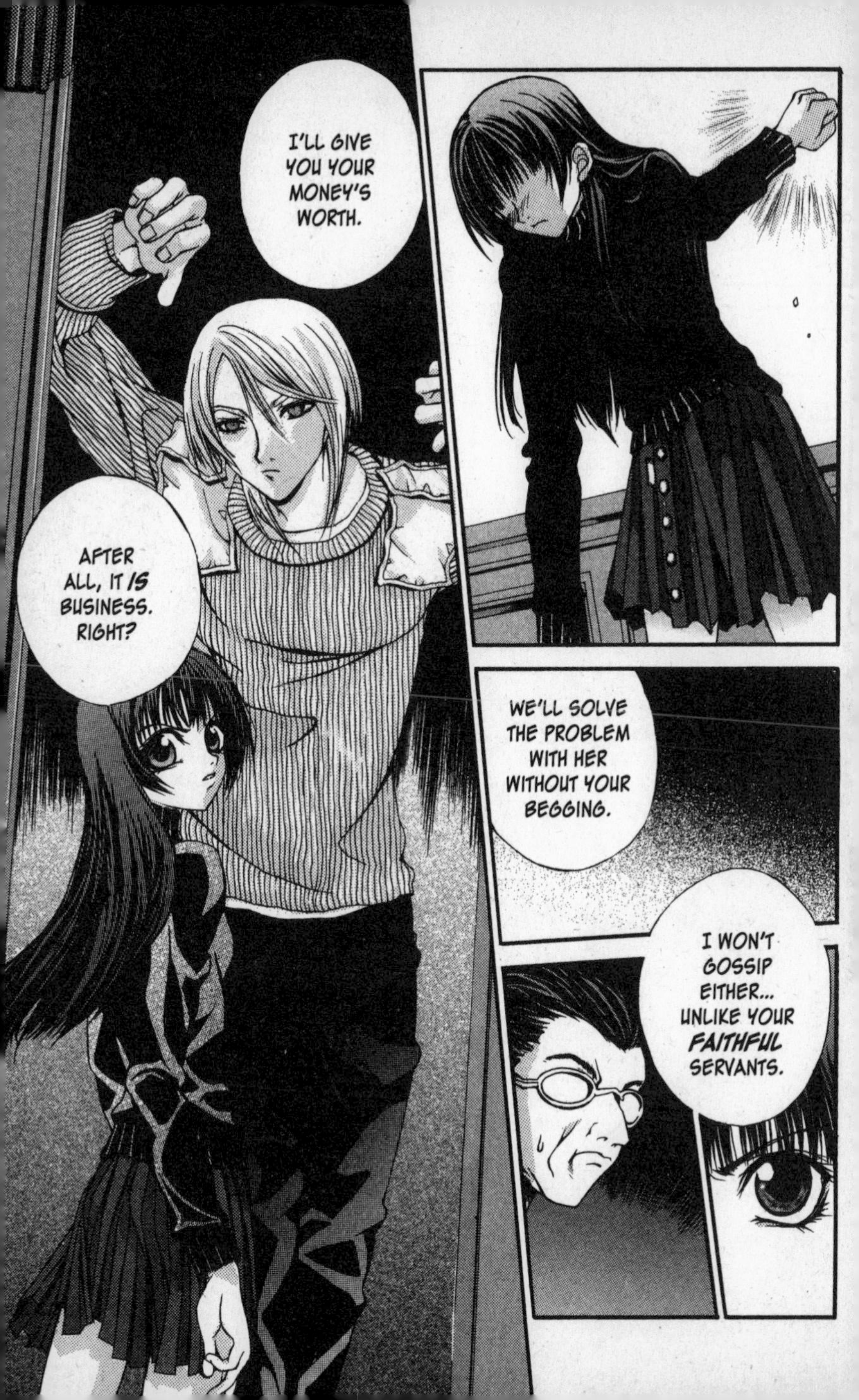
WE'LL SOLVE THE PROBLEM WITH HER WITHOUT YOUR BEGGING.
I WON'T GOSSIP EITHER... UNLIKE YOUR FAITHFUL SERVANTS.
I'LL GIVE YOU YOUR MONEY'S WORTH.
AFTER ALL, IT IS BUSINESS. RIGHT?

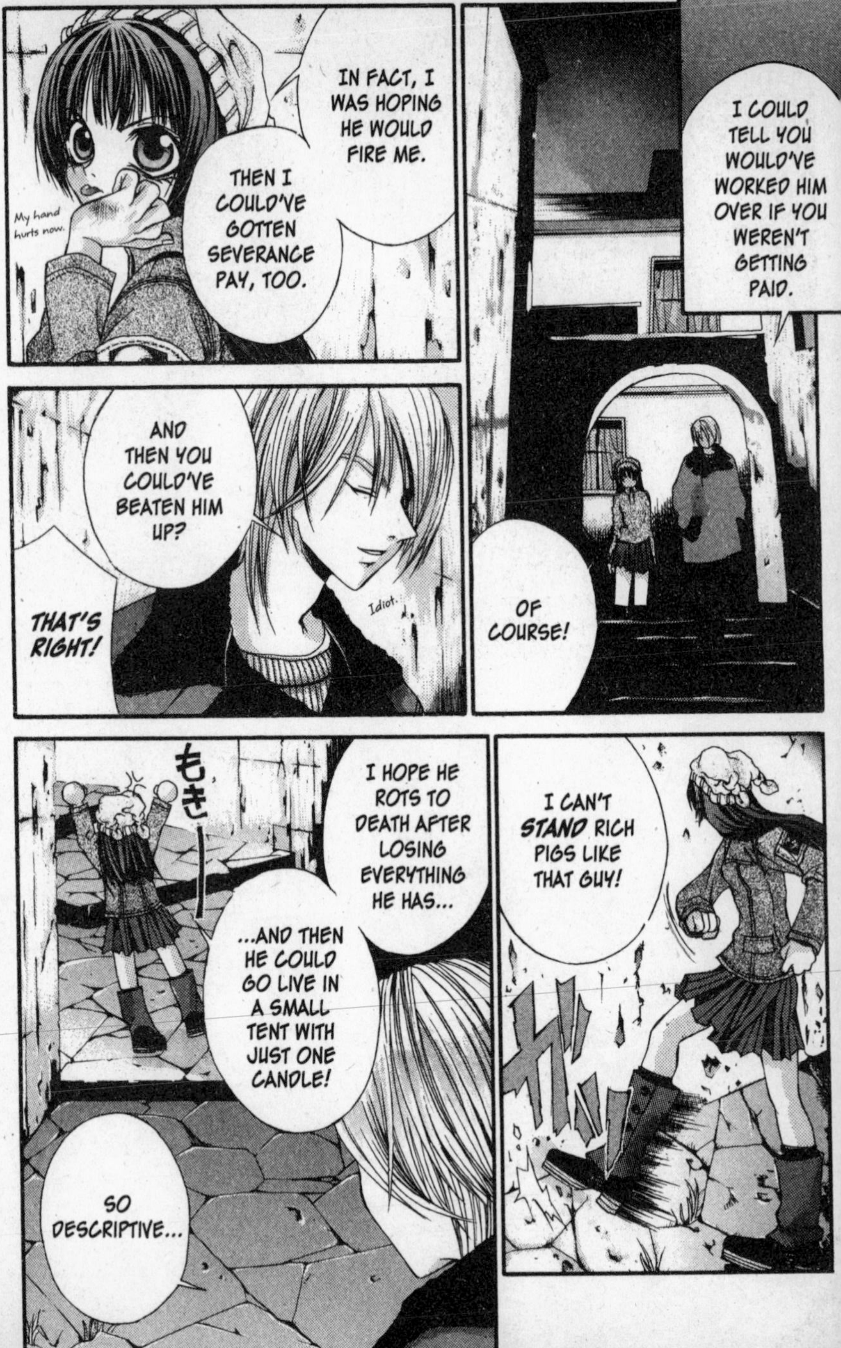
I COULD TELL YOU WOULD'VE WORKED HIM OVER IF YOU WEREN'T GETTING PAID.
OF COURSE!
IN FACT, I WAS HOPING HE WOULD FIRE ME.
THEN I COULD'VE GOTTEN SEVERANCE PAY, TOO.
My hand hurts now.
AND THEN YOU COULD'VE BEATEN HIM UP?
THAT'S RIGHT!
Idiot.
I CAN'T STAND RICH PIGS LIKE THAT GUY!
I HOPE HE ROTS TO DEATH AFTER LOSING EVERYTHING HE HAS...
...AND THEN HE COULD GO LIVE IN A SMALL TENT WITH JUST ONE CANDLE!
もき
SO DESCRIPTIVE...

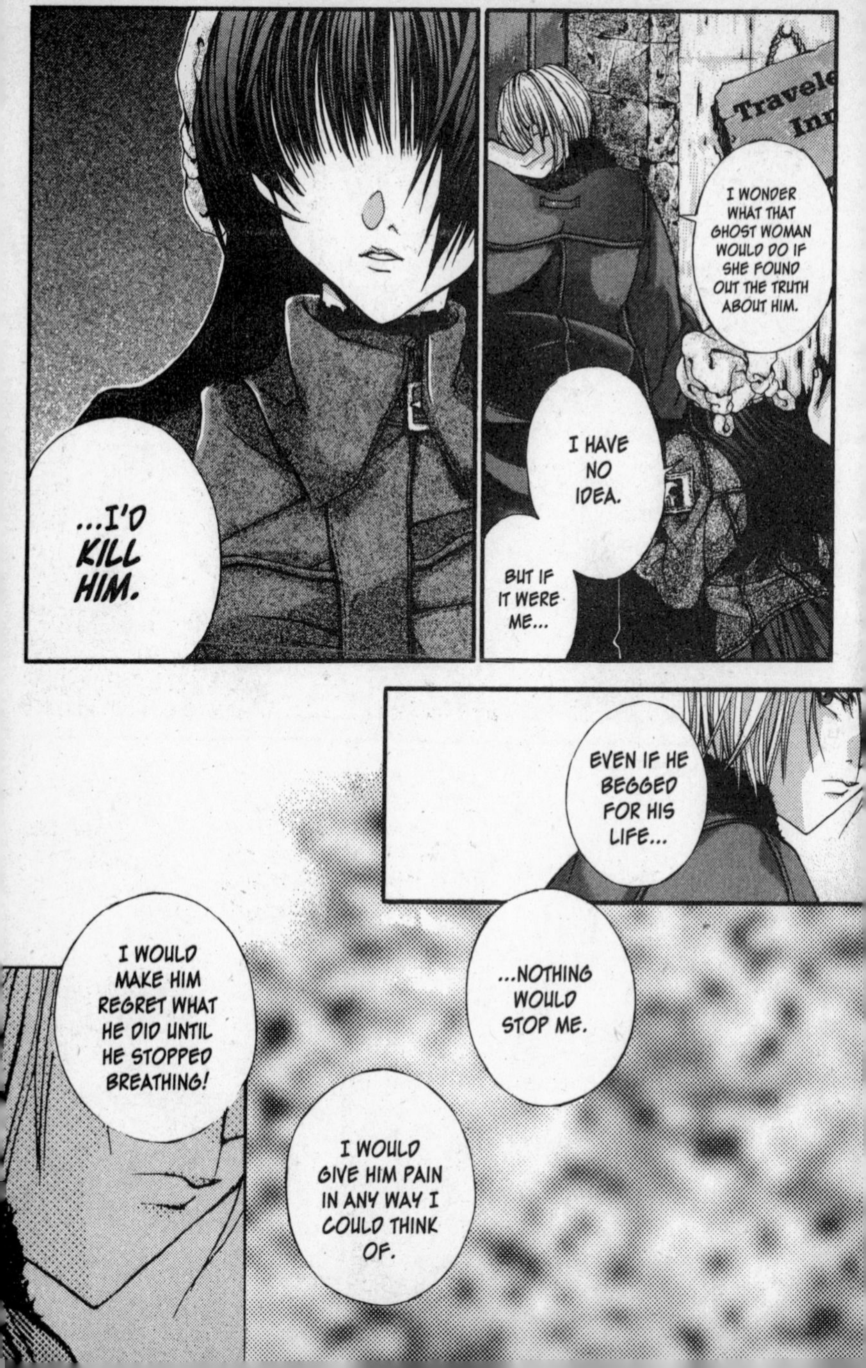
I WONDER WHAT THAT GHOST WOMAN WOULD DO IF SHE FOUND OUT THE TRUTH ABOUT HIM.
I HAVE NO IDEA.
BUT IF IT WERE ME...
...I'D KILL HIM.
EVEN IF HE BEGGED FOR HIS LIFE...
...NOTHING WOULD STOP ME.
I WOULD MAKE HIM REGRET WHAT HE DID UNTIL HE STOPPED BREATHING!
I WOULD GIVE HIM PAIN IN ANY WAY I COULD THINK OF.

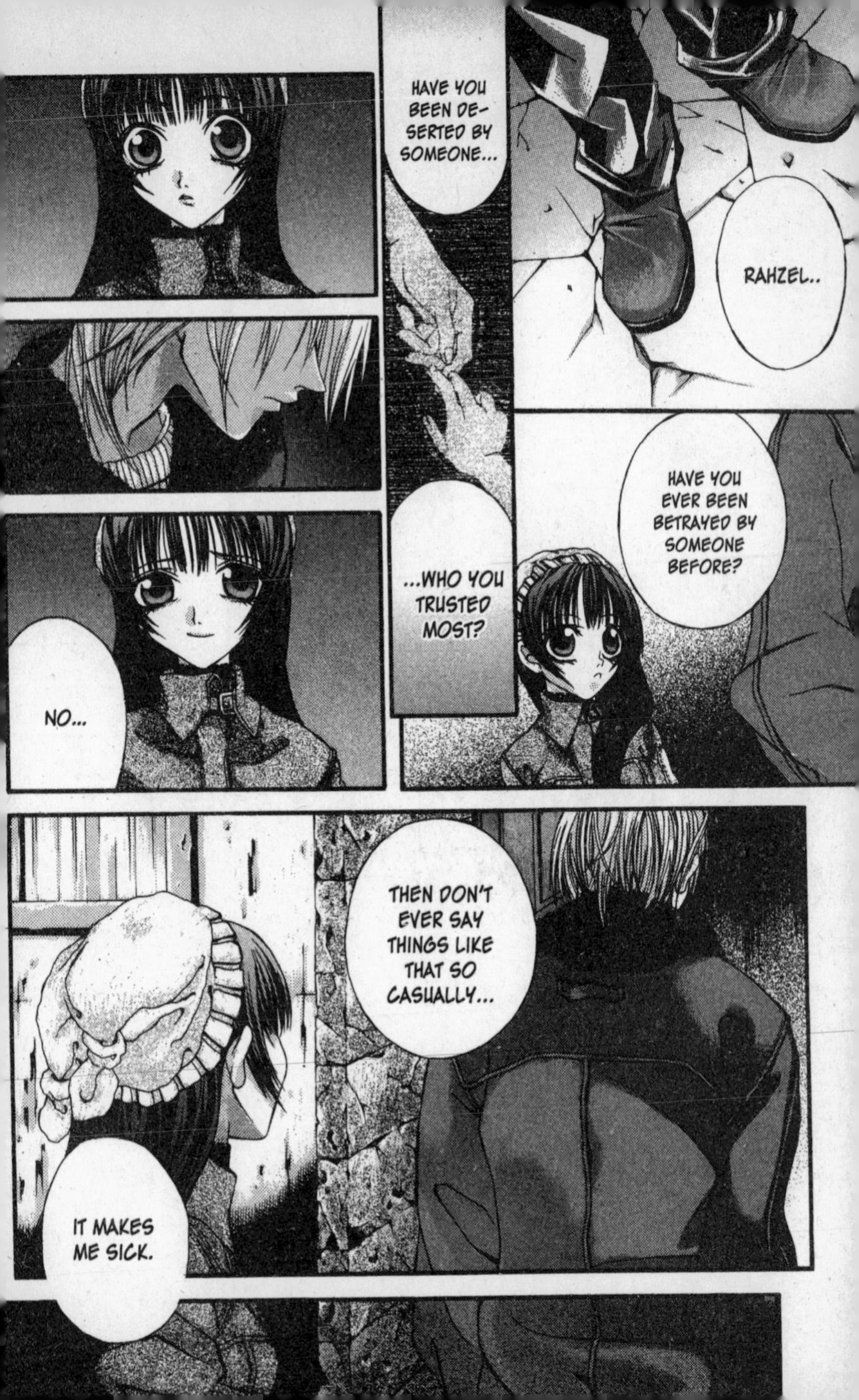
RAHZEL..
HAVE YOU EVER BEEN BETRAYED BY SOMEONE BEFORE?
HAVE YOU BEEN DE-SERTED BY SOMEONE...
...WHO YOU TRUSTED MOST?
NO...
THEN DON'T EVER SAY THINGS LIKE THAT SO CASUALLY...
IT MAKES ME SICK.

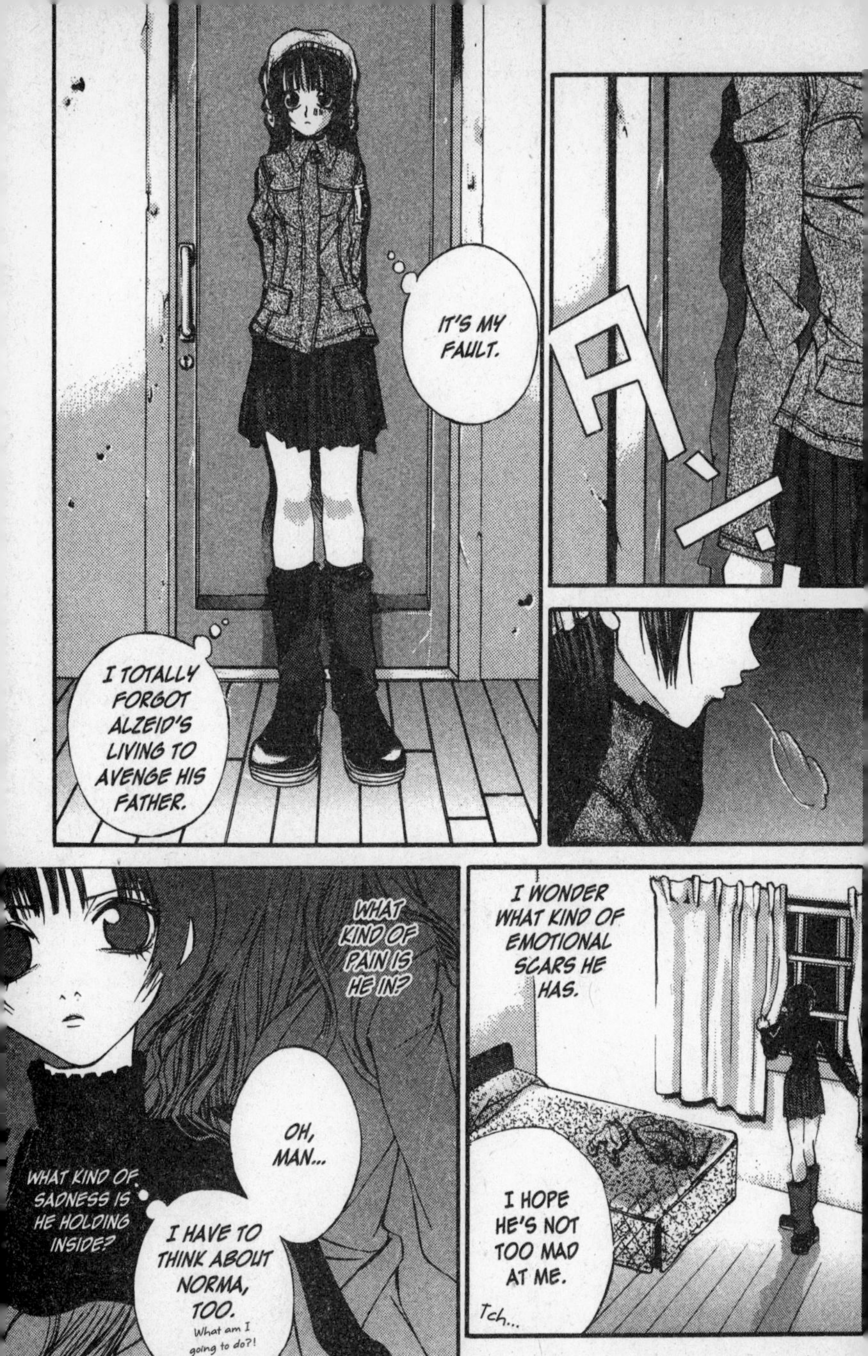

IT'S MY FAULT.
I TOTALLY FORGOT ALZEID'S LIVING TO AVENGE HIS FATHER.
I WONDER WHAT KIND OF EMOTIONAL SCARS HE HAS.
I HOPE HE'S NOT TOO MAD AT ME.
Tch...
WHAT KIND OF PAIN IS HE IN?
OH, MAN...
I HAVE TO THINK ABOUT NORMA, TOO.
What am I going to do?!
WHAT KIND OF SADNESS IS HE HOLDING INSIDE?

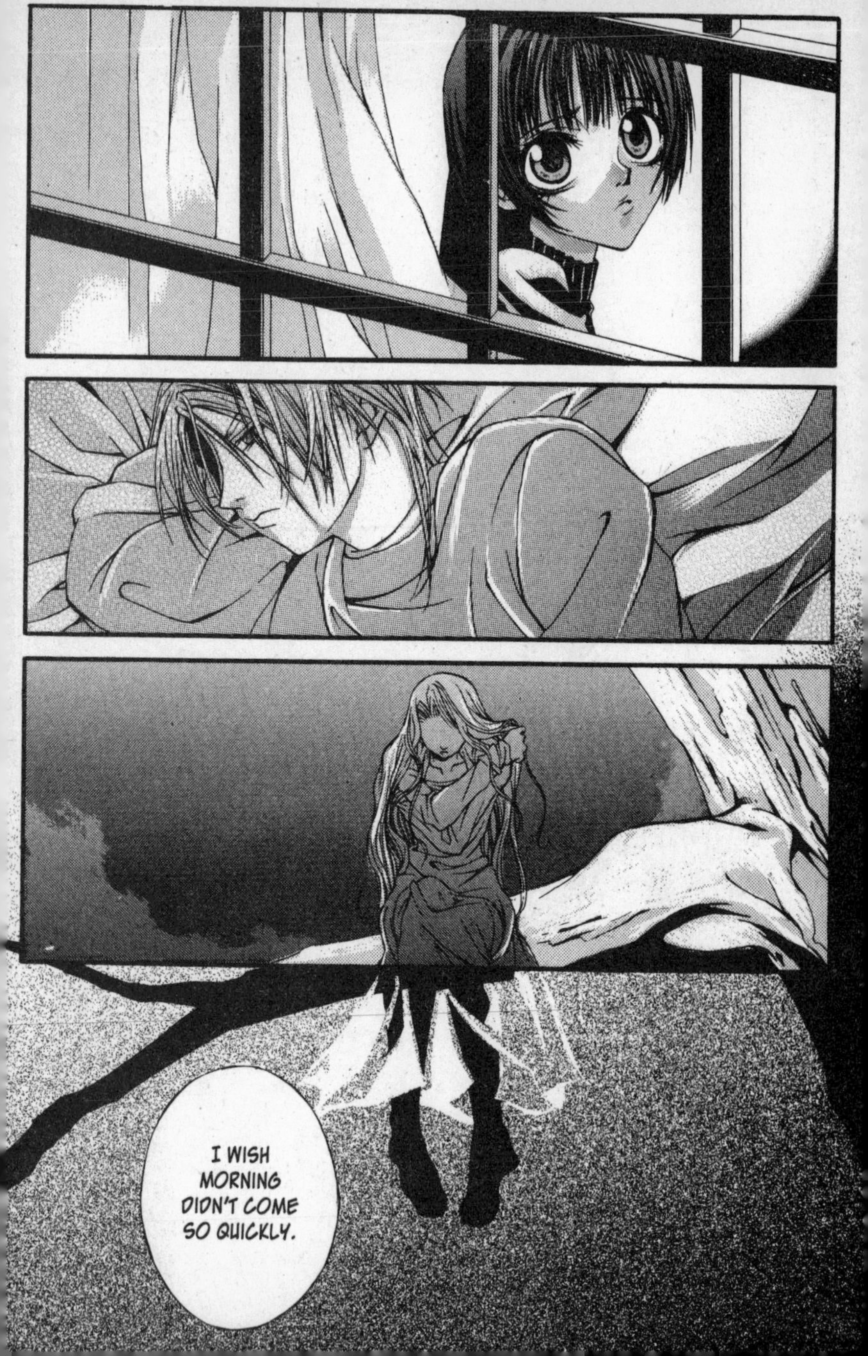
I WISH MORNING DIDN'T COME SO QUICKLY.

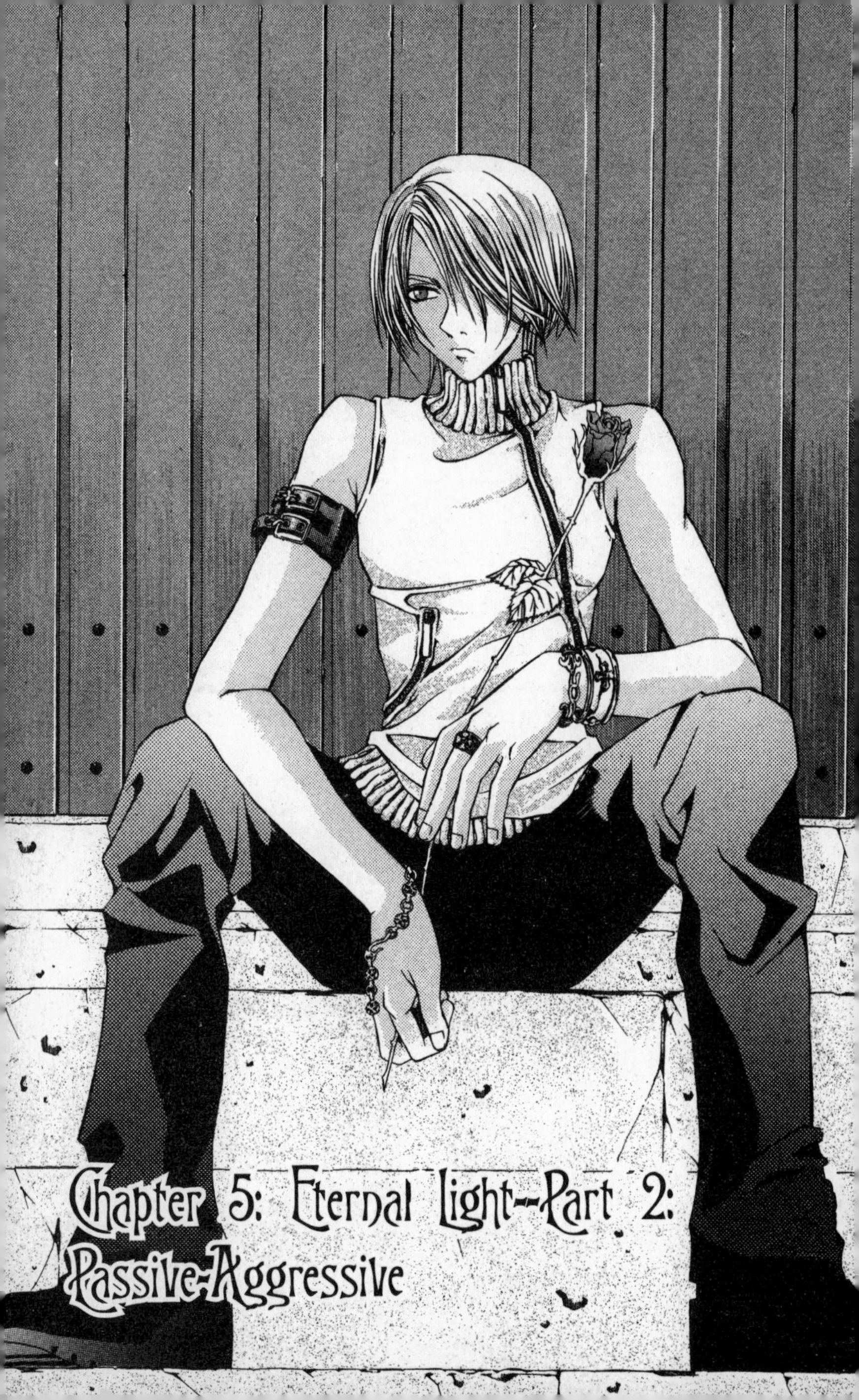
Chapter 5: Eternal Light--Part 2:
Passive-Aggressive

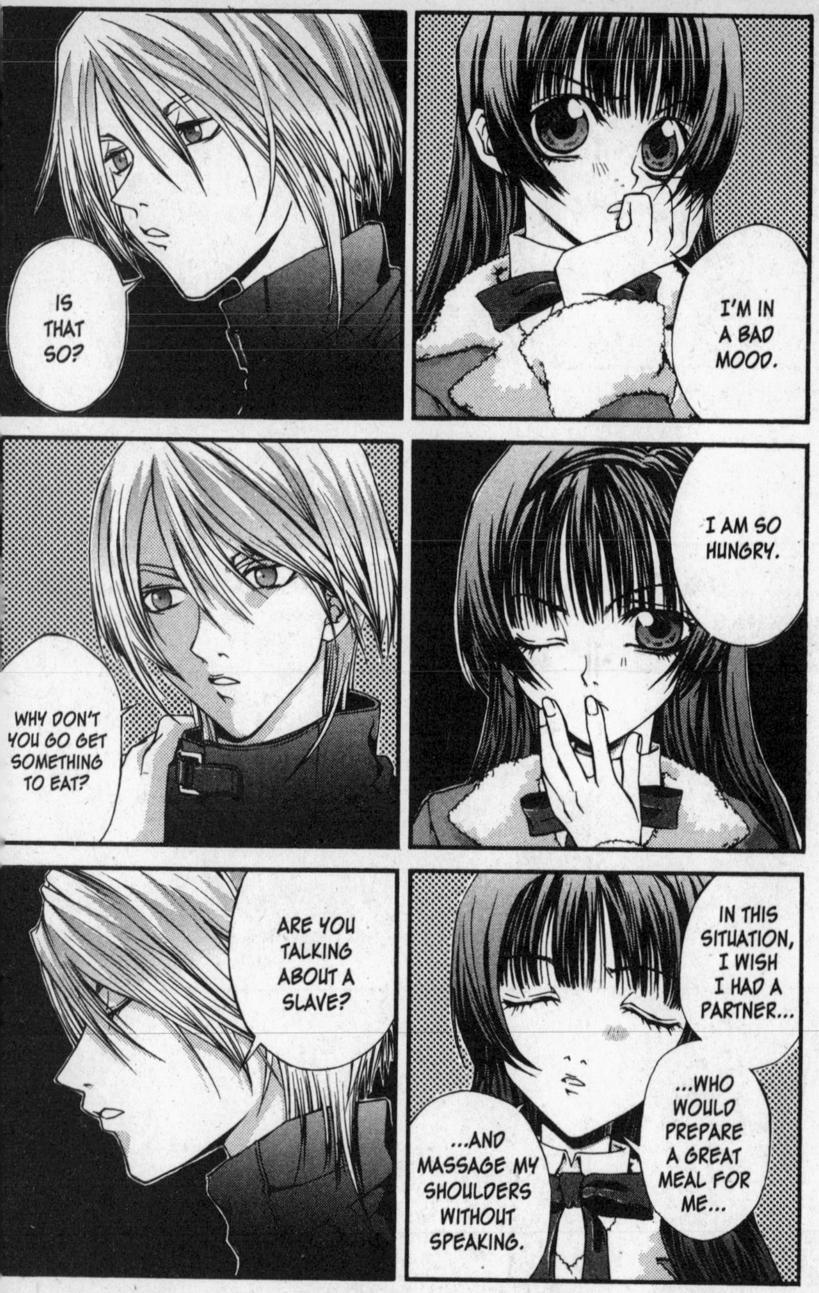
I'M IN A BAD MOOD.
IS THAT SO?
I AM SO HUNGRY.
WHY DON'T YOU GO GET SOMETHING TO EAT?
IN THIS SITUATION, I WISH I HAD A PARTNER...
...WHO WOULD PREPARE A GREAT MEAL FOR ME...
...AND MASSAGE MY SHOULDERS WITHOUT SPEAKING.
ARE YOU TALKING ABOUT A SLAVE?

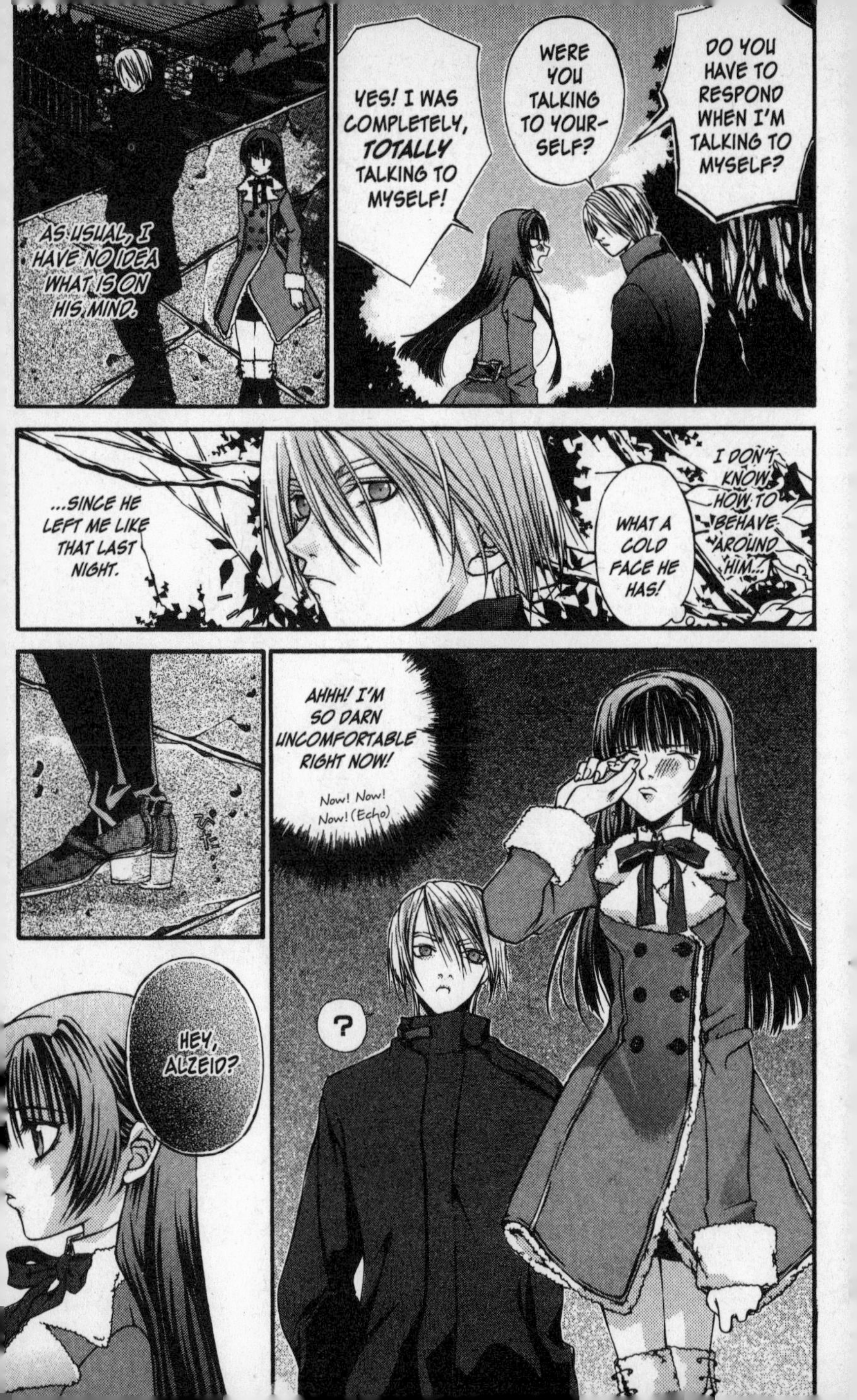
DO YOU HAVE TO RESPOND WHEN I'M TALKING TO MYSELF?
WERE YOU TALKING TO YOUR-SELF?
YES! I WAS COMPLETELY, TOTALLY TALKING TO MYSELF!
AS USUAL, I HAVE NO IDEA WHAT IS ON HIS MIND.
I DON'T KNOW HOW TO BEHAVE AROUND HIM...
WHAT A COLD FACE HE HAS!
...SINCE HE LEFT ME LIKE THAT LAST NIGHT.
AHHH! I'M SO DARN UNCOMFORTABLE RIGHT NOW!
Now! Now! Now! (Echo)
?
HEY, ALZEID?

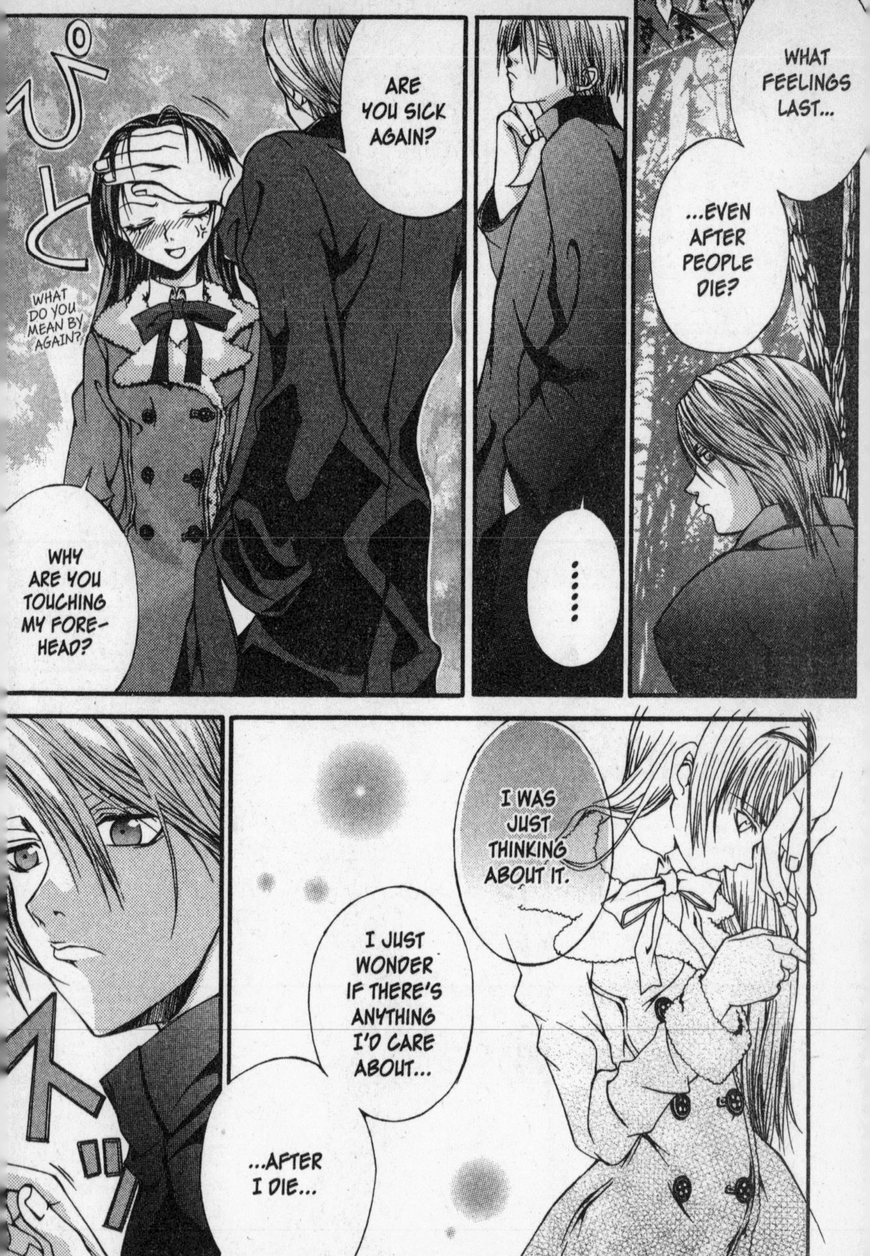
WHAT FEELINGS LAST...
...EVEN AFTER PEOPLE DIE?
.....
ARE YOU SICK AGAIN?
ぴと
WHAT DO YOU MEAN BY AGAIN?
WHY ARE YOU TOUCHING MY FORE-HEAD?
I WAS JUST THINKING ABOUT IT.
I JUST WONDER IF THERE'S ANYTHING I'D CARE ABOUT...
...AFTER I DIE...

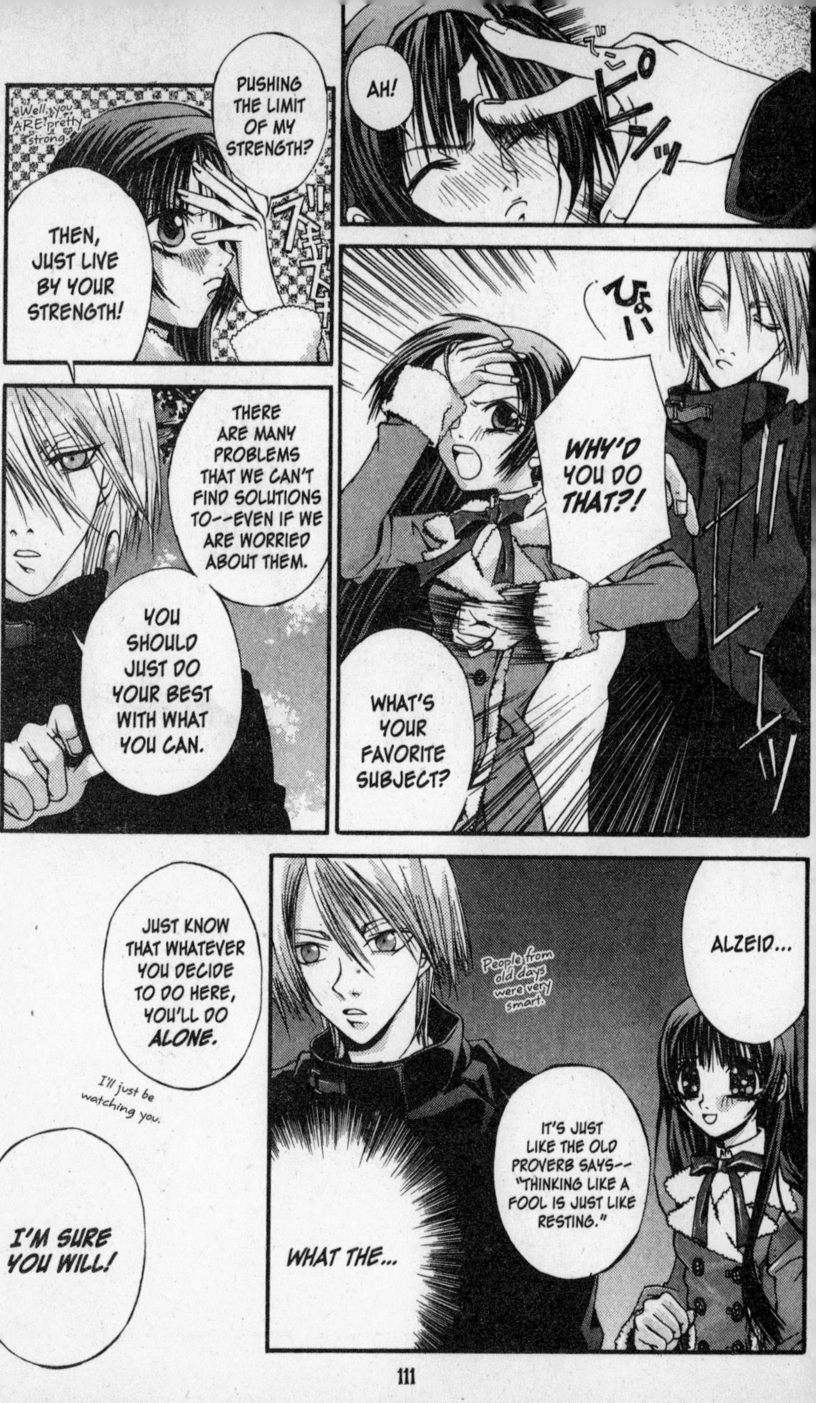
AH!
PUSHING THE LIMIT OF MY STRENGTH?
Well, you ARE pretty strong.
THEN, JUST LIVE BY YOUR STRENGTH!
WHY'D YOU DO THAT?!
WHAT'S YOUR FAVORITE SUBJECT?
THERE ARE MANY PROBLEMS THAT WE CAN'T FIND SOLUTIONS TO--EVEN IF WE ARE WORRIED ABOUT THEM.
YOU SHOULD JUST DO YOUR BEST WITH WHAT YOU CAN.
ALZEID...
IT'S JUST LIKE THE OLD PROVERB SAYS--"THINKING LIKE A FOOL IS JUST LIKE RESTING."
People from old days were very smart.
WHAT THE...
JUST KNOW THAT WHATEVER YOU DECIDE TO DO HERE, YOU'LL DO ALONE.
I'll just be watching you.
I'M SURE YOU WILL!

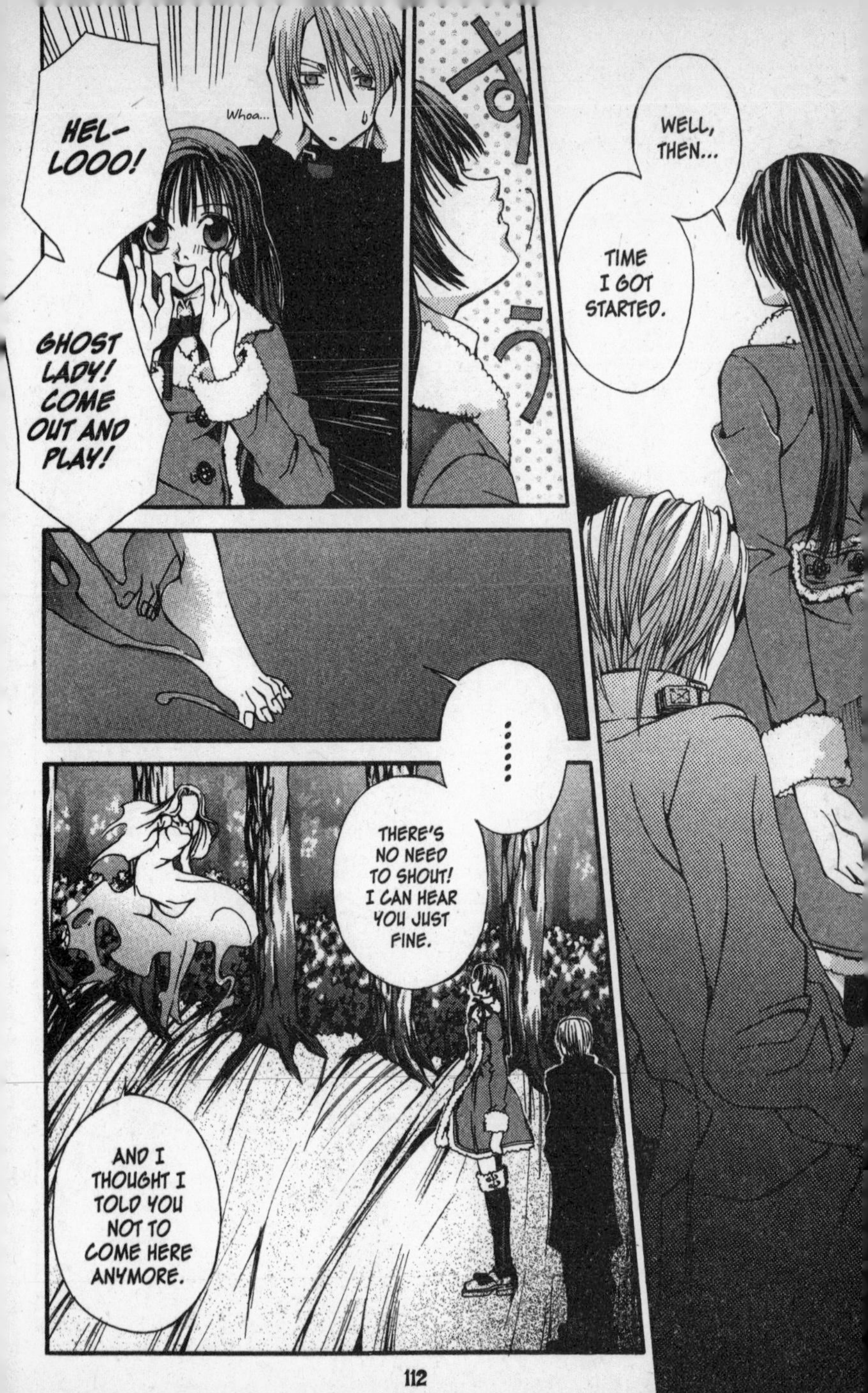

WELL, THEN...
TIME I GOT STARTED.
Whoa...
HEL-LOOO!
GHOST LADY! COME OUT AND PLAY!
......
THERE'S NO NEED TO SHOUT! I CAN HEAR YOU JUST FINE.
AND I THOUGHT I TOLD YOU NOT TO COME HERE ANYMORE.

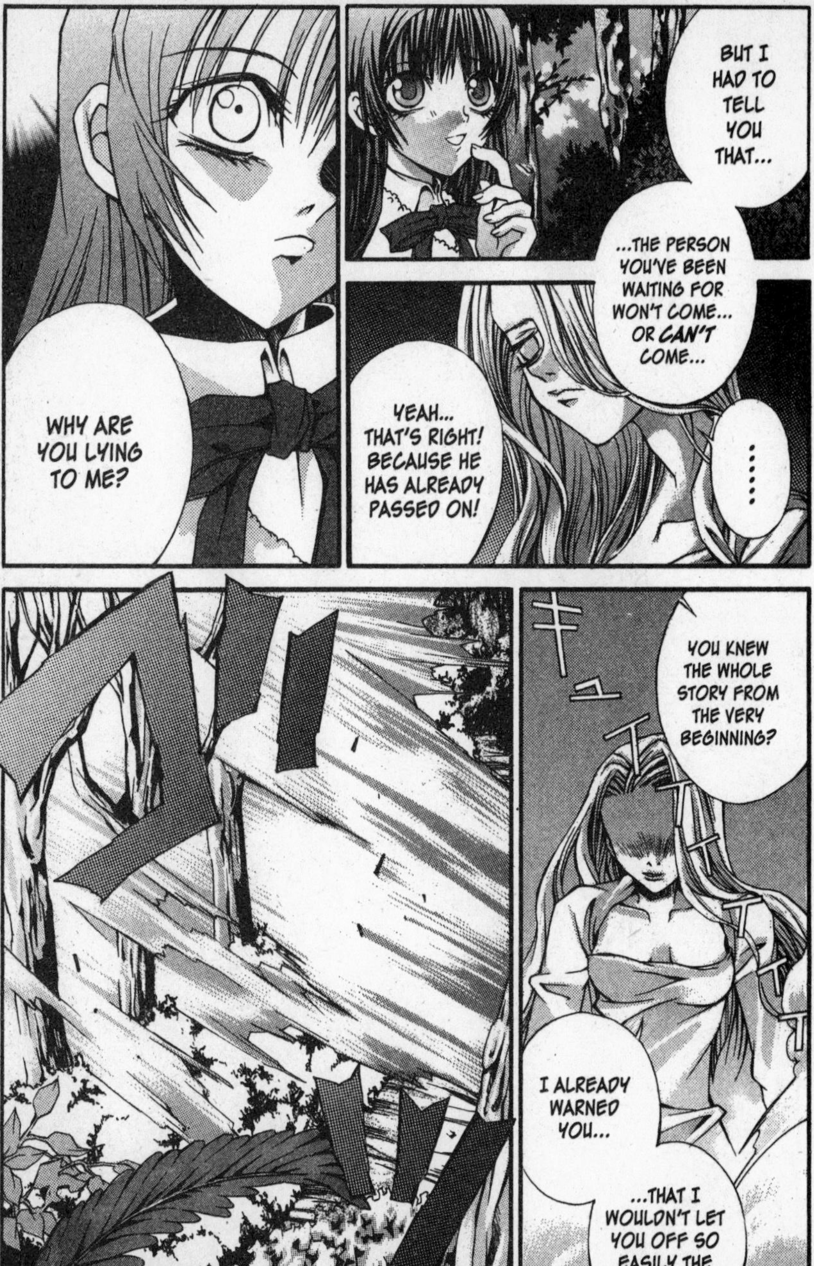
BUT I HAD TO TELL YOU THAT...
...THE PERSON YOU'VE BEEN WAITING FOR WON'T COME... OR **CAN'T** COME...
......
YEAH... THAT'S RIGHT! BECAUSE HE HAS ALREADY PASSED ON!
WHY ARE YOU LYING TO ME?
キュ
YOU KNEW THE WHOLE STORY FROM THE VERY BEGINNING?
I ALREADY WARNED YOU...
...THAT I WOULDN'T LET YOU OFF SO EASILY THE NEXT TIME!

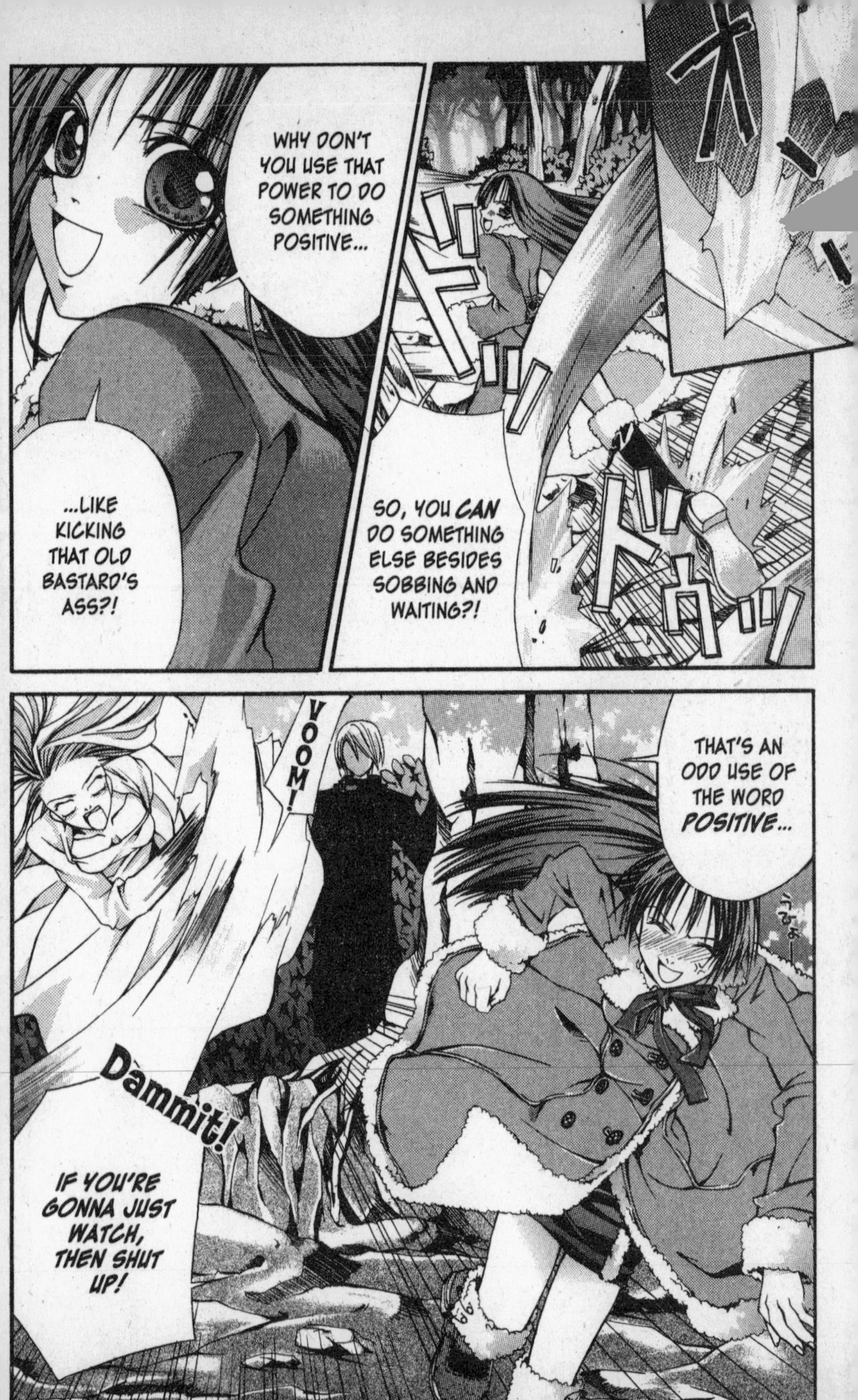

SO, YOU CAN DO SOMETHING ELSE BESIDES SOBBING AND WAITING?!
WHY DON'T YOU USE THAT POWER TO DO SOMETHING POSITIVE...
...LIKE KICKING THAT OLD BASTARD'S ASS?!
THAT'S AN ODD USE OF THE WORD POSITIVE...
VOOM!
Dammit!
IF YOU'RE GONNA JUST WATCH, THEN SHUT UP!

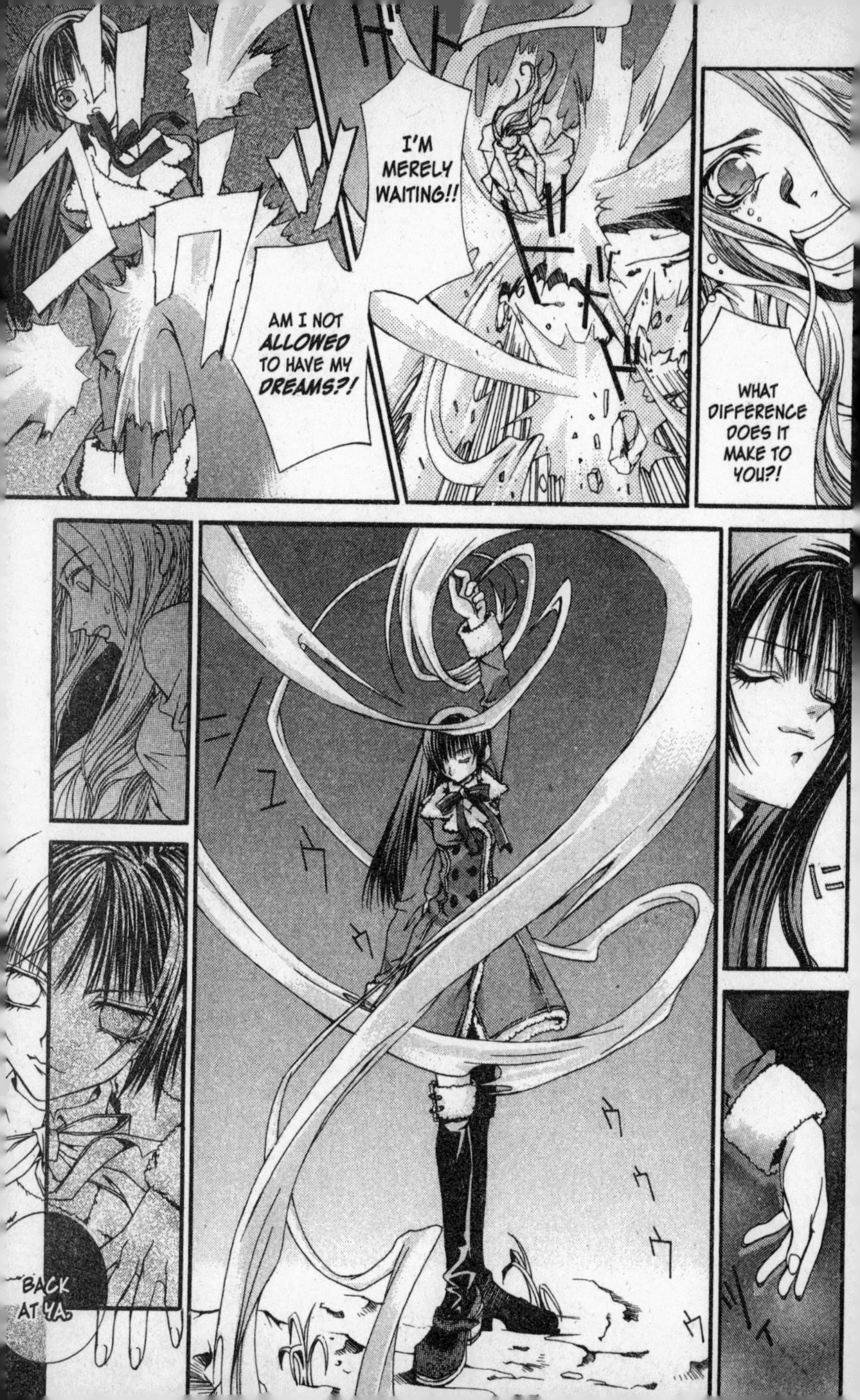
WHAT DIFFERENCE DOES IT MAKE TO YOU?!
I'M MERELY WAITING!!
AM I NOT ALLOWED TO HAVE MY DREAMS?!
BACK AT YA.

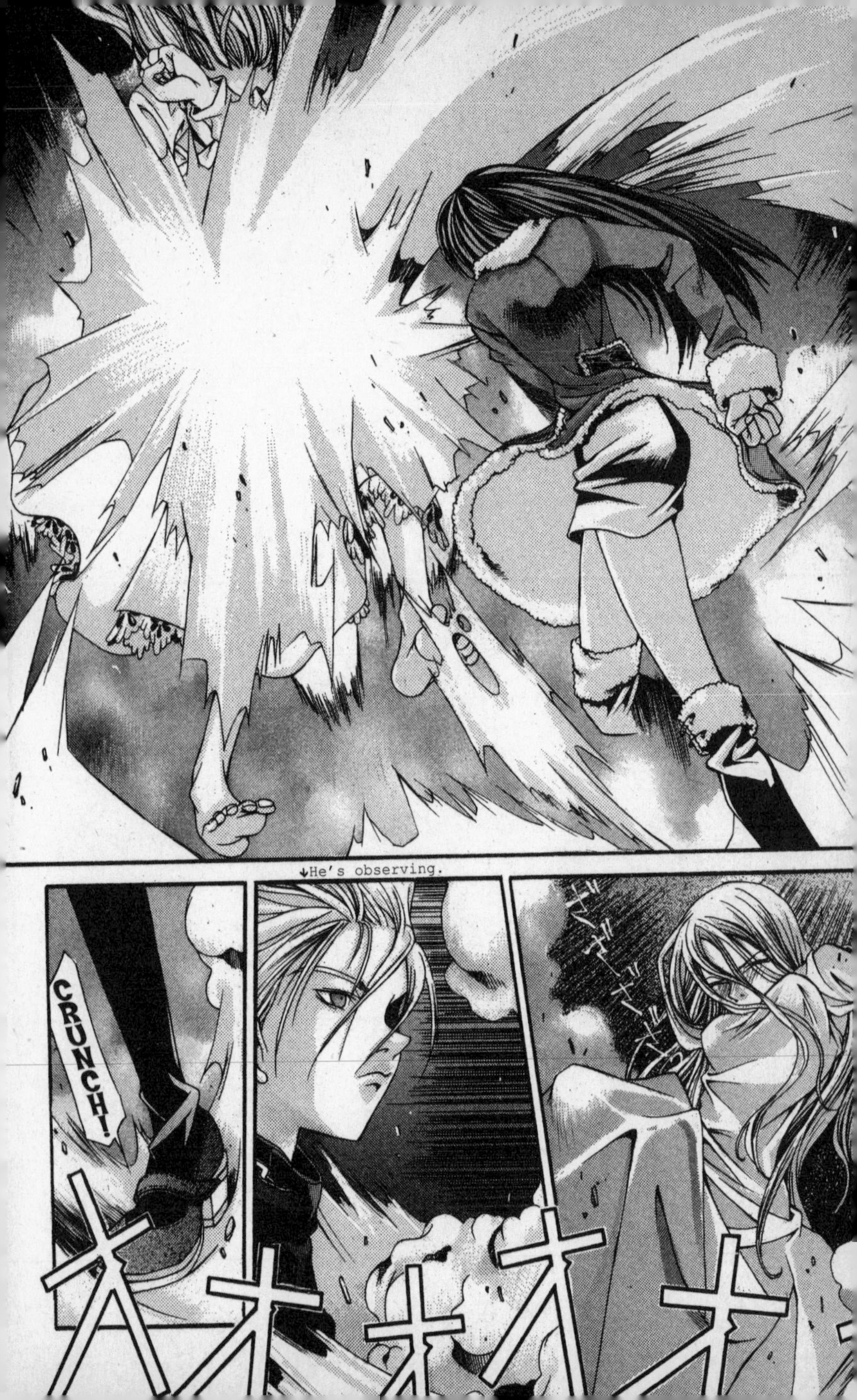
↓He's observing.
CRUNCH!

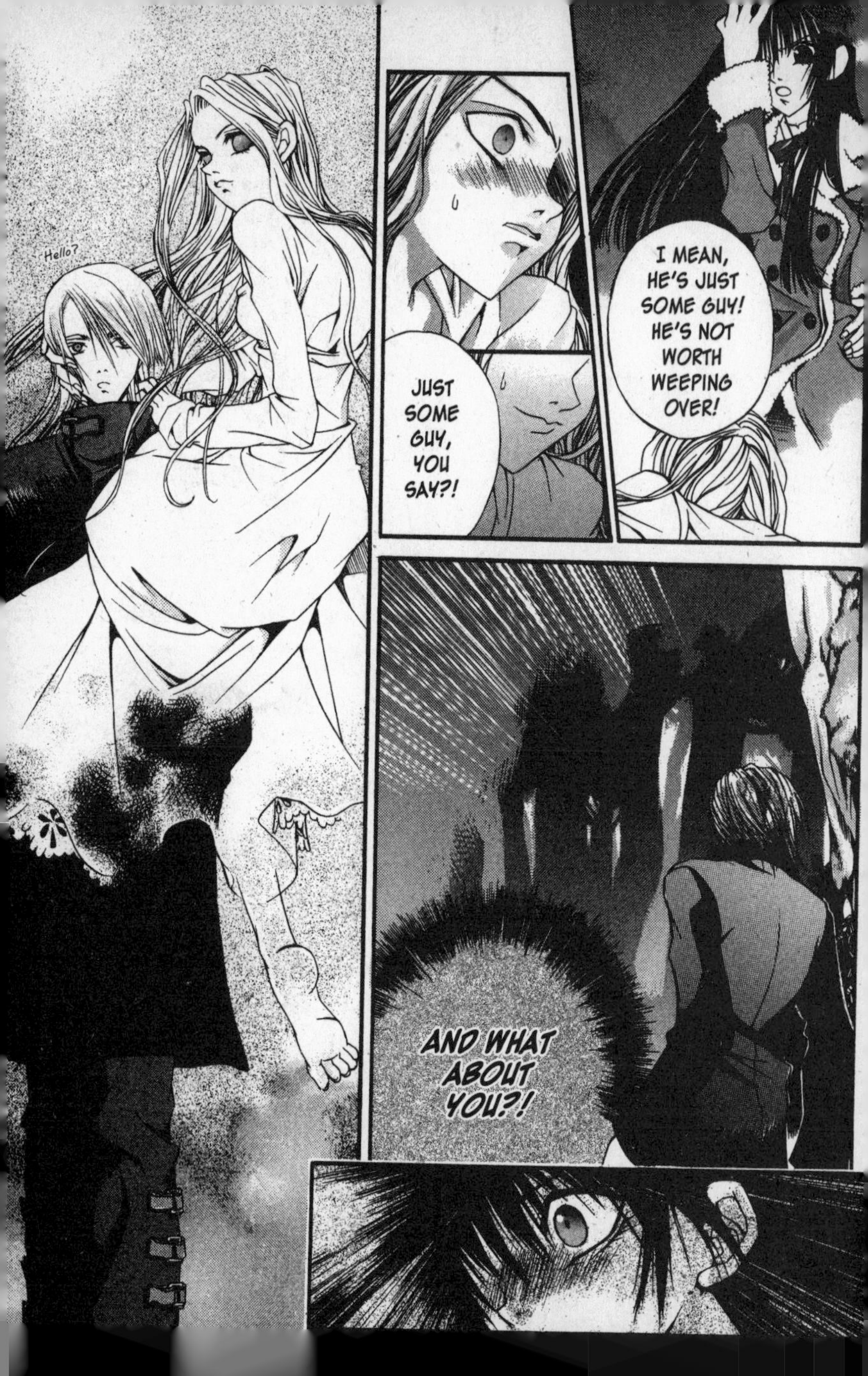
I MEAN, HE'S JUST SOME GUY! HE'S NOT WORTH WEEPING OVER!
JUST SOME GUY, YOU SAY?!
AND WHAT ABOUT YOU?!
Hello?

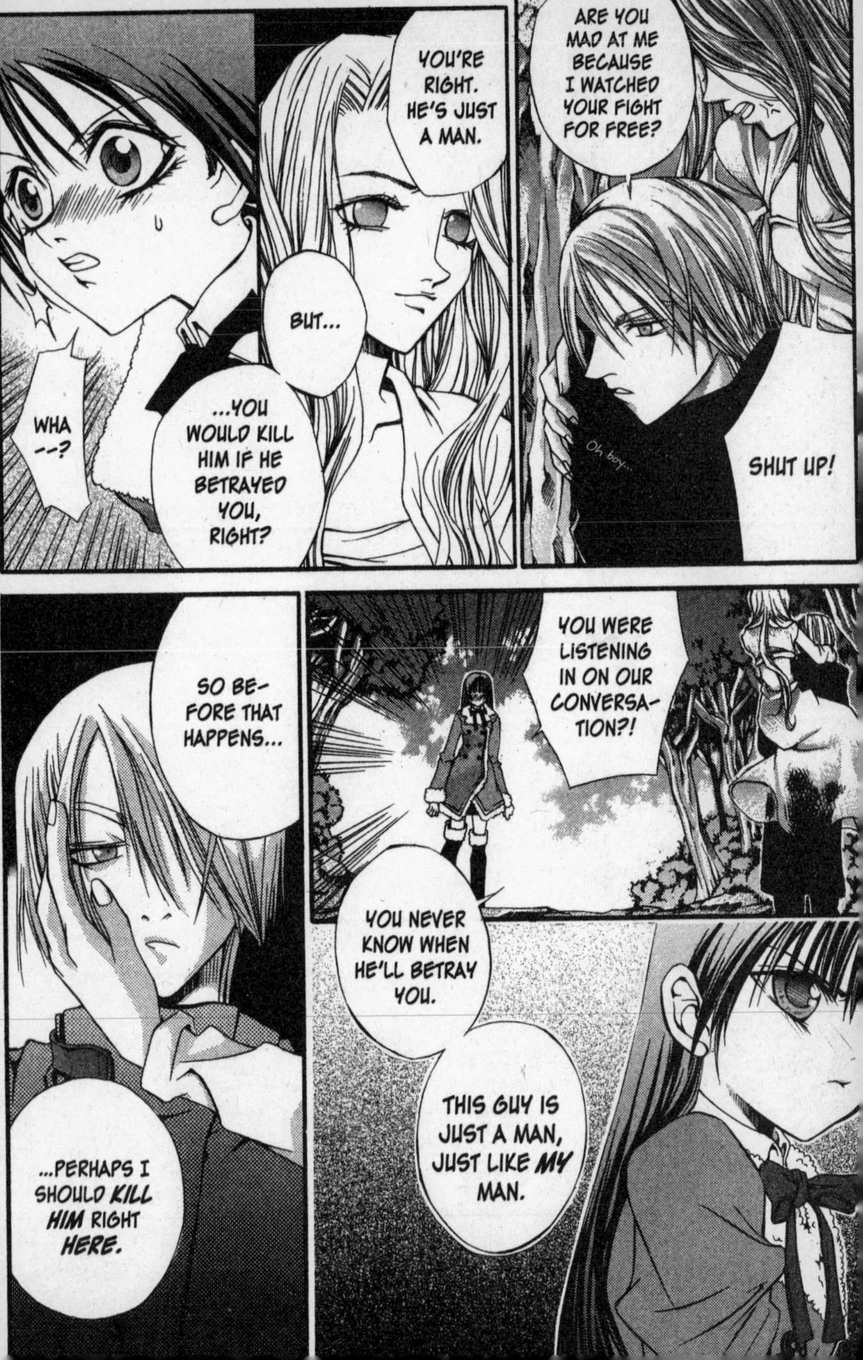
ARE YOU MAD AT ME BECAUSE I WATCHED YOUR FIGHT FOR FREE?
Oh boy...
SHUT UP!
YOU'RE RIGHT. HE'S JUST A MAN.
BUT...
...YOU WOULD KILL HIM IF HE BETRAYED YOU, RIGHT?
WHA--?
YOU WERE LISTENING IN ON OUR CONVERSA-TION?!
YOU NEVER KNOW WHEN HE'LL BETRAY YOU.
THIS GUY IS JUST A MAN, JUST LIKE *MY* MAN.
SO BE-FORE THAT HAPPENS...
...PERHAPS I SHOULD *KILL HIM* RIGHT *HERE*.

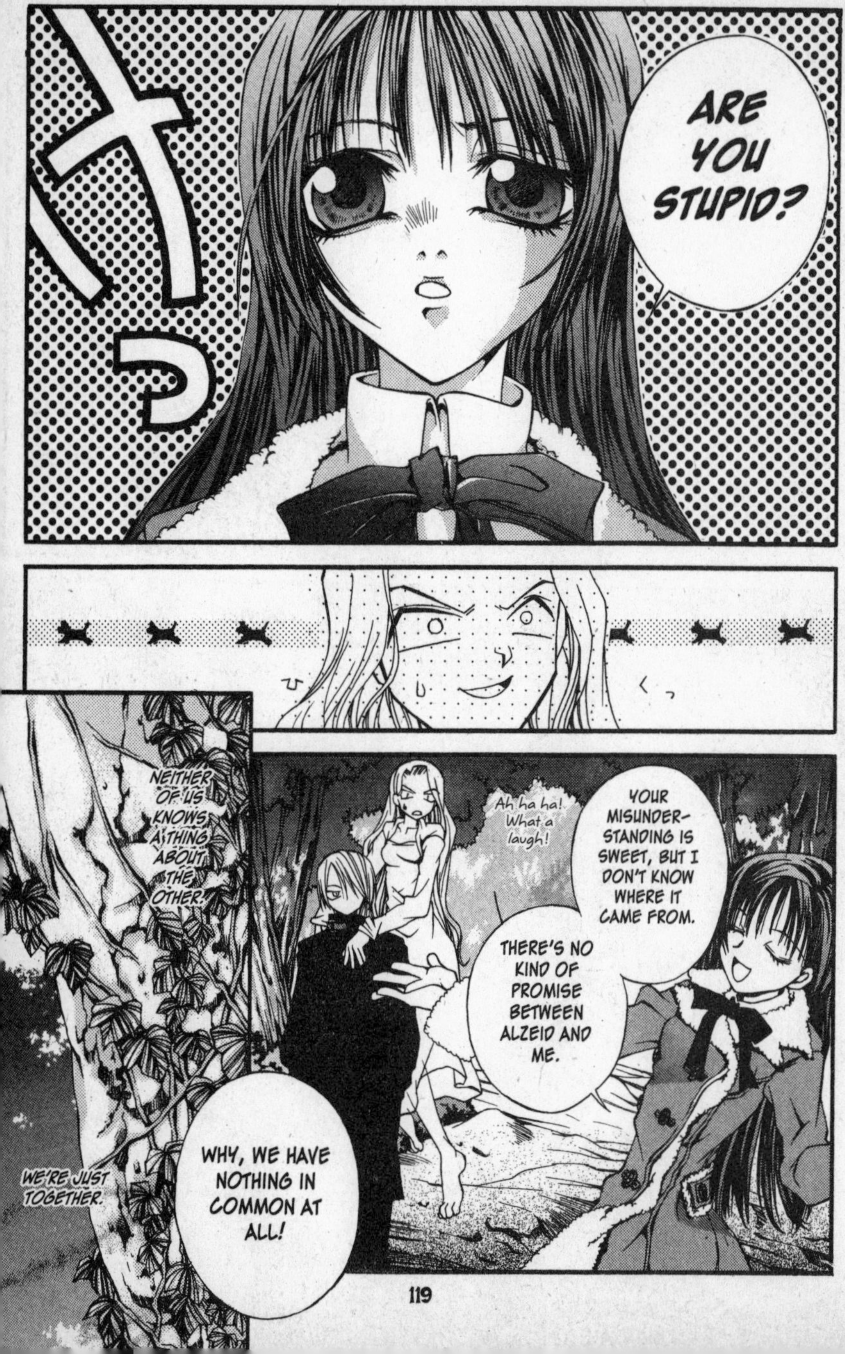

ARE YOU STUPID?
YOUR MISUNDERSTANDING IS SWEET, BUT I DON'T KNOW WHERE IT CAME FROM.
Ah ha ha! What a laugh!
THERE'S NO KIND OF PROMISE BETWEEN ALZEID AND ME.
WHY, WE HAVE NOTHING IN COMMON AT ALL!
NEITHER OF US KNOWS A THING ABOUT THE OTHER.
WE'RE JUST TOGETHER.

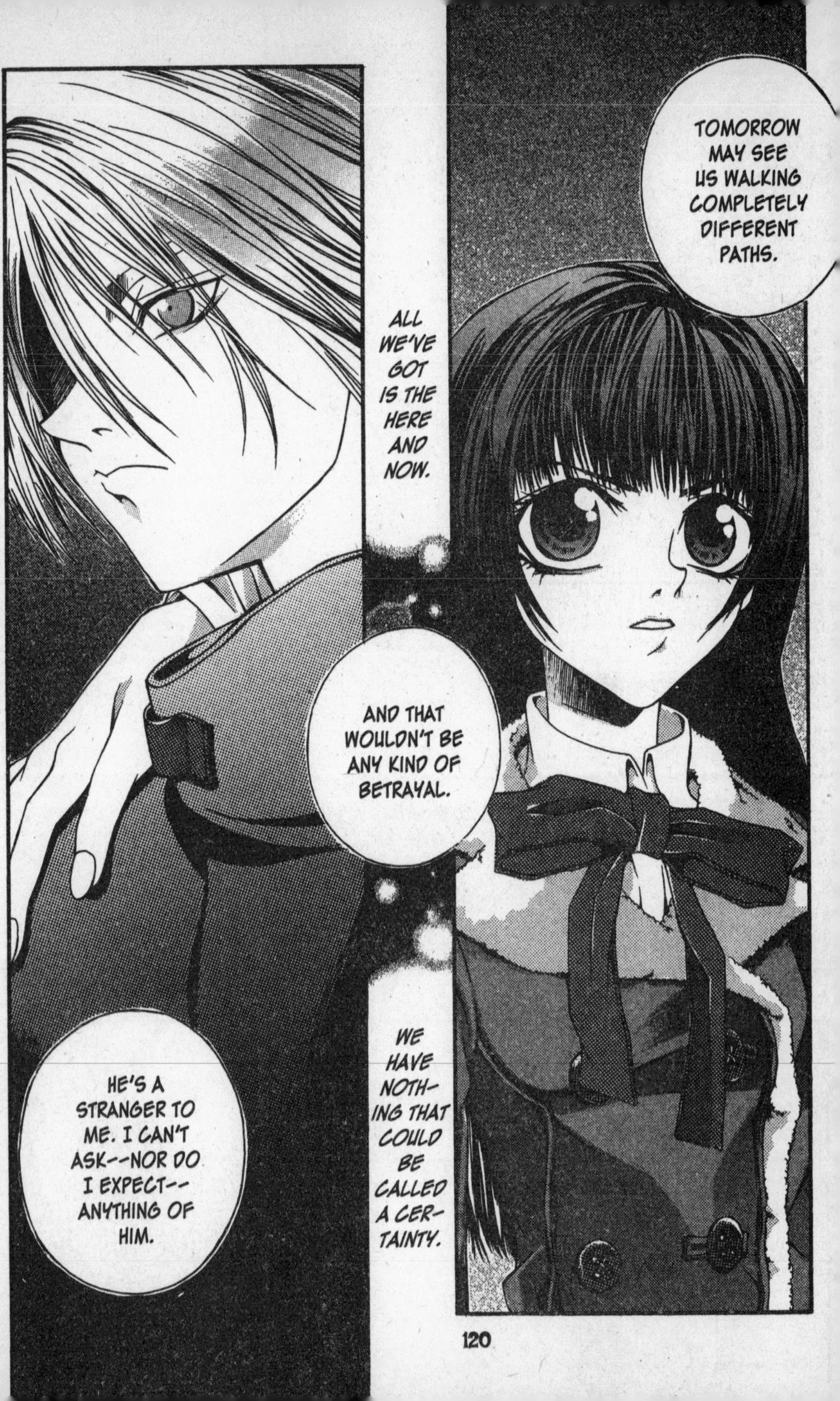
TOMORROW MAY SEE US WALKING COMPLETELY DIFFERENT PATHS.
ALL WE'VE GOT IS THE HERE AND NOW.
AND THAT WOULDN'T BE ANY KIND OF BETRAYAL.
WE HAVE NOTHING THAT COULD BE CALLED A CERTAINTY.
HE'S A STRANGER TO ME. I CAN'T ASK--NOR DO I EXPECT--ANYTHING OF HIM.

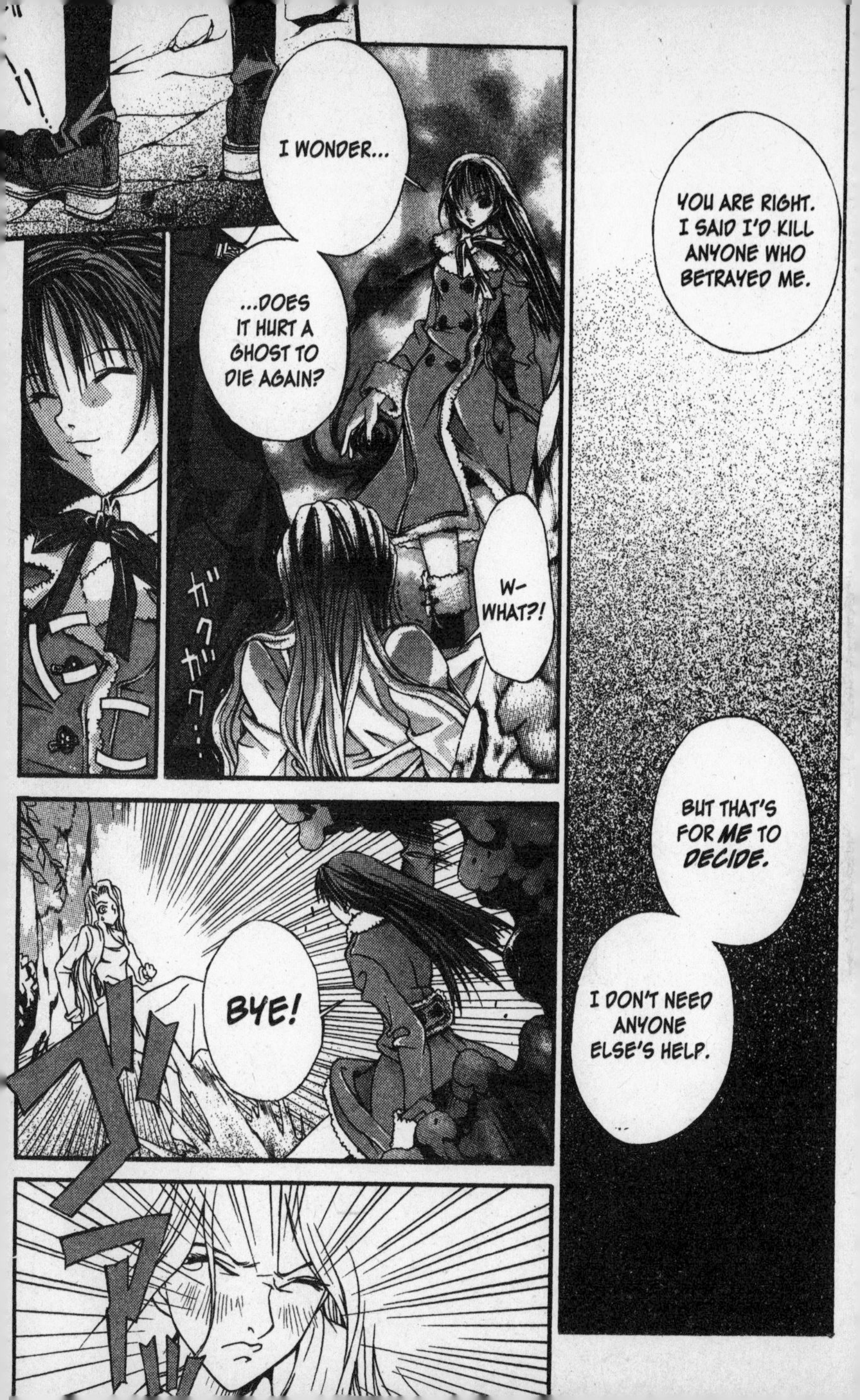
YOU ARE RIGHT. I SAID I'D KILL ANYONE WHO BETRAYED ME.
BUT THAT'S FOR *ME* TO *DECIDE.*
I DON'T NEED ANYONE ELSE'S HELP.
I WONDER...
...DOES IT HURT A GHOST TO DIE AGAIN?
W- WHAT?!
ガクガク…
BYE!

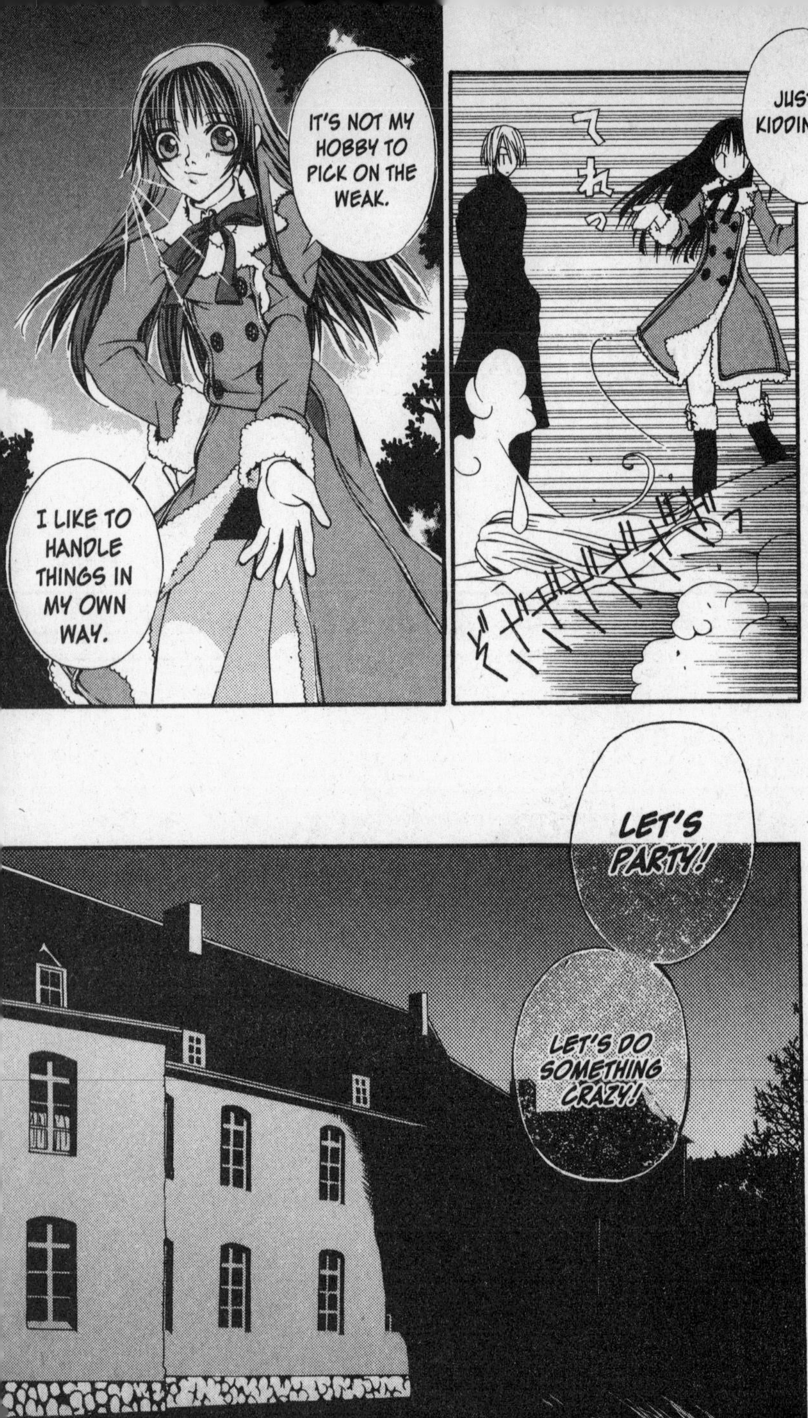
JUST KIDDING!
IT'S NOT MY HOBBY TO PICK ON THE WEAK.
I LIKE TO HANDLE THINGS IN MY OWN WAY.
LET'S PARTY!
LET'S DO SOMETHING CRAZY!

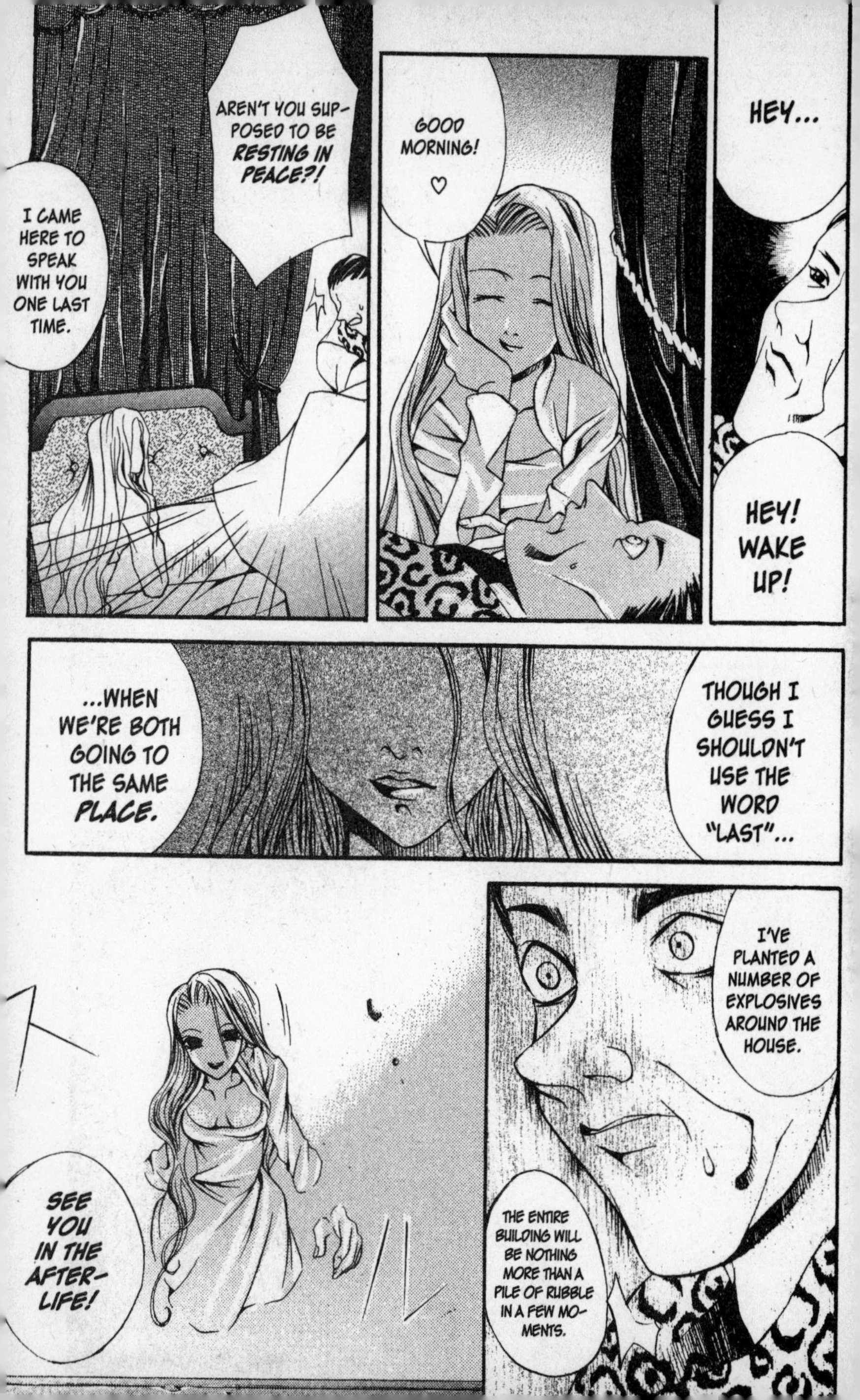
HEY...
HEY! WAKE UP!
GOOD MORNING! ♡
AREN'T YOU SUP-POSED TO BE RESTING IN PEACE?!
I CAME HERE TO SPEAK WITH YOU ONE LAST TIME.
THOUGH I GUESS I SHOULDN'T USE THE WORD "LAST"...
...WHEN WE'RE BOTH GOING TO THE SAME PLACE.
I'VE PLANTED A NUMBER OF EXPLOSIVES AROUND THE HOUSE.
THE ENTIRE BUILDING WILL BE NOTHING MORE THAN A PILE OF RUBBLE IN A FEW MO-MENTS.
SEE YOU IN THE AFTER-LIFE!

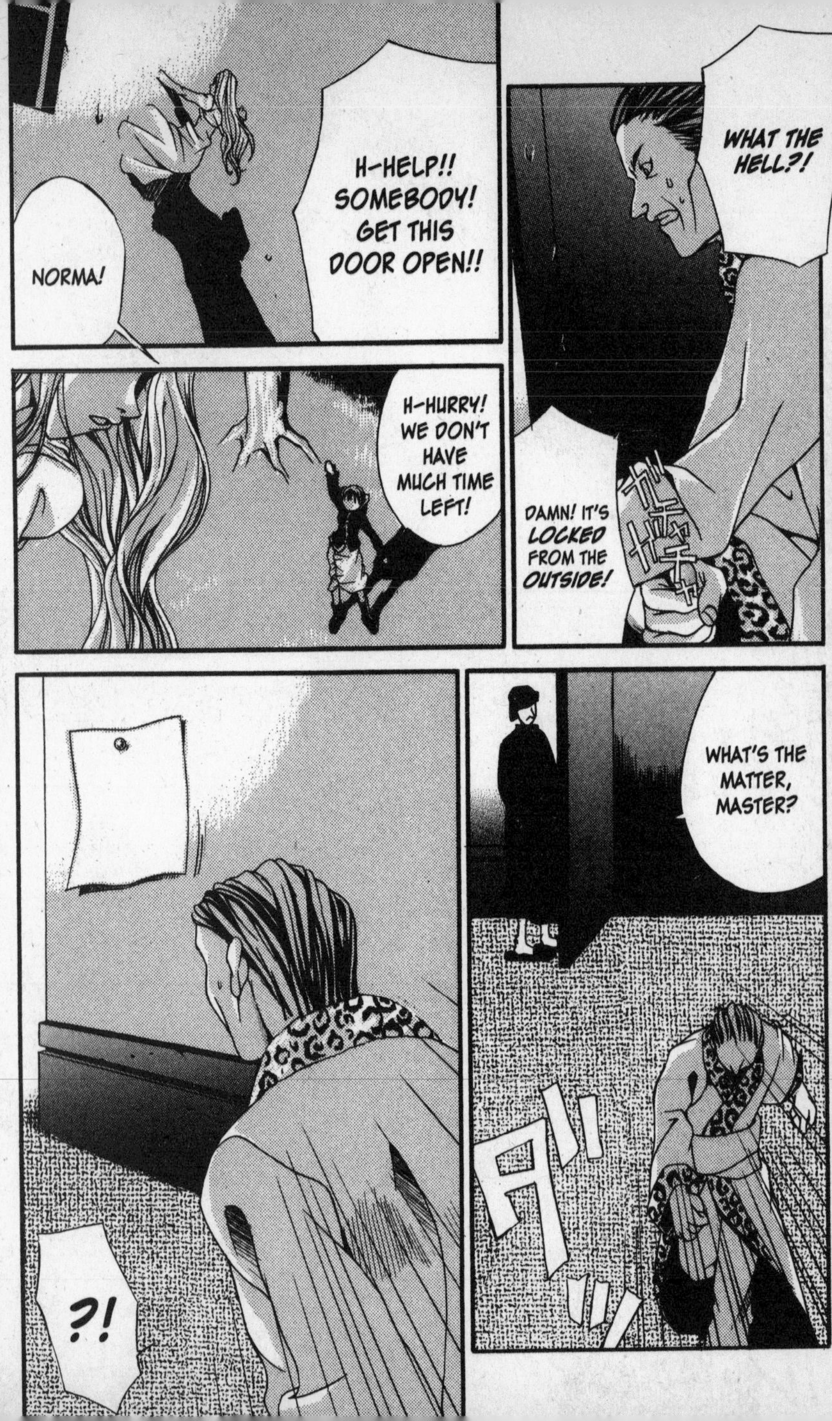
WHAT THE HELL?!
DAMN! IT'S LOCKED FROM THE OUTSIDE!
H-HELP!! SOMEBODY! GET THIS DOOR OPEN!!
NORMA!
H-HURRY! WE DON'T HAVE MUCH TIME LEFT!
WHAT'S THE MATTER, MASTER?
ダッ
?!

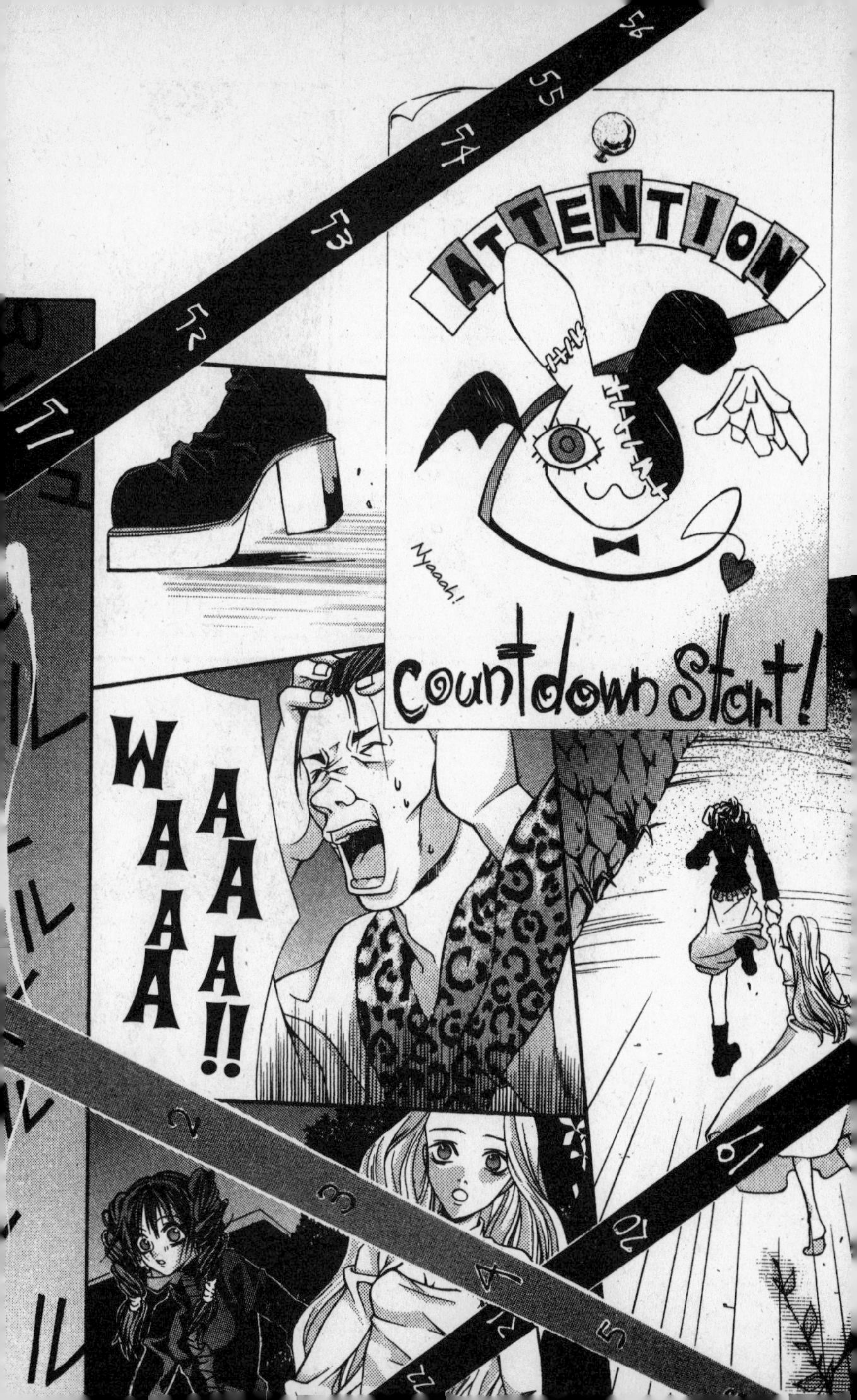
56 55 54 53 52 51
ATTENTION
Nyaaah!
Countdown Start!
WAAAAAAA!!

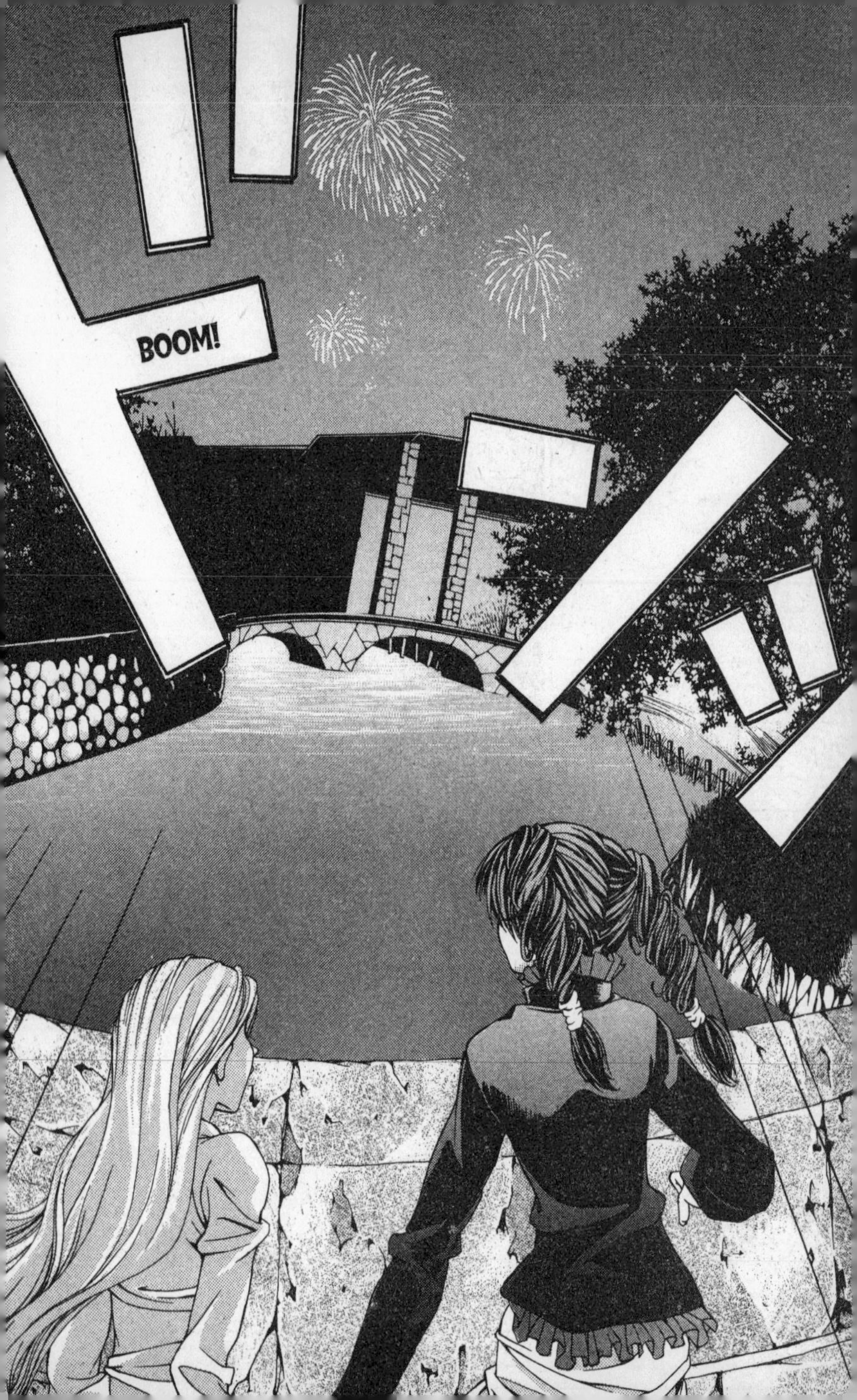
BOOM!

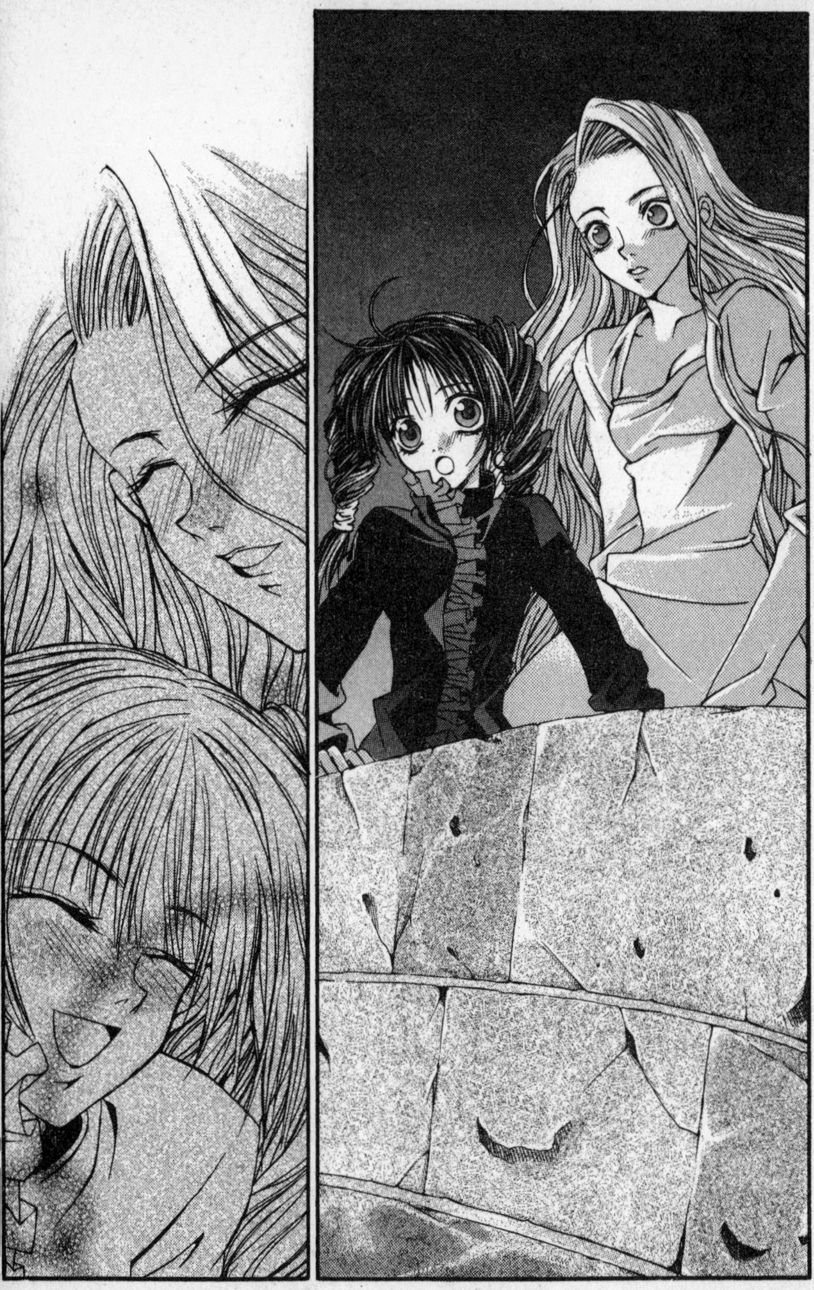

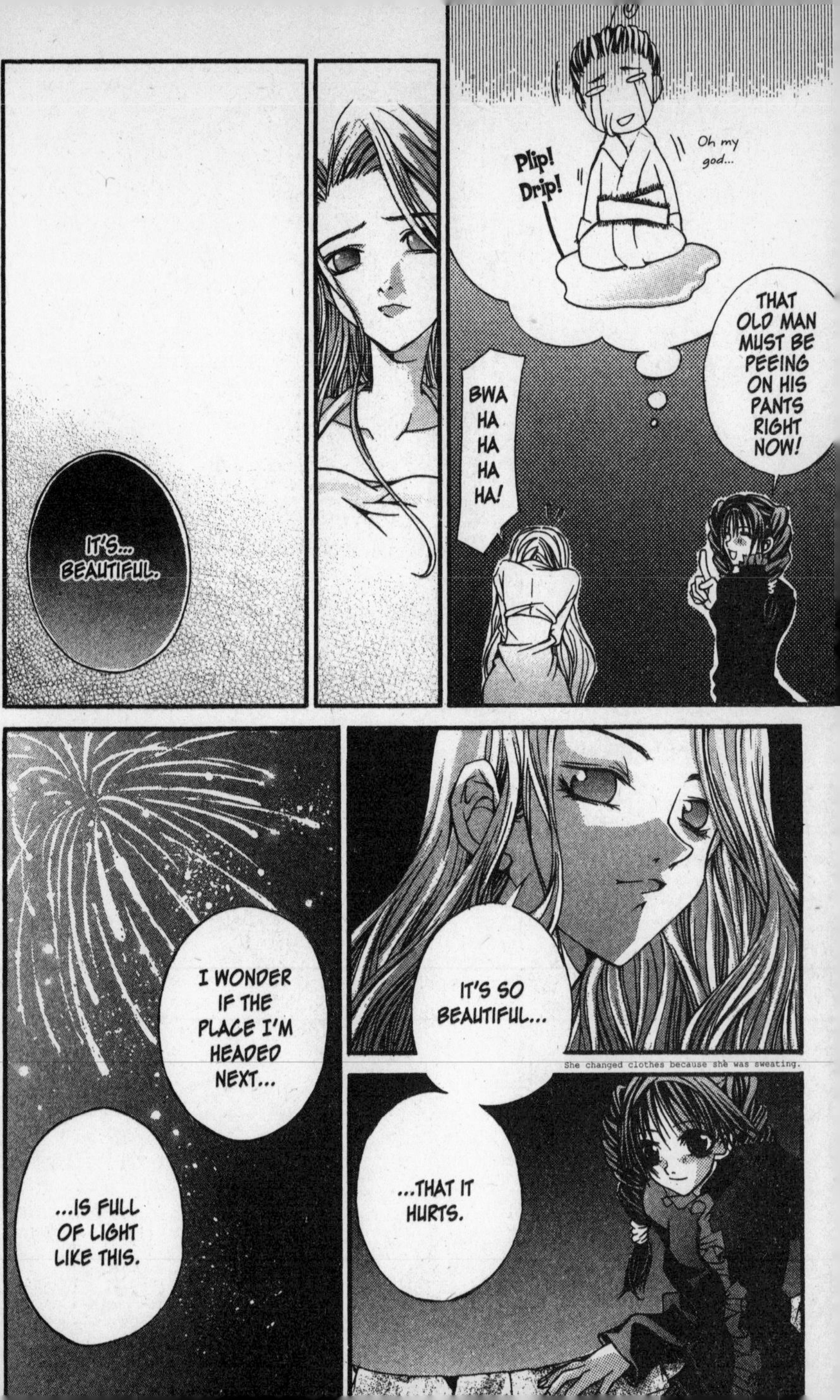
Oh my god...
Plip! Drip!
THAT OLD MAN MUST BE PEEING ON HIS PANTS RIGHT NOW!
BWA HA HA HA HA!
IT'S... BEAUTIFUL.
IT'S SO BEAUTIFUL...
She changed clothes because she was sweating.
...THAT IT HURTS.
I WONDER IF THE PLACE I'M HEADED NEXT...
...IS FULL OF LIGHT LIKE THIS.

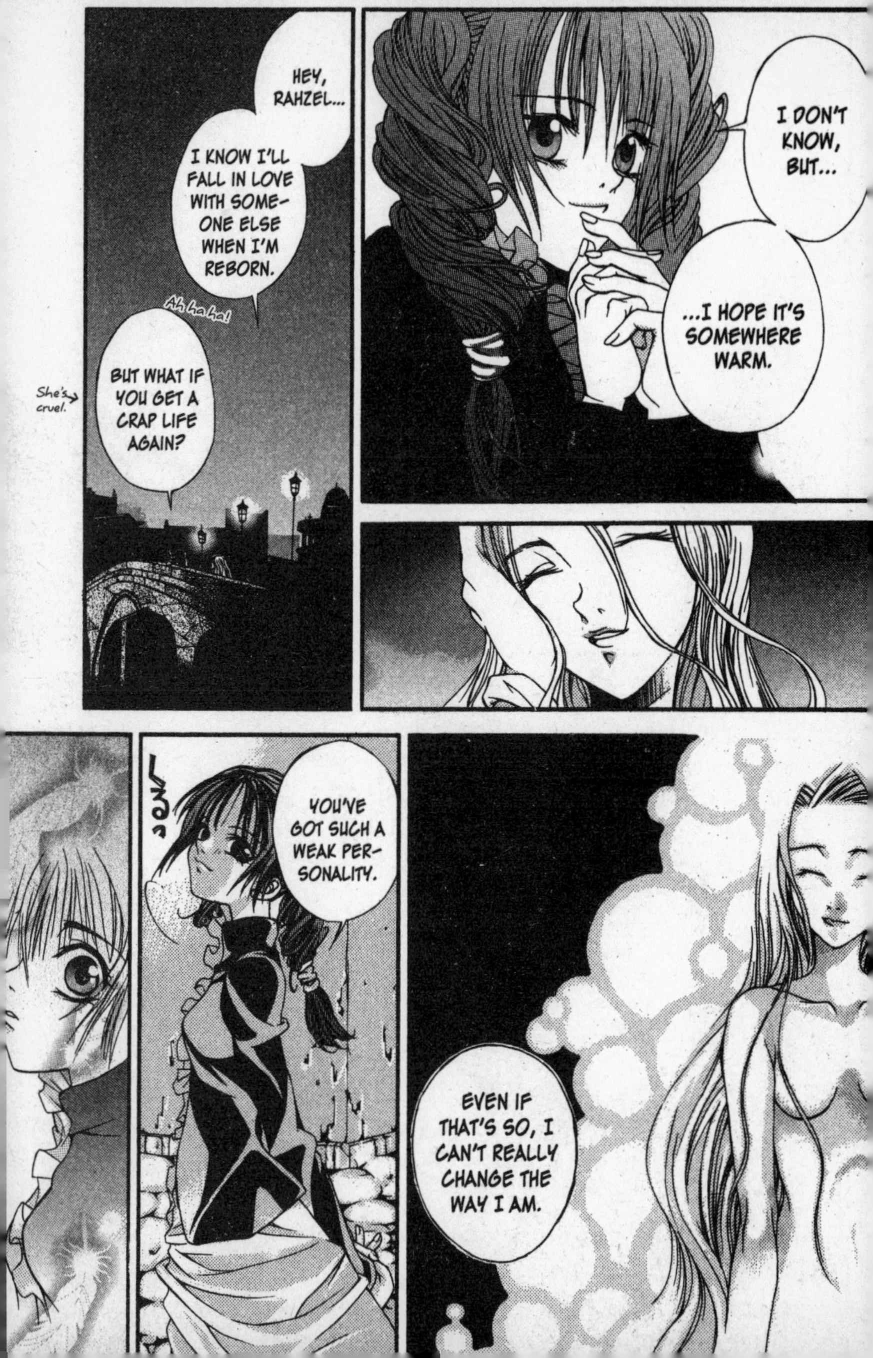
HEY, RAHZEL...
I KNOW I'LL FALL IN LOVE WITH SOME-ONE ELSE WHEN I'M REBORN.
Ah ha ha!
BUT WHAT IF YOU GET A CRAP LIFE AGAIN?
She's cruel.
I DON'T KNOW, BUT...
...I HOPE IT'S SOMEWHERE WARM.
YOU'VE GOT SUCH A WEAK PER-SONALITY.
EVEN IF THAT'S SO, I CAN'T REALLY CHANGE THE WAY I AM.

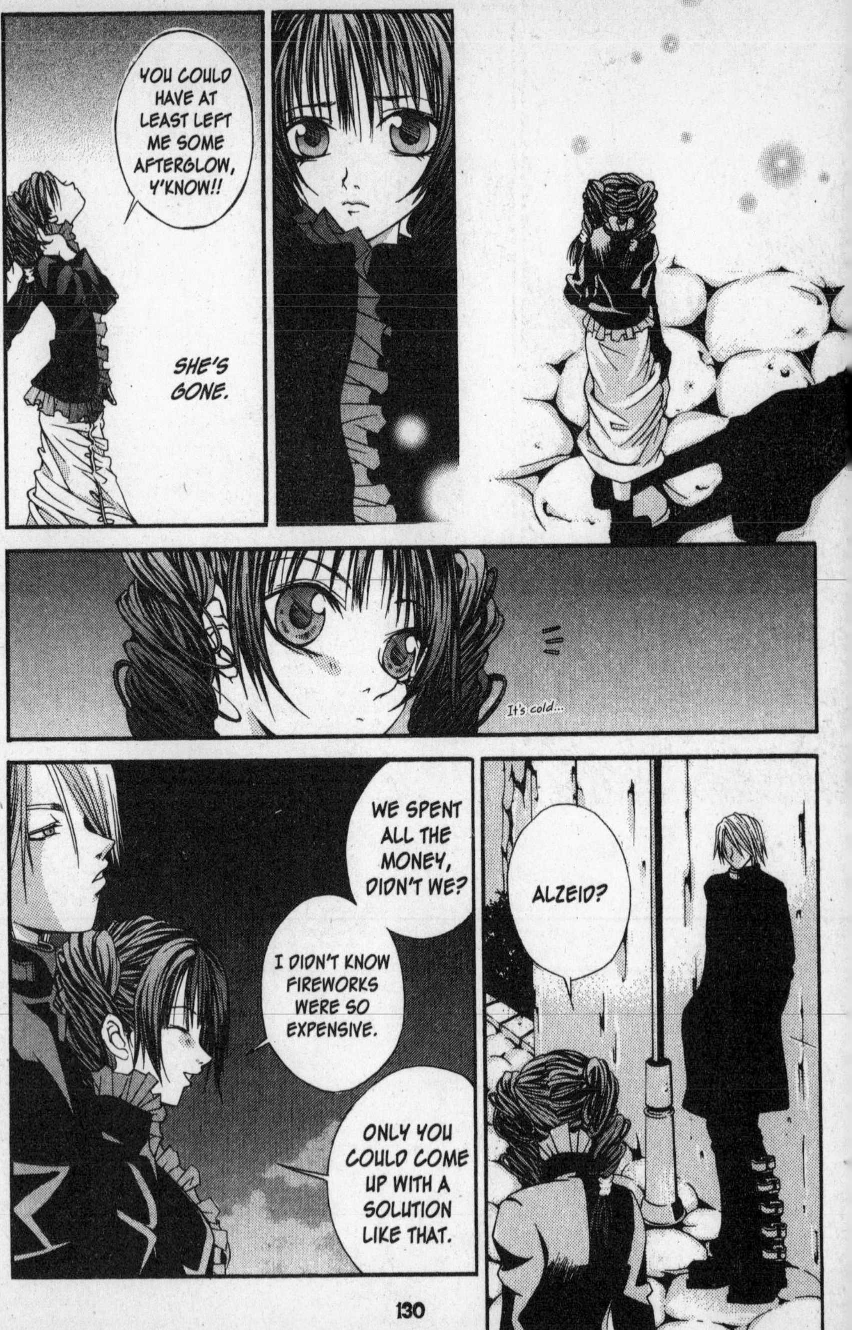
YOU COULD HAVE AT LEAST LEFT ME SOME AFTERGLOW, Y'KNOW!!
SHE'S GONE.
It's cold...
ALZEID?
WE SPENT ALL THE MONEY, DIDN'T WE?
I DIDN'T KNOW FIREWORKS WERE SO EXPENSIVE.
ONLY YOU COULD COME UP WITH A SOLUTION LIKE THAT.

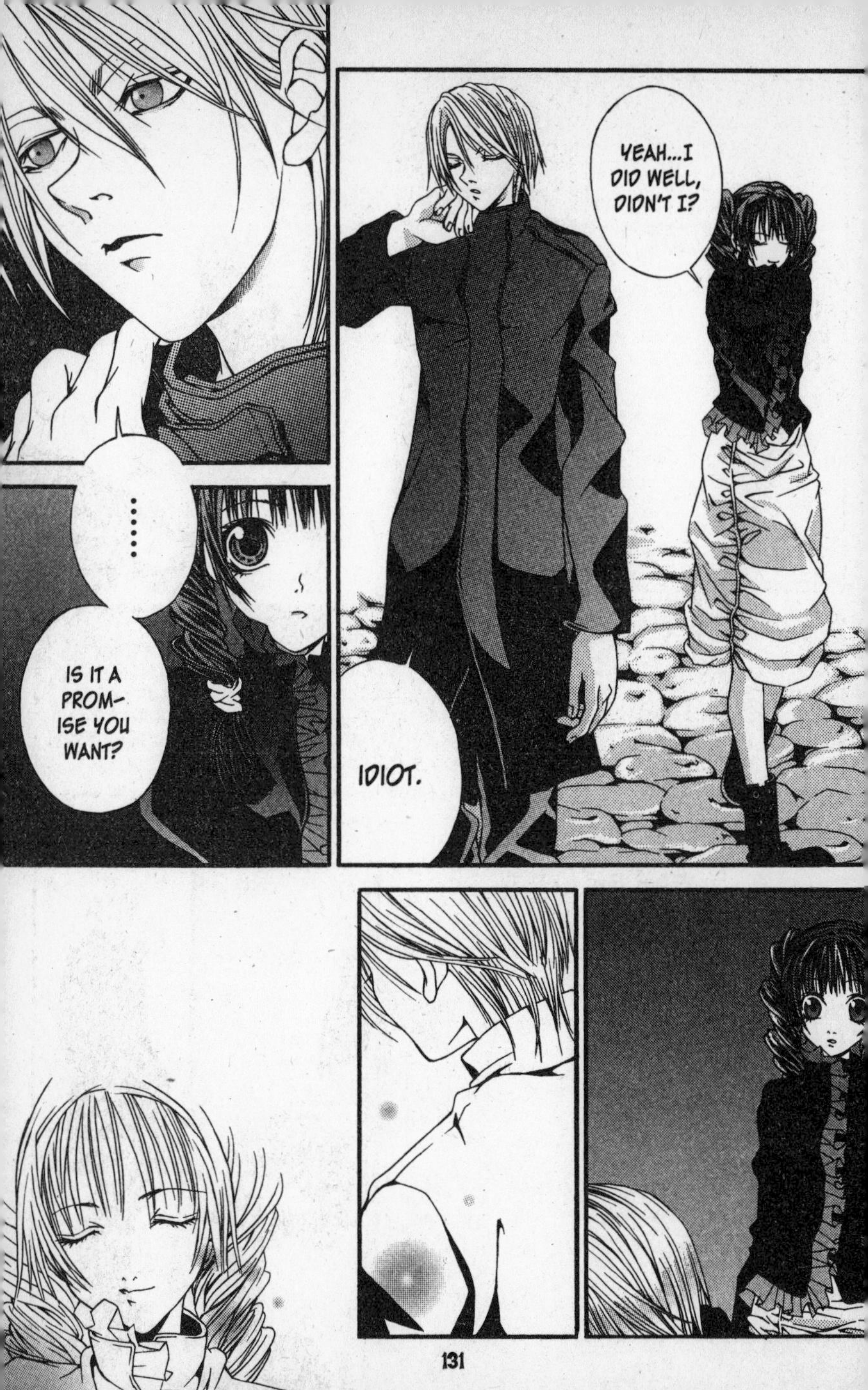
YEAH...I DID WELL, DIDN'T I?
IDIOT.
......
IS IT A PROM-ISE YOU WANT?

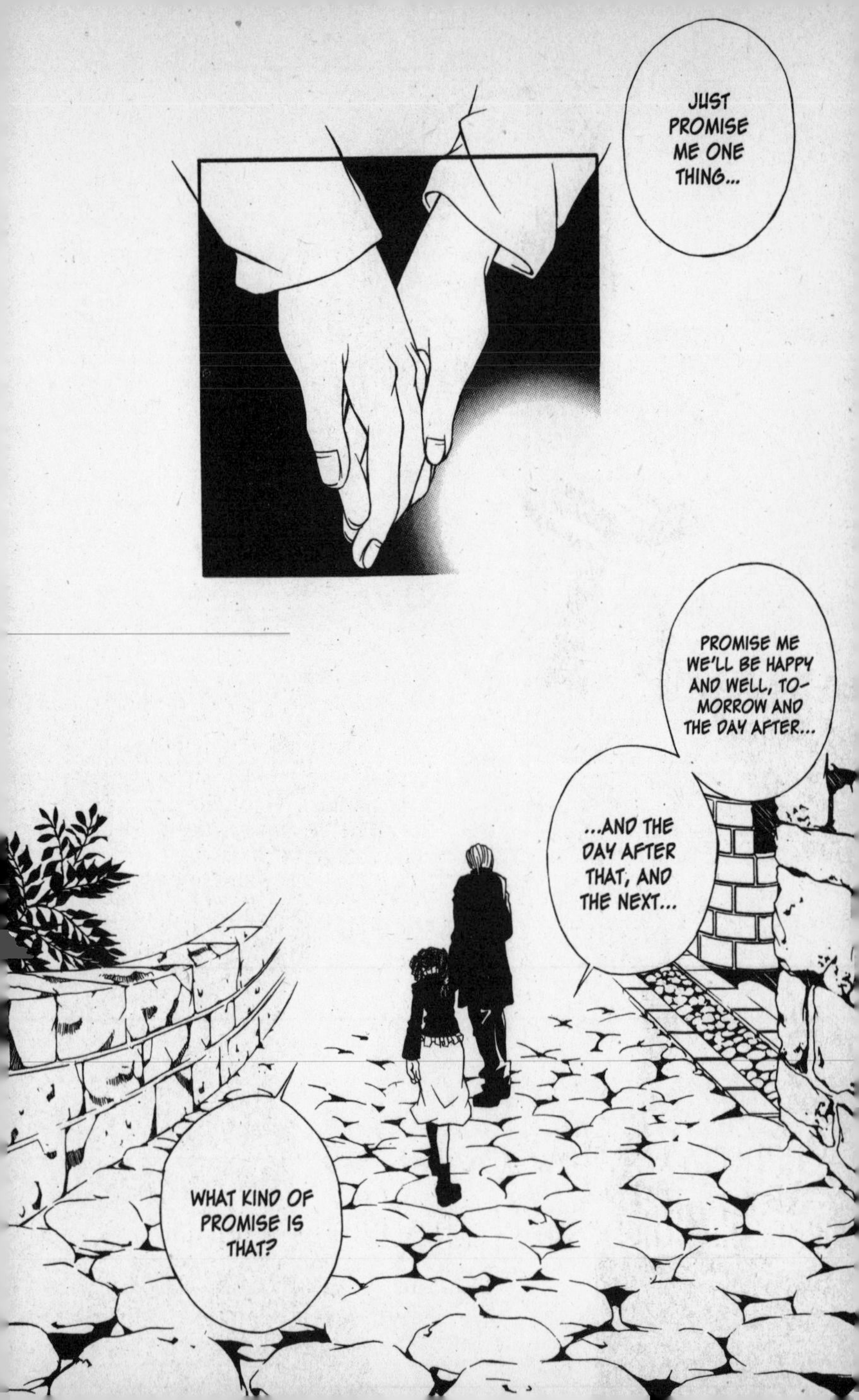
JUST PROMISE ME ONE THING...
PROMISE ME WE'LL BE HAPPY AND WELL, TO-MORROW AND THE DAY AFTER...
...AND THE DAY AFTER THAT, AND THE NEXT...
WHAT KIND OF PROMISE IS THAT?

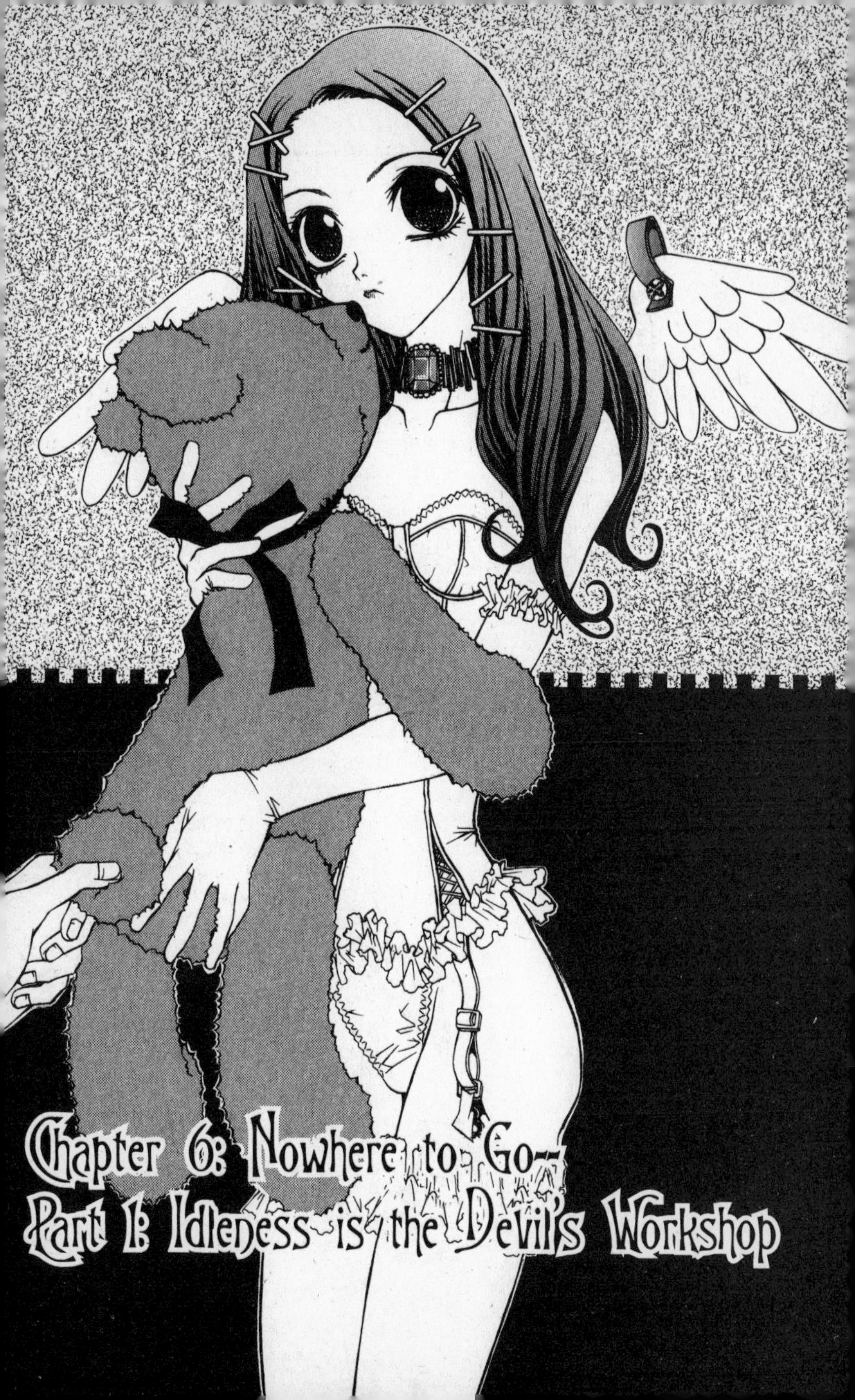

Chapter 6: Nowhere to Go– Part 1: Idleness is the Devil's Workshop

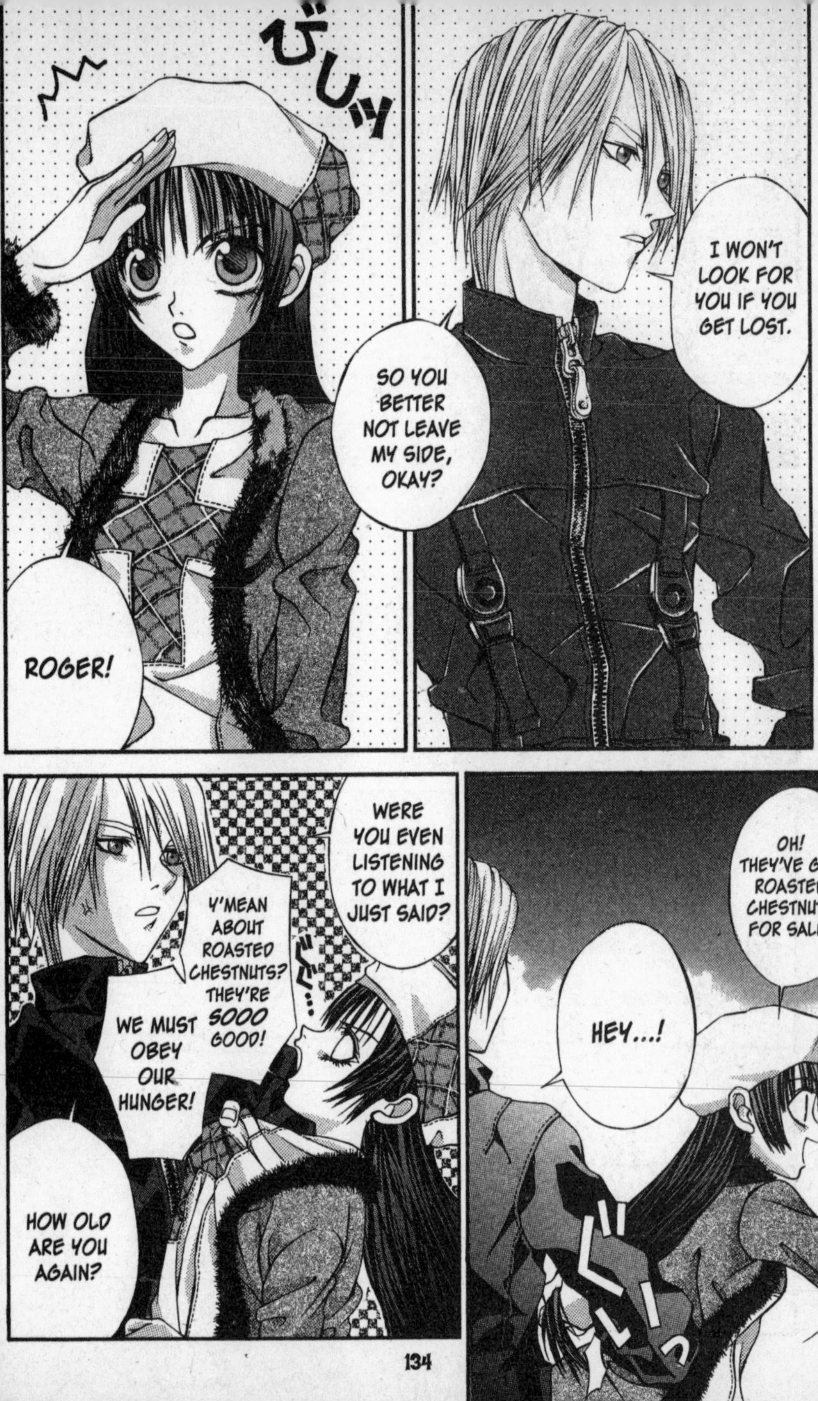
I WON'T LOOK FOR YOU IF YOU GET LOST.
SO YOU BETTER NOT LEAVE MY SIDE, OKAY?
びしッ
ROGER!
OH! THEY'VE GOT ROASTED CHESTNUTS FOR SALE!
HEY...!
WERE YOU EVEN LISTENING TO WHAT I JUST SAID?
Y'MEAN ABOUT ROASTED CHESTNUTS? THEY'RE SOOO GOOD!
WE MUST OBEY OUR HUNGER!
HOW OLD ARE YOU AGAIN?

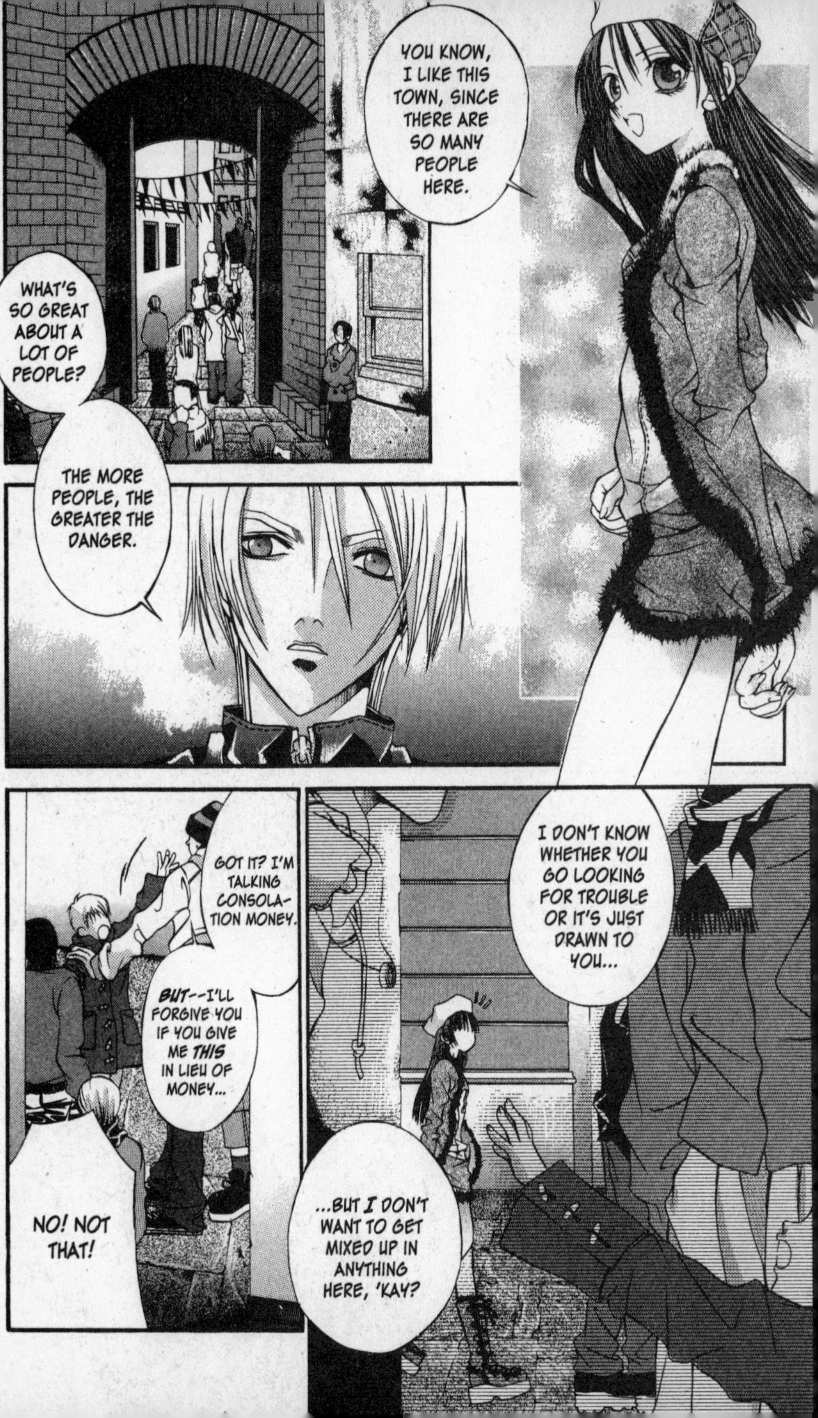
YOU KNOW, I LIKE THIS TOWN, SINCE THERE ARE SO MANY PEOPLE HERE.
WHAT'S SO GREAT ABOUT A LOT OF PEOPLE?
THE MORE PEOPLE, THE GREATER THE DANGER.
I DON'T KNOW WHETHER YOU GO LOOKING FOR TROUBLE OR IT'S JUST DRAWN TO YOU...
...BUT *I* DON'T WANT TO GET MIXED UP IN ANYTHING HERE, 'KAY?
GOT IT? I'M TALKING CONSOLATION MONEY.
BUT--I'LL FORGIVE YOU IF YOU GIVE ME *THIS* IN LIEU OF MONEY...
NO! NOT THAT!

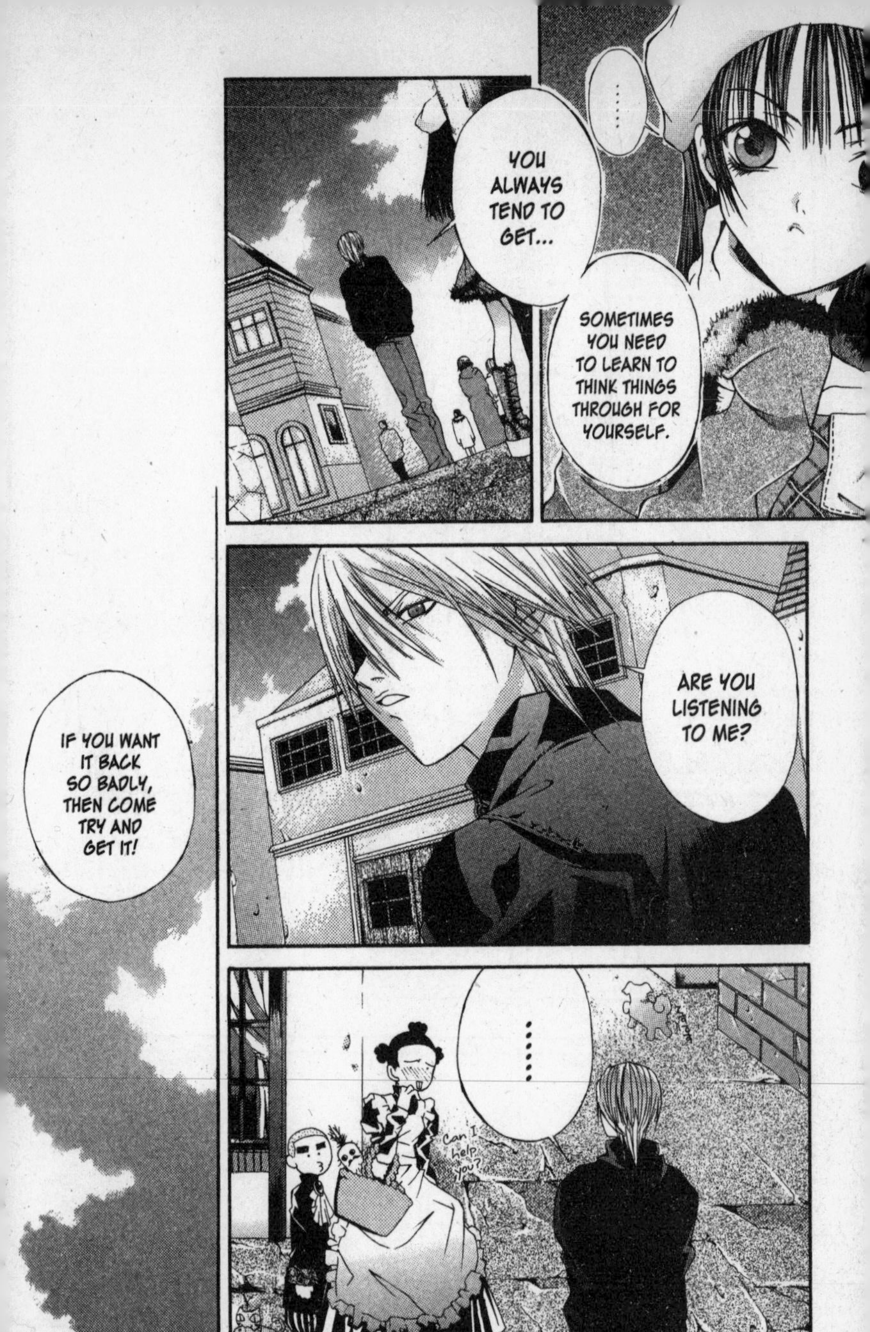
......
YOU ALWAYS TEND TO GET...
SOMETIMES YOU NEED TO LEARN TO THINK THINGS THROUGH FOR YOURSELF.
ARE YOU LISTENING TO ME?
IF YOU WANT IT BACK SO BADLY, THEN COME TRY AND GET IT!
......
Can I help you?

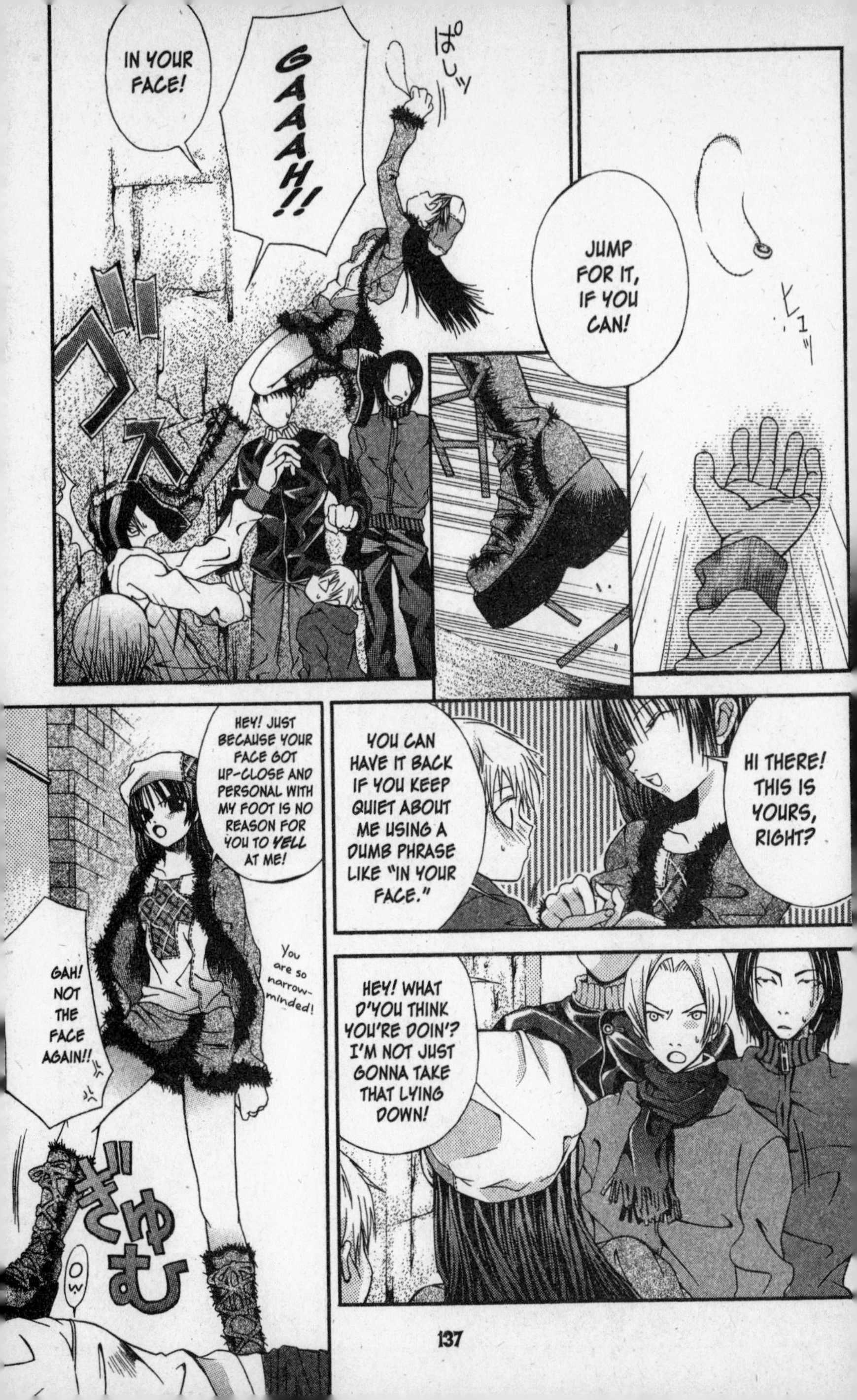
JUMP FOR IT, IF YOU CAN!
ぱしッ
IN YOUR FACE!
GAAAAH!!
HI THERE! THIS IS YOURS, RIGHT?
YOU CAN HAVE IT BACK IF YOU KEEP QUIET ABOUT ME USING A DUMB PHRASE LIKE "IN YOUR FACE."
HEY! WHAT D'YOU THINK YOU'RE DOIN'? I'M NOT JUST GONNA TAKE THAT LYING DOWN!
HEY! JUST BECAUSE YOUR FACE GOT UP-CLOSE AND PERSONAL WITH MY FOOT IS NO REASON FOR YOU TO YELL AT ME!
You are so narrow-minded!
GAH! NOT THE FACE AGAIN!!
ぎゅむ
OW

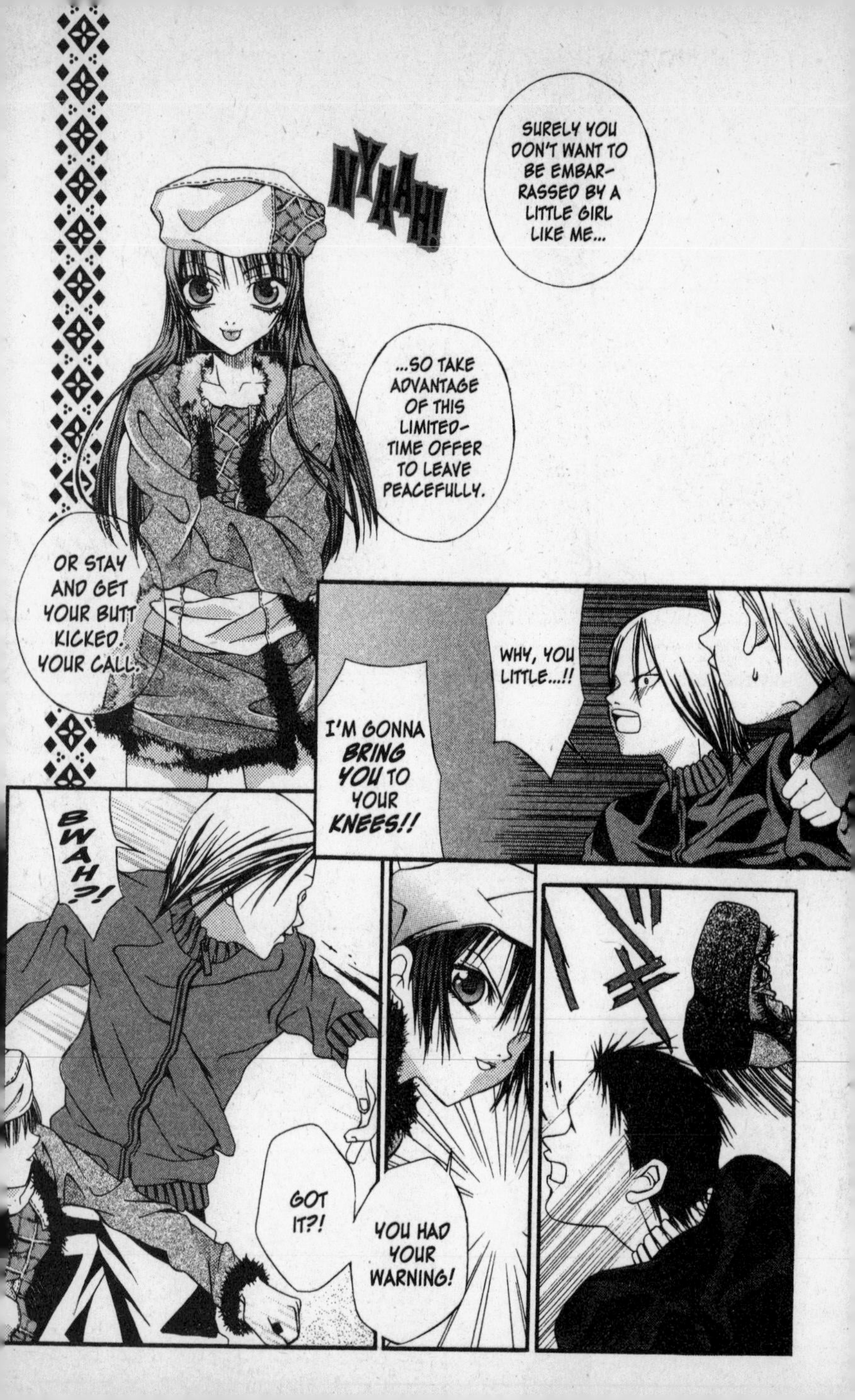
SURELY YOU DON'T WANT TO BE EMBAR-RASSED BY A LITTLE GIRL LIKE ME...
NYAAH!
...SO TAKE ADVANTAGE OF THIS LIMITED-TIME OFFER TO LEAVE PEACEFULLY.
OR STAY AND GET YOUR BUTT KICKED. YOUR CALL.
WHY, YOU LITTLE...!!
I'M GONNA **BRING YOU** TO YOUR **KNEES!!**
YOU HAD YOUR WARNING!
GOT IT?!
BWAH?!

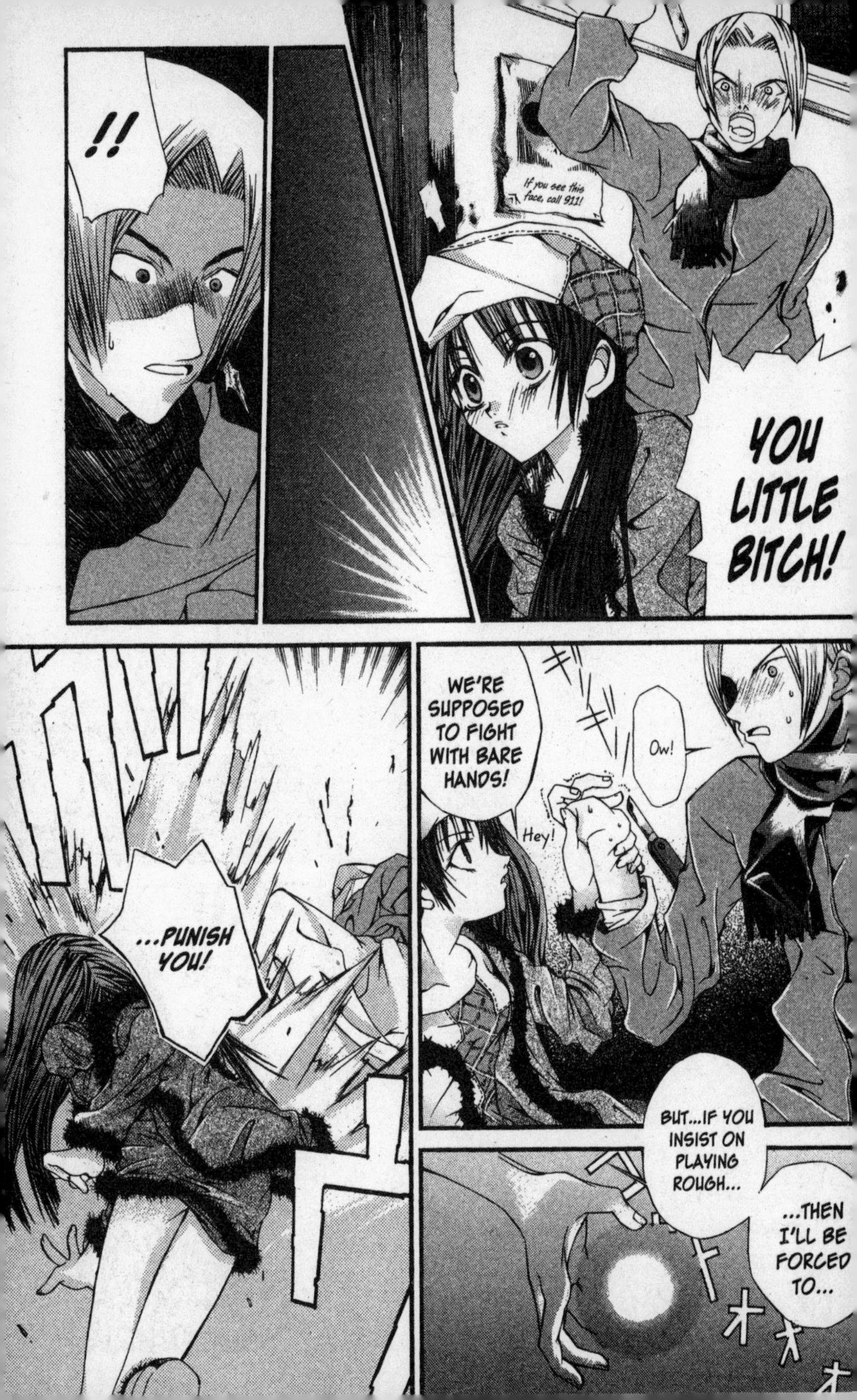
If you see this face, call 911!
YOU LITTLE BITCH!
!!
WE'RE SUPPOSED TO FIGHT WITH BARE HANDS!
Ow!
Hey!
BUT...IF YOU INSIST ON PLAYING ROUGH...
...THEN I'LL BE FORCED TO...
...PUNISH YOU!

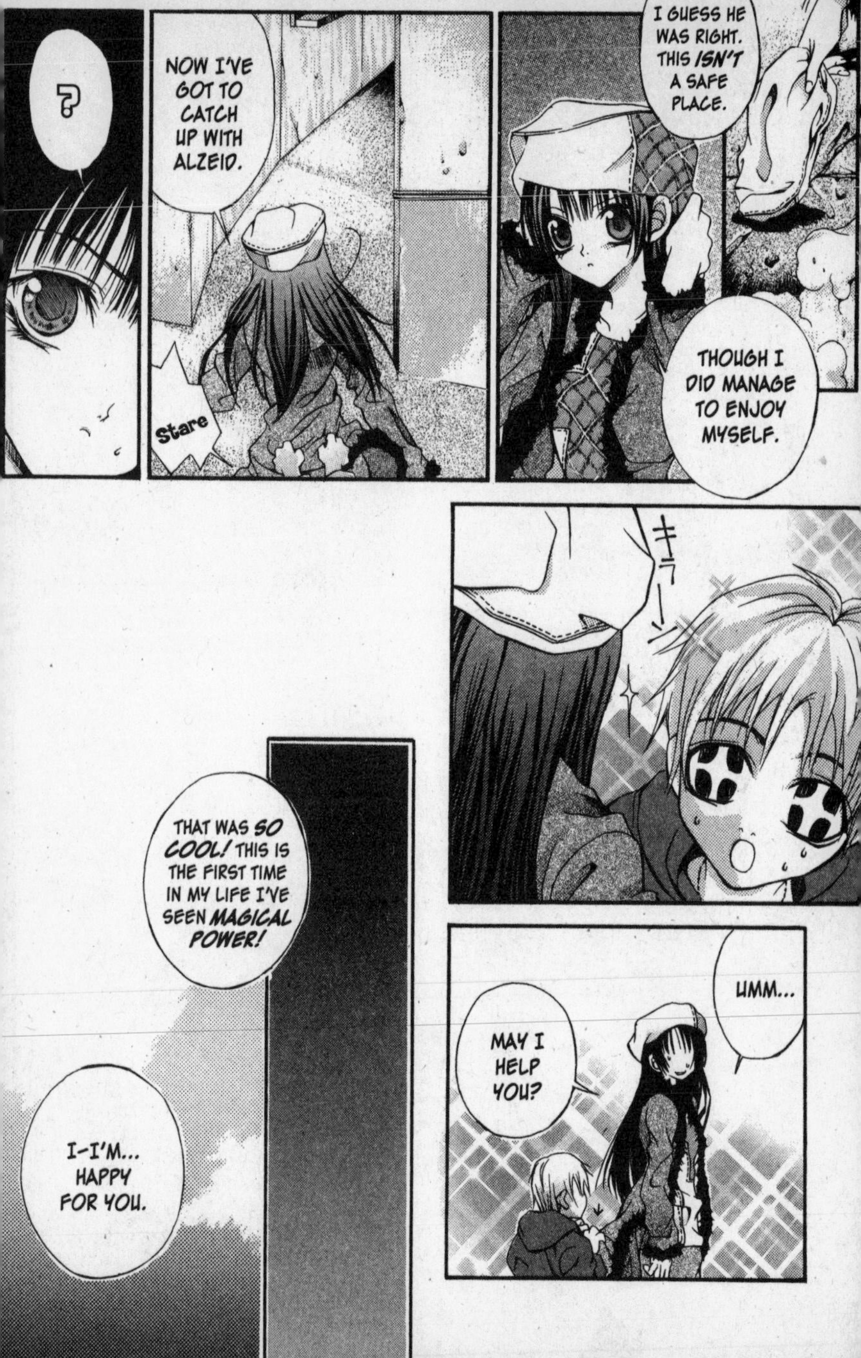
I GUESS HE WAS RIGHT. THIS ISN'T A SAFE PLACE.
THOUGH I DID MANAGE TO ENJOY MYSELF.
NOW I'VE GOT TO CATCH UP WITH ALZEID.
Stare
?
UMM...
MAY I HELP YOU?
THAT WAS SO COOL! THIS IS THE FIRST TIME IN MY LIFE I'VE SEEN MAGICAL POWER!
I-I'M... HAPPY FOR YOU.

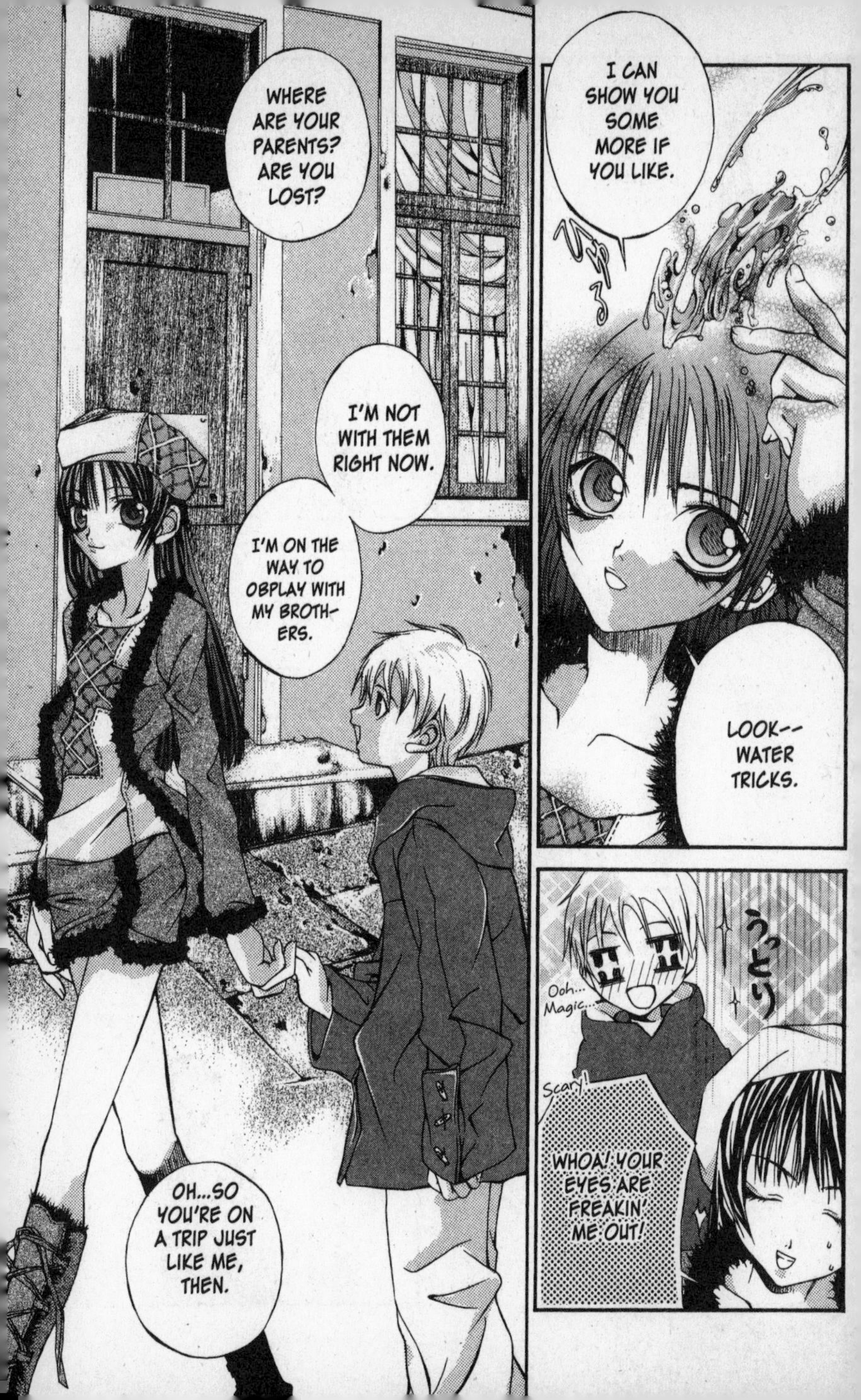
I CAN SHOW YOU SOME MORE IF YOU LIKE.
LOOK-- WATER TRICKS.
うっとり
Ooh... Magic...
Scary!
WHOA! YOUR EYES ARE FREAKIN' ME OUT!
WHERE ARE YOUR PARENTS? ARE YOU LOST?
I'M NOT WITH THEM RIGHT NOW.
I'M ON THE WAY TO OBPLAY WITH MY BROTH-ERS.
OH...SO YOU'RE ON A TRIP JUST LIKE ME, THEN.

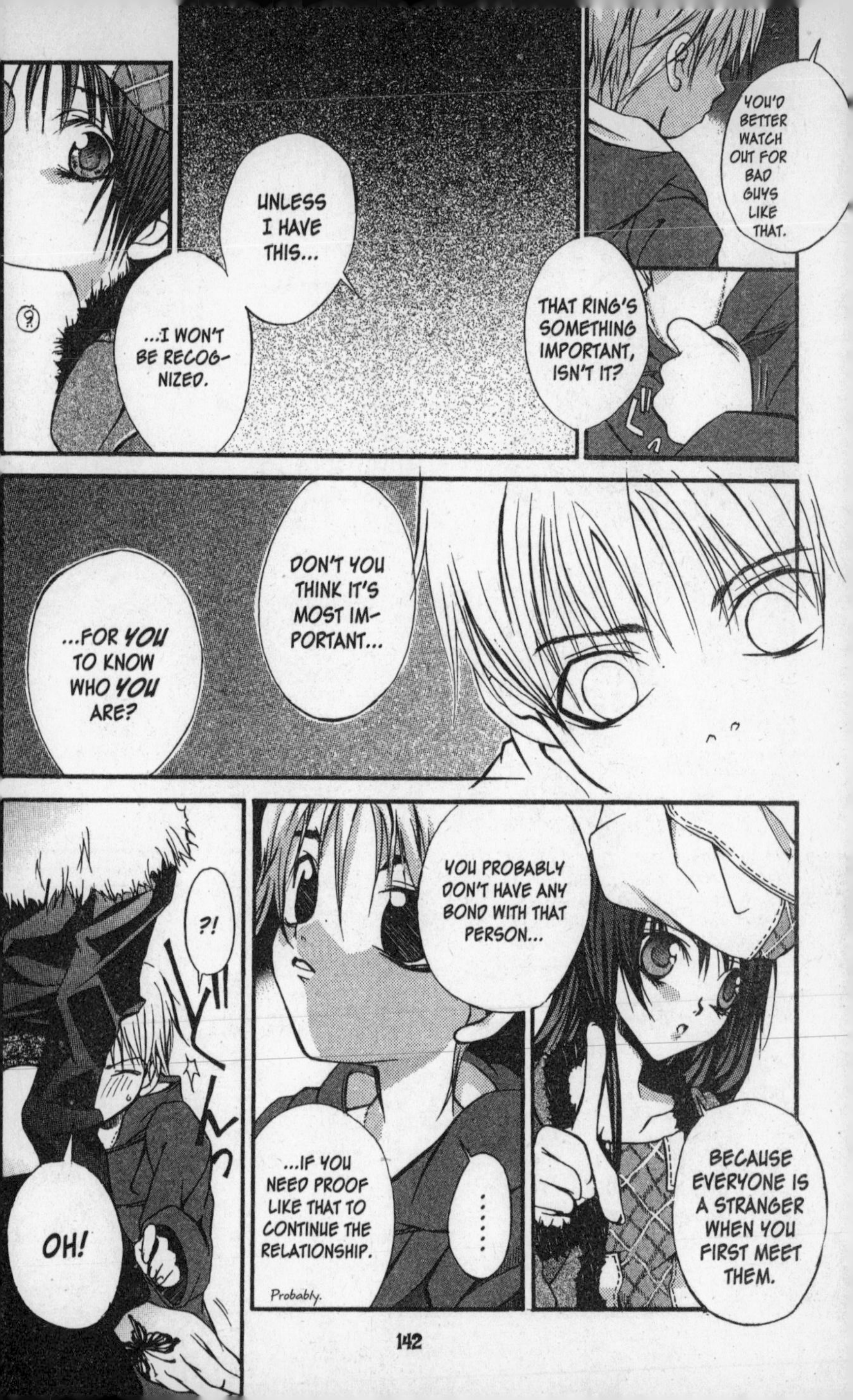
YOU'D BETTER WATCH OUT FOR BAD GUYS LIKE THAT.
THAT RING'S SOMETHING IMPORTANT, ISN'T IT?
UNLESS I HAVE THIS...
...I WON'T BE RECOG-NIZED.
DON'T YOU THINK IT'S MOST IM-PORTANT...
...FOR *YOU* TO KNOW WHO *YOU* ARE?
YOU PROBABLY DON'T HAVE ANY BOND WITH THAT PERSON...
BECAUSE EVERYONE IS A STRANGER WHEN YOU FIRST MEET THEM.
......
...IF YOU NEED PROOF LIKE THAT TO CONTINUE THE RELATIONSHIP.
Probably.
?!
OH!

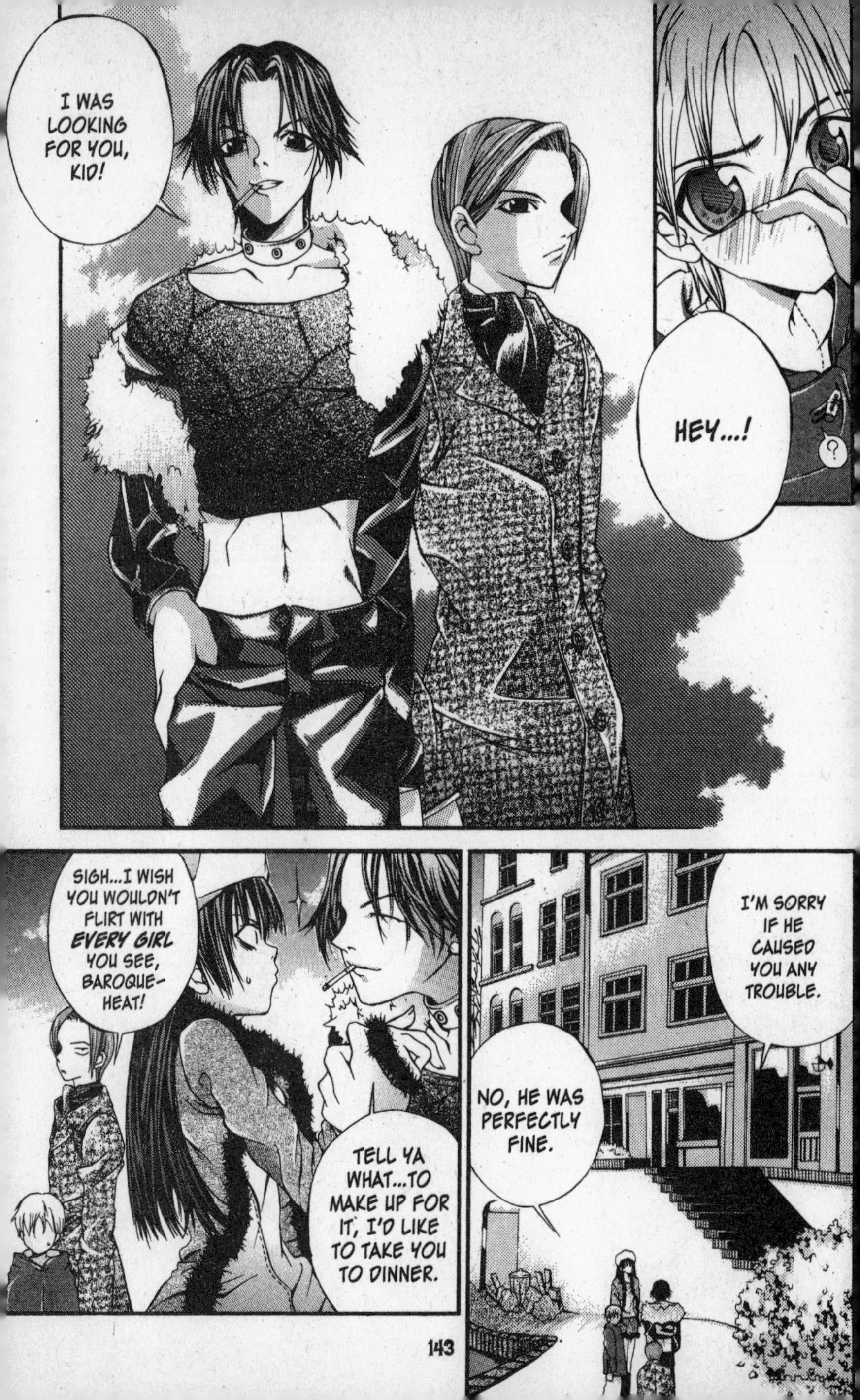
HEY...!
?
I WAS LOOKING FOR YOU, KID!
I'M SORRY IF HE CAUSED YOU ANY TROUBLE.
NO, HE WAS PERFECTLY FINE.
SIGH...I WISH YOU WOULDN'T FLIRT WITH *EVERY GIRL* YOU SEE, BAROQUE-HEAT!
TELL YA WHAT...TO MAKE UP FOR IT, I'D LIKE TO TAKE YOU TO DINNER.

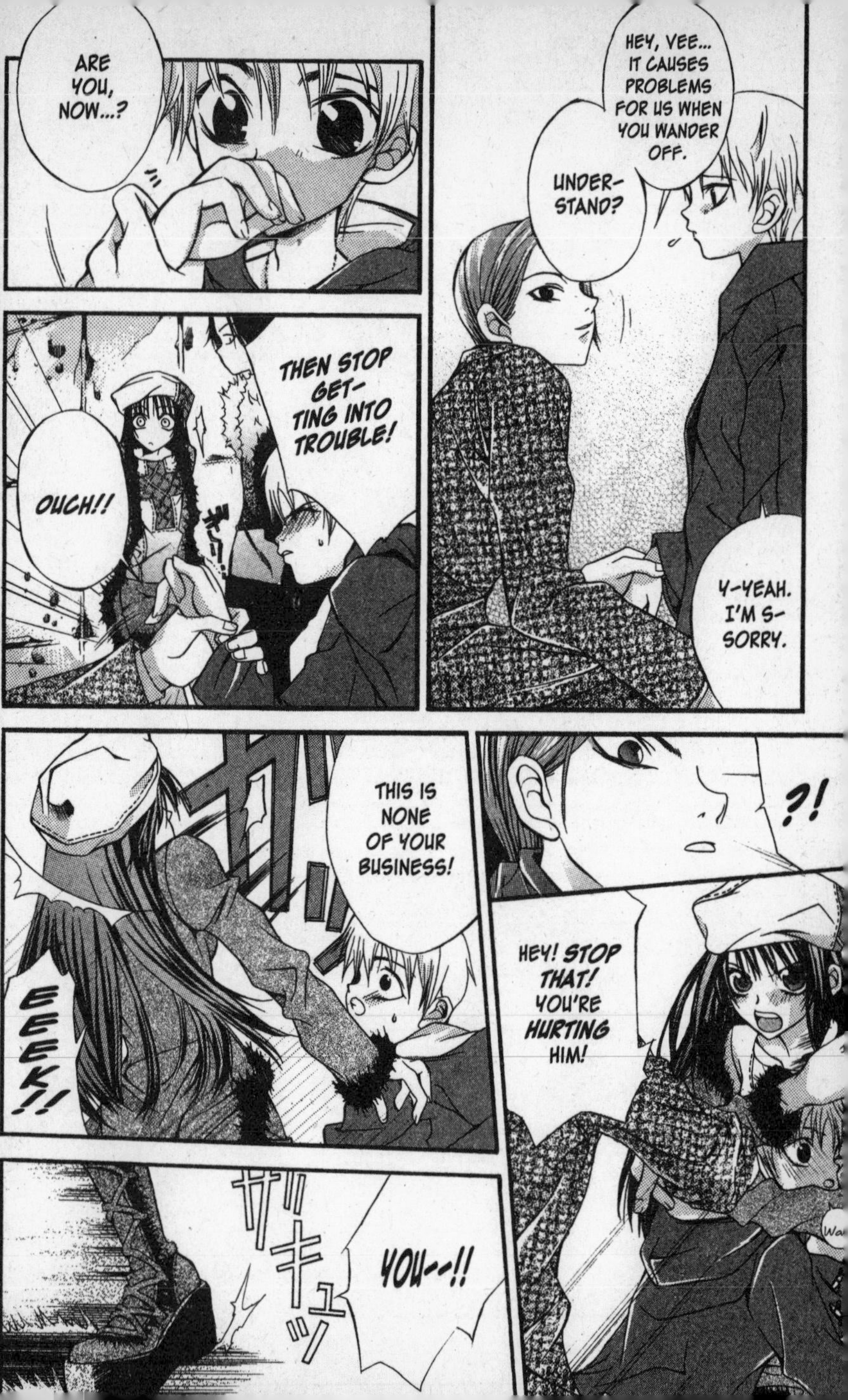
HEY, VEE... IT CAUSES PROBLEMS FOR US WHEN YOU WANDER OFF.
UNDER-STAND?
Y-YEAH. I'M S-SORRY.
ARE YOU, NOW...?
THEN STOP GET-TING INTO TROUBLE!
OUCH!!
?!
THIS IS NONE OF YOUR BUSINESS!
EEEEK!!
HEY! STOP THAT! YOU'RE HURTING HIM!
YOU--!!

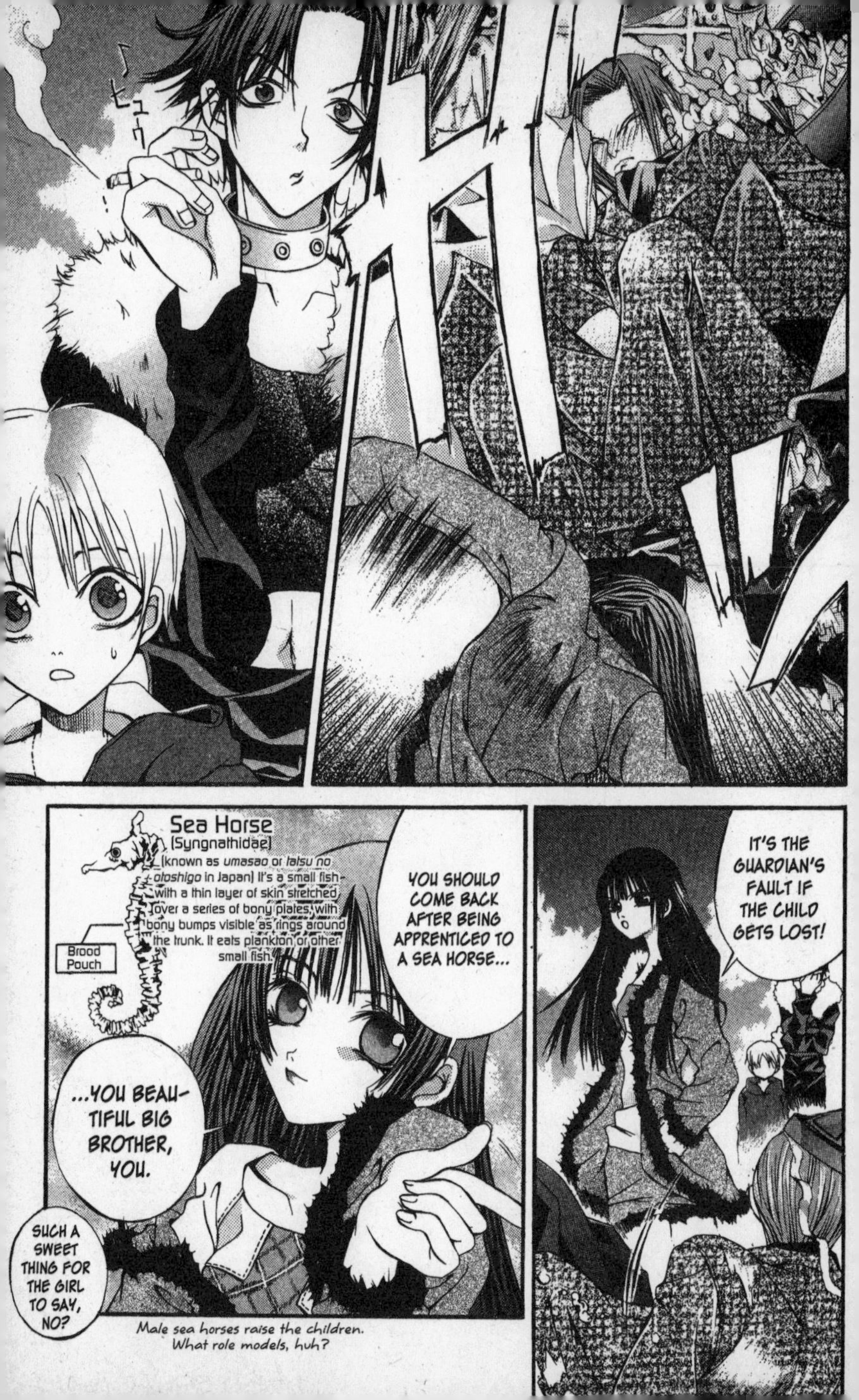
ヒュウ
IT'S THE GUARDIAN'S FAULT IF THE CHILD GETS LOST!
Sea Horse
(Syngnathidae)
(known as *umasao* or *tatsu no otoshigo* in Japan) It's a small fish with a thin layer of skin stretched over a series of bony plates, with bony bumps visible as rings around the trunk. It eats plankton or other small fish.
Brood Pouch
YOU SHOULD COME BACK AFTER BEING APPRENTICED TO A SEA HORSE...
...YOU BEAUTIFUL BIG BROTHER, YOU.
SUCH A SWEET THING FOR THE GIRL TO SAY, NO?
Male sea horses raise the children. What role models, huh?

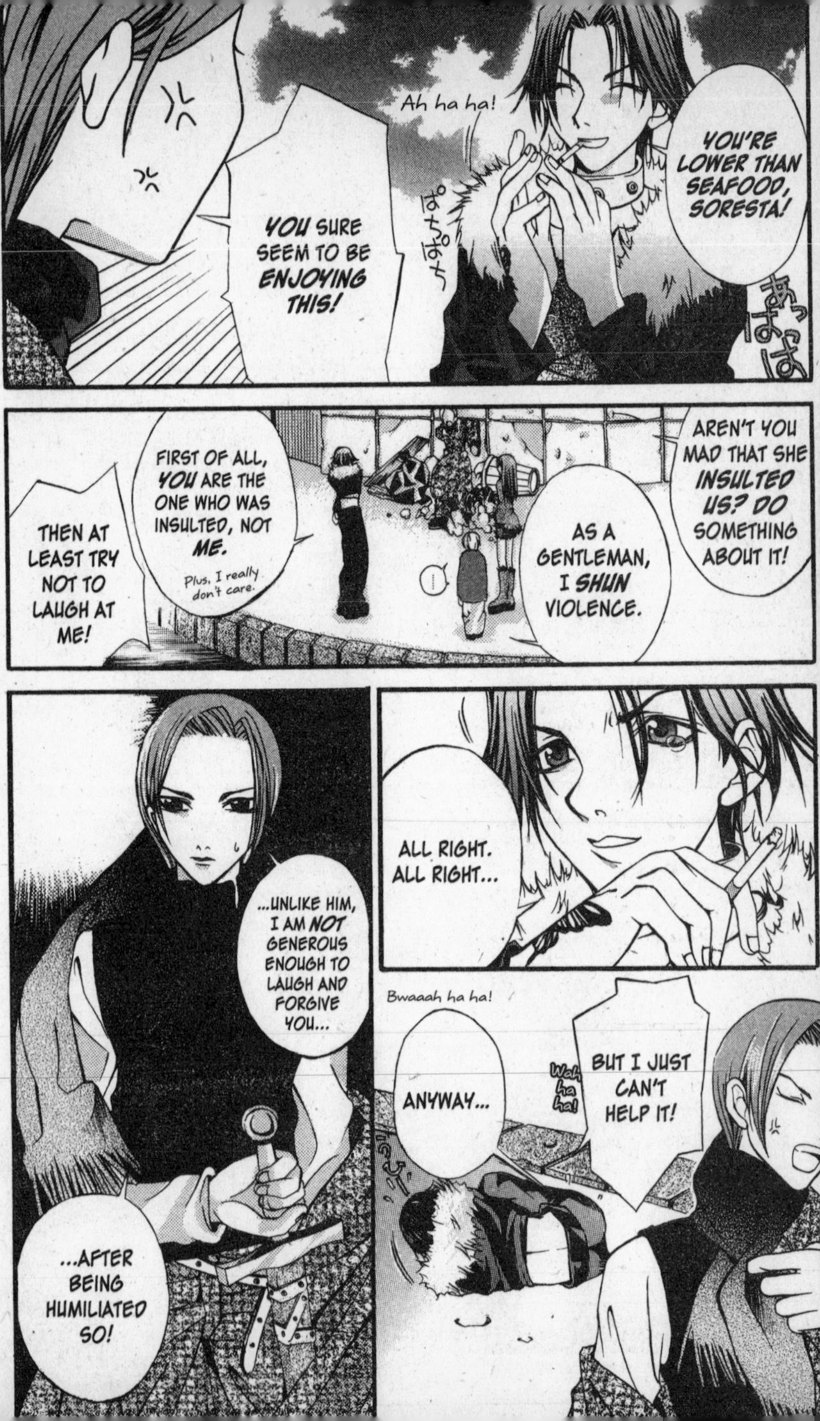
YOU'RE LOWER THAN SEAFOOD, SORESTA!
あっはっは
Ah ha ha!
ぱちぱち
YOU SURE SEEM TO BE ENJOYING THIS!
AREN'T YOU MAD THAT SHE INSULTED US? DO SOMETHING ABOUT IT!
AS A GENTLEMAN, I SHUN VIOLENCE.
...
FIRST OF ALL, YOU ARE THE ONE WHO WAS INSULTED, NOT ME.
Plus, I really don't care.
THEN AT LEAST TRY NOT TO LAUGH AT ME!
ALL RIGHT. ALL RIGHT...
BUT I JUST CAN'T HELP IT!
Wah ha ha!
Bwaaah ha ha!
ANYWAY...
...UNLIKE HIM, I AM NOT GENEROUS ENOUGH TO LAUGH AND FORGIVE YOU...
...AFTER BEING HUMILIATED SO!

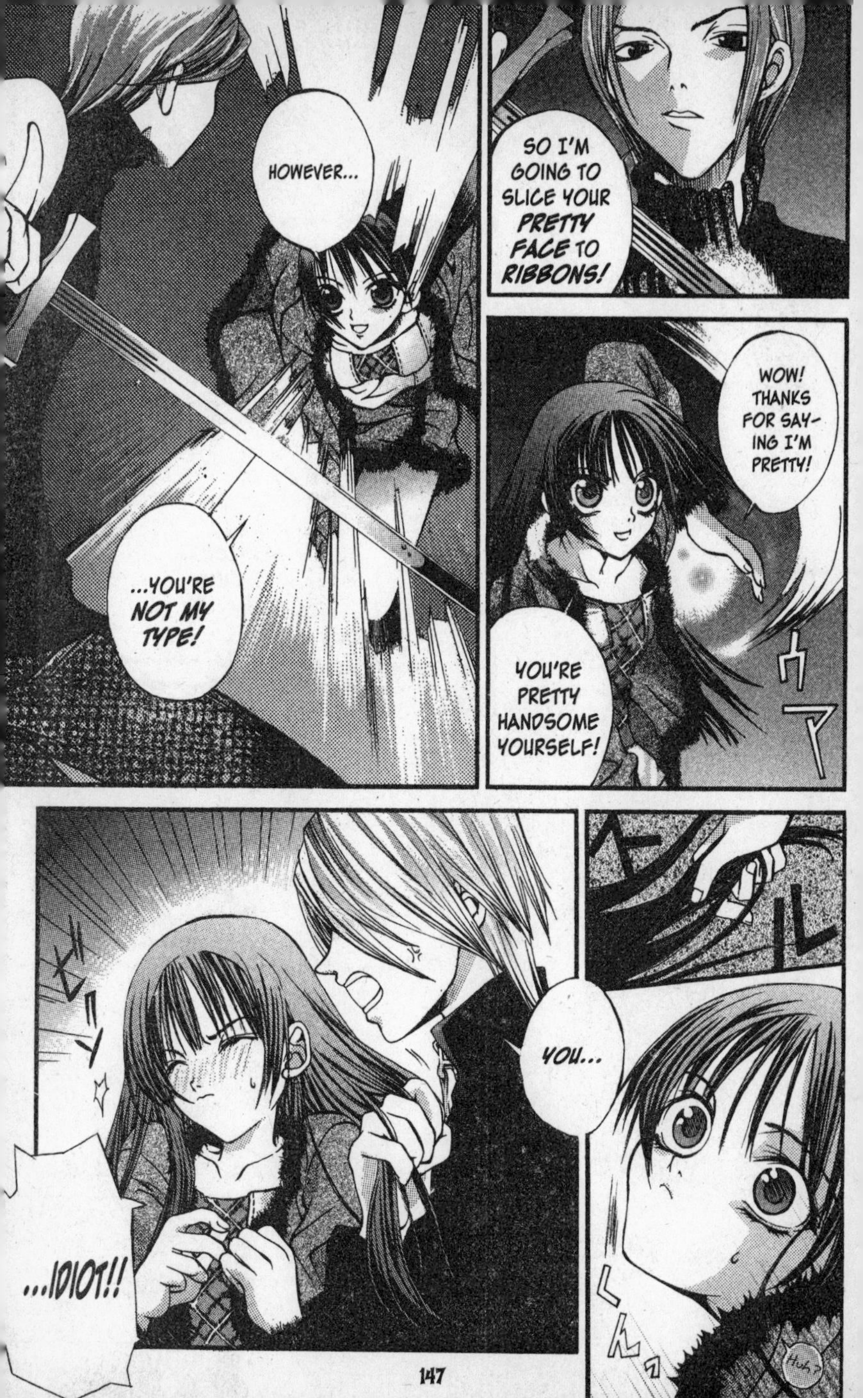
SO I'M GOING TO SLICE YOUR PRETTY FACE TO RIBBONS!
WOW! THANKS FOR SAYING I'M PRETTY!
YOU'RE PRETTY HANDSOME YOURSELF!
HOWEVER...
...YOU'RE NOT MY TYPE!
YOU...
Huh?
...IDIOT!!

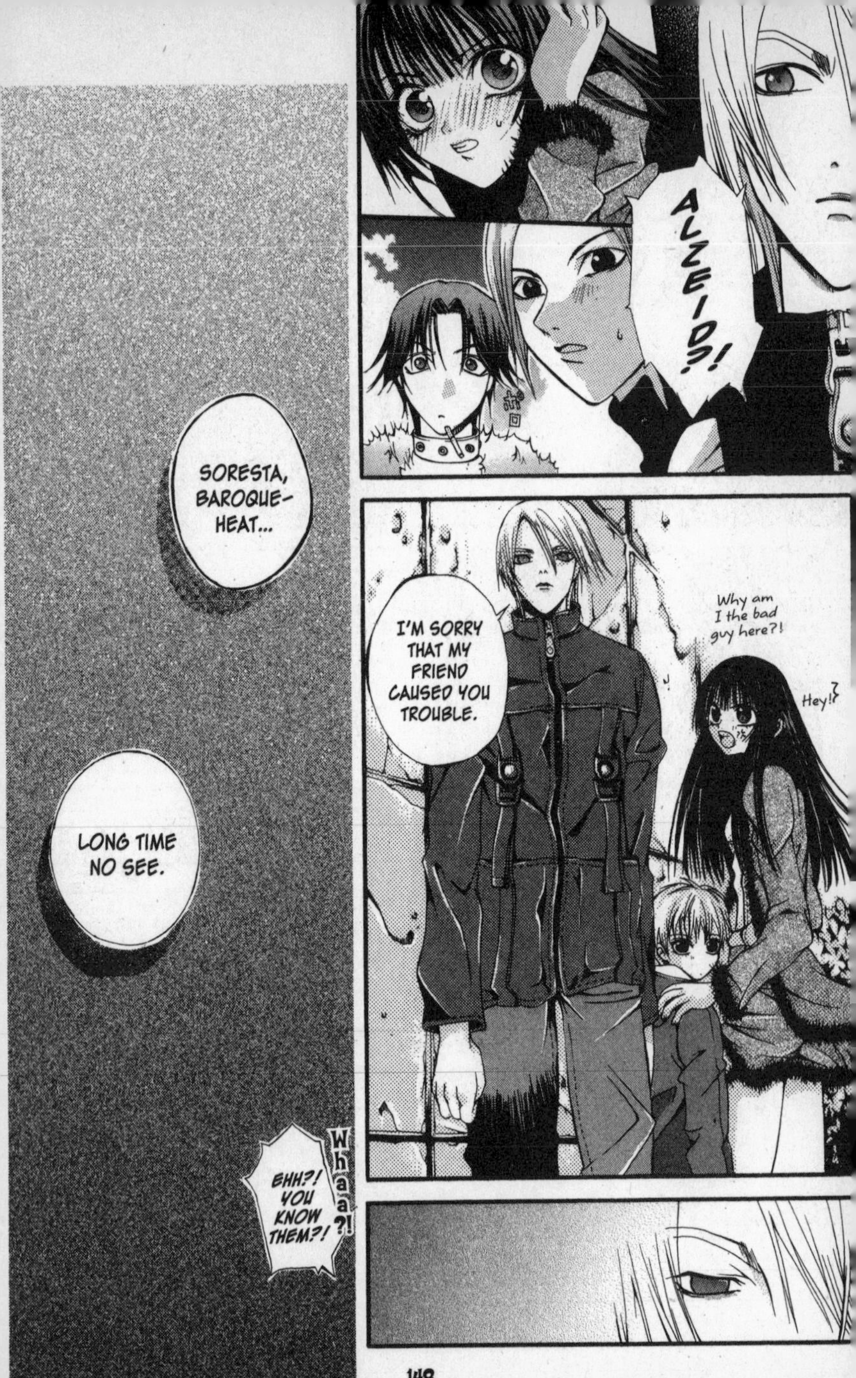
ALZEIDS?!
Why am I the bad guy here?!
Hey!?
I'M SORRY THAT MY FRIEND CAUSED YOU TROUBLE.
SORESTA, BAROQUE-HEAT...
LONG TIME NO SEE.
Whaaa?!
EHH?! YOU KNOW THEM?!

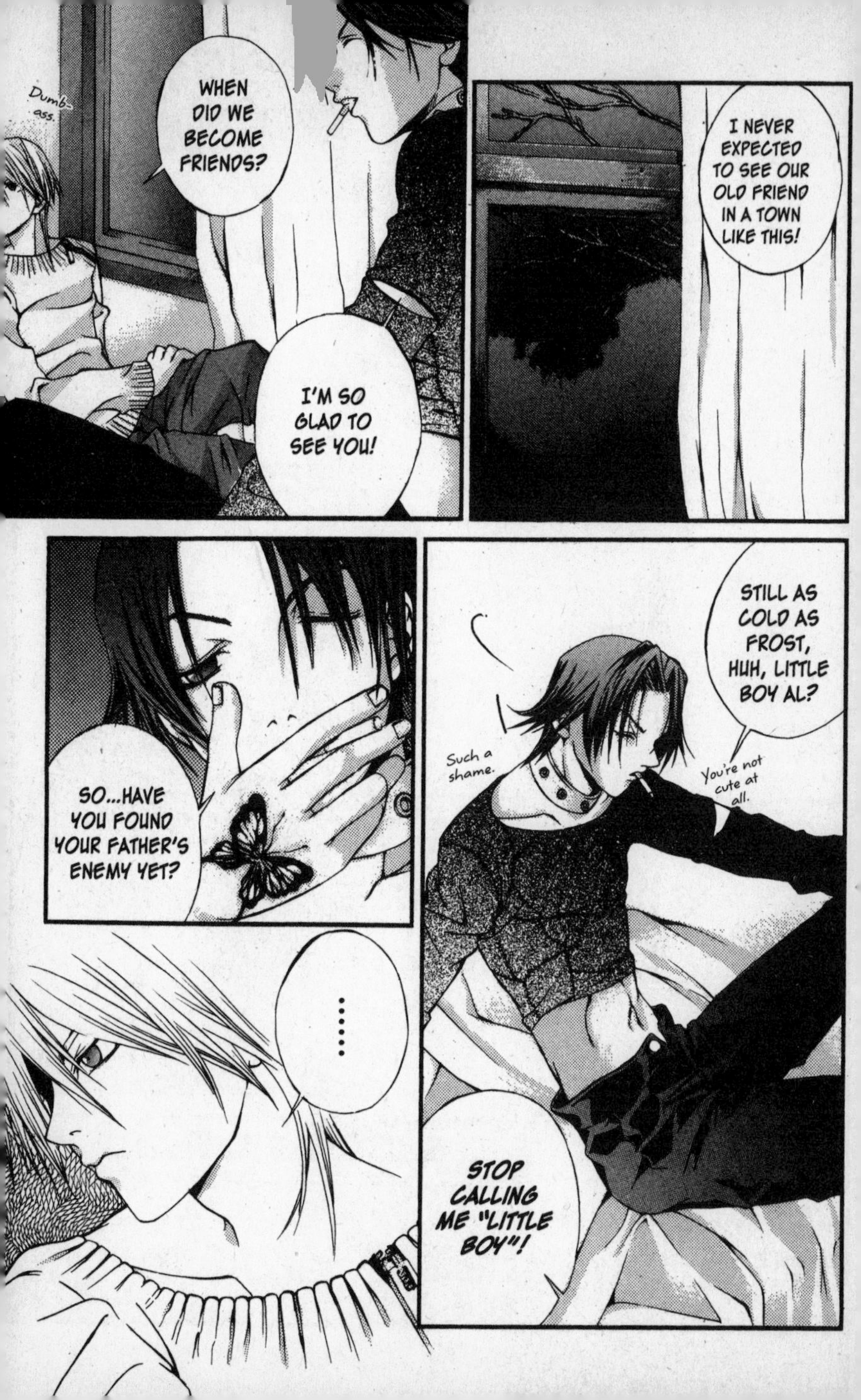

I NEVER EXPECTED TO SEE OUR OLD FRIEND IN A TOWN LIKE THIS!
WHEN DID WE BECOME FRIENDS?
Dumb-ass.
I'M SO GLAD TO SEE YOU!
STILL AS COLD AS FROST, HUH, LITTLE BOY AL?
You're not cute at all.
Such a shame.
STOP CALLING ME "LITTLE BOY"!
SO...HAVE YOU FOUND YOUR FATHER'S ENEMY YET?
......

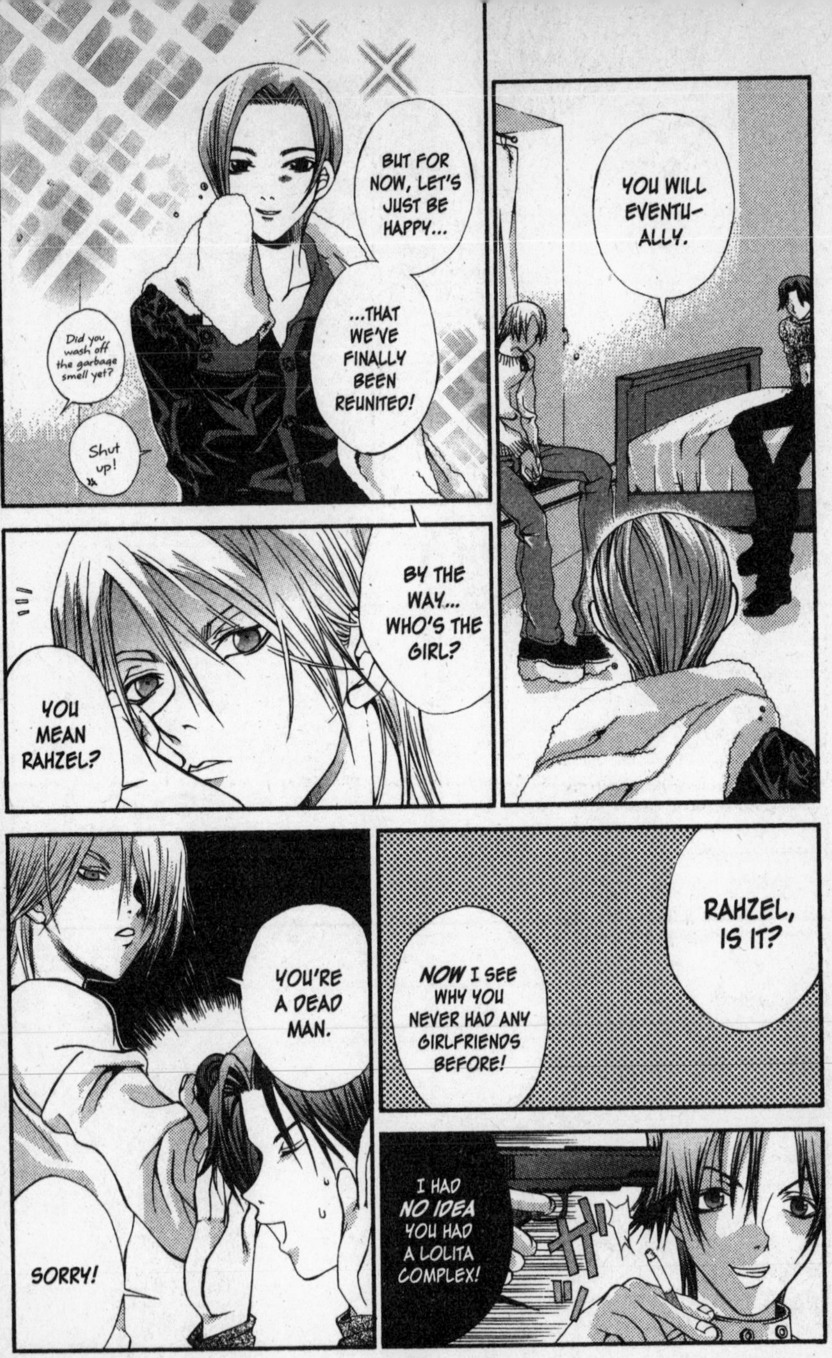

YOU WILL EVENTU-ALLY.
BUT FOR NOW, LET'S JUST BE HAPPY...
...THAT WE'VE FINALLY BEEN REUNITED!
Did you wash off the garbage smell yet?
Shut up!
BY THE WAY... WHO'S THE GIRL?
YOU MEAN RAHZEL?
RAHZEL, IS IT?
NOW I SEE WHY YOU NEVER HAD ANY GIRLFRIENDS BEFORE!
I HAD NO IDEA YOU HAD A LOLITA COMPLEX!
YOU'RE A DEAD MAN.
SORRY!

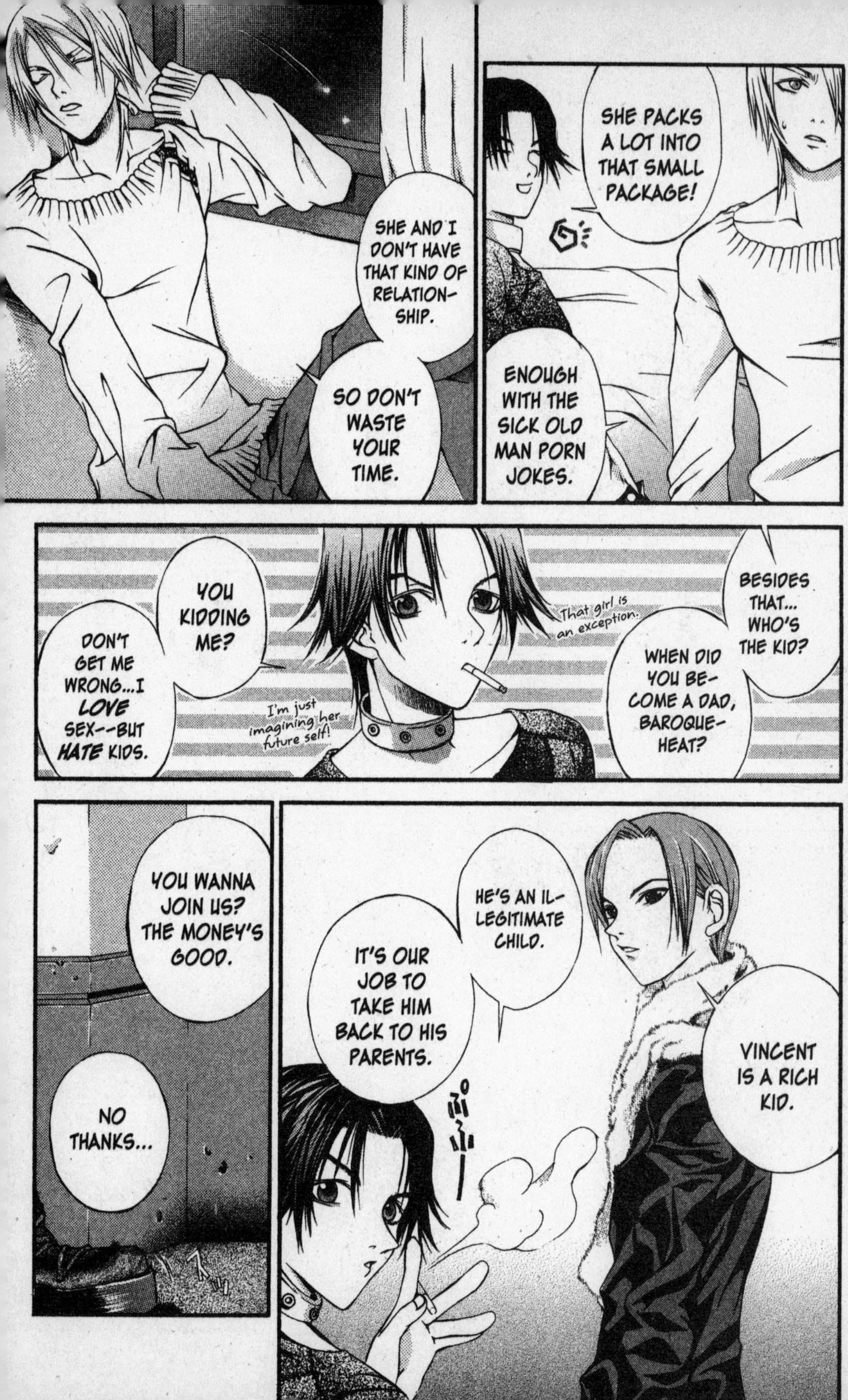
SHE PACKS A LOT INTO THAT SMALL PACKAGE!
ENOUGH WITH THE SICK OLD MAN PORN JOKES.
SHE AND I DON'T HAVE THAT KIND OF RELATION-SHIP.
SO DON'T WASTE YOUR TIME.
BESIDES THAT... WHO'S THE KID?
WHEN DID YOU BE-COME A DAD, BAROQUE-HEAT?
That girl is an exception.
YOU KIDDING ME?
I'm just imagining her future self!
DON'T GET ME WRONG...I *LOVE* SEX--BUT *HATE* KIDS.
VINCENT IS A RICH KID.
HE'S AN IL-LEGITIMATE CHILD.
IT'S OUR JOB TO TAKE HIM BACK TO HIS PARENTS.
YOU WANNA JOIN US? THE MONEY'S GOOD.
NO THANKS...

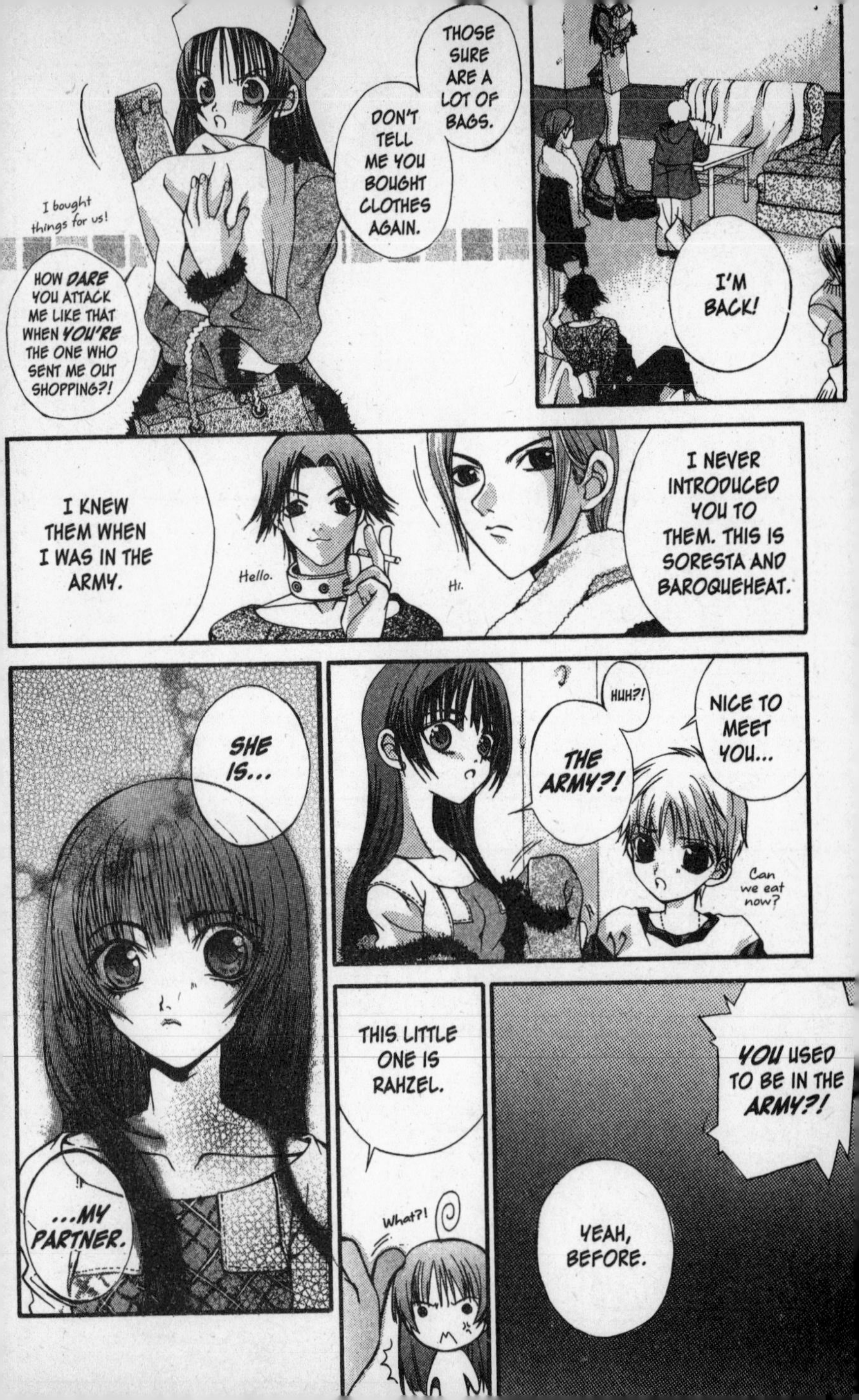
I'M BACK!
THOSE SURE ARE A LOT OF BAGS.
DON'T TELL ME YOU BOUGHT CLOTHES AGAIN.
I bought things for us!
HOW *DARE* YOU ATTACK ME LIKE THAT WHEN *YOU'RE* THE ONE WHO SENT ME OUT SHOPPING?!
I NEVER INTRODUCED YOU TO THEM. THIS IS SORESTA AND BAROQUEHEAT.
Hi.
Hello.
I KNEW THEM WHEN I WAS IN THE ARMY.
NICE TO MEET YOU...
HUH?!
THE ARMY?!
Can we eat now?
YOU USED TO BE IN THE *ARMY?!*
YEAH, BEFORE.
THIS LITTLE ONE IS RAHZEL.
What?!
SHE IS...
...MY PARTNER.

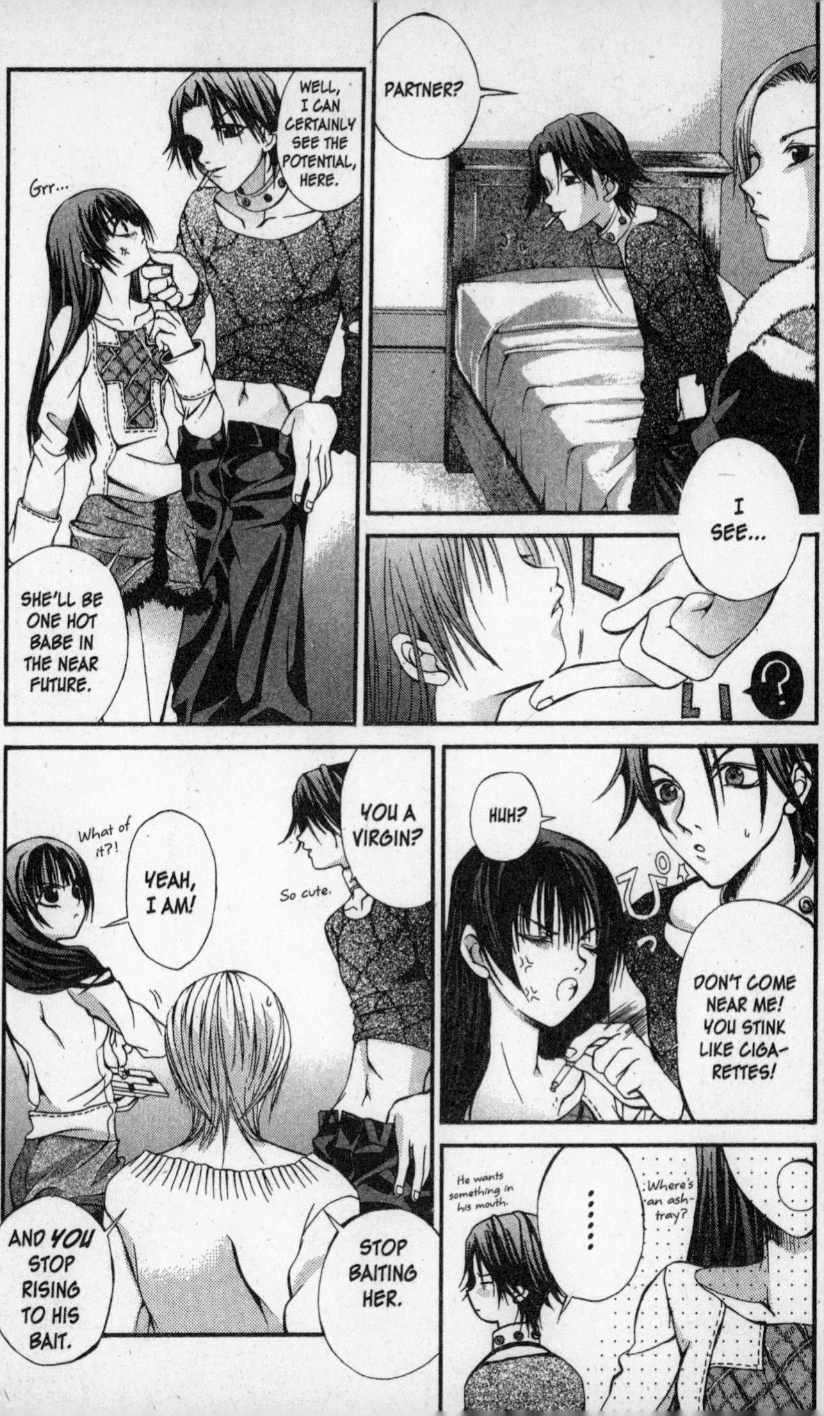
PARTNER?
I SEE...
?
WELL, I CAN CERTAINLY SEE THE POTENTIAL, HERE.
Grr...
SHE'LL BE ONE HOT BABE IN THE NEAR FUTURE.
HUH?
DON'T COME NEAR ME! YOU STINK LIKE CIGA-RETTES!
Where's an ash-tray?
......
He wants something in his mouth.
YOU A VIRGIN?
So cute.
YEAH, I AM!
What of it?!
STOP BAITING HER.
AND YOU STOP RISING TO HIS BAIT.

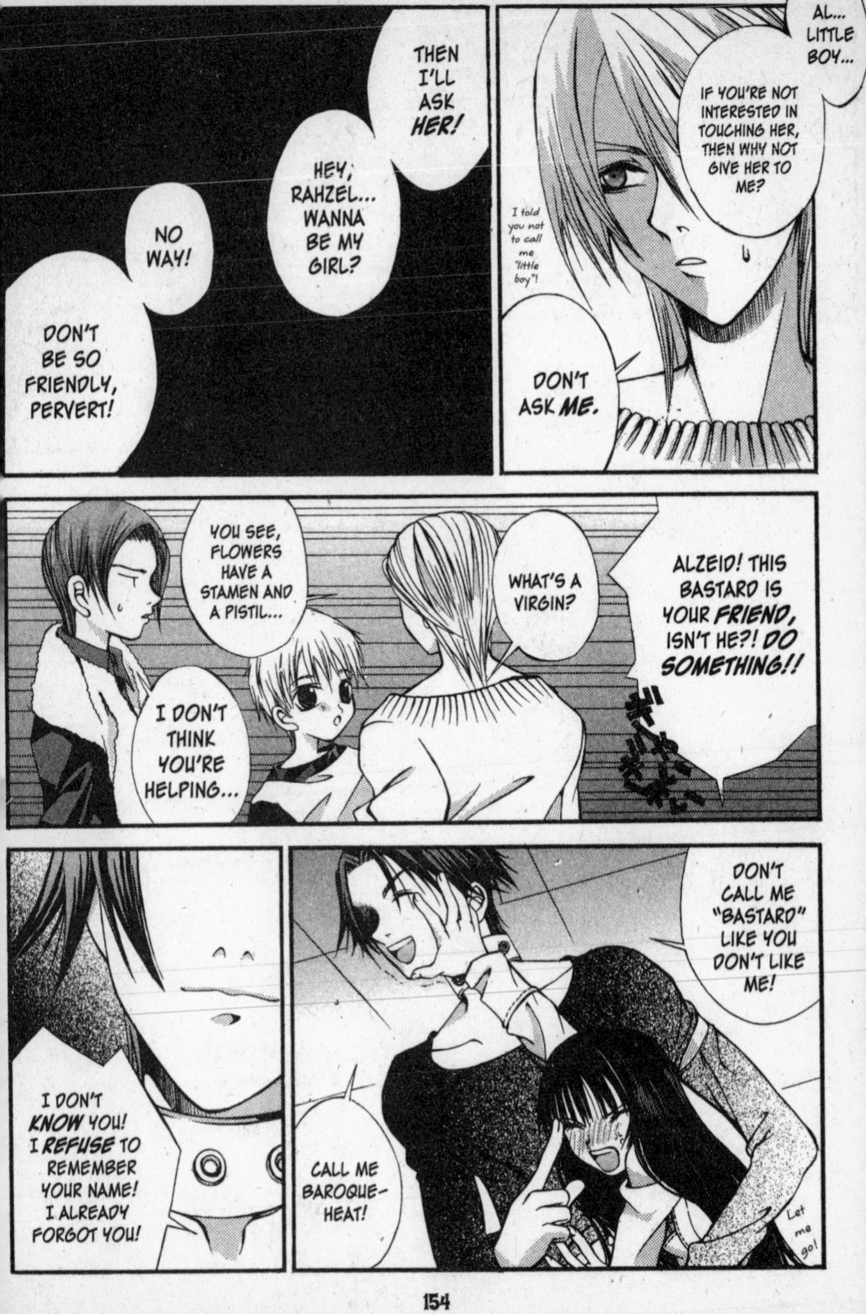
AL, AL... LITTLE BOY...
IF YOU'RE NOT INTERESTED IN TOUCHING HER, THEN WHY NOT GIVE HER TO ME?
I told you not to call me "little boy"!
DON'T ASK ME.
THEN I'LL ASK HER!
HEY, RAHZEL... WANNA BE MY GIRL?
NO WAY!
DON'T BE SO FRIENDLY, PERVERT!
ALZEID! THIS BASTARD IS YOUR FRIEND, ISN'T HE?! DO SOMETHING!!
WHAT'S A VIRGIN?
YOU SEE, FLOWERS HAVE A STAMEN AND A PISTIL...
I DON'T THINK YOU'RE HELPING...
DON'T CALL ME "BASTARD" LIKE YOU DON'T LIKE ME!
Let me go!
CALL ME BAROQUE-HEAT!
I DON'T KNOW YOU! I REFUSE TO REMEMBER YOUR NAME! I ALREADY FORGOT YOU!

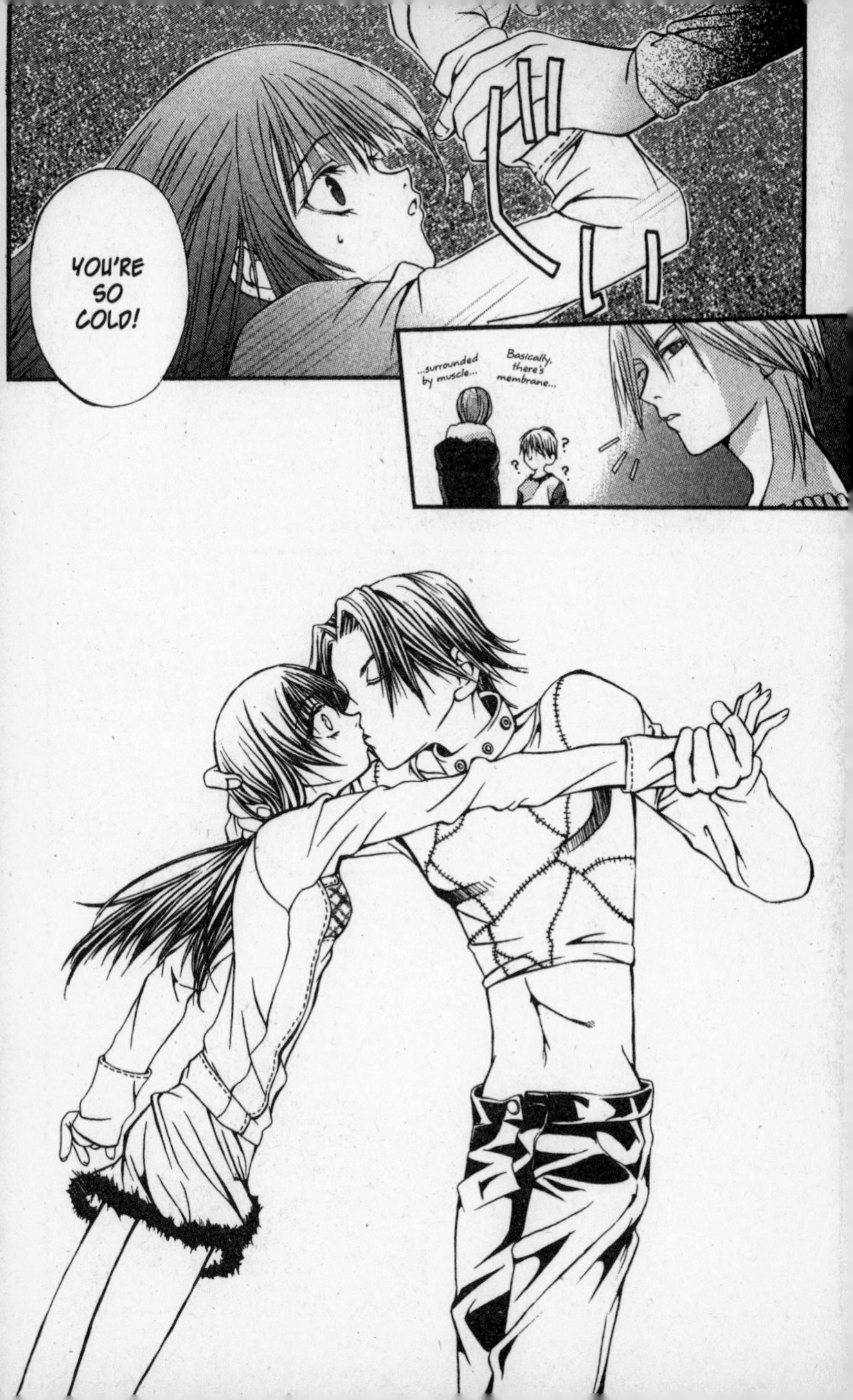
YOU'RE SO COLD!
Basically, there's membrane...
...surrounded by muscle...

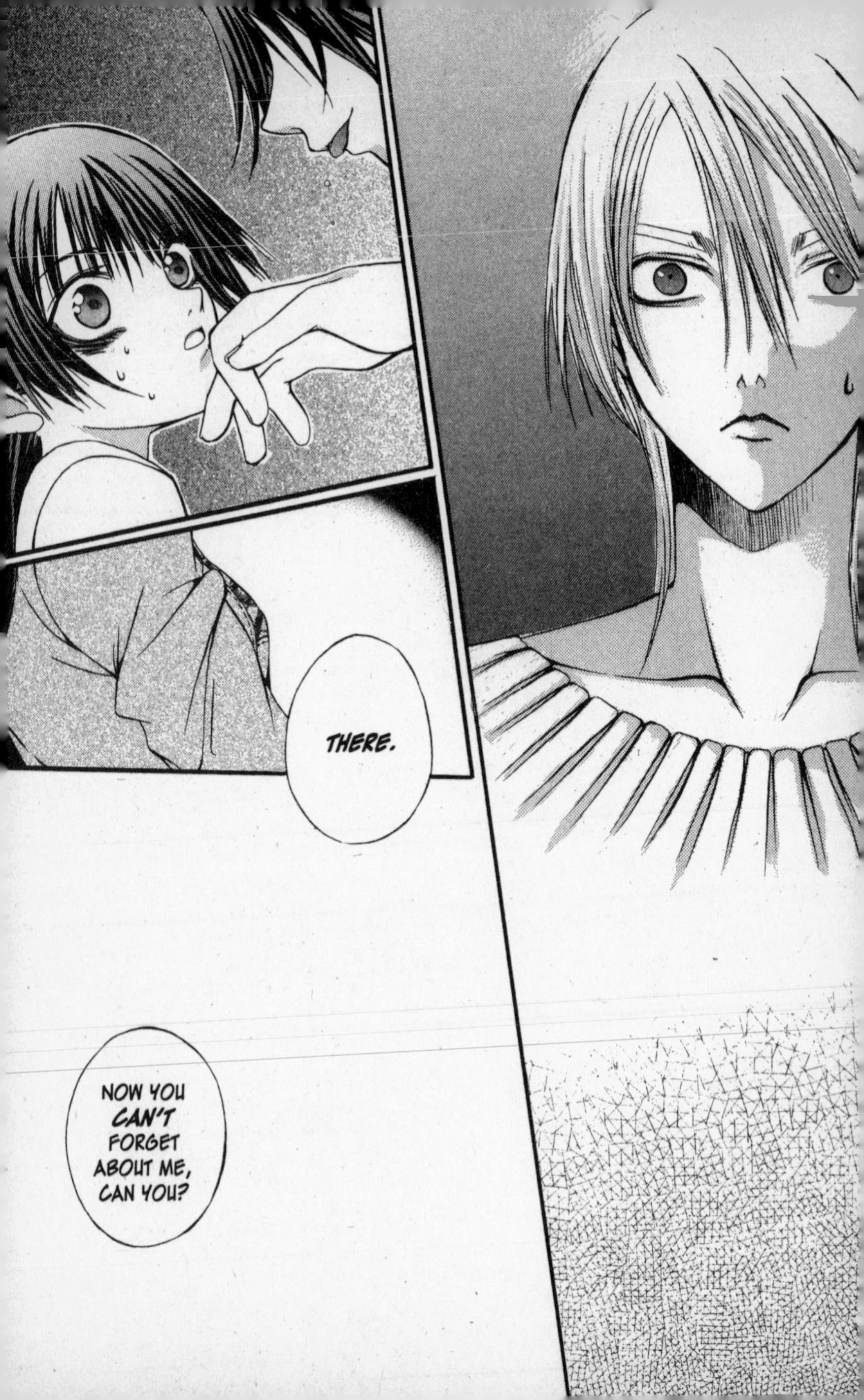
THERE.
NOW YOU CAN'T FORGET ABOUT ME, CAN YOU?

Chapter 7: Nowhere to Go~Part 2: Gamble

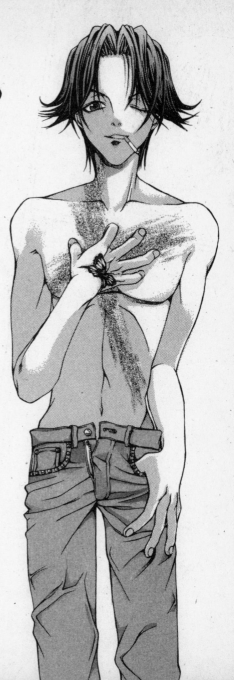

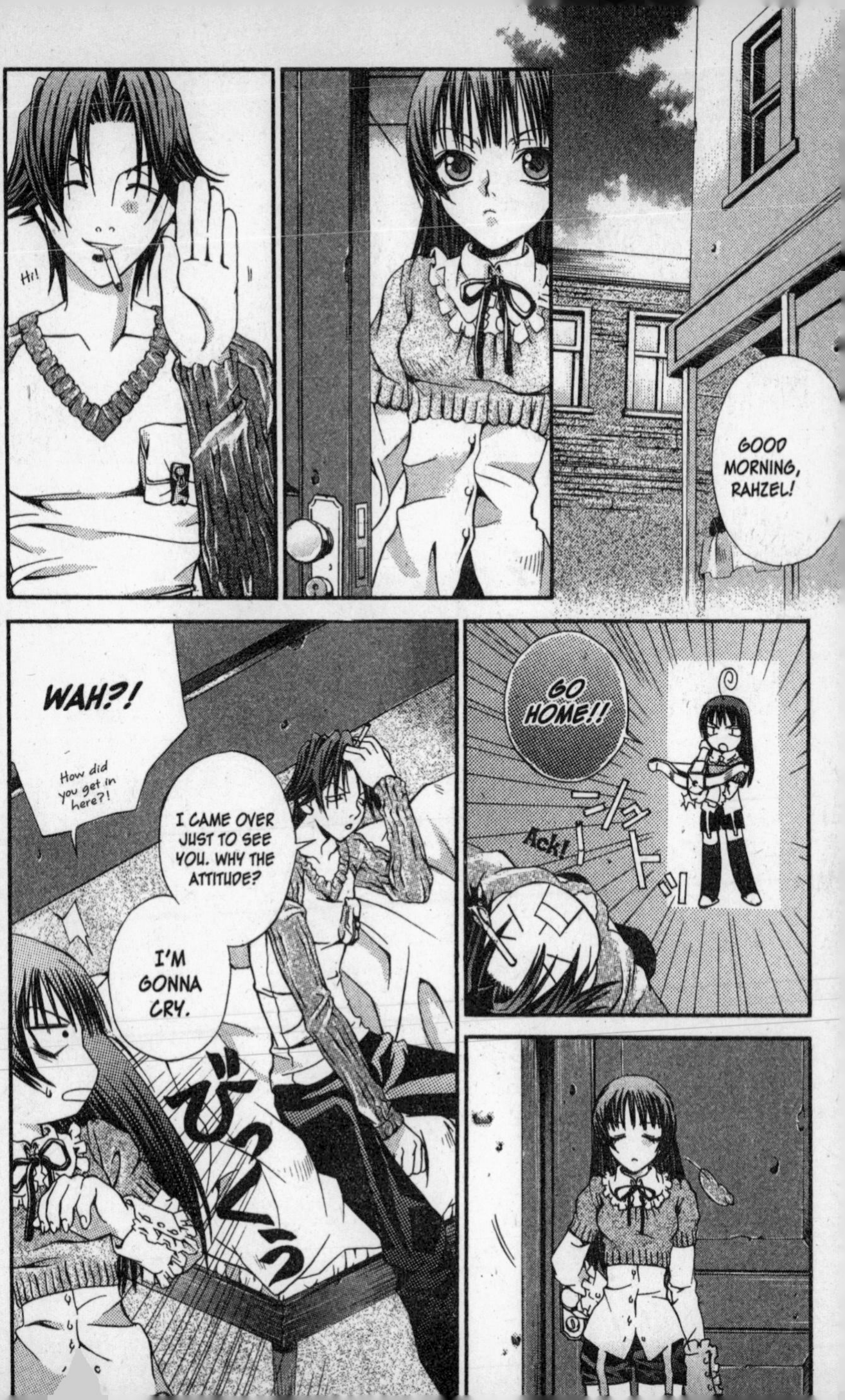
GOOD MORNING, RAHZEL!
Hi!
GO HOME!!
Ack!
WAH?!
How did you get in here?!
I CAME OVER JUST TO SEE YOU. WHY THE ATTITUDE?
I'M GONNA CRY.

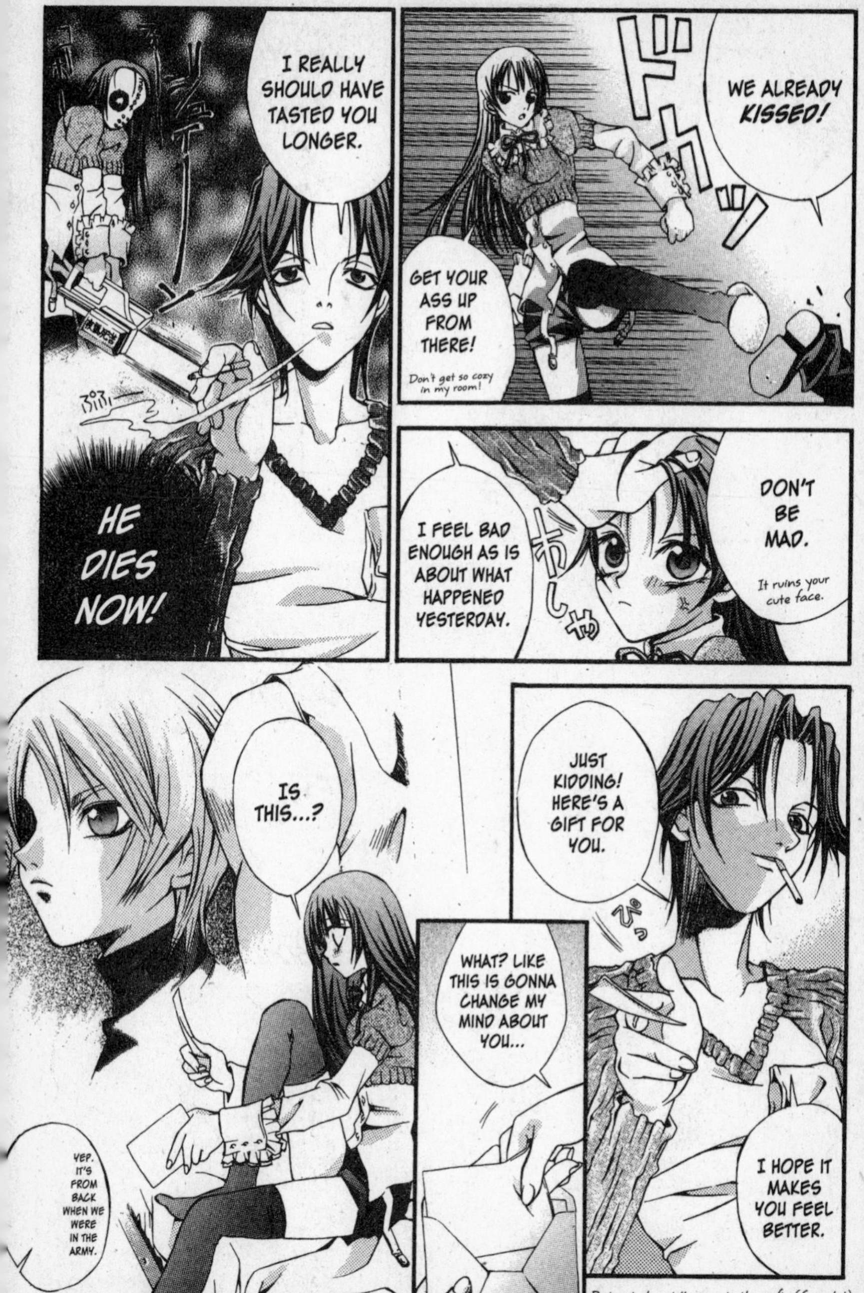
WE ALREADY KISSED!
GET YOUR ASS UP FROM THERE!
Don't get so cozy in my room!
DON'T BE MAD.
It ruins your cute face.
I FEEL BAD ENOUGH AS IS ABOUT WHAT HAPPENED YESTERDAY.
I REALLY SHOULD HAVE TASTED YOU LONGER.
HE DIES NOW!
JUST KIDDING! HERE'S A GIFT FOR YOU.
I HOPE IT MAKES YOU FEEL BETTER.
WHAT? LIKE THIS IS GONNA CHANGE MY MIND ABOUT YOU...
IS THIS...?
YEP. IT'S FROM BACK WHEN WE WERE IN THE ARMY.
But yet she still accepts the gift. (Greedy!)

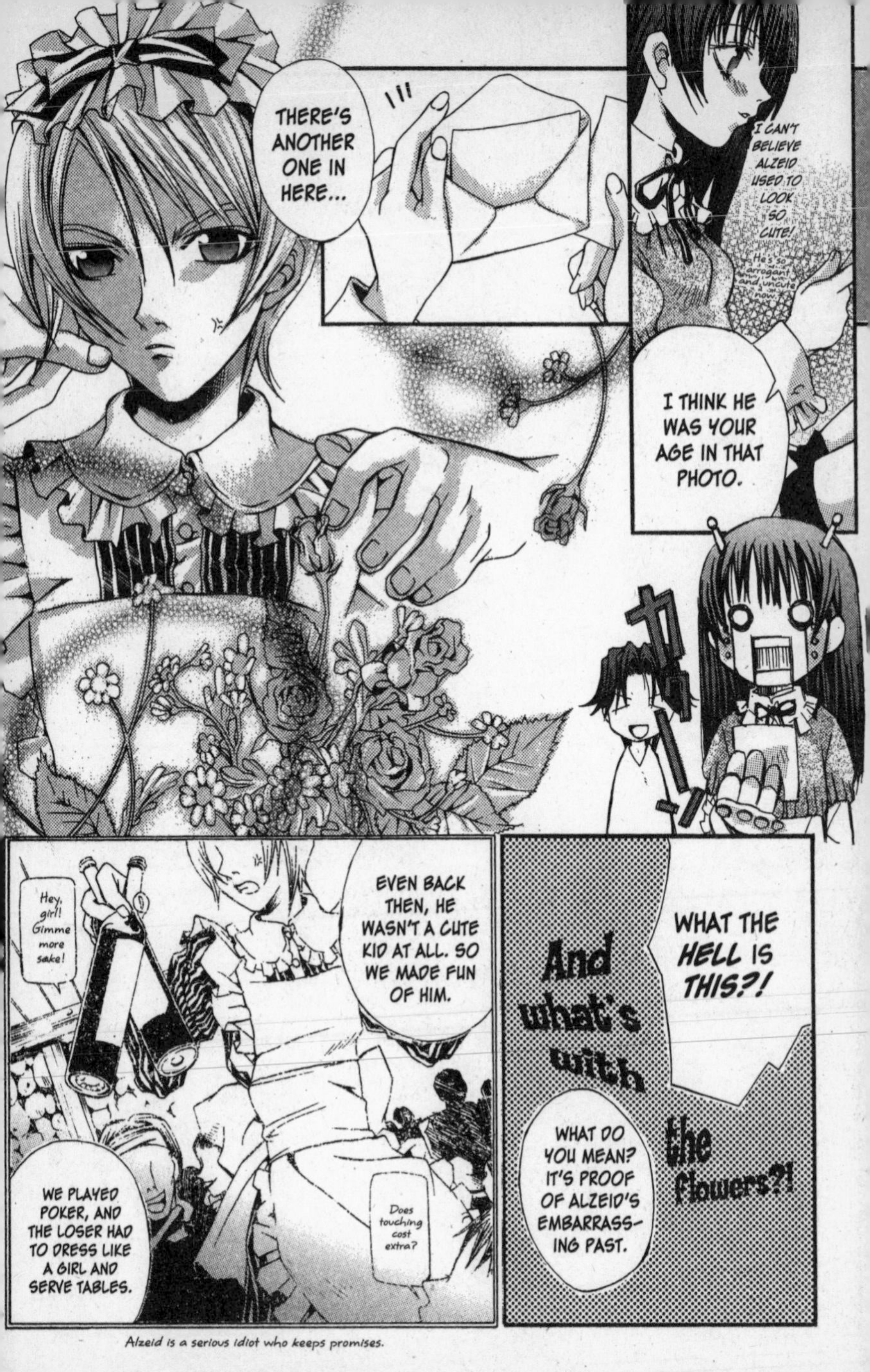
I CAN'T BELIEVE ALZEID USED TO LOOK SO CUTE!
He's so arrogant and uncute now.
I THINK HE WAS YOUR AGE IN THAT PHOTO.
THERE'S ANOTHER ONE IN HERE...
WHAT THE HELL IS THIS?!
And what's with the flowers?!
WHAT DO YOU MEAN? IT'S PROOF OF ALZEID'S EMBARRASSING PAST.
EVEN BACK THEN, HE WASN'T A CUTE KID AT ALL. SO WE MADE FUN OF HIM.
Hey, girl! Gimme more sake!
Does touching cost extra?
WE PLAYED POKER, AND THE LOSER HAD TO DRESS LIKE A GIRL AND SERVE TABLES.

Alzeid is a serious idiot who keeps promises.

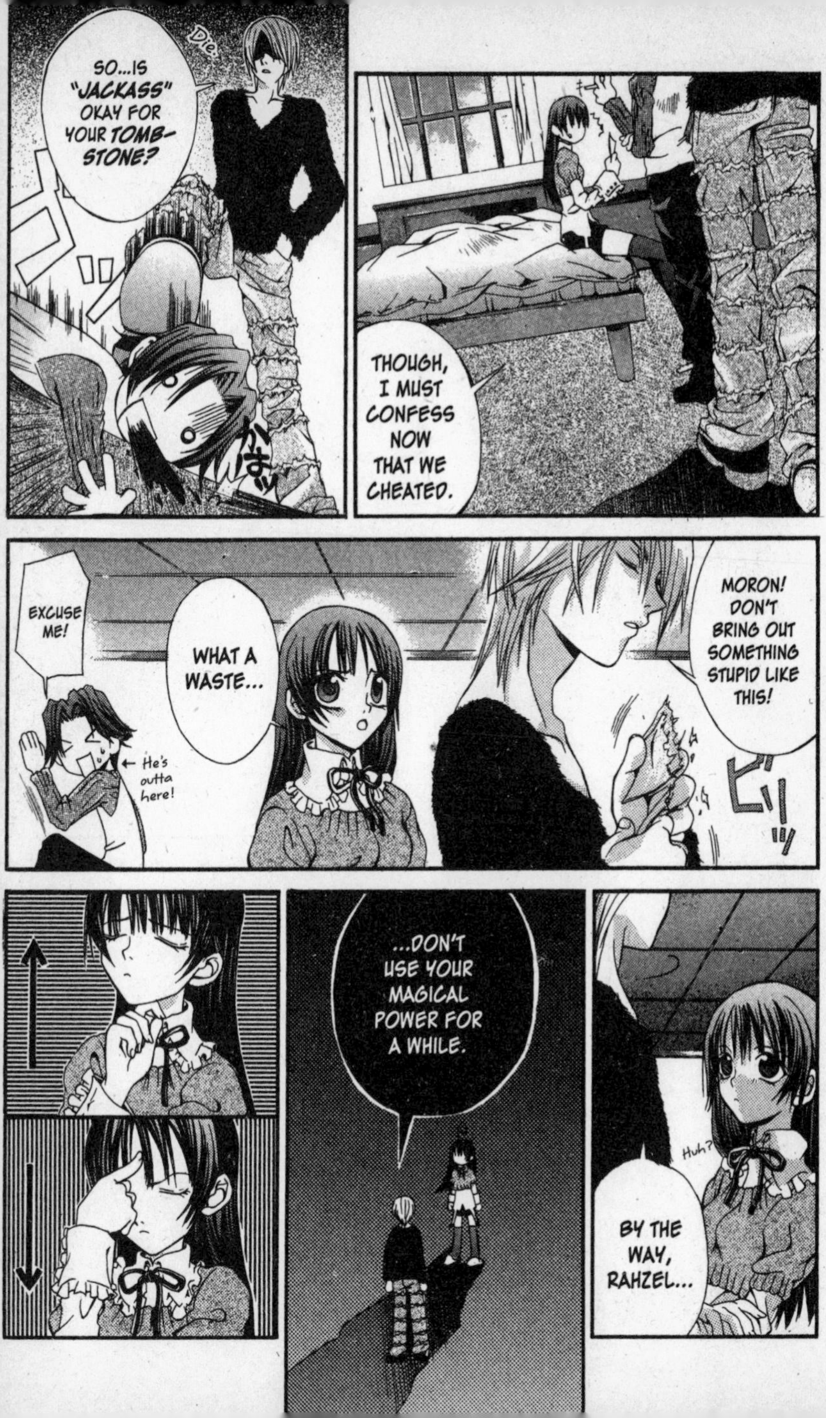
THOUGH, I MUST CONFESS NOW THAT WE CHEATED.
Die.
SO...IS "JACKASS" OKAY FOR YOUR TOMBSTONE?
MORON! DON'T BRING OUT SOMETHING STUPID LIKE THIS!
WHAT A WASTE...
EXCUSE ME!
← He's outta here!
Huh?
BY THE WAY, RAHZEL...
...DON'T USE YOUR MAGICAL POWER FOR A WHILE.

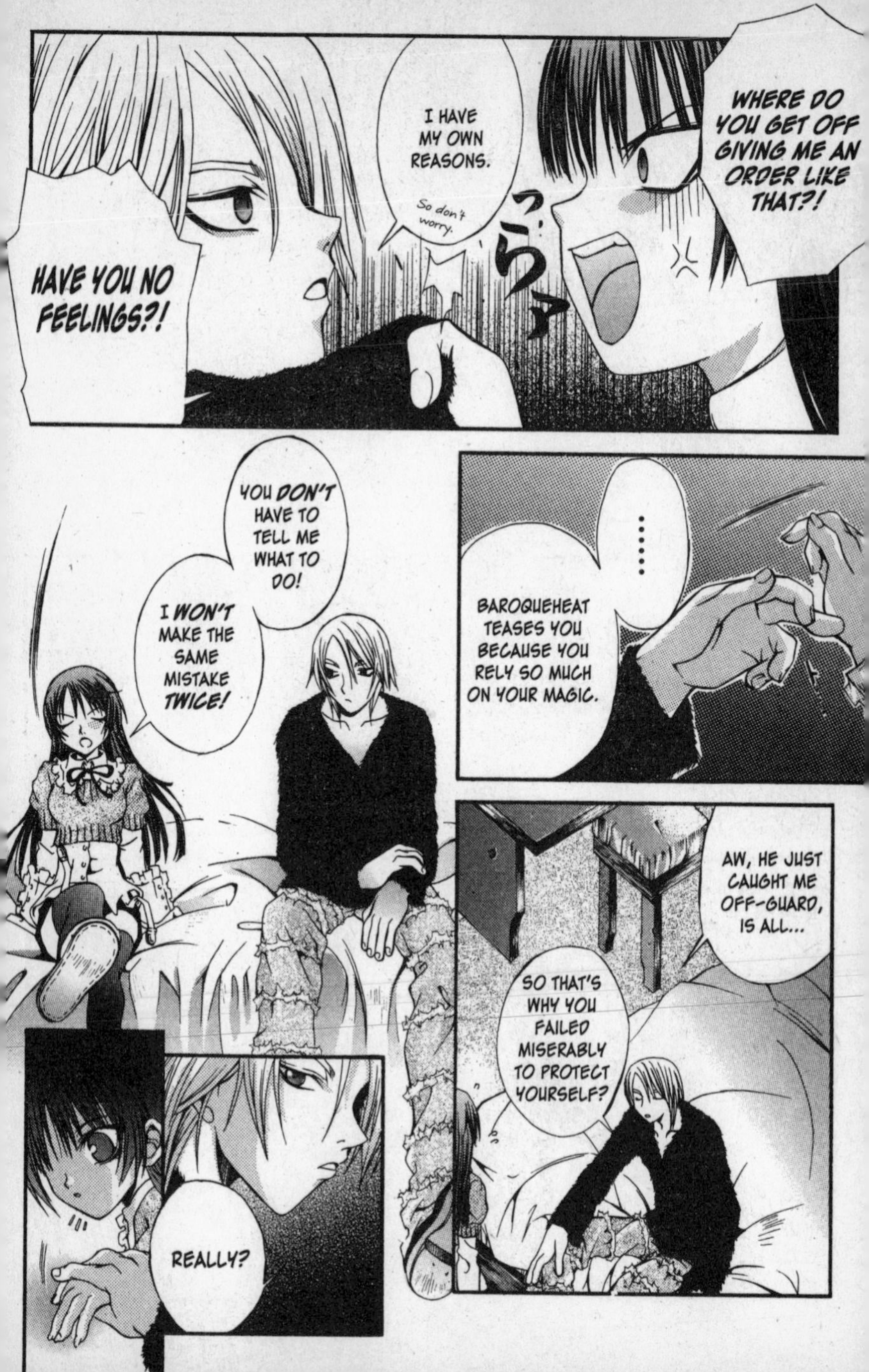
WHERE DO YOU GET OFF GIVING ME AN ORDER LIKE THAT?!
I HAVE MY OWN REASONS.
So don't worry.
HAVE YOU NO FEELINGS?!
......
BAROQUEHEAT TEASES YOU BECAUSE YOU RELY SO MUCH ON YOUR MAGIC.
AW, HE JUST CAUGHT ME OFF-GUARD, IS ALL...
SO THAT'S WHY YOU FAILED MISERABLY TO PROTECT YOURSELF?
YOU DON'T HAVE TO TELL ME WHAT TO DO!
I WON'T MAKE THE SAME MISTAKE TWICE!
REALLY?

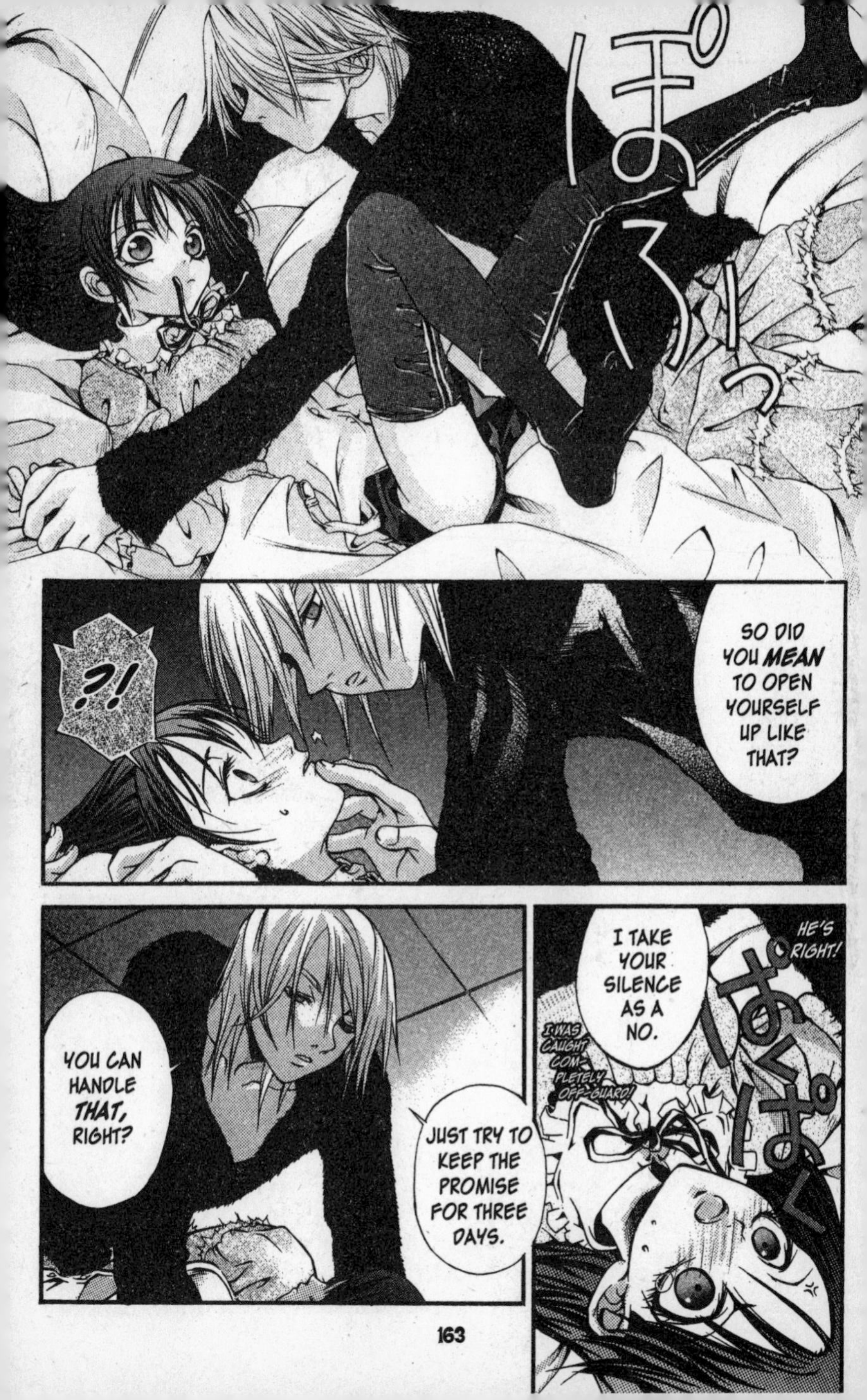
ぽふっ
SO DID YOU *MEAN* TO OPEN YOURSELF UP LIKE THAT?
?!
I TAKE YOUR SILENCE AS A NO.
HE'S RIGHT!
I WAS CAUGHT COMPLETELY OFF-GUARD!
JUST TRY TO KEEP THE PROMISE FOR THREE DAYS.
YOU CAN HANDLE *THAT*, RIGHT?

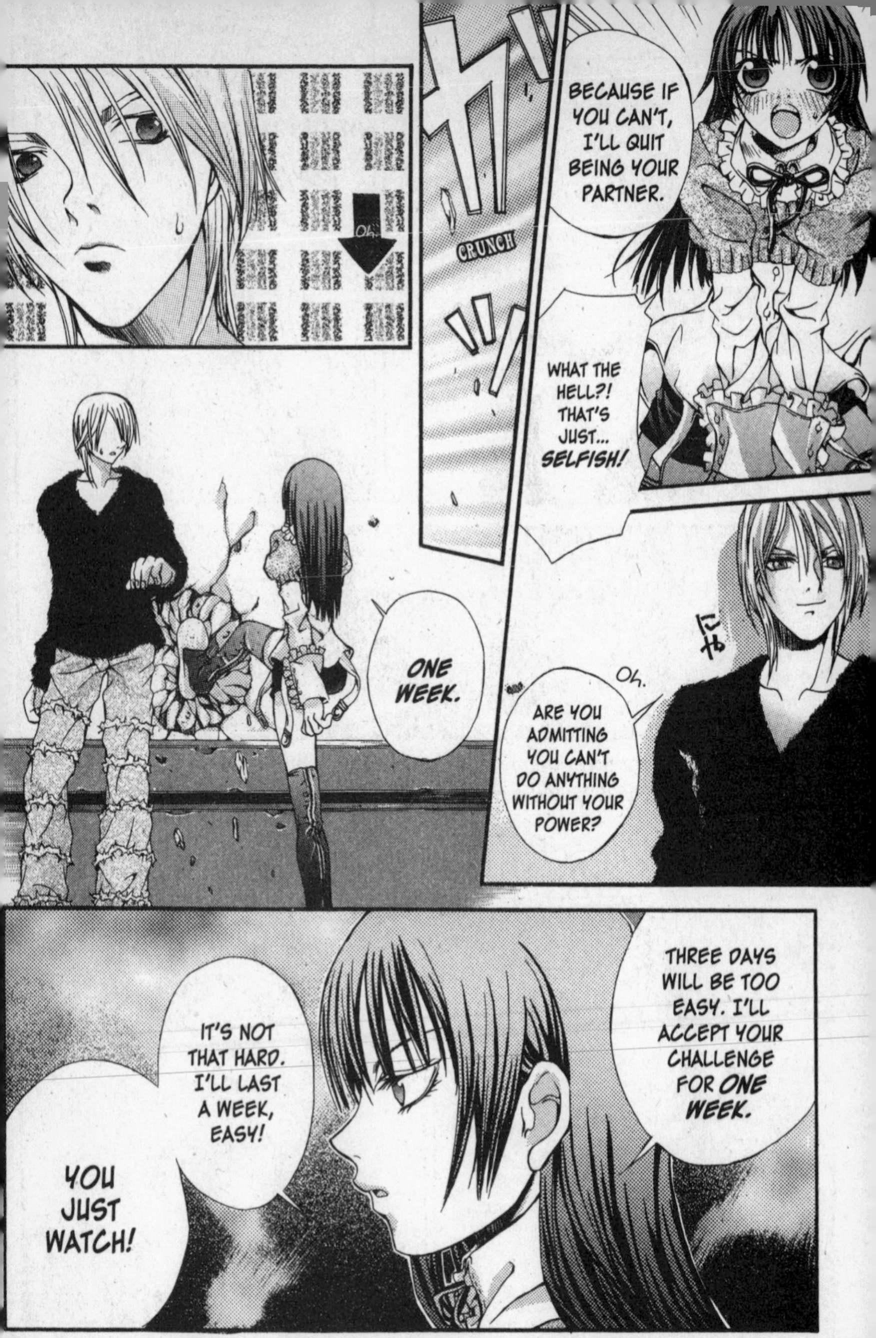
BECAUSE IF YOU CAN'T, I'LL QUIT BEING YOUR PARTNER.
WHAT THE HELL?! THAT'S JUST... SELFISH!
Oh.
ARE YOU ADMITTING YOU CAN'T DO ANYTHING WITHOUT YOUR POWER?
CRUNCH
Oh.
ONE WEEK.
THREE DAYS WILL BE TOO EASY. I'LL ACCEPT YOUR CHALLENGE FOR ONE WEEK.
IT'S NOT THAT HARD. I'LL LAST A WEEK, EASY!
YOU JUST WATCH!

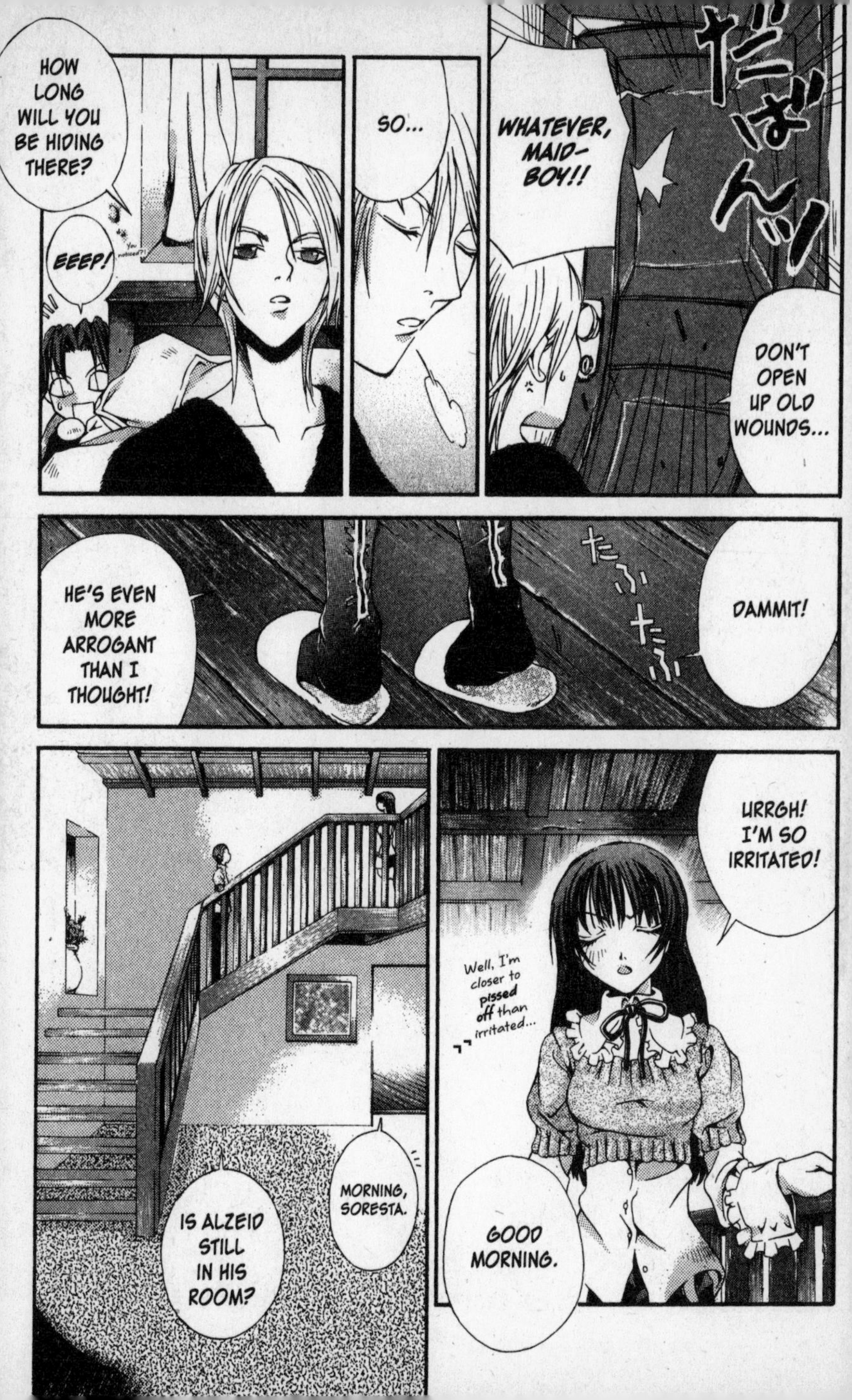
だばんッ!
WHATEVER, MAID-BOY!!
DON'T OPEN UP OLD WOUNDS...
SO...
HOW LONG WILL YOU BE HIDING THERE?
EEEP!
You noticed?!
DAMMIT!
たふたふ
HE'S EVEN MORE ARROGANT THAN I THOUGHT!
URRGH! I'M SO IRRITATED!
Well, I'm closer to pissed off than irritated...
GOOD MORNING.
MORNING, SORESTA.
IS ALZEID STILL IN HIS ROOM?

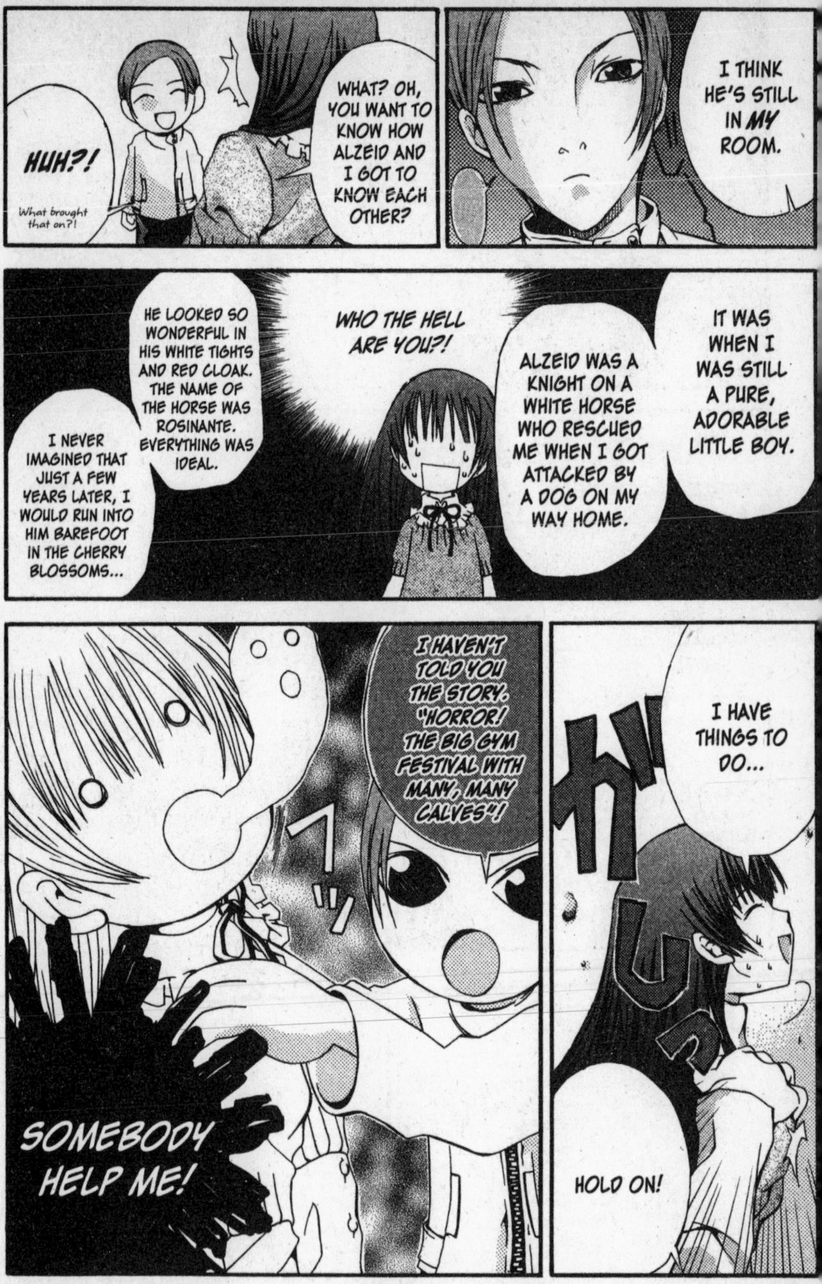
I THINK HE'S STILL IN *MY* ROOM.
WHAT? OH, YOU WANT TO KNOW HOW ALZEID AND I GOT TO KNOW EACH OTHER?
HUH?!
What brought that on?!
IT WAS WHEN I WAS STILL A PURE, ADORABLE LITTLE BOY.
ALZEID WAS A KNIGHT ON A WHITE HORSE WHO RESCUED ME WHEN I GOT ATTACKED BY A DOG ON MY WAY HOME.
WHO THE HELL ARE YOU?!
HE LOOKED SO WONDERFUL IN HIS WHITE TIGHTS AND RED CLOAK. THE NAME OF THE HORSE WAS ROSINANTE. EVERYTHING WAS IDEAL.
I NEVER IMAGINED THAT JUST A FEW YEARS LATER, I WOULD RUN INTO HIM BAREFOOT IN THE CHERRY BLOSSOMS...
I HAVE THINGS TO DO...
HOLD ON!
I HAVEN'T TOLD YOU THE STORY. "HORROR! THE BIG GYM FESTIVAL WITH MANY, MANY CALVES"!
SOMEBODY HELP ME!

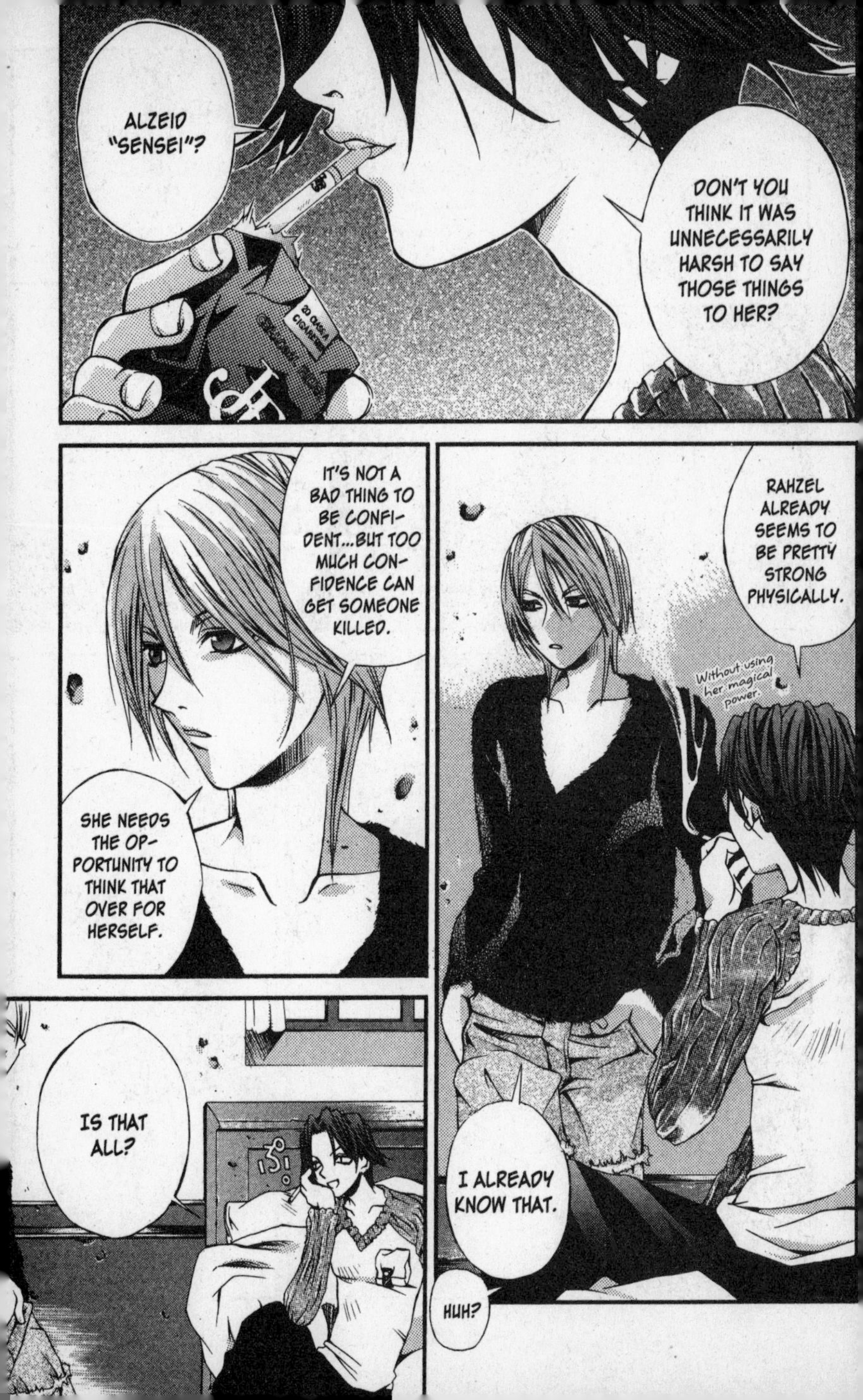
ALZEID "SENSEI"?
DON'T YOU THINK IT WAS UNNECESSARILY HARSH TO SAY THOSE THINGS TO HER?
RAHZEL ALREADY SEEMS TO BE PRETTY STRONG PHYSICALLY.
Without using her magical power.
I ALREADY KNOW THAT.
HUH?
IT'S NOT A BAD THING TO BE CONFI-DENT...BUT TOO MUCH CON-FIDENCE CAN GET SOMEONE KILLED.
SHE NEEDS THE OP-PORTUNITY TO THINK THAT OVER FOR HERSELF.
IS THAT ALL?

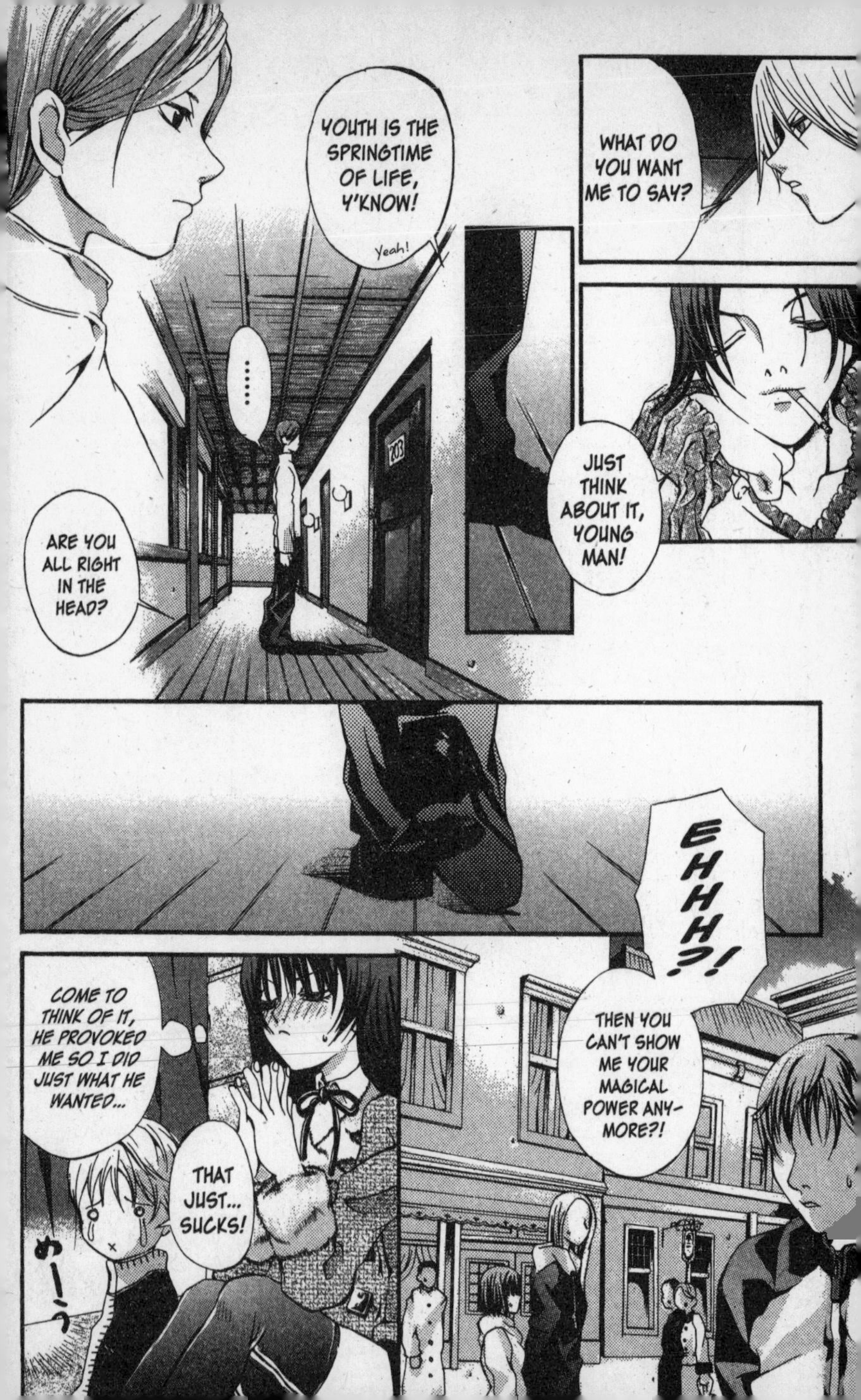
WHAT DO YOU WANT ME TO SAY?
JUST THINK ABOUT IT, YOUNG MAN!
YOUTH IS THE SPRINGTIME OF LIFE, Y'KNOW!
Yeah!
......
ARE YOU ALL RIGHT IN THE HEAD?
EHHHH?!
THEN YOU CAN'T SHOW ME YOUR MAGICAL POWER ANY-MORE?!
COME TO THINK OF IT, HE PROVOKED ME SO I DID JUST WHAT HE WANTED...
THAT JUST... SUCKS!
めーっ

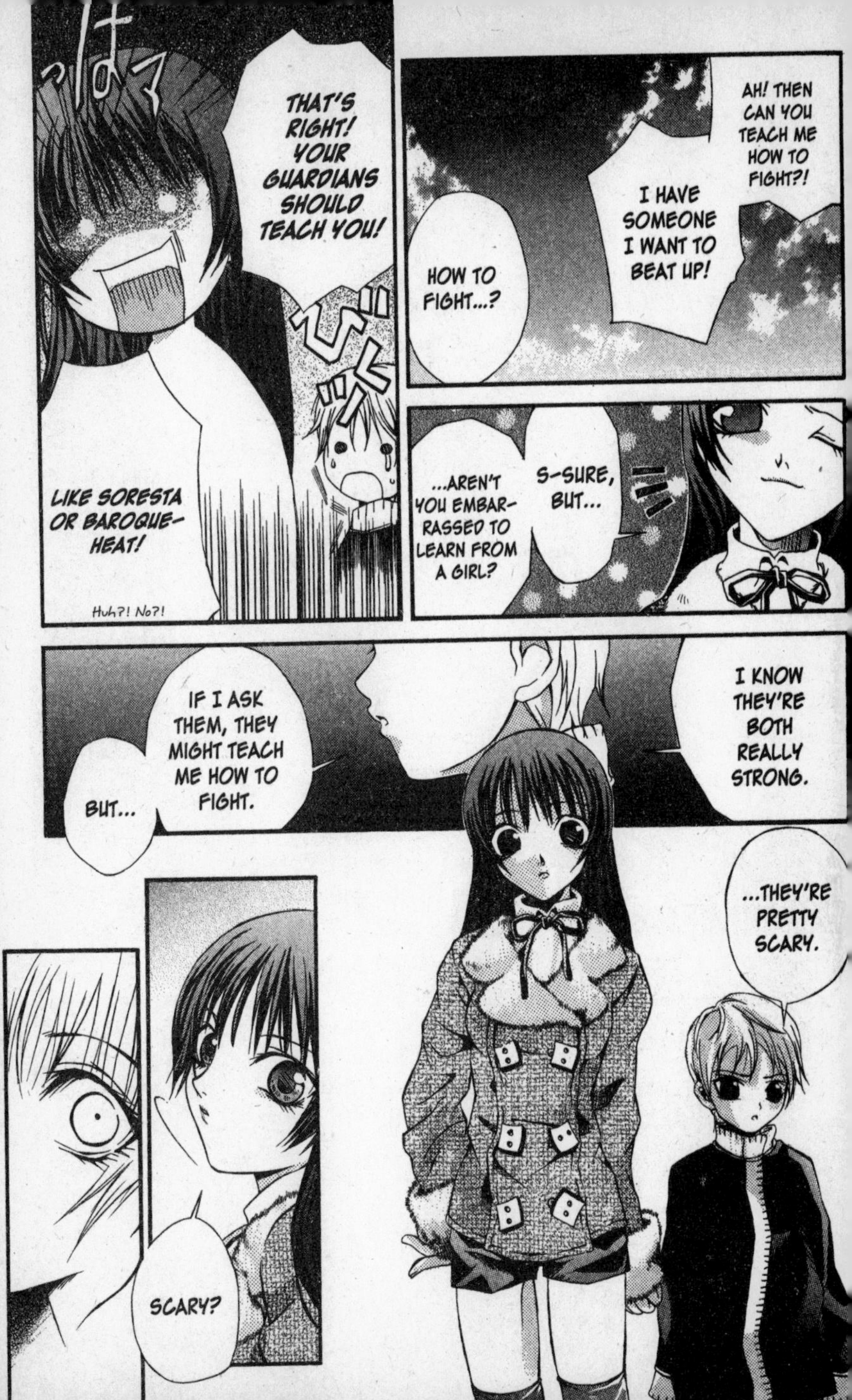
AH! THEN CAN YOU TEACH ME HOW TO FIGHT?!
I HAVE SOMEONE I WANT TO BEAT UP!
HOW TO FIGHT...?
S-SURE, BUT...
...AREN'T YOU EMBAR-RASSED TO LEARN FROM A GIRL?
THAT'S RIGHT! YOUR GUARDIANS SHOULD TEACH YOU!
LIKE SORESTA OR BAROQUE-HEAT!
Huh?! No?!
I KNOW THEY'RE BOTH REALLY STRONG.
IF I ASK THEM, THEY MIGHT TEACH ME HOW TO FIGHT.
BUT...
...THEY'RE PRETTY SCARY.
SCARY?

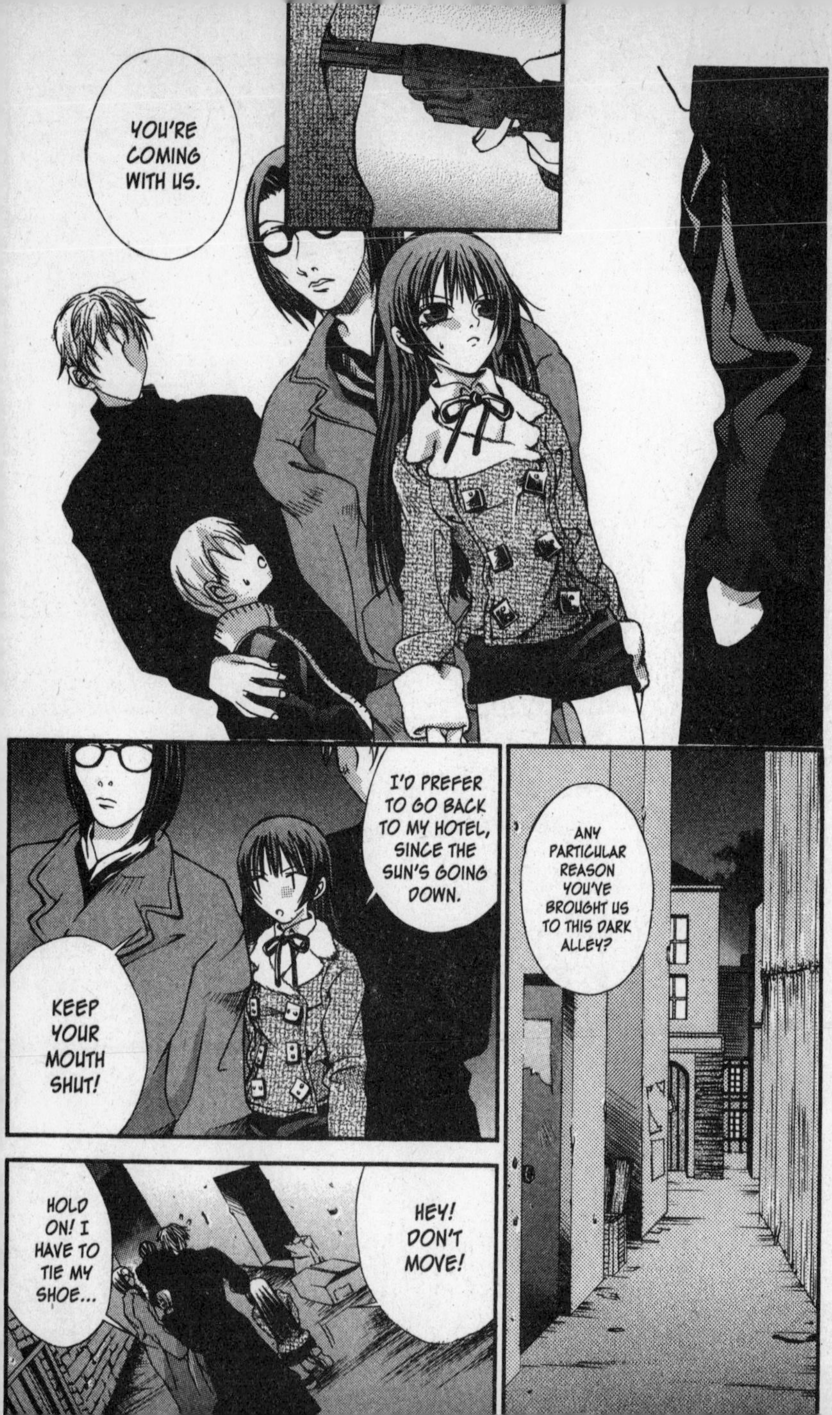
YOU'RE COMING WITH US.
ANY PARTICULAR REASON YOU'VE BROUGHT US TO THIS DARK ALLEY?
I'D PREFER TO GO BACK TO MY HOTEL, SINCE THE SUN'S GOING DOWN.
KEEP YOUR MOUTH SHUT!
HEY! DON'T MOVE!
HOLD ON! I HAVE TO TIE MY SHOE...

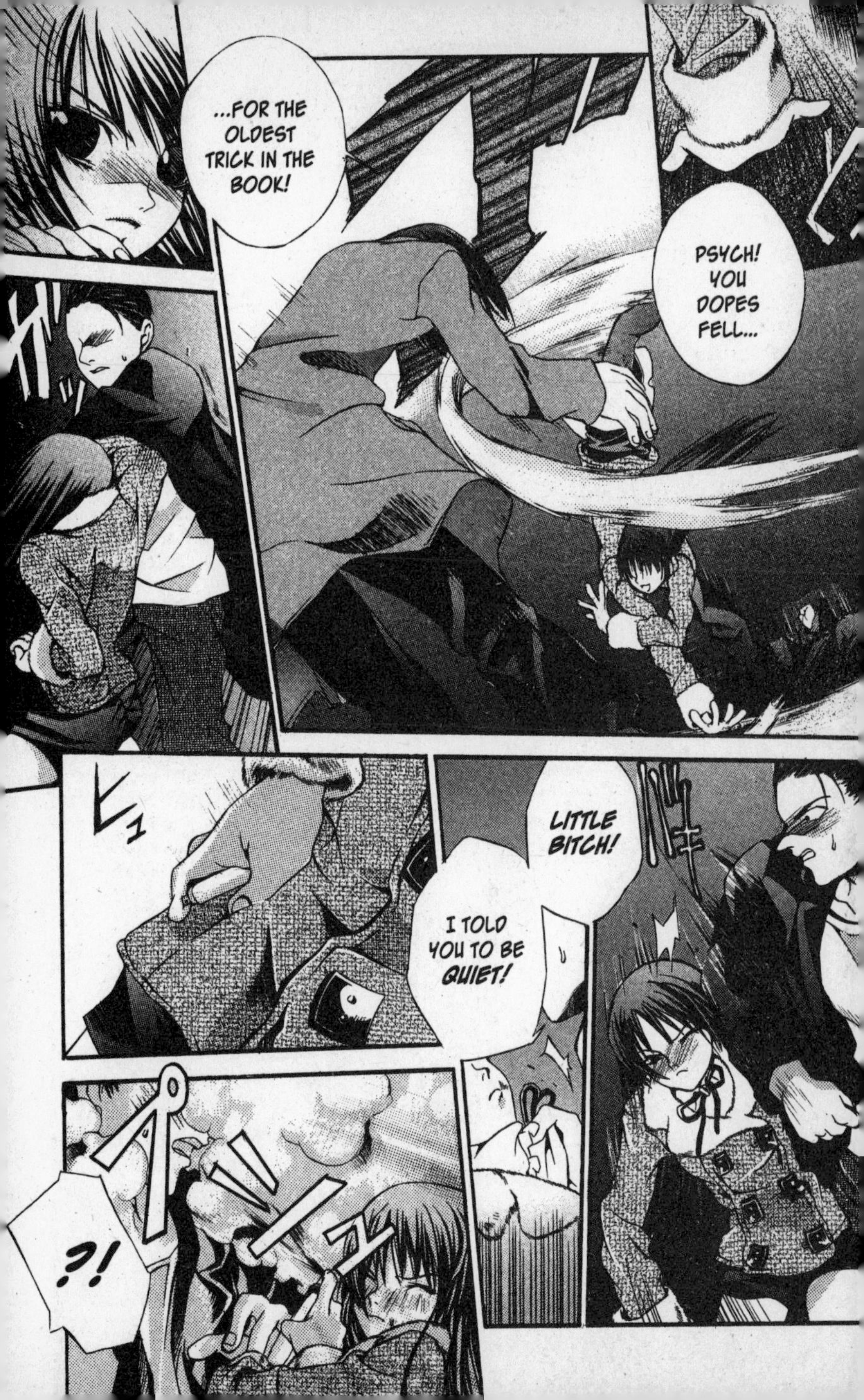
PSYCH! YOU DOPES FELL...
...FOR THE OLDEST TRICK IN THE BOOK!
LITTLE BITCH!
I TOLD YOU TO BE QUIET!
?!

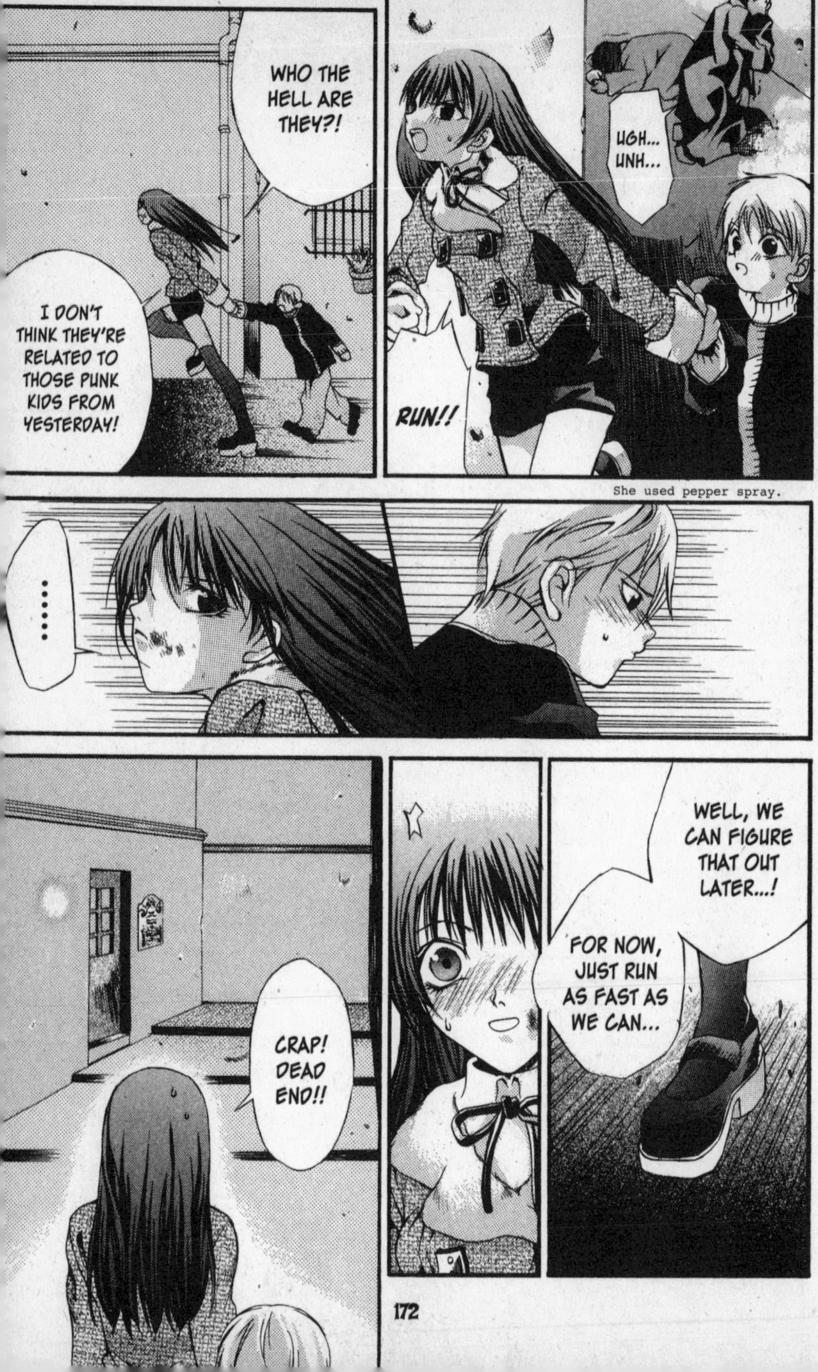
UGH... UNH...
RUN!!
She used pepper spray.
WHO THE HELL ARE THEY?!
I DON'T THINK THEY'RE RELATED TO THOSE PUNK KIDS FROM YESTERDAY!
......
WELL, WE CAN FIGURE THAT OUT LATER...!
FOR NOW, JUST RUN AS FAST AS WE CAN...
CRAP! DEAD END!!

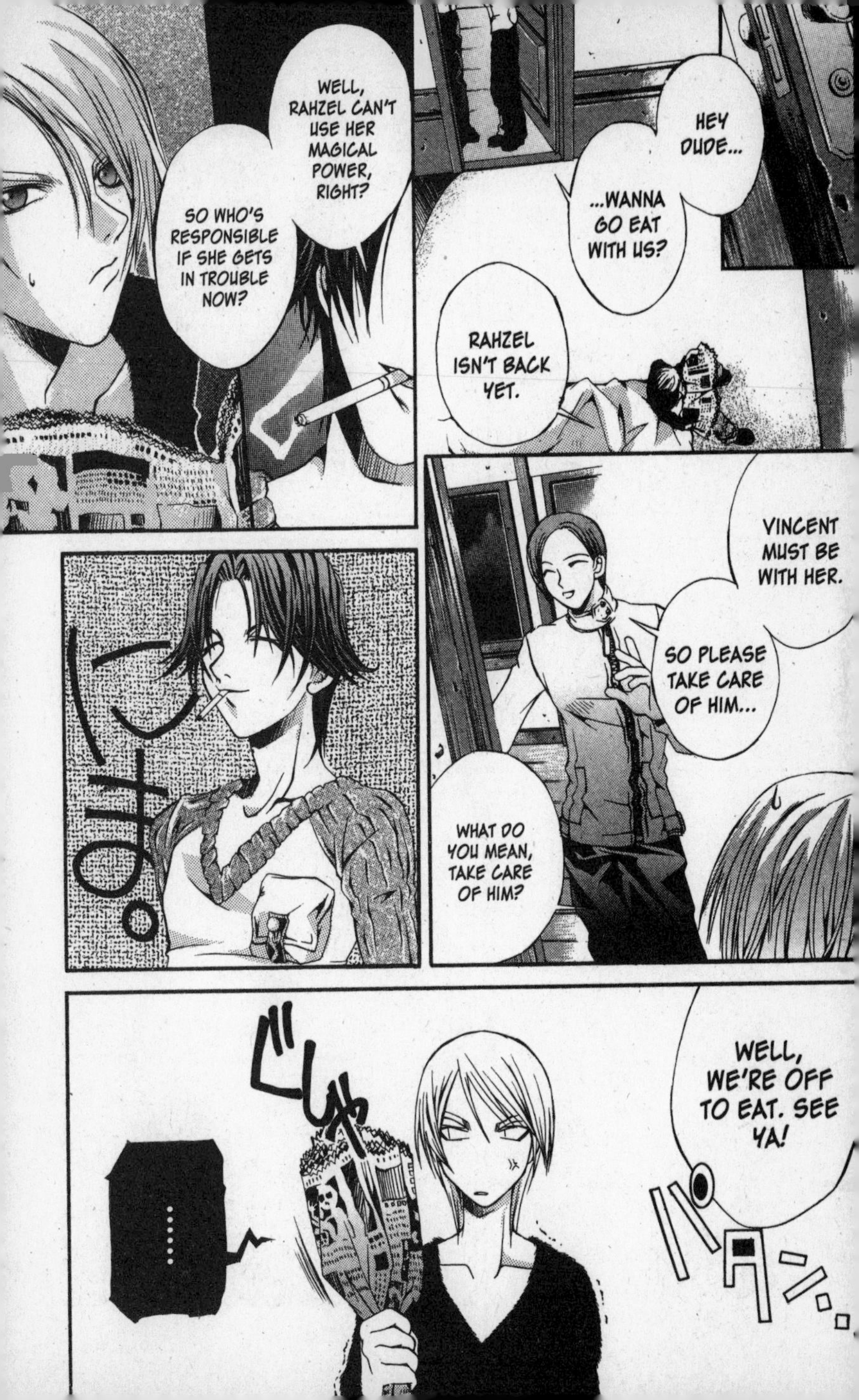
HEY DUDE...
...WANNA GO EAT WITH US?
RAHZEL ISN'T BACK YET.
WELL, RAHZEL CAN'T USE HER MAGICAL POWER, RIGHT?
SO WHO'S RESPONSIBLE IF SHE GETS IN TROUBLE NOW?
VINCENT MUST BE WITH HER.
SO PLEASE TAKE CARE OF HIM...
WHAT DO YOU MEAN, TAKE CARE OF HIM?
WELL, WE'RE OFF TO EAT. SEE YA!
ぐしゃ
......

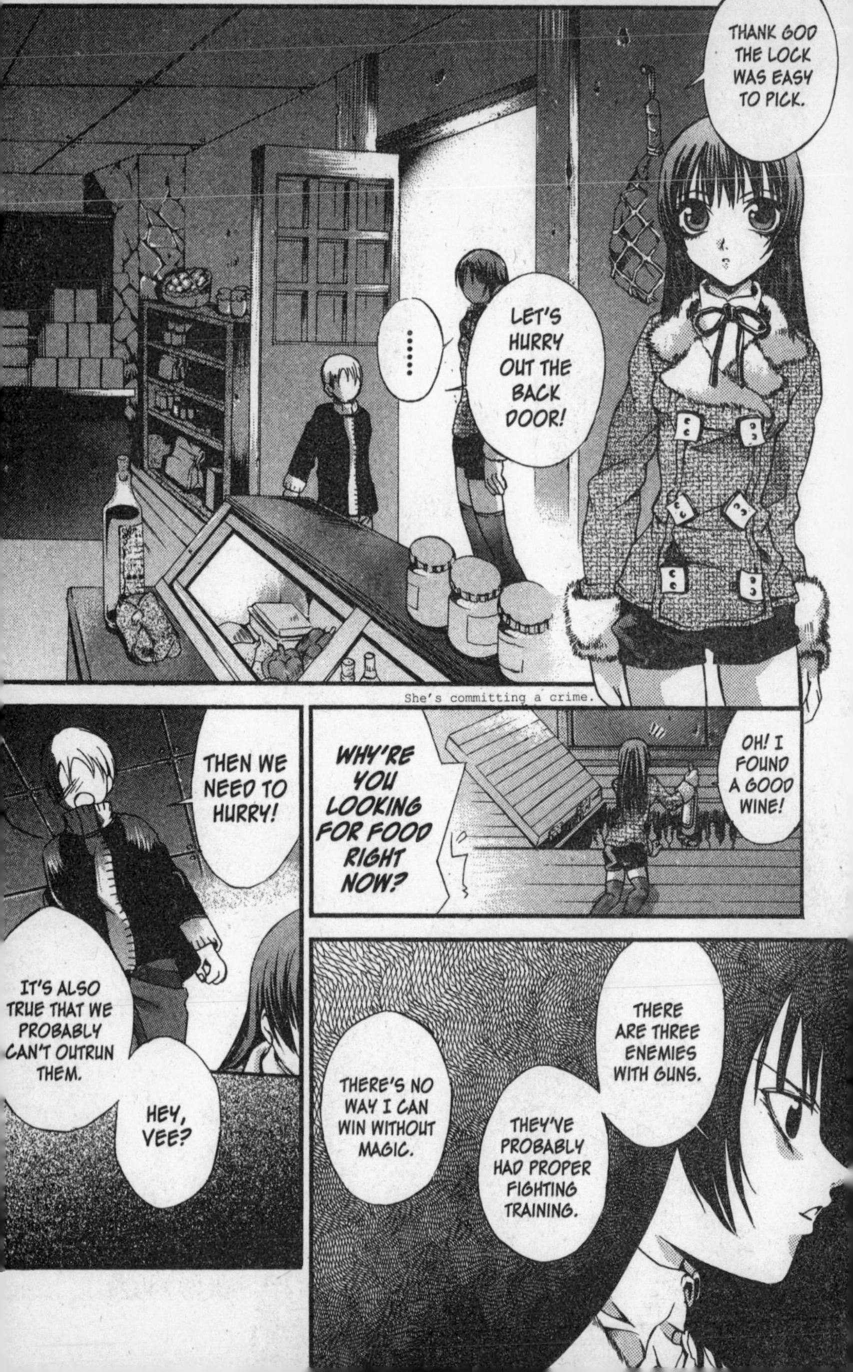
THANK GOD THE LOCK WAS EASY TO PICK.
LET'S HURRY OUT THE BACK DOOR!
......
She's committing a crime.
OH! I FOUND A GOOD WINE!
WHY'RE YOU LOOKING FOR FOOD RIGHT NOW?
THERE ARE THREE ENEMIES WITH GUNS.
THEY'VE PROBABLY HAD PROPER FIGHTING TRAINING.
THERE'S NO WAY I CAN WIN WITHOUT MAGIC.
THEN WE NEED TO HURRY!
IT'S ALSO TRUE THAT WE PROBABLY CAN'T OUTRUN THEM.
HEY, VEE?

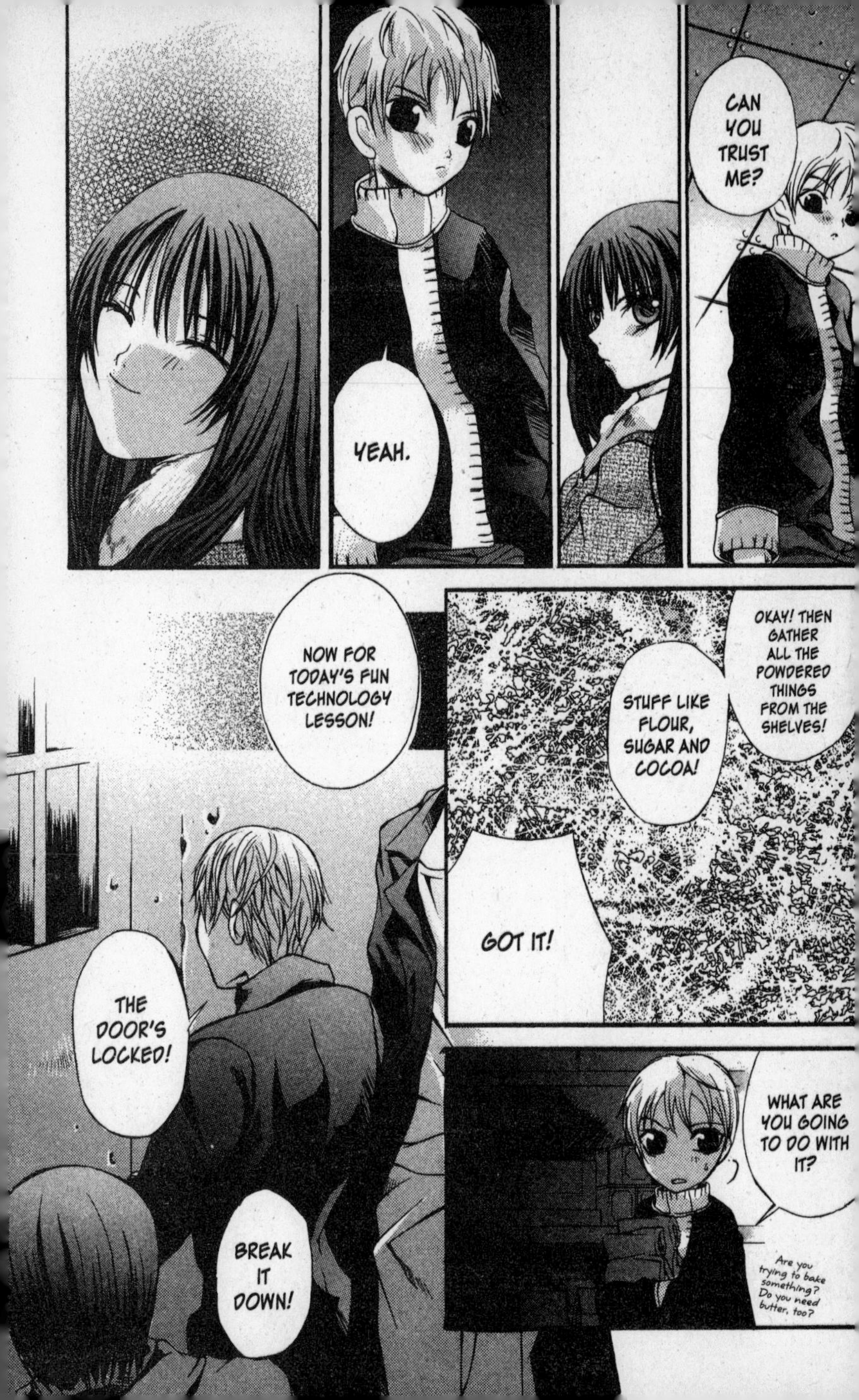
CAN YOU TRUST ME?
YEAH.
OKAY! THEN GATHER ALL THE POWDERED THINGS FROM THE SHELVES!
STUFF LIKE FLOUR, SUGAR AND COCOA!
GOT IT!
WHAT ARE YOU GOING TO DO WITH IT?
Are you trying to bake something? Do you need butter, too?
NOW FOR TODAY'S FUN TECHNOLOGY LESSON!
THE DOOR'S LOCKED!
BREAK IT DOWN!

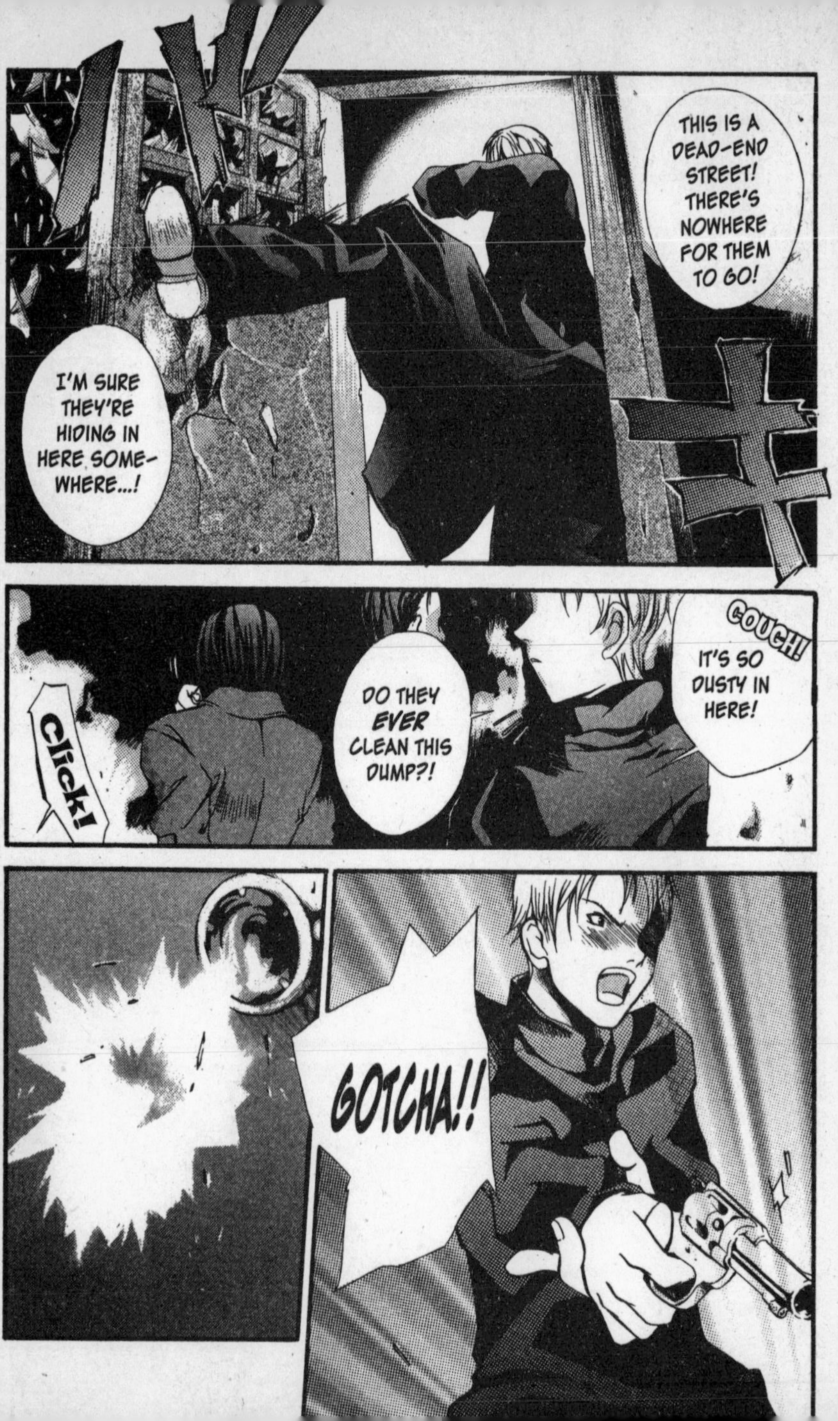
THIS IS A DEAD-END STREET! THERE'S NOWHERE FOR THEM TO GO!
I'M SURE THEY'RE HIDING IN HERE SOME-WHERE...!
COUGH!
IT'S SO DUSTY IN HERE!
DO THEY *EVER* CLEAN THIS DUMP?!
Click!
GOTCHA!!

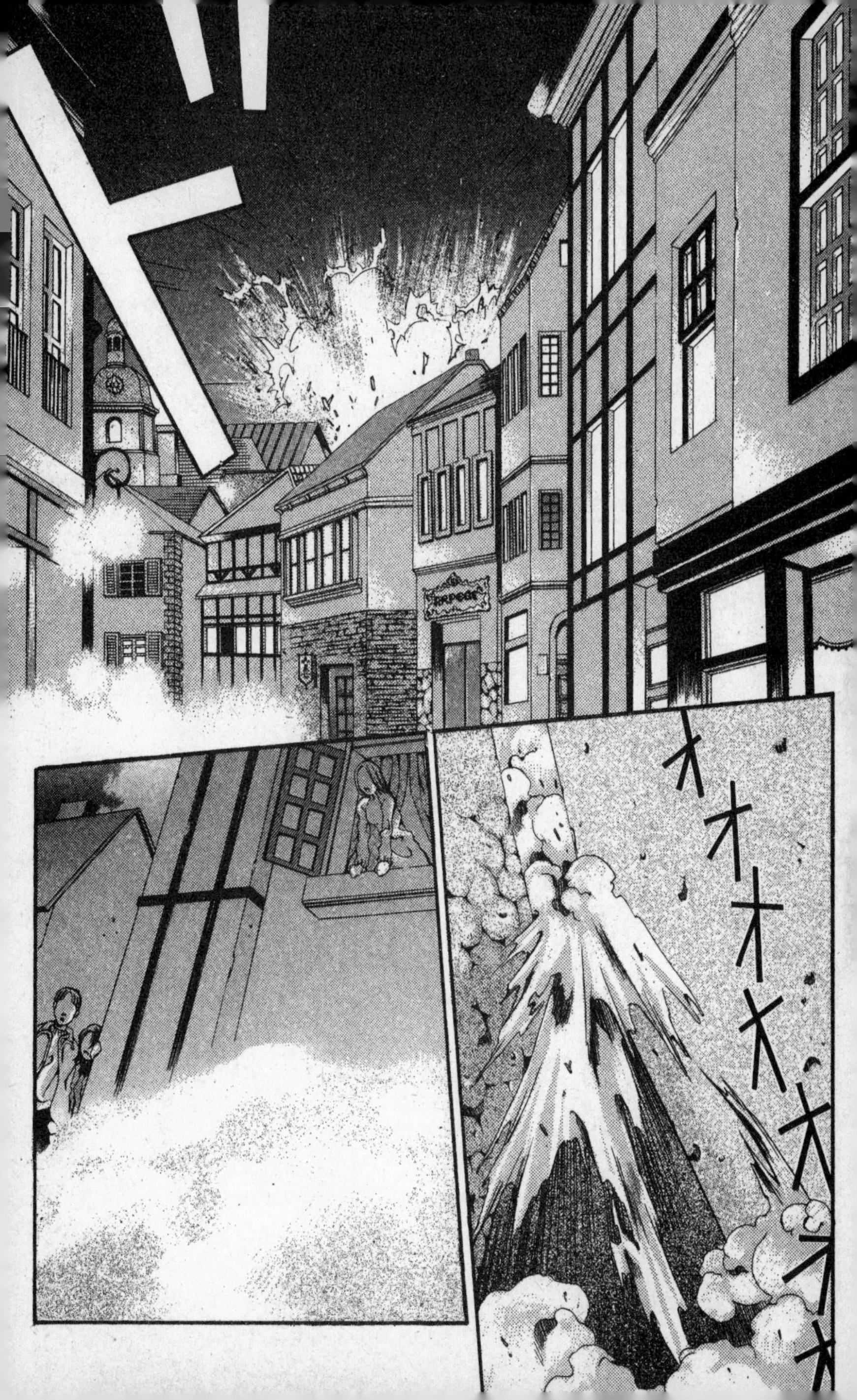
ド
オオオオオオ

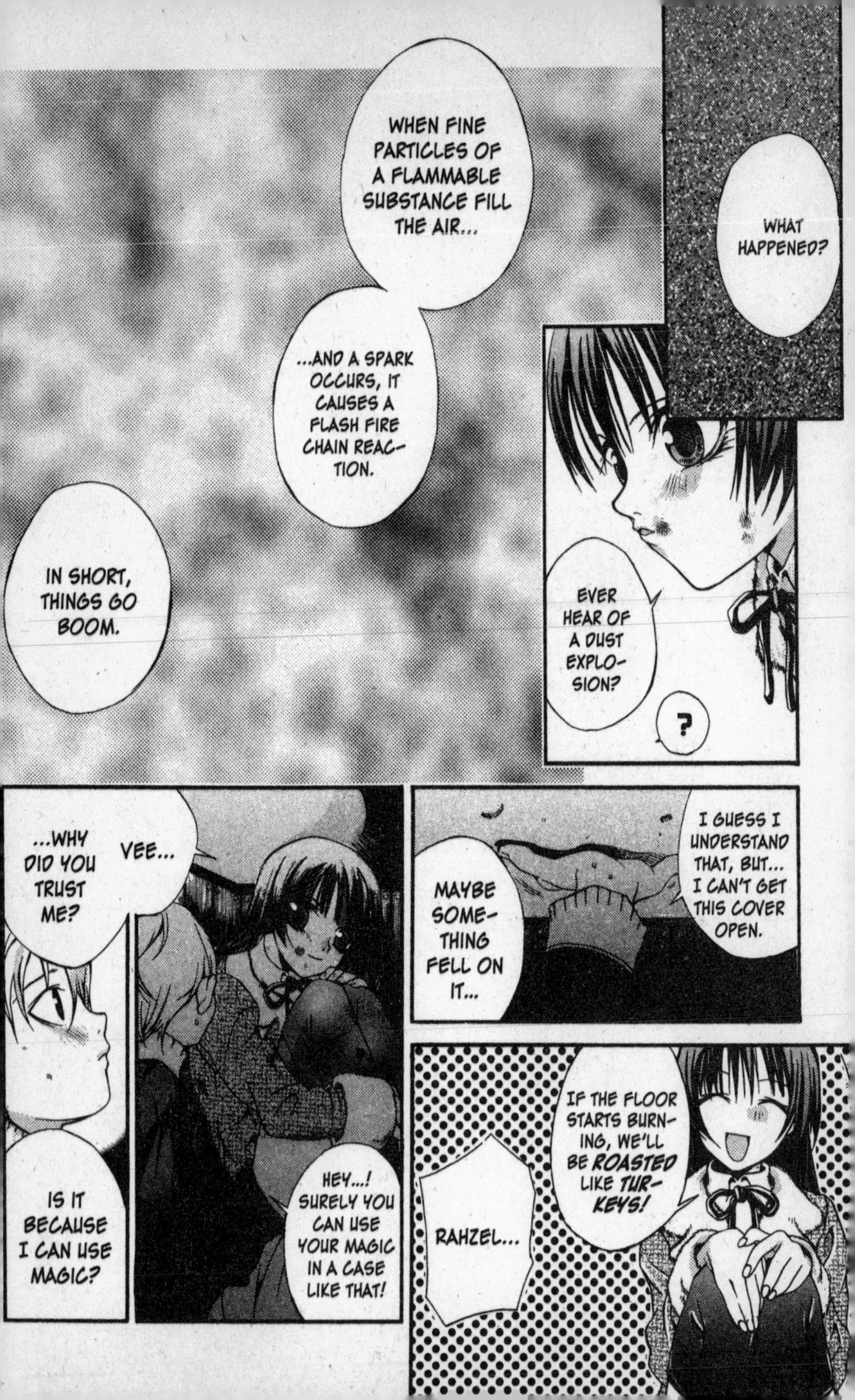
WHAT HAPPENED?
EVER HEAR OF A DUST EXPLOSION?
?
WHEN FINE PARTICLES OF A FLAMMABLE SUBSTANCE FILL THE AIR...
...AND A SPARK OCCURS, IT CAUSES A FLASH FIRE CHAIN REAC-TION.
IN SHORT, THINGS GO BOOM.
I GUESS I UNDERSTAND THAT, BUT... I CAN'T GET THIS COVER OPEN.
MAYBE SOME-THING FELL ON IT...
IF THE FLOOR STARTS BURN-ING, WE'LL BE *ROASTED* LIKE *TUR-KEYS!*
RAHZEL...
VEE...
...WHY DID YOU TRUST ME?
HEY...! SURELY YOU CAN USE YOUR MAGIC IN A CASE LIKE THAT!
IS IT BECAUSE I CAN USE MAGIC?

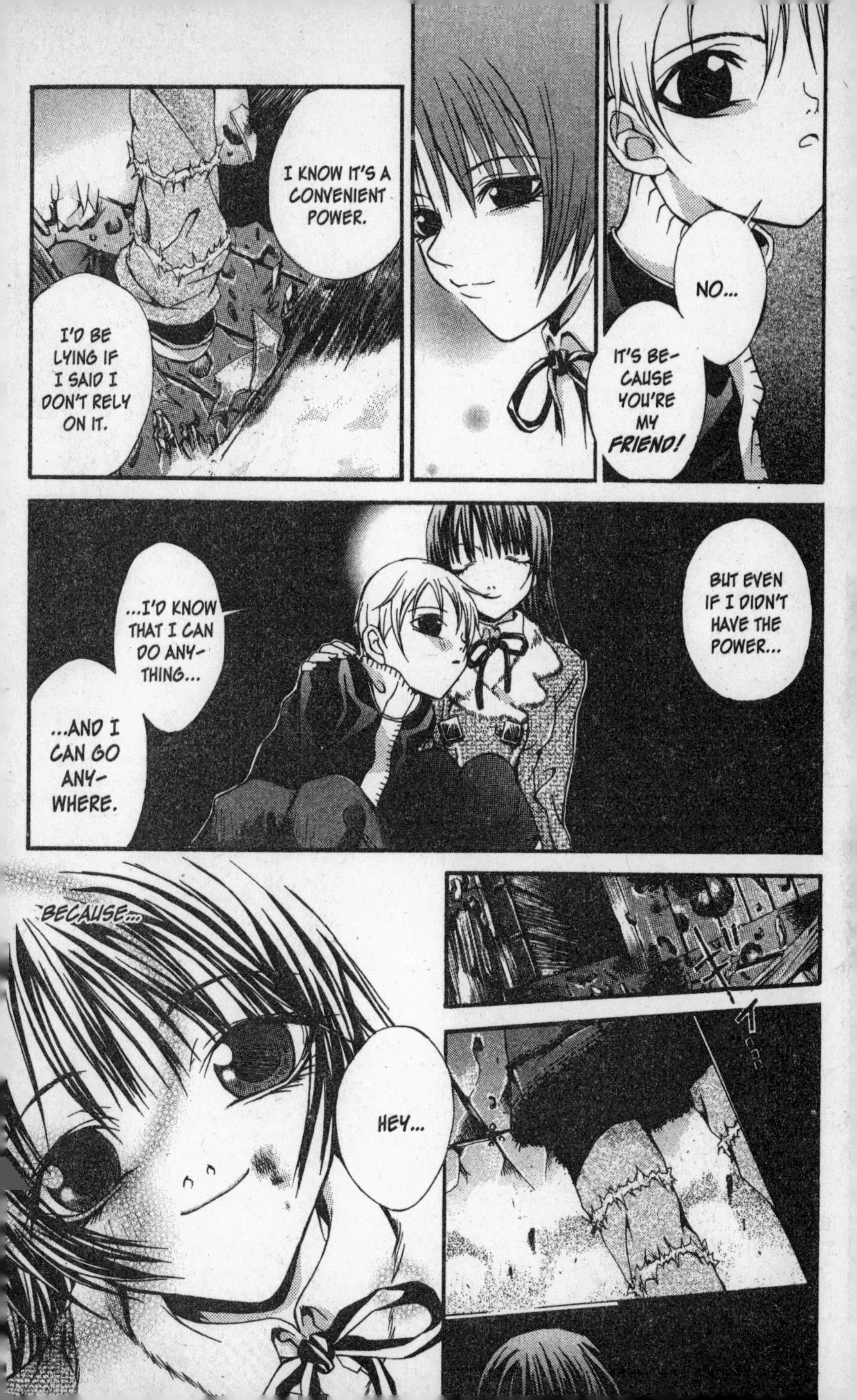
NO...
IT'S BE-CAUSE YOU'RE MY FRIEND!
I KNOW IT'S A CONVENIENT POWER.
I'D BE LYING IF I SAID I DON'T RELY ON IT.
BUT EVEN IF I DIDN'T HAVE THE POWER...
...I'D KNOW THAT I CAN DO ANY-THING...
...AND I CAN GO ANY-WHERE.
BECAUSE...
HEY...

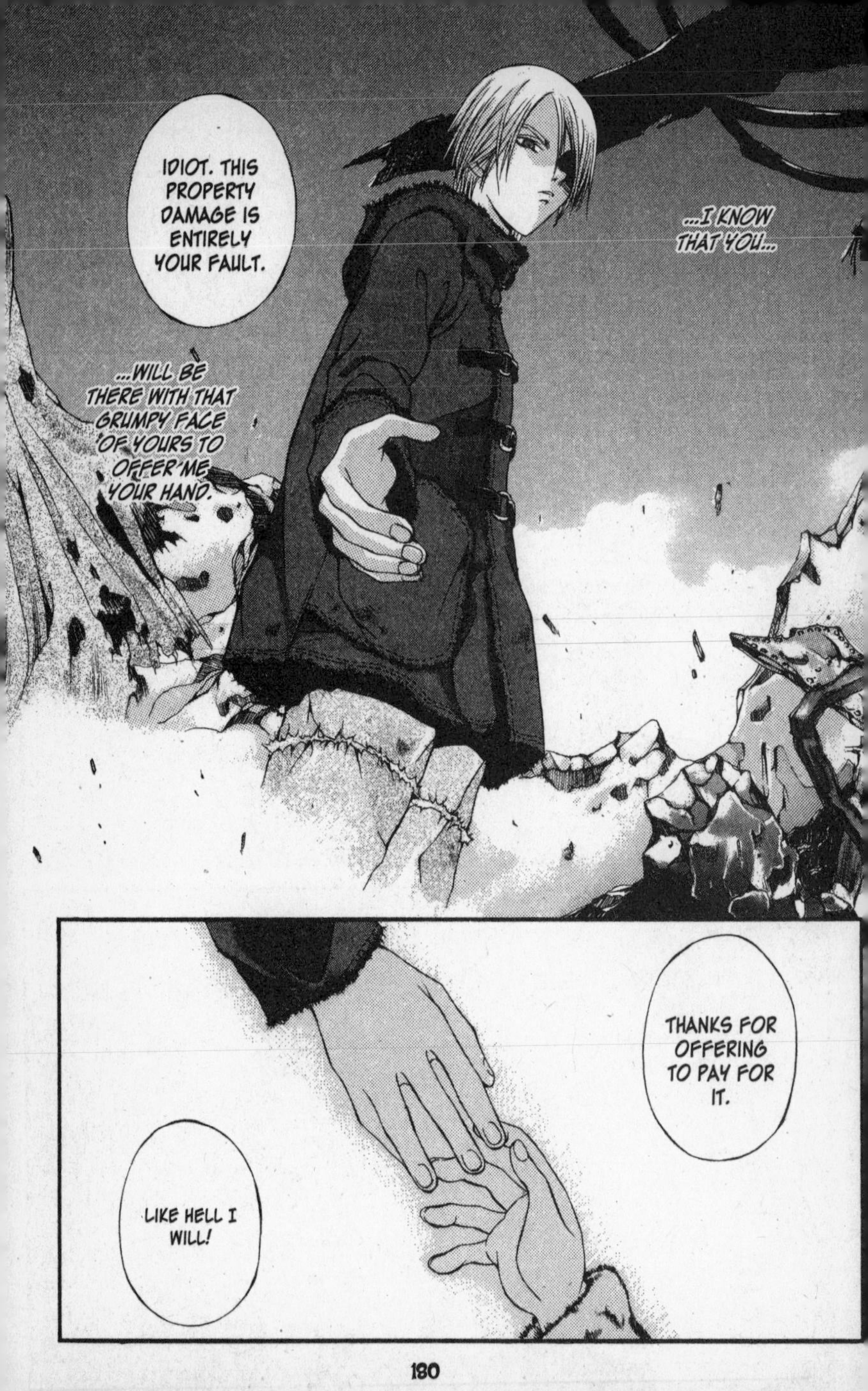
...I KNOW THAT YOU...
IDIOT. THIS PROPERTY DAMAGE IS ENTIRELY YOUR FAULT.
...WILL BE THERE WITH THAT GRUMPY FACE OF YOURS TO OFFER ME YOUR HAND.
THANKS FOR OFFERING TO PAY FOR IT.
LIKE HELL I WILL!

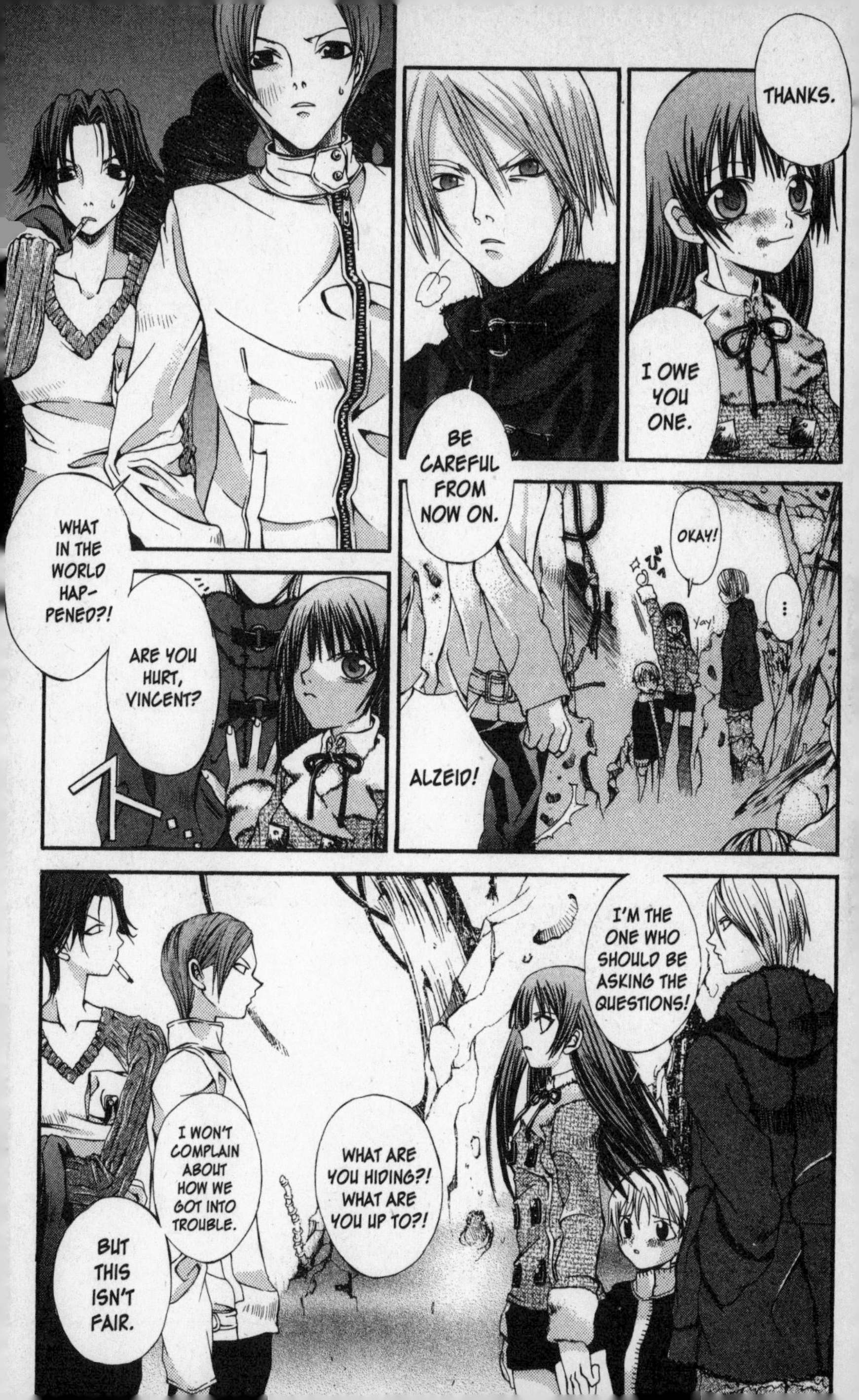
THANKS.
I OWE YOU ONE.
BE CAREFUL FROM NOW ON.
OKAY!
Yay!
...
ALZEID!
WHAT IN THE WORLD HAP-PENED?!
ARE YOU HURT, VINCENT?
I'M THE ONE WHO SHOULD BE ASKING THE QUESTIONS!
WHAT ARE YOU HIDING?! WHAT ARE YOU UP TO?!
I WON'T COMPLAIN ABOUT HOW WE GOT INTO TROUBLE.
BUT THIS ISN'T FAIR.

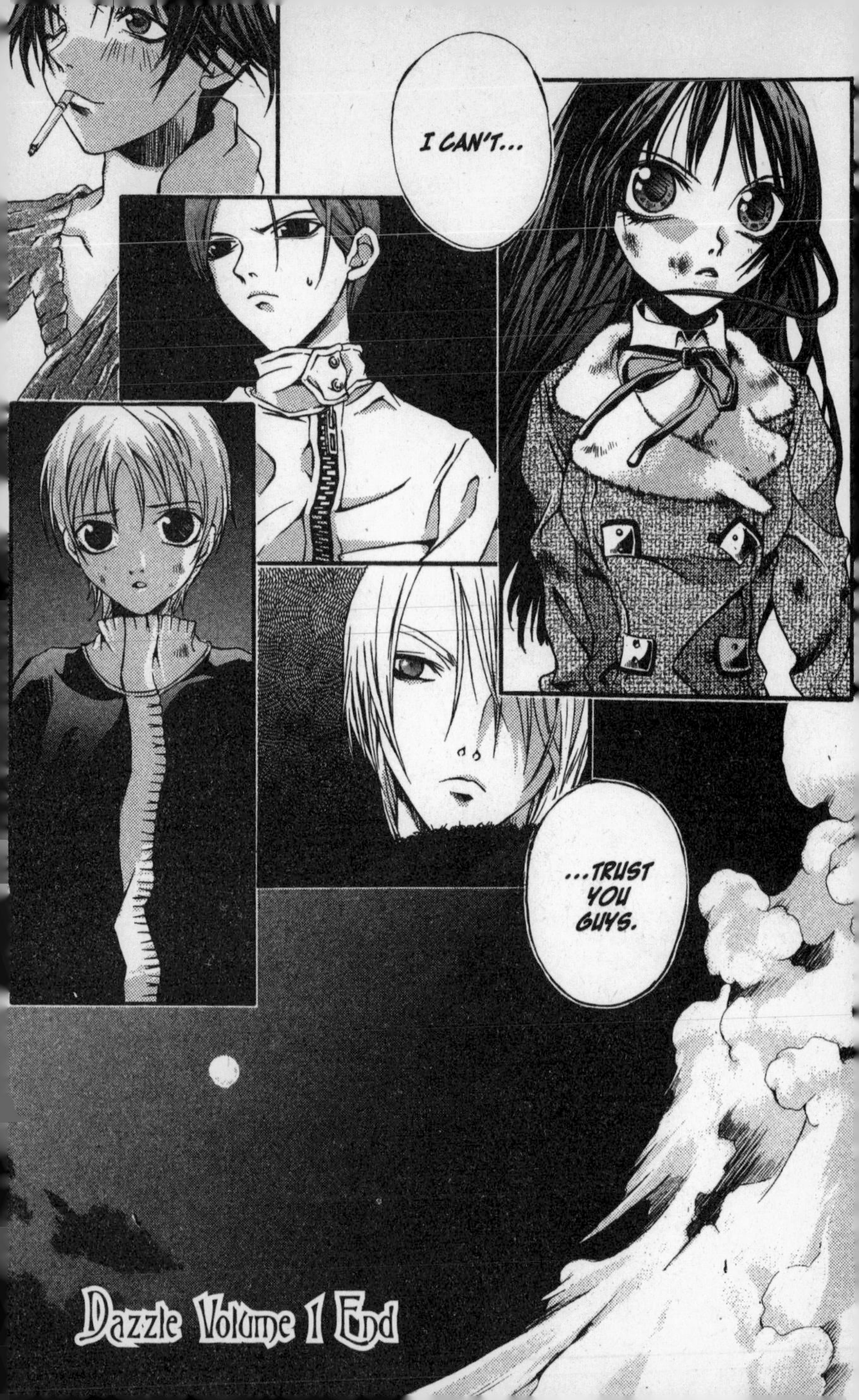
I CAN'T...
...TRUST YOU GUYS.
Dazzle Volume 1 End

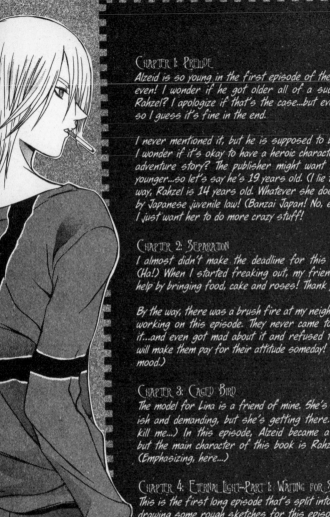

CHAPTER 1: PRELUDE

Alzeid is so young in the first episode of the story! Childlike, even! I wonder if he got older all of a sudden because of Rahzel? I apologize if that's the case...but everyone gets old, so I guess it's fine in the end.

I never mentioned it, but he is supposed to be 24 years old. I wonder if it's okay to have a heroic character this old in an adventure story? The publisher might want us to make him younger...so let's say he's 19 years old. (I lie too much.) By the way, Rahzel is 14 years old. Whatever she does will be allowed by Japanese juvenile law! (Banzai Japan! No, enough of that...) I just want her to do more crazy stuff!

CHAPTER 2: SEPARATION

I almost didn't make the deadline for this second episode! (Ha!) When I started freaking out, my friends came over to help by bringing food, cake and roses! Thank you all!

By the way, there was a brush fire at my neighbor's while I was working on this episode. They never came to apologize about it...and even got mad about it and refused to move away! I'll will make them pay for their attitude someday! (I'm in a fighting mood.)

CHAPTER 3: CAGED BIRD

The model for Lina is a friend of mine. She's not quite so self ish and demanding, but she's getting there. (She's going to kill me...) In this episode, Alzeid became a main character, but the main character of this book is Rahzel. **Rahzel**, okay? (Emphasizing, here...)

CHAPTER 4: ETERNAL LIGHT--PART 1: WAITING FOR SPRING

This is the first long episode that's split into two. When I was drawing some rough sketches for this episode, I heard some noise from the stereo--but it was unplugged! It was so scary! (It has happened again a few times since then.) Help! If anyone knows how this is happening, please contact me! Help me!

Chapter 5: Eternal Light--Part 2: Passive-Aggressive
From where I live, I can see the fireworks from Tokyo Disneyland. Disney people are so bourgeois! (Violent word!)

The title page of this episode was originally done just in pen and ink. It might have been cooler if I'd kept it that way.

Chapter 6: Nowhere to Go--Part 1: Idleness Is the Devil's Workshop
I confess--there was no way I could make the deadline on this episode. So I cried for help to my friend who has nothing to do with the manga business and made her do some toning. I also asked her to change her moving date. I am such a devil! I'm almost as much a devil as Sugino-san, my editor. She's evil, but so reliable! Love you, Sugino-san! (I'm sure she'll forgive me for saying stuff like that.)

It's been six months since I started working on this story. I'm definitely at my limit as far as how much work I can do by myself, but my place is too small for an assistant. You probably won't believe this, but I am drawing manga on my dresser! (It's like I'm drawing on a cardboard box.) And that's not all! My chair is a designer's chair with three legs. I fall off it all the time!

Chapter 7: Nowhere to Go--Part 2: Gamble
Here I introduced the drawing of Alzeid wearing an angel costume. I wonder if fans will hate me for drawing something like that? Now I'm nervous...

Intermission: Heart's Outline
How come I have to draw somebody's sleeping face instead of being asleep myself? Sometimes when I feel like that, there are so many tears in my eyes I can't see to draw manga. (It's already summertime, but in the manga I'm still drawing wintertime.) When it comes to sleeping, I often think about stories in my bed, but then I fall sleep so quickly and can't remember anything. (Are you kidding me?) I would like to get some feedback from you. I just feel sad if I don't get any feedback on my work. Oh! And thanks to all my fans who send me letters all the time! That's my source of energy! I love you all! I write replies slowly, but surely...so please be patient!

Well, see you in Volume 2! More like...you'll see me! Okay! See ya!

Minari Endoh

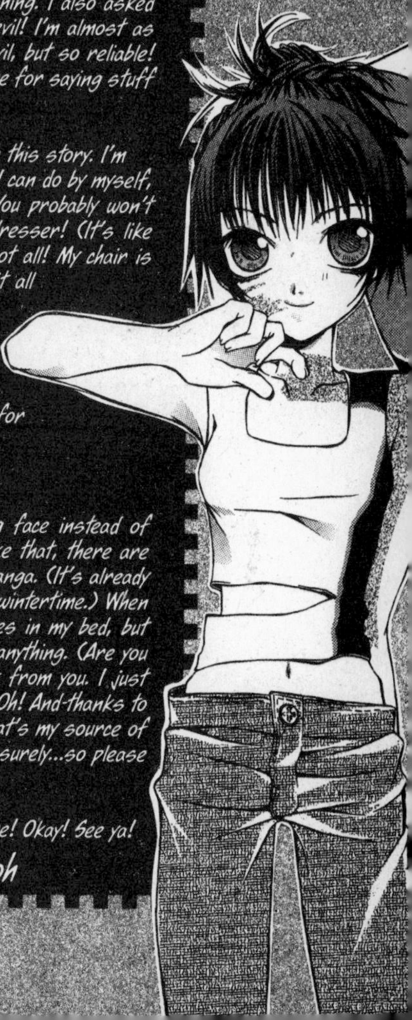

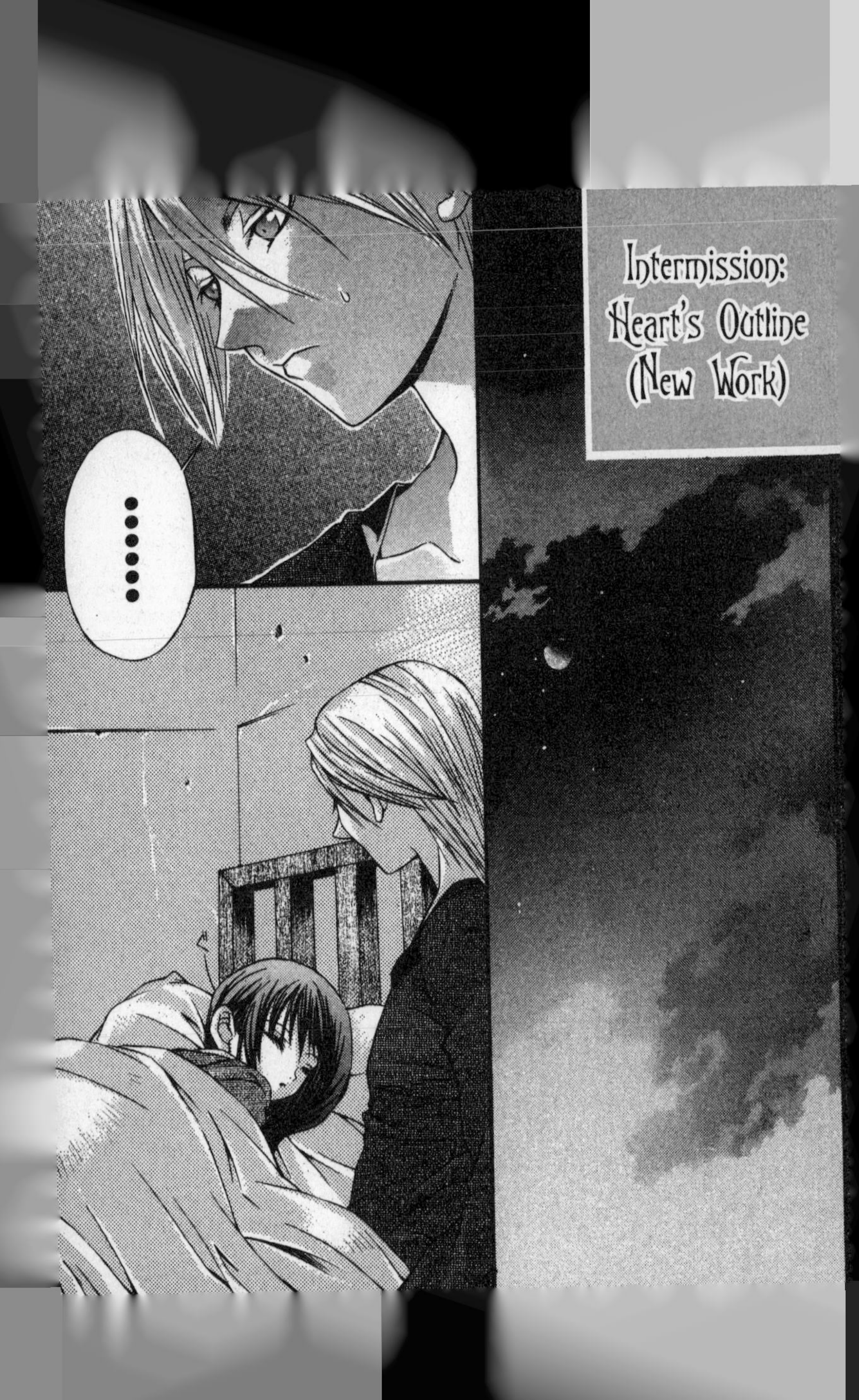
Intermission: Heart's Outline (New Work)
......

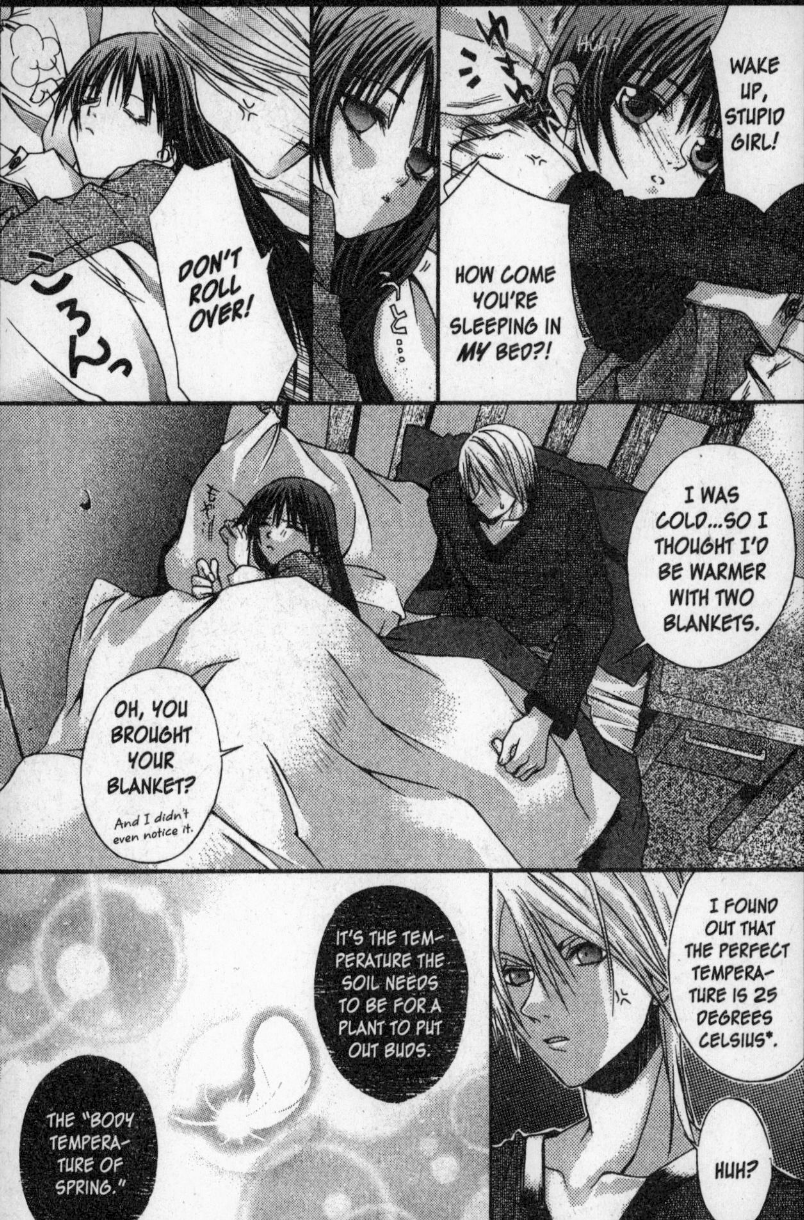
WAKE UP, STUPID GIRL!
HOW COME YOU'RE SLEEPING IN MY BED?!
DON'T ROLL OVER!
I WAS COLD...SO I THOUGHT I'D BE WARMER WITH TWO BLANKETS.
OH, YOU BROUGHT YOUR BLANKET?
And I didn't even notice it.
I FOUND OUT THAT THE PERFECT TEMPERATURE IS 25 DEGREES CELSIUS*.
HUH?
IT'S THE TEMPERATURE THE SOIL NEEDS TO BE FOR A PLANT TO PUT OUT BUDS.
THE "BODY TEMPERATURE OF SPRING."

*25 °C = 77 °F

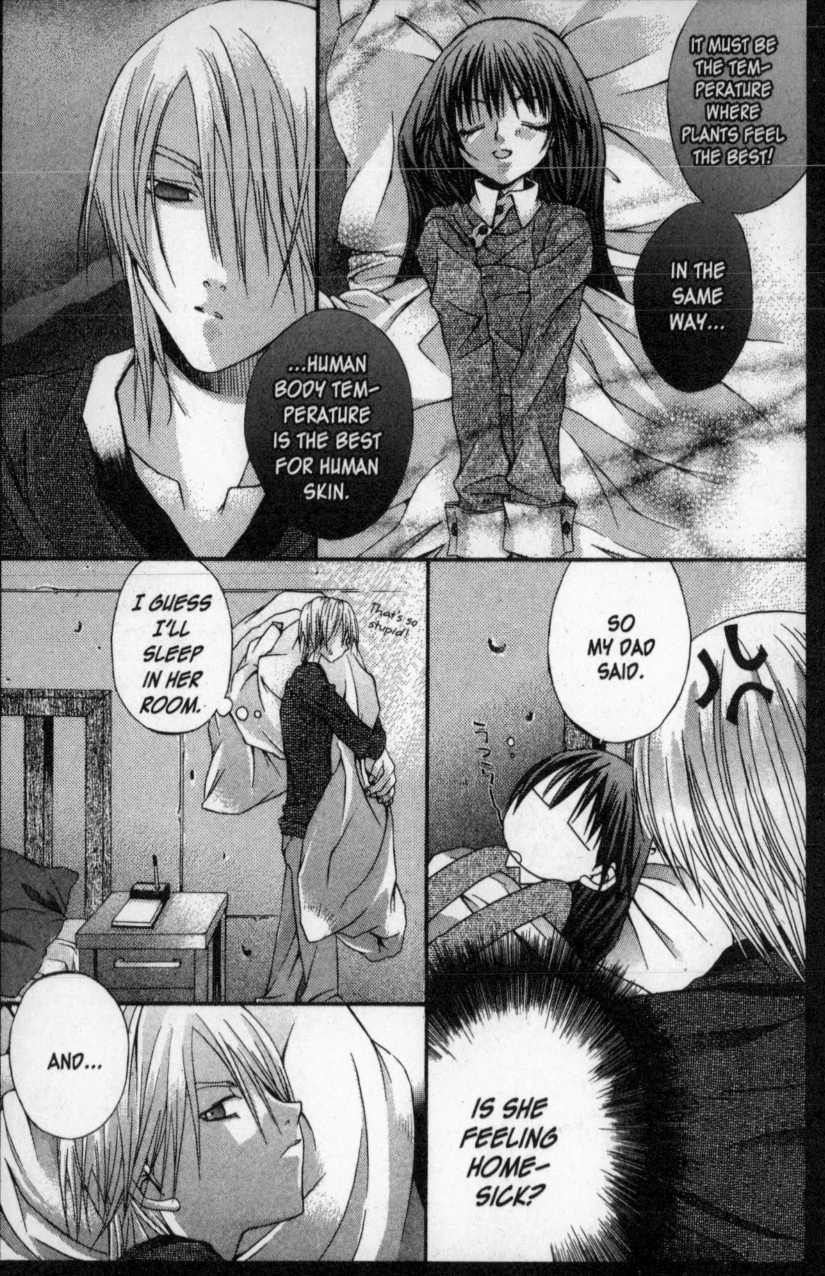
IT MUST BE THE TEMPERATURE WHERE PLANTS FEEL THE BEST!
IN THE SAME WAY...
...HUMAN BODY TEMPERATURE IS THE BEST FOR HUMAN SKIN.
SO MY DAD SAID.
I GUESS I'LL SLEEP IN HER ROOM.
That's so stupid!
IS SHE FEELING HOMESICK?
AND...

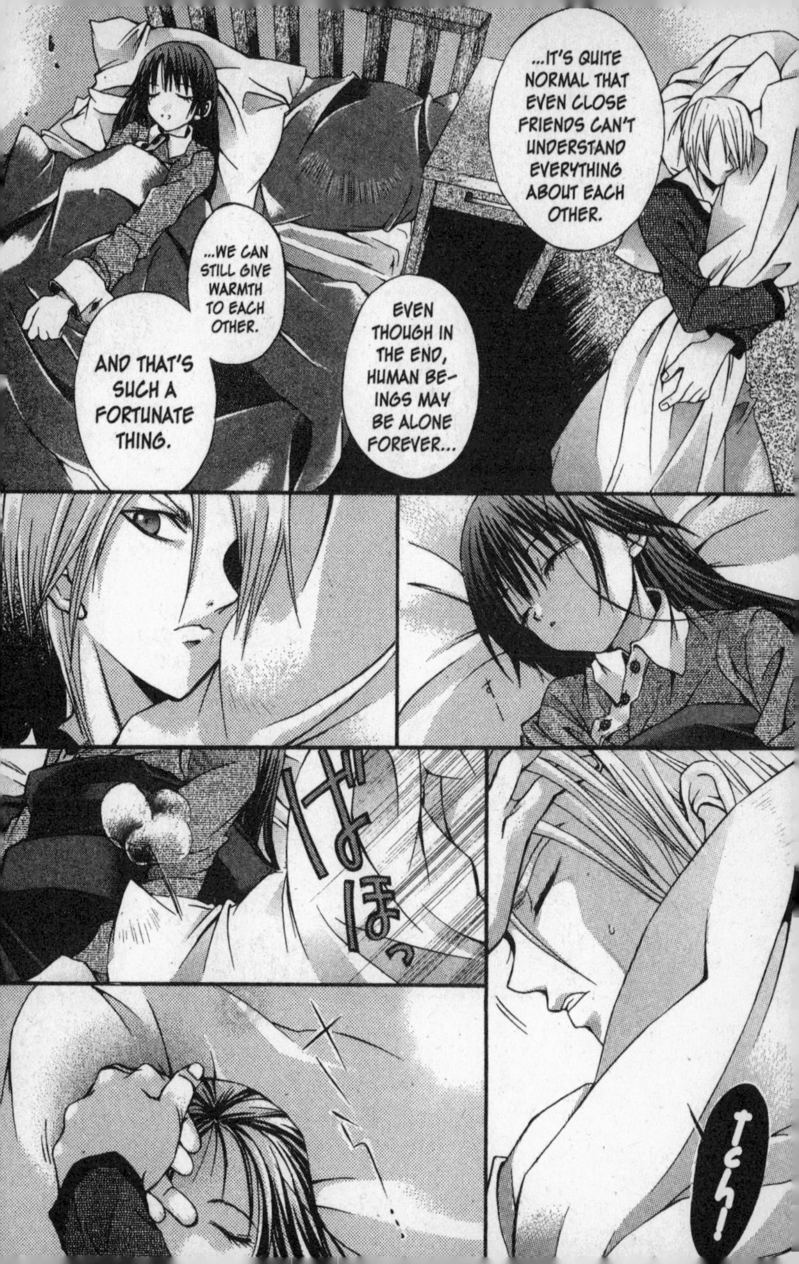
...IT'S QUITE NORMAL THAT EVEN CLOSE FRIENDS CAN'T UNDERSTAND EVERYTHING ABOUT EACH OTHER.
EVEN THOUGH IN THE END, HUMAN BE-INGS MAY BE ALONE FOREVER...
...WE CAN STILL GIVE WARMTH TO EACH OTHER.
AND THAT'S SUCH A FORTUNATE THING.
TCH!

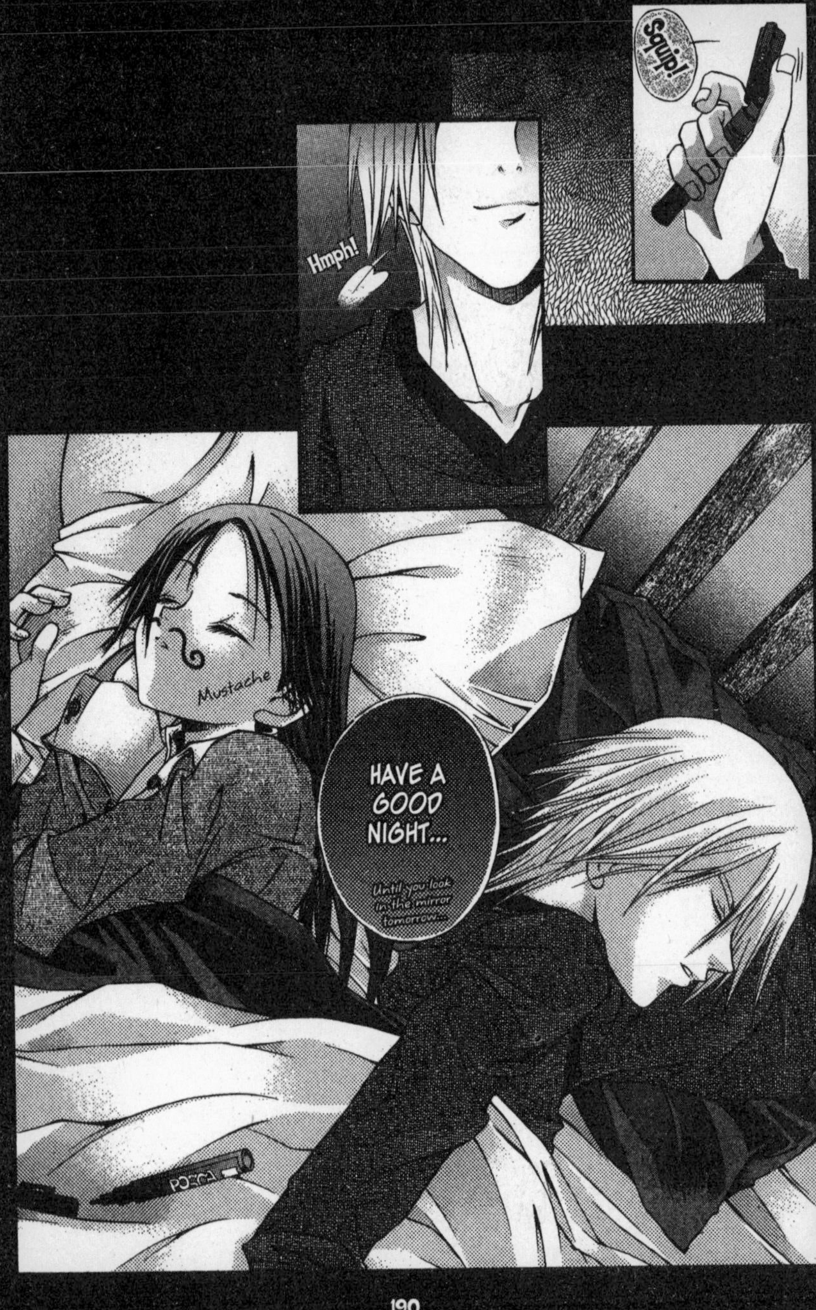
Squip!
Hmph!
Mustache
HAVE A GOOD NIGHT...
Until you look in the mirror tomorrow...
PORCA

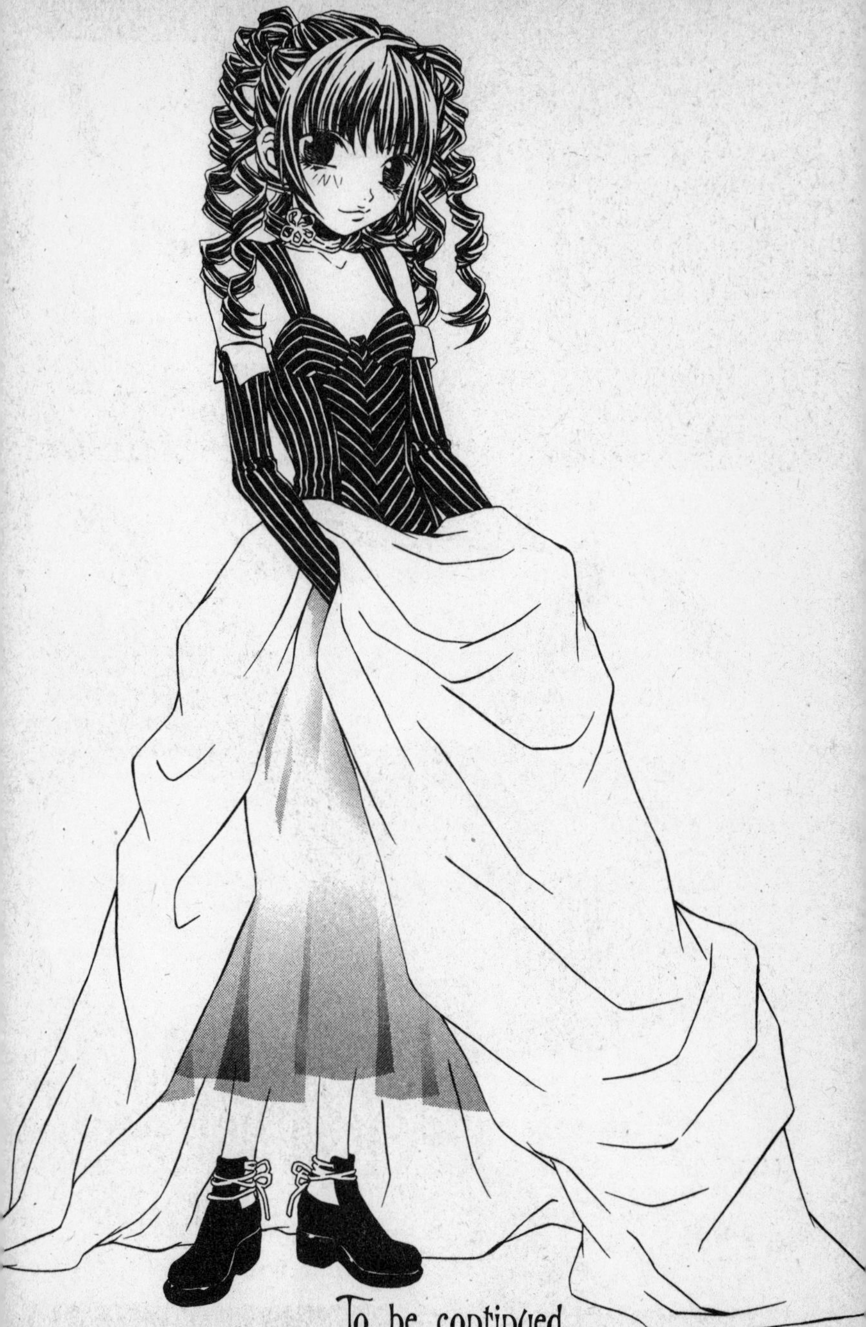

To be continued...

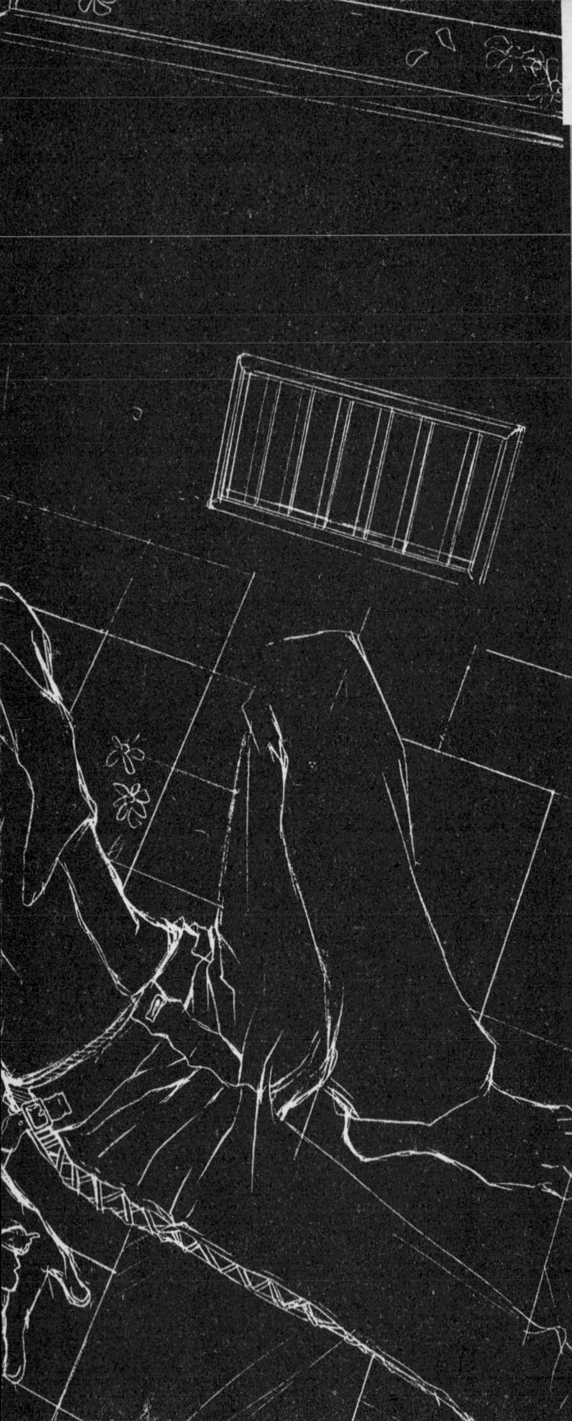

New Postscript

I am so embarrassed...I just want to dig a hole to hide in! I've switched publishers--so my books are going to be republished! But the first book was published two years ago, and my first story came out three years ago. It was my first serial manga, and I was very nervous and confused back then. But I still love Dazzle! I still love myself, even though my work was terrible! (Am I a narcissist?) I apologize to the people who purchased the old version from the previous publisher. I don't know how to thank you enough if you repurchased the newer version from the new publisher. Thank you very, very much!

Right now the continuing story of Rahzel's adventure is published in Comic Zero Sum from the publisher Ichijinsha. She's being stupid as usual. Please check them out!

By the way, the character profile drawing looks rough not on purpose, but because I didn't have enough time to finish. (Don't admit it!) And also, my handwriting is terrible. (No, stop admitting your mistakes!) I put it off until the last minute, and caused a lot of trouble for all the people at work. (Self-criticism.) Next time I will definitely do it right for sure!

I would like to thank all the people who helped me to create Dazzle--as well as all the people who read this book! Thank you very much!

Minari Endoh

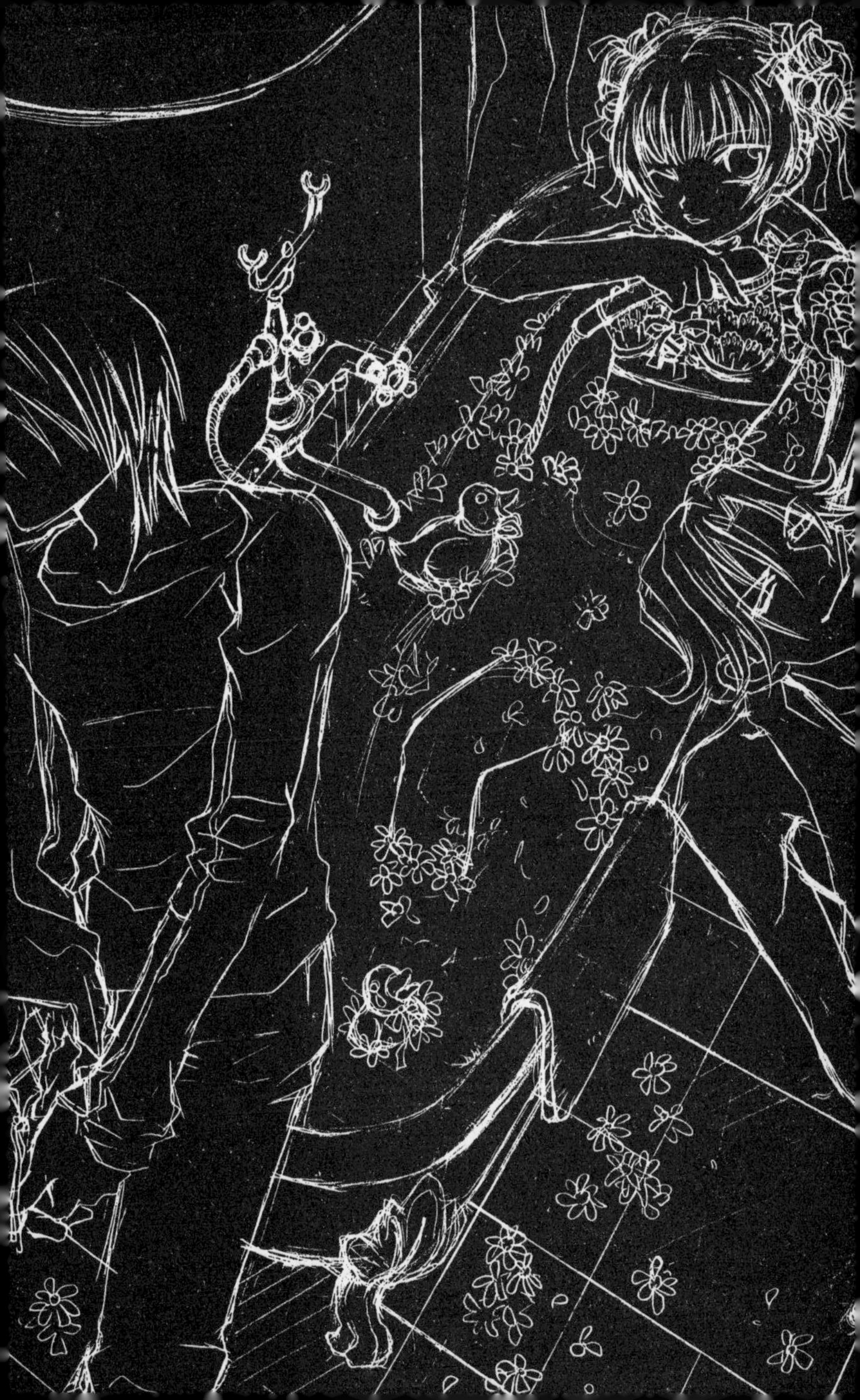

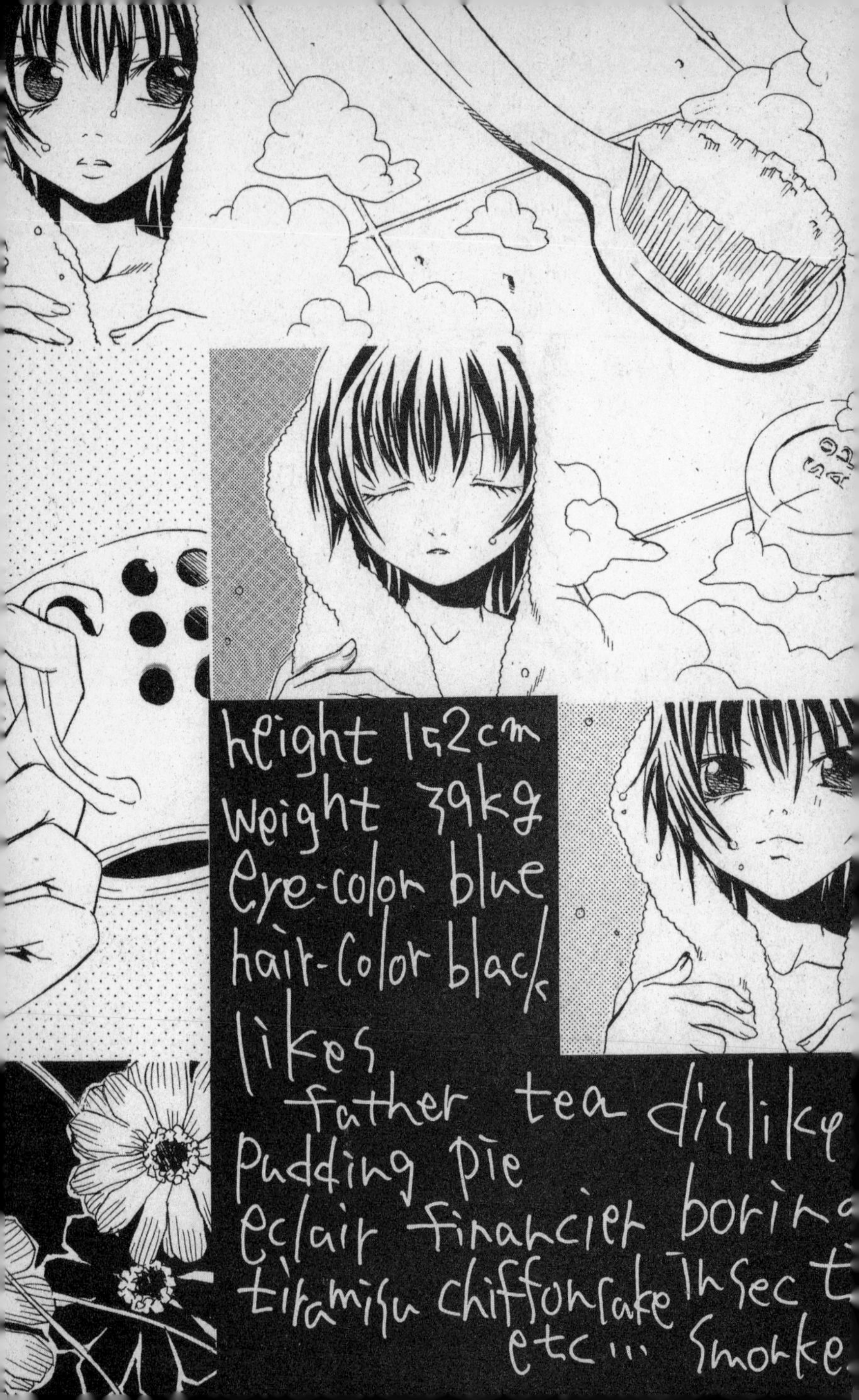
height 152cm
weight 39kg
eye-color blue
hair-color black
likes
father tea
pudding pie
eclair financier
tiramisu chiffoncake
etc...
dislike
borin
insect
smoke

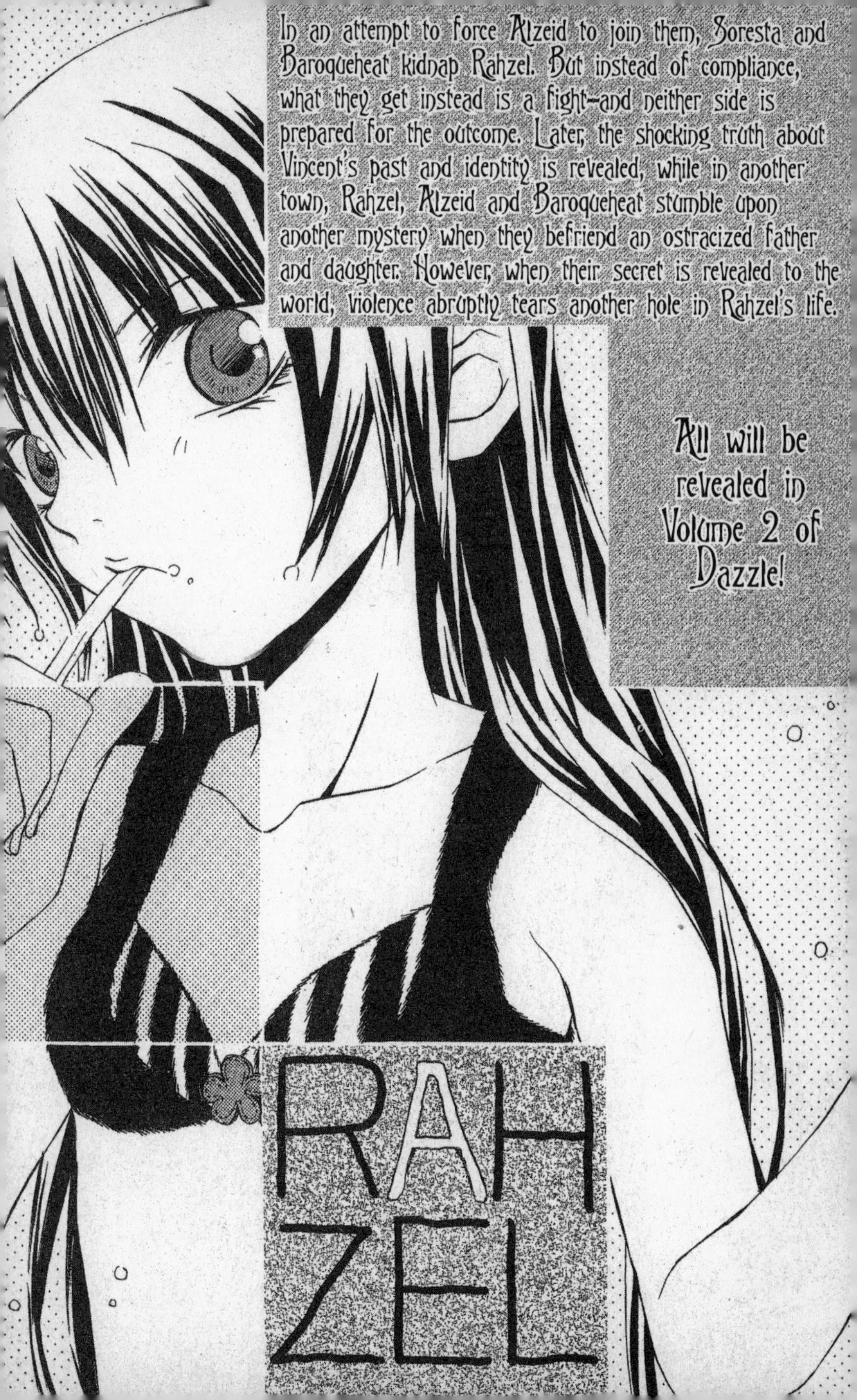
In an attempt to force Alzeid to join them, Soresta and Baroqueheat kidnap Rahzel. But instead of compliance, what they get instead is a fight—and neither side is prepared for the outcome. Later, the shocking truth about Vincent's past and identity is revealed, while in another town, Rahzel, Alzeid and Baroqueheat stumble upon another mystery when they befriend an ostracized father and daughter. However, when their secret is revealed to the world, violence abruptly tears another hole in Rahzel's life.
All will be revealed in Volume 2 of Dazzle!
RAH ZEL

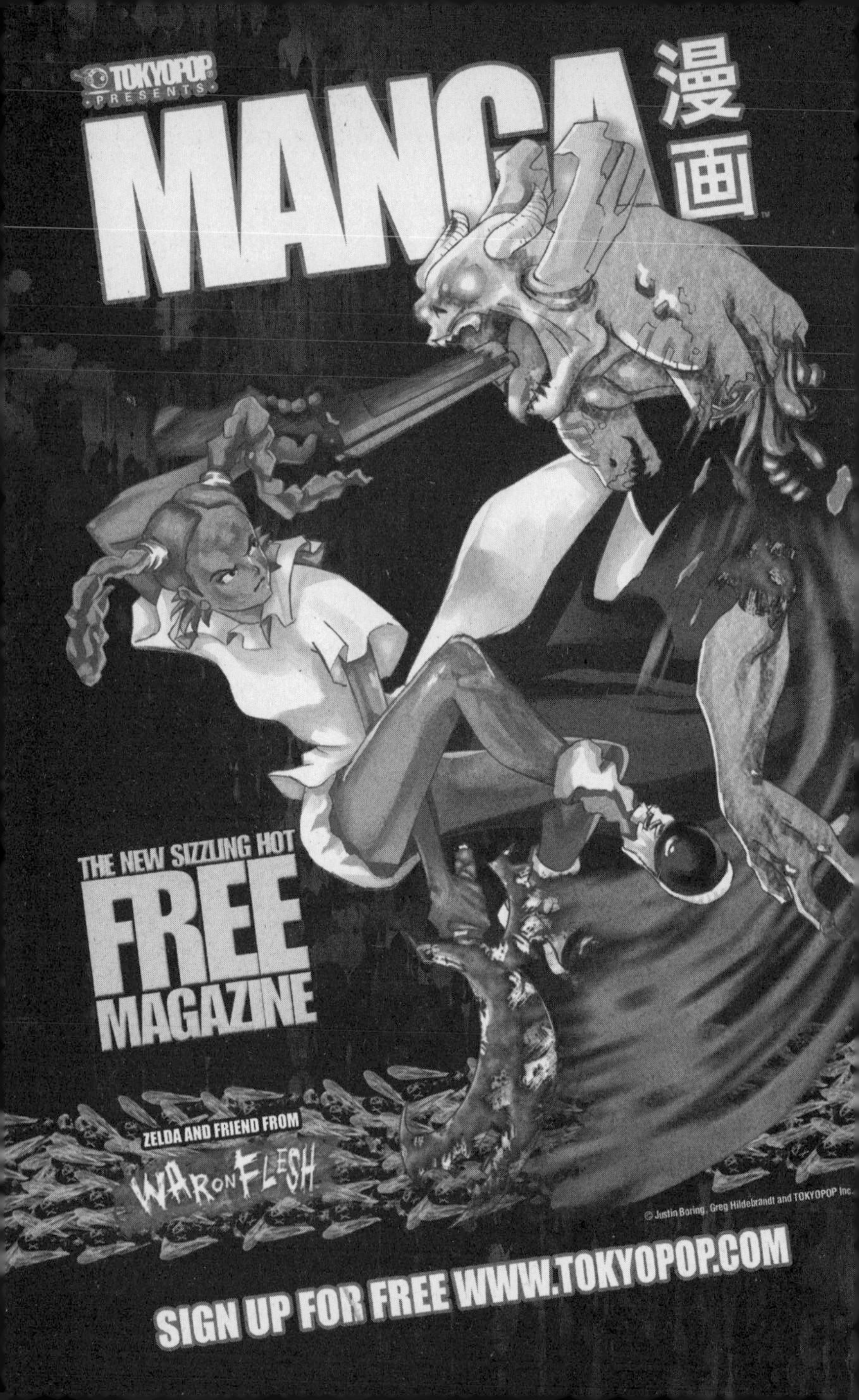

TOKYOPOP PRESENTS
MANGA 漫画
THE NEW SIZZLING HOT
FREE
MAGAZINE
ZELDA AND FRIEND FROM
WAR ON FLESH
© Justin Boring, Greg Hildebrandt and TOKYOPOP Inc.
SIGN UP FOR FREE WWW.TOKYOPOP.COM

TOKYOPOP SHOP

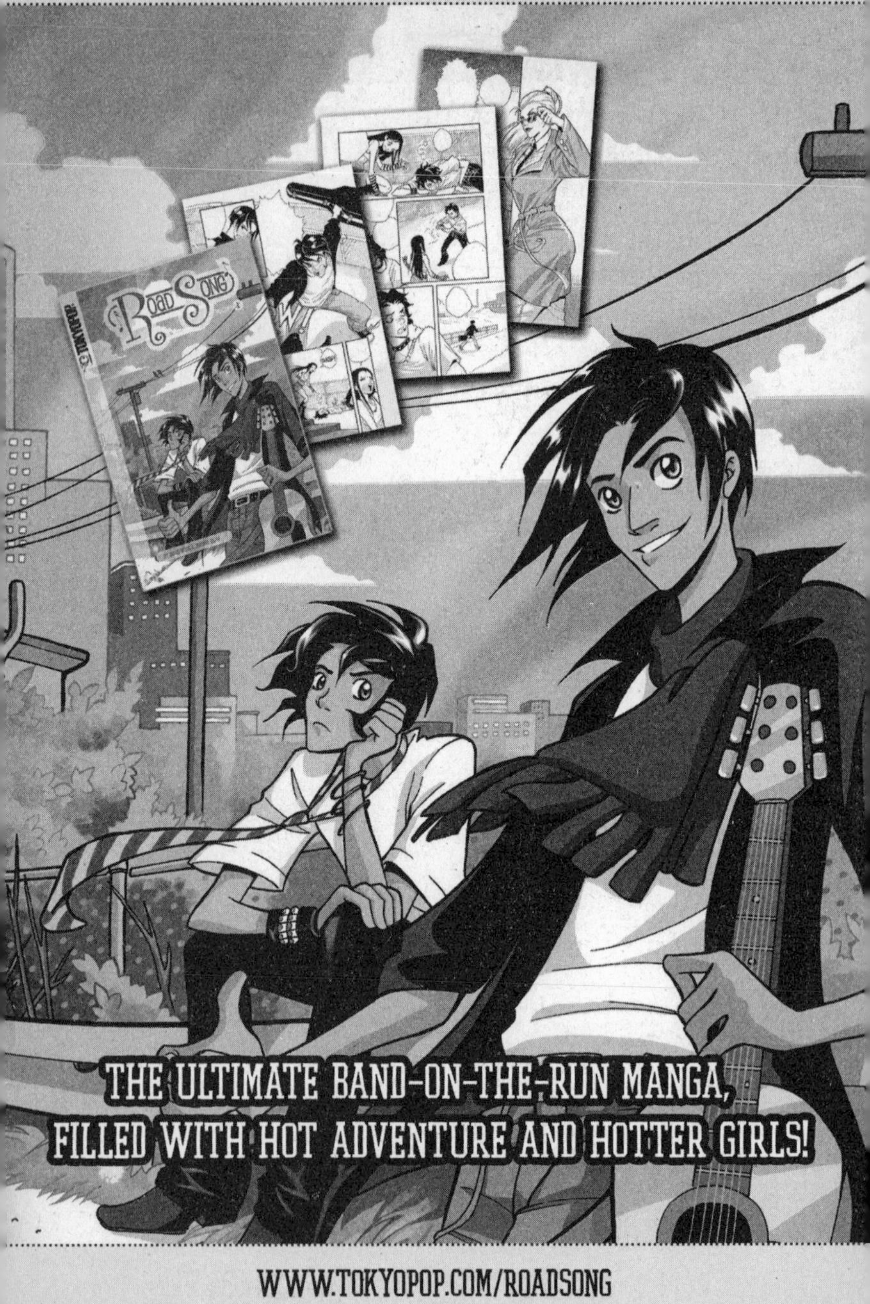
RoadSong
TOKYOPOP
THE ULTIMATE BAND-ON-THE-RUN MANGA,
FILLED WITH HOT ADVENTURE AND HOTTER GIRLS!

Music...mystery...and Murder!

Road Song

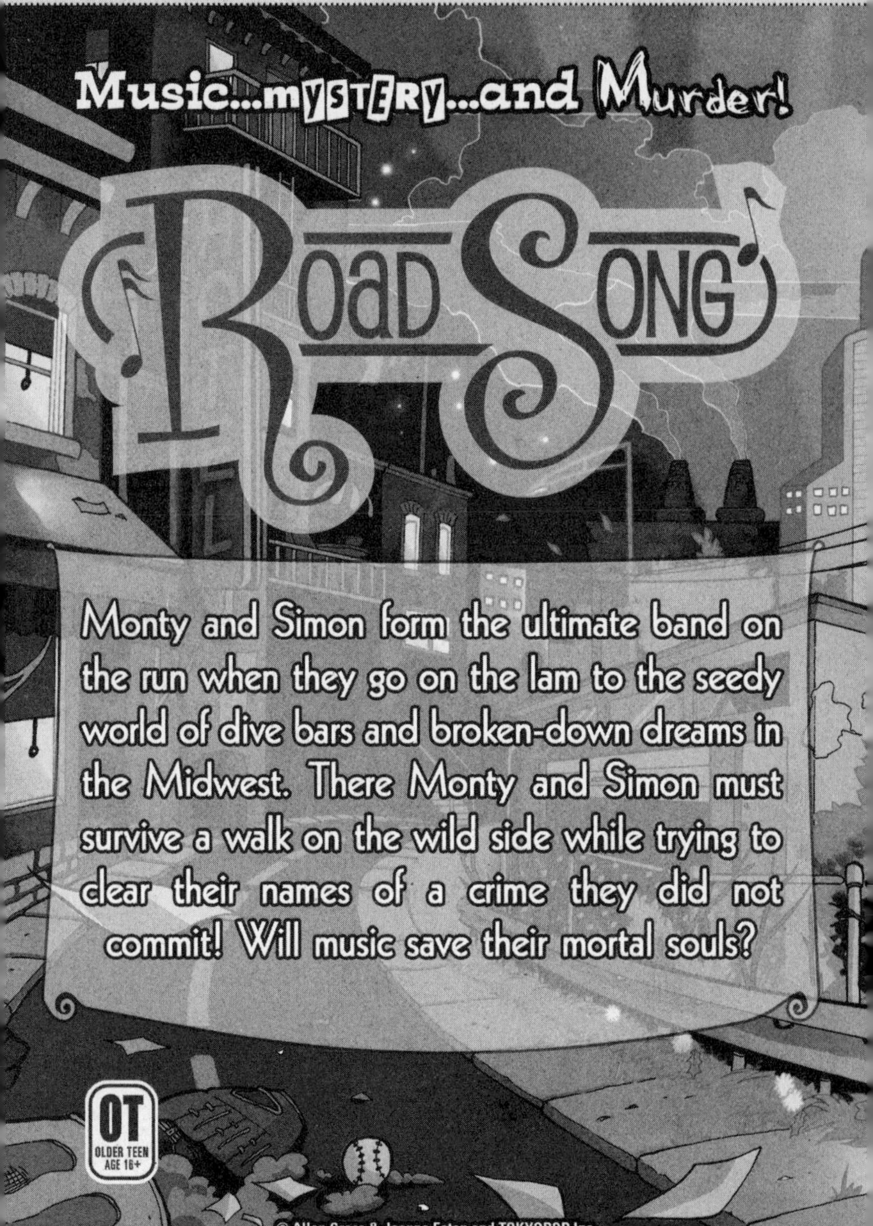

Monty and Simon form the ultimate band on the run when they go on the lam to the seedy world of dive bars and broken-down dreams in the Midwest. There Monty and Simon must survive a walk on the wild side while trying to clear their names of a crime they did not commit! Will music save their mortal souls?

OT
OLDER TEEN
AGE 16+

READ A CHAPTER OF THE MANGA ONLINE FOR FREE:

STOP!

This is the back of the book.
You wouldn't want to spoil a great ending!

This book is printed "manga-style," in the authentic Japanese right-to-left format. Since none of the artwork has been flipped or altered, readers get to experience the story just as the creator intended. You've been asking for it, so TOKYOPOP® delivered: authentic, hot-off-the-press, and far more fun!

DIRECTIONS

If this is your first time reading manga-style, here's a quick guide to help you understand how it works.

It's easy... just start in the top right panel and follow the numbers. Have fun, and look for more 100% authentic manga from TOKYOPOP®!